Also in the Variorum Collected Studies Series:

A. RUPERT HALL
Newton, his Friends and his Foes

ROBERT FOX
The Culture of Science in France, 1770-1900

R.W. HOME
Electricity and Experimental Physics in Eighteenth-Century Europe

ROSHDI RASHED
Optique et mathématiques
Recherches sur l'histoire de la pensée scientifique en arabe

JOHN M. RIDDLE
Quid Pro Quo:
Studies in the History of Drugs

GUY BEAUJOUAN
Science médiévale d'Espagne et d'alentour

GUY BEAUJOUAN
'Par raison de nombres'
L'art du calcul et les savoirs scientifiques médiévaux

CURTIS WILSON
Astronomy from Keplar to Newton

ALLEN G. DEBUS
Chemistry, Alchemy and the New Philosophy, 1550-1700

GERARD L'E. TURNER
Scientific Instruments and Experimental Philosophy, 1500-1850

BRUCE S. EASTWOOD
Astronomy and Optics from Pliny to Decartes

WALTER PAGEL
From Paracelsus to Van Helmont
Studies in Renaissance Medicine and Science

WILLIAM A. WALLACE
Galileo, the Jesuits, and the Medieval Aristotle

After Newton:
Essays on Natural Philosophy

P. M. Harman

After Newton:
Essays on Natural Philosophy

VARIORUM

This edition copyright © 1993 by P. M. Harman.

Published by VARIORUM
Ashgate Publishing Limited
Gower House, Croft Road,
Aldershot, Hampshire GU11 3HR
Great Britain

Ashgate Publishing Company
Old Post Road
Brookfield, Vermont 05036
USA

ISBN 0-86078-348-0

A CIP catalogue record for this book is available from the British Library.

This Variorum edition is printed on acid-free paper.

Printed by   Galliard (Printers) Ltd
Great Yarmouth, Norfolk
Great Britain

COLLECTED STUDIES SERIES CS389

CONTENTS

Preface   ix

Acknowledgements   xii

PART I: FROM NEWTON TO FARADAY

I   Newtonian forces and Lockean powers: concepts of matter in eighteenth-century thought   233–306

    (In collaboration with J.E. McGuire)

    Historical Studies in the Physical Sciences 3. Philadelphia, Pennsylvania: University of Pennsylvania Press, 1971

II   'Nature is a perpetual worker': Newton's aether and eighteenth-century natural philosophy   1–25
    Ambix 20. Cambridge, 1973

III   Ether and imponderables   61–83
    Conceptions of Ether: Studies in the History of Ether Theories, 1740–1900, edited by G.N. Cantor and M.J.S. Hodge. Cambridge: Cambridge University Press, 1981

IV   Voluntarism and immanence: conceptions of nature in eighteenth-century thought   271–283
    Journal of the History of Ideas 39. Philadelphia, Pennsylvania, 1978

V   Conversion of forces and the conservation energy   147–161
    Centaurus 18. Copenhagen: Munksgaard International Publishers Ltd., 1974

| VI | Faraday's theories of matter and electricity
*The British Journal for the History of
Science 5. London, 1971* | 235–257 |

PART II: FROM LEIBNIZ TO HELMHOLTZ

VII	'Geometry and nature': Leibniz and Johann Bernoulli's theory of motion *Centaurus 21. Copenhagen: Munksgaard International Publishers Ltd., 1977*	1–26
VIII	Dynamics and intelligibility: Bernoulli and MacLaurin *Metaphysics and Philosophy of Science in the Seventeenth and Eighteenth Centuries: Essays in Honour of Gerd Buchdahl, edited by R.S. Woolhouse. Dordrecht: Kluwer Academic Publishers, 1988*	213–225
IX	Concepts of inertia: Newton to Kant *Religion, Science and Worldview: Essays in Honor of Richard S. Westfall, edited by M.J. Osler and P.L. Farber. Cambridge: Cambridge University Press, 1985*	119–133
X	Force and inertia: Euler and Kant's *Metaphysical Foundations of Natural Science* *Nature Mathematized: Historical and Philosophical Case Studies in Classical Modern Natural Philosophy, edited by W.R. Shea. Dordrecht: D. Reidel Publishing Company, 1983*	229–249
XI	Mayer's concept of 'force': the 'axis' of a new science of physics *Historical Studies in the Physical Sciences 7. Princeton, New Jersey: Princeton University Press, 1976*	277–296

| XII | Helmholtz and Kant: the metaphysical foundations of *Über die Erhaltung der Kraft*
 Studies in History and Philosophy of Science 5. London, 1974 | 205–238 |

Index 1–3

This book contains xii + 315 pages

PUBLISHER'S NOTE

The articles in this volume, as in all others in the Collected Studies Series, have not been given a new, continuous pagination. In order to avoid confusion, and to facilitate their use where these same studies have been referred to elsewhere, the original pagination has been maintained wherever possible.

Each article has been given a Roman number in order of appearance, as listed in the Contents. This number is repeated on each page and quoted in the index entries.

PREFACE

The papers collected in this volume are concerned with a major transition in natural philosophy in the period 1700–1850: from Newton's concept of passive matter activated by ethereal and 'active' principles, to the conception of nature as a self-contained system regulated by powers internal to the natural order. The development of energy and field concepts in the physics of this period is viewed in relation to this profound shift in sensibility in a broader natural philosophy.

The papers are divided into two parts. Those in the first part are concerned with the philosophical and theological dimensions of matter theory in British natural philosophy, and trace a rich tradition of speculation about the nature of matter, ether and force, a tradition initiated by Newton's speculative writings. This tradition of matter theory is shown to have played a part in shaping the emergence of energy and field concepts. The second part of this volume is concerned with the Leibnizian and Kantian critiques of Newtonian natural philosophy, and with the transition from Leibnizian 'living force', with its complex associations as an agent intrinsic to the natural order, to Helmholtz's principle of the conservation of energy, which is shown to have been explicated with reference to the Kantian metaphysics of nature.

The book as a whole is therefore concerned with aspects of the nature and growth of Newtonianism and with the conceptual diversity (and departure from 'Newtonian' principles) of the physics of the period 1700–1850. The two parts of the book complement each other, revealing parallels and dissimilarities between rival traditions of natural philosophy.

On gathering these papers to form a collection of essays, I am naturally led to reflect on their import. The passage of time, the appearance of subsequent historical work on topics bearing on the themes of these papers, as well as my own absorption in other (and rather different) studies, lead me to reflect on the truism that published work is fixed in time, cast off from the later development of its author. Nevertheless, the methodology here adopted, that of the history of ideas (and the application of philosophical analysis to the history of science), still seems to me to have relevance to the themes discussed here, subtle discourses in natural philosophy that cannot be readily translated into present-day analogues. The problems described here relate to questions that have a complex relation to the general scientific practice of the period. While the relation of these debates in natural philosophy to their scientific context is by no means ignored (especially in Essays III, V, VI, VII and XII), the focus here is not on scientific practice, but rather on a matrix of ideas in a broader natural philosophy which is however relevant to an understanding of the development of physics in the Newtonian period.

When I began work on these topics more than twenty years ago, this dimension to the physics of the Newtonian period was frequently alluded to in the literature. But in the absence of detailed historical analysis, reference to the 'influence' of philosophical traditions on the physics of this period often seemed unconvincing and even confused, and was regularly dismissed as irrelevant by historians of physics. The studies collected here were undertaken in an attempt to remedy this gap in historical understanding, and to do so by a close attention to the structure and intellectual context of the systems of natural philosophy of the period.

I do not however intend to imply that the history of physics between 1700 and 1850 should or can be construed as the unravelling of a net of conceptual tangles, or in terms of the filiation of ideas through the diverse systems of natural philosophy of the period. I would not claim that the problems of natural philosophy examined in this volume are the most significant elements in the emergence of energy principles, or in Faraday's theory of the physical field; nor indeed in Kant's critique of the philosophical assumptions of Newtonian physics. But if these systems of natural philosophy did not determine scientific practice, their enunciation did constrain its form, and shaped the structure of scientific thought in the period. In discussing traditions of natural philosophy I do not intend to unduly emphasise continuity, to seemingly assimilate into a common tradition systems of thought that are too diverse for such an integration. The natural philosophers of the period did however themselves construct their arguments in relation to perceived intellectual traditions; and if continuity of discourse is one theme here, the conceptual diversity of the systems of natural philosophy is another.

One theme of the work collected here, on the philosophical structure of 'classical' physics, has been further developed in my book *Metaphysics and Natural Philosophy: the Problem of Substance in Classical Physics* (Harvester Press, 1982). The argument there is wider in chronological range but is more restricted and focused in its thematic coverage. This earlier volume elaborates one theme of the present collection of papers, and stands in complement to it. I should also mention one further feature of this volume of essays: except for Essays

VIII, IX and X the papers collected here were published under my former name P.M. Heimann.

My work on the history of natural philosophy owes its initial inspiration to my fruitful association with Ted McGuire. Our collaboration in writing the first of the papers here reproduced (for which I acknowledge his generous permission) emboldened me to investigate these topics. McGuire's seminal work on Newton's natural philosophy helped to shape the direction of my initial inquiries, and his intellectual daring encouraged my endeavours by example. Later in exploring Kantian themes I was indebted to the advice of Gerd Buchdahl, a stimulating experience.

In reproducing the papers in this volume I have corrected some trivial typographical and factual errors in the originals. On one occasion (in Essay II) I have deleted a sentence which contains an assertion that now seems to me to be false. Otherwise the papers appear as written.

Lancaster, 1992　　　　　　　　　　　　　　　　　　　　P.M. HARMAN

ACKNOWLEDGEMENTS

I am grateful to the following publishers, institutions and journals for permission to reproduce the studies included in this volume: the University of Pennsylvania Press, Philadelphia (for study I); the Society for the History of Alchemy and Chemistry (II); the Cambridge University Press, Cambridge (III, IX); the *Journal of the History of Ideas* (IV); Munksgaard International Publishers Ltd, Copenhagen (V, VII); the British Society for the History of Science (VI); Kluwer Academic Publishers, Dordrecht (VIII, X); Princeton University Press, Princeton (XI); Pergamon Press PLC (XII).

Full bibliographic details of the original publications are given in the Contents page.

Newtonian Forces and Lockean Powers: Concepts of Matter in Eighteenth-Century Thought

BY P. M. HEIMANN AND J. E. MC GUIRE

INTRODUCTION

The interpretation of eighteenth-century natural philosophy presents special difficulties. Though Newton's work was frequently lauded as providing the key to unlock the secrets of nature, the form of this key is not immediately apparent. Indeed, the extension, modification, and—on occasion—the rejection of Newtonian principles often appear obscure. Furthermore, the influence of other seventeenth-century systems of thought on eighteenth-century natural philosophy is still a crucial question awaiting analysis. In this study we are concerned with speculative British natural philosophy in the post-Newtonian period; but even within these limits the problems of interpretation are enormous. In what follows we attempt to explore theories of matter and force which in part arose out of the Newtonian tradition. This study is not intended as a delineation of the meaning of "Newtonianism" in eighteenth-century natural philosophy. We are concerned to examine a number of related themes in the thought of the period, themes surrounding discussions of the nature of matter. We will contend that many interpretations of nature arose from an intellectual revolution which was philosophical in character, as well as from the impact of scientific events. We will be concerned to analyze an important debate between philosophers

I

such as David Hume and Thomas Reid and natural philosophers such as Joseph Priestley and James Hutton. We will therefore discuss a number of connected problems that are well represented within the scientific thought of this period, but we do not intend to imply that the important change in epistemology which we delineate necessarily applies to eighteenth-century scientific thought as a whole. There is as yet no well-defined historiography of eighteenth-century science, and the conclusions of this study, which have important implications for the thought of the period, must remain suggestive.

It is a commonplace in eighteenth-century historical studies that there was a divorce between the general intellectual thought of the period and science.[1] Indeed, this view supposes that the metaphysical reorientation fundamental to seventeenth-century science provided the basic philosophical framework of eighteenth-century science.[2] The results of this study will suggest some limitations to this consensus of historical opinion. In our view the intellectual revolution in epistemology and ontology as manifested in certain features of the science of this period is as significantly "revolutionary" as that of the seventeenth century. As in the seventeenth century, new theories of science were developed in close connection with new systems of philosophy. Seen in this way, the "scientific revolution" will appear less uniquely "revolutionary" than has been supposed hitherto. The group of eighteenth-century thinkers we discuss were concerned with philosophical problems in connection with science no less than were the *virtuosi* of the seventeenth century.

In a recent study Schofield has argued for a strict dichotomy between the tradition of imponderable fluids and that of inter-

---

1. A clear statement of this opinion can be found in Peter Gay's stimulating *The Enlightenment: An Interpretation,* Vol. 2: *The Science of Freedom* (London, 1970), pp. 159 f: "The irresistible propulsion of modern scientific inquiry was towards positivism, toward the elimination of metaphysics, and the clean separation of facts and values, foreshadowed by Bacon, implied by Newton, triumphantly announced by Hume, taken for granted by the leading scientists of the late eighteenth century. Scientific thinking exacted the stripping away of theological, metaphysical, aesthetic, and ethical admixtures that had been a constituent part of science since the Greeks."
2. The extensive literature on the "scientific revolution"—for example, E. J. Dijksterhuis, *The Mechanization of the World Picture,* trans. C. Dikshoorn (Oxford, 1961), and A. Koyré, *Newtonian Studies* (London, 1965)—almost presupposes this view.

particulate forces in this period;[3] in the present paper we will question the overall validity of this interpretation. The main purpose of this paper is to show the different ways in which certain thinkers conceived the essence of matter as being constituted by attractive and repulsive "powers," a conception of nature which underlies both the tradition of imponderable fluids and that of interparticulate forces. Given this claim for the implications of the notion of "power" in the period, some indication of its significance is in order. Though eighteenth-century thinkers are not entirely unambiguous in their use of this term, it is likely that their mode of employing it arises in part from John Locke's *Essay Concerning Human Understanding* (1690). Contextually, what eighteenth-century thinkers generally mean when they use the term "power" is this: to ascribe a power to a material object is to assert what it can or cannot do in virtue of its intrinsic nature in relation to specifiable extrinsic circumstances, leaving open a complete characterization of the object's constitution in virtue of which it is held to be endowed with powers. This conception of matter involved the notion of activity in nature which contrasts with the general seventeenth-century emphasis on the passivity of material entities. This is borne out by the fact that thinkers like Descartes, Hobbes, and Boyle viewed powers as being noninherent in matter; that is, "powers" are not ascribable to bodies in and of themselves. Rather, powers are manifested only when bodies are in specifiable relations with one another; i.e., the sun has the power actively to melt wax if wax is present, and the wax to melt only when heat is present. This conception of power is very different from that widely held in the eighteenth century where powers were conceived as being substantively present in entities, thus defining the entities' essence in

---

3. Robert E. Schofield, *Mechanism and Materialism: British Natural Philosophy in An Age of Reason* (Princeton, 1970). Schofield asserts a rigid dichotomy throughout the natural philosophy of the period between "mechanists" who sought the "causation for all the phenomena of nature . . . [in] the primary particles of an undifferentiable matter . . . [their] combinations . . . their motions, and the forces of attraction and repulsion between them which determine those motions" and "materialists" who believed "that the causes of phenomena inhere in unique substances, each possessing as an essential property the power to convey . . . some characteristic quality (*ibid.*, pp. 15 f.). This dichotomy may illuminate some aspects of the period, but the ideas of many thinkers cannot be categorized in this way. For example, see Notes 43 and 193 below.

I

terms of inherent activity. The eighteenth-century view must also be distinguished from the doctrines of *vis insita* found in the writings of Newton and Leibniz and, in general, in theories of *conatus*.

The notion of the passivity of matter, matter as an entity embodying the lowest degree of reality and perfection, is fundamental to Newton's philosophy, since he superadded to infinitesimally small particles immaterial forces as the agents of change in nature. Newton argued that compound bodies were extremely porous. For him, forces operating in void space came to have more significance as the properties of interstitial particles became less important for explaining phenomena. Fundamental to the operation of forces was his concept of "active principle," the manifestation of God's agency in the world. The notion of "active principle" became transformed during the eighteenth century into that of "active substances," which, like the active principles in Newton's natural philosophy, were employed to explain the activity and operations of nature. However, a concept that Newton had employed to establish God's causal connection with nature became transformed into a concept used to support a theory of the balance of nature, a view which conceived nature as a self-contained system independent of divine intervention. These ideas appear very clearly in the work of James Hutton, whose system of nature falls within the tradition of theories of imponderable fluids. We will argue that Newton's aether of the 1717/18 *Opticks* was to have a significant influence on such theories. This aether was not a "mechanical"aether designed to explain phenomena by contact action, but in the limit its interstitial particles were conceived as vanishingly small, the centers of forces operating throughout void space. Thus, James Hutton associated attractive and repulsive forces with different phenomenal entities—identifying the attractive force with ordinary matter and the repulsive force with the imponderable fluids of heat, light, electricity, and phlogiston—and he went on to conceive the essence of such phenomenal entities as constituted by powers.

The theories of reality developed by men like Priestley and Hutton were consciously based on a rigorously empirical epistemology, with close attention to the foundations of scientific knowledge. In arguing that sensory experience only provided evidence of resisting powers, these thinkers denied that the essence of matter was solidity. In so doing they were to reject the traditional categories of seventeenth-century science, even one as fundamental as the primary and secondary quality distinction.

The increasingly important role which forces came to have in Newton's philosophy of nature was to have important consequences. His emphasis on the significance of forces, in his mind closely associated with the paucity of solid matter in the universe, was to lead Priestley to reject the theory that solid particles constituted the essence of matter. In addition, Priestley argued that in conjunction with extension, repulsive and attractive powers were the essence of matter. This view was to lead to the seminal idea that matter was no more than forces diffused through space, and we will indicate that this in part was to shape Faraday's concept of the physical field.

I

Without going into the well-known details of changes in the Queries of the *Opticks* early in the eighteenth century,[4] Newton's general view (both there and in related documents) of the nature of force is as follows. Appealing to the "analogy of Nature," he held that as a long-range force like gravity operates between gross bodies and their particles, so numerous short-range forces operate between various hierarchies of homogeneous particles which comprise visible matter and its *differentiae*.[5] Though he was never entirely unambiguous as to their ontological status, Newton did not consider forces

4. See A. Koyré, "Etudes Newtoniennes. II—Les queries de l'Optique," *Archs. Int. Hist. Sci., 14* (1960), 15-29; H. Guerlac, "Francis Hauksbee, expérimentateur au profit de Newton," *ibid., 16* (1963), 113-128; *id.,* "Sir Isaac and the ingenious Mr. Hauksbee," *Mélanges Alexandre Koyré,* ed. I. B. Cohen and R. Taton, 2 vols. (Paris, 1964), *1,* 228-253; *id.,* "Newton's Optical Ether," *Notes and Records of the Royal Society, 22* (1967), 45-57.

5. In the third Rule of Philosophizing, which he prefixed to the third Book of the *Principia* in 1713, Newton stated that "The qualities of bodies which cannot be intended and remitted, and which apply to all bodies on which it is possible to set up experiments, are qualities of all bodies universally," appealing to "the analogy of Nature, which uses to be simple, and always consonant to itself." (Sir Isaac Newton, *The Mathematical Principles of Natural Philosophy,* trans. B. Motte, 2 vols. [London, 1729], *2,* 203.) In the earliest draft of the Rule he wrote that "The laws (and properties) of all bodies on which it is possible to institute experiments, are laws (and properties) of all bodies whatsoever," a clear statement of a general analogy between macro- and micro-phenomena. (Trinity College Library, N.Q. 16.200.) For the full text see J. E. McGuire, "The Origin of Newton's Doctrine of Essential Qualities," *Centaurus, 12* (1968), 236.

I

as either secondary qualities or as material substances. In and of themselves they were closer in nature to the immaterial, though of course their effects could be ascertained in relation to material entities. Moreover, since force was not a secondary quality it did not arise from matter, nor was it in any way reducible to the interactions of bodies or particles. Like his view of space—neither a quality nor a substance—Newton tended to regard force as in a category of its own. Viewed within the Neoplatonic framework of his thought, force was closer to space than to matter, as a dynamic principle of divine operation, since force and space were respectively an expression, in the realm of nature, of God's spiritual power and existence. Moreover, as force and space were not in the category of substance they did not satisfy criteria for material existence such as impenetrability and three-dimensionality. Newton's view that force and space exist in a realm categorically different from matter will be seen as significant for later eighteenth-century thought.[6]

In terms of this ontology, Newton tended to hold that interparticulate forces were dispositional in nature, being able to transform from one "state" to another. For example, in Query 31 of the *Opticks* he stated that the "attractive Force [of particles] can reach but to a small distance from them . . . where Attraction ceases, there a repulsive Virtue ought to succeed."[7] All particles of matter were thus conceived as being surrounded by envelopes of various forces which, by entering into combinations, changed the configuration of the internal layers of particles of any given body so as to alter its manifest properties. With the primacy of force foremost in his mind, Newton was more concerned, in explaining the interactions and visible properties of matter, with the way in which particles were rearranged than with their geometrical properties. Though he was never able to quantify these interstitial forces

---

6. For a discussion of Newton's distinction between body and space see J. E. McGuire, "Body and Void and Newton's *De Mundi Systemate:* Some New Sources," *Arch. Hist. Exact Sci.,* 3 (1966), 206-248. For Newton's concept of force see McGuire, "Force, Active Principles and Newton's Invisible Realm," *Ambix,* 15 (1968), 154-208. For a discussion of Newton's concept of space see also F. E. L. Priestley, "The Clarke-Leibniz Controversy," *The Methodological Heritage of Newton,* ed. Robert E. Butts and John W. Davis (Oxford, 1970), pp. 34-56.

7. Isaac Newton, *Opticks or a Treatise of the Reflections, Refractions, Inflections & Colours of Light* ([Dover edition, based on the 4th edition of 1730], New York, 1952), p. 395.

by establishing measurable parameters, they were to be treated more exactly by early disciples such as the Keills and Freind. Newton's theory of the paucity of matter in the universe in relation to the void was fundamental to his theory of forces, for the forces were held to operate within the internal vacuities of matter. The paucity of matter was clearly connected in Newton's mind with the way in which forces arrange the constituents of matter. His commitment to the void was thus closely associated with his belief in the primacy of force.[8]

Important to Newton's conception of force was his notion of active principles, which were the general mode of causation of divine agency in the natural world. Though active principles were sometimes used as a cognate for force, more often they were used as a general term to denote the cause or causes of any particular force. Though at one level forces were natural agents in the world, at another they, like matter, were dependent on and manifestations of the agency of God. Though Newton tended to interchange the terms "force" and "active principle," it is important to notice that he used a contextually meaningful distinction between the two. Though forces are causes they are not, of course, a fundamental cause like God. Unlike many later thinkers, Newton held it meaningful to ask: what is the cause or causes of any given force, itself a cause at another level of being? Therefore one of his central problems was the ontological problem of the causation of force, and "active principle" was the term he used, in various contexts, to designate this category of problem. Though God, in virtue of divine concurrence, was the ultimate cause and sustainer of all natural entities, active principles, though at one stage identified with God, by the time of publication of the 1717/18 edition of the *Opticks* referred to processes in the physical world which were linked with physical and chemical phenomena.[9] This chain of thought carried the implication that many of the propensities of these principles were yet to be discovered. As there was a hierarchy of forces in nature, so presumably, for Newton, there was a hierarchy of natural causes related to them which could be known in principle. This contention is less surprising when it is realized that Newton was concerned to

---

8. See McGuire, "Body and Void," *op. cit.* (Note 6).
9. See McGuire, "Force, Active Principles," *op. cit.* (Note 6).

maintain the primacy of the spiritual and spirituous in nature, as is evident by his designating matter as ontologically imperfect, a conception which he associated with the paucity of matter and with the primacy of force in nature. Newton's conception of the paucity of matter is significant for understanding the eighteenth-century view of the relationship between matter conceived as "power" and the vacuity of the universe. If resistance is not related to solidity, as was the view of many eighteenth-century thinkers, and given the Newtonian assumption of the paucity of solid particles in relation to void space, natural philosophers like Joseph Priestley could consider it but a small step to reduce solid matter to powers which could affect the senses. This presupposes a non-Newtonian assumption, namely, that the nature of matter is active resistance rather than passive solidity.

It is clear that Newton uses the term "active principles" in a more embracing sense than "force." The term "aether" of the 1717 *Opticks* stands for a type of "active principle," though these terms as well are not strictly interchangeable. This aether is another attempt at solving the ontological problem of the causation of force. Thus, far from being synonymous with "force," the term "active principle" refers to yet another putative cause of forces like gravity.

A proper understanding of this aether hypothesis is imperative for comprehending much of later scientific thought in Britain. Without going into the vexed question of why this aether was introduced into the later Queries, its main characteristics are these. Being particulate in structure, it is described in the following terms: "rare," "subtile," "elastick," that which "dilates and contracts," "condenses," has graduated "density," and "vibrates."[10] By its subtlety it appears to diffuse through space, by its rarity to produce no resistance to material motions. Moreover, in terms of the graduated elastic density of the aether, in Query 21 Newton suggested that it was rarer in the pores of bodies than in surrounding space. Therefore the differential density between any two places would *cause* any two bodies to move toward one another, as from a denser to a rarer medium.

10. Newton, *Opticks,* pp. 348 ff.

NEWTONIAN FORCES AND LOCKEAN POWERS

There are, however, more fundamental aspects of this aether, the implications of which have yet to be appreciated, which had important historical consequences. The 1717 hypothesis is a "force-aether," and though this has been recognized by Newtonian scholars,[11] its true nature as a putative cause of gravitation has not. The key to this lies in the following passage from Query 21:

> As Attraction is stronger in small Magnets than in great ones in proportion to their Bulk, and in Gravity is greater in the Surfaces of small Planets than in those of great ones in proportion to their bulk, and small Bodies are agitated much more by electric attraction than great ones; so the smallness of the Rays of Light may contribute very much to the power of the Agent by which they are refracted. And so if any one should suppose that *Aether* (like our *Air*) may contain Particles which endeavour to recede from one another (for I do not know what this *Aether* is) and that its Particles are exceedingly smaller than those of air, or even than those of Light: The exceeding smallness of its Particles may contribute to the greatness of the force by which those Particles may recede from one another, and thereby make that Medium exceedingly more rare and elastick than Air, and by consequence exceedingly less able to resist the motions of Projectiles, and exceedingly more able to press upon gross Bodies, by endeavouring to expand it self.[12]

Without doubt Newton distinguishes between the gross aether itself, a "medium" having properties such as "rarity" and "elasticity," and its composition. The microstructure of this aether is crucially important. Arguing analogically Newton concludes that its particles are probably smaller than those of the rays of light, so that just as a small magnet has more force in proportion to its bulk than a large magnet, the tiny aethereal particles give rise to forces having great intensity in relation to their size. This relation between smallness of size and greatness of force is partly a consequence of Newton's doctrine regarding the porosity of matter. As the pores of any given physical entity decrease in size and number, so its solid parts concentrate more and more to a central point, ending theoretically in the total solidity of the remaining infinitesimal particles. Accord-

---

11. See Arnold Thackray, *Atoms and Powers: An Essay on Newtonian Matter-Theory and the Development of Chemistry* (Cambridge, Mass., 1970), p. 28.
12. *Opticks*, pp. 351 f.

ingly, since the quantity of matter is concentrated, it will give rise to a force having great intensity in relation to size; as John Keill puts it, "the attraction will not be so strong, when a particle of a given magnitude has several pores, as when it is entirely solid."[13] Size thus becomes an important factor when particles of absolute solidity are considered. In view of Newton's argument by analogy, the possibility is open that in the limit the dimensions of particles would be vanishingly small, leaving space containing interparticulate forces clustering around changing networks of foci.[14] Thus, with an extension of the argument, reduction of matter through the paucity of particles and their smallness embodies the existence of force throughout space; that is, an aethereal "medium" is dynamic in nature, not a mechanical fluid.[15] This line of reasoning is made explicit by Priestley.

From the point of view of particle size and porosity, these are the implications of the "force-aether." Moreover, Newton is not adumbrating a "mechanist" aether, but attempting to reduce, through the gross features of the aether, action-at-a-distance forces such as gravitation to a single monolithic repulsive force. In the light of this analysis it is clear that action at a distance is a doctrine which never seriously troubled Newton. For him it was an intelligible mode of action, something that actually occurs in *rerum natura*. While "brute inanimate" matter could not act across space, interstitial forces could, since their mode of existence was that of filling and operating in space. These are the basic entities of the aether, constituting its distinctive ontological character, and they are privileged in status since

---

13. See John Keill, "In qua Leges Attractionis aliaque Physices Principia traduntur," *Philosophical Transactions*, 26 (1708/9), 104 (Theorem 14).

14. See McGuire, "Force, Active Principles," *op. cit.* (Note 6).

15. This distinction between the aethereal medium which embodies the existence of force throughout space and a mechanical fluid underlies much eighteenth-century natural philosophy. Bryan Robinson's *Dissertation on the Aether of Sir Isaac Newton* (Dublin, 1743) is in many ways a unique work. It develops a mechanical treatment, in terms of the sizes of aether particles, the density of the aether, and the force between the particles, of how the aether is supposed to cause gravitation, elasticity, heat, cohesion and fermentation, and the phenomena of optics. Robinson's aether must be sharply distinguished from theories involving the imponderable fluid "aethers" of light, electricity, and heat. As we will show, such theories have relation to Newton's "force aether" rather than to a "mechanical fluid" of the kind supposed by Robinson.

they cannot in turn be explained.[16] Thus, we are in a position to see that not only was Newton's aether nonmechanical but that it was truly dynamic in character with respect to its operation between the aether's particles. Hence the gross properties of the aethereal medium are merely phenomenal manifestations of a microstructure embodying only repulsive forces acting between vanishingly small particles. Viewing the aether in this way, Newton's theory of a nearly matterless universe is preserved. This interpretation of the aether is strengthened by remarks on a manuscript of six folio sheets in which Newton develops some "Observations" on Hauksbee's experiments on electrical phenomena, intended for the 1717/18 edition of the *Opticks*. In defining his "very subtle active substance or medium," Newton says: "To distinguish this Medium from the bodies which flote in it, & from their effluvia & emanations & from the air, I will hence forward call it Aether & by the word bodies I will understand the bodies which flote in it, taking this name not in the sense of the modern metaphysicians, but in the sense of the common people."[17] Newton's firm reference to what he understands by the term "body" is almost certainly related to definitions of body and void which were intended to preface Book III of the third edition of the *Principia*. These were probably written late in 1716 at the same time

16. With important differences of emphasis, we are in basic agreement with Laurens Laudan regarding the nature of Newton's aether. See Roger H. Stuewer, ed., *Historical and Philosophical Perspectives of Science* (Minneapolis, 1970), pp. 230-238. Newton's thought certainly functioned on many levels—the descriptive, the architectonic, the regulative, the teleological—and appealed to the transcendental harmonies of nature in wrestling with the problem of the intelligibility of action-at-a-distance. See Gerd Buchdahl, "History of Science and Criteria of Choice," *ibid.*, pp. 204-230. Nevertheless, the 1717/18 aether theory taken on its own merits seems to claim that the mechanists are maintaining that action at a distance, to be made intelligible and acceptable, must be reduced to, or explained in terms of, collision, impacts, or some other sort of contact action. But as is clear from the above analysis, Newton's aether is basically structured in terms of intense repulsive forces *between* the aether particles. Thus, these sorts of forces explain the gross features of the macro-aether. And it is crucial to mention that Newton never offered aetherial or mechanical explanations for short-range distance forces with which the *Opticks* abounds. It is difficult to believe, then, that Newton was attempting to meet his critics by supplying them with a "mechanical" explanation of gravity. The basic ontology of his aether is nonmechanist, and it is in no way necessarily related to the theological model which embodies God operating on matter with void space as his sensorium. For Newton this sort of explanation is in the category of teleology.

17. University Library, Cambridge, Add. 3970.9, fol. 623r.

I

as the "Observations." Like the "Observations," these definitions oppose the metaphysical views of the Cartesians and Leibnizians regarding body. Body is defined as "everything that can be moved and touched, in which there is resistance to tangible things ... it is indeed in this sense that the common people always accept the word."[18] Thus Newton makes a clear and unambiguous distinction between matter and the aether. Moreover, since the basic action of this aether is by means of repulsive forces between infinitely small particles, the analogy with the proportionality of any given quantity of matter to gravitation does not apply to its microstructure. This is clear since the smaller the particle the more intense is the force. Moreover, the analogy applies only to the density of the aether in a descriptive sense, since in placing the aether in an entirely different category from matter the proportionalities between mass, inertia, and gravitation are not ascribable to the former. Indeed, there is evidence to show that Newton may have thought the 1717 aether to be noninertial in character.[19] Moreover, since impulsive action is a necessary condition of a mechanical hypothesis, the 1717 aether is clearly not mechanical. It might be thought, however, that Newton is merely outlining a possible explanation of force in terms of force, and thus opening a regress. This is not the case. The repulsive force of the aether is not only different in its mode of action from large-scale attractive forces, but it is related to matter in a fundamentally dif-

18. University Library, Cambridge, Add. 3965.13, fol. 422^r. For full Latin text and translation of the definition see McGuire, "Body and Void," *op. cit.* (Note 6), pp. 246 f, 220 f.
19. Any mechanical aether would give rise to conceptual difficulties. The differential density of the aether was supposed to cause gravity, but the exact application of the inverse-square laws indicated a nonresisting void (see J. Lohne, "Newton's 'Proof' of the Sine Law and Mathematical Principles of Colours," *Arch. Hist. Exact Sci., 1* [1961], 402). Again, the mode of transmission of such impulses is obscure (see McGuire, "Body and Void," *op. cit.* [Note 6], 231). A "mechanical" fluid aether of the kind supposed by the Cartesians is, for Newton, a physical impossibility, and for this reason he states the difference between "aether" and "body"; indeed, he even speculates in a draft letter to Leibniz that this aether is "a substance in which bodies move and flote without resistance & which therefore has no *vis inertiae,* but acts by other laws than those that are mechanical" (U.L.C. Add. 3968.17, fol. 257^r, quoted in McGuire, "Force, Active Principles," *op. cit.* [Note 6], 203). To escape from some of the difficulties arising from the supposition of an impulsive aether, William Jones argued that by impulse Newton meant an "incorporeal" cause (*An Essay on the first Principles of Natural Philosophy* [London, 1762], p. 24), supposing *"immaterial impulses* in a vacuum" for the explanation of gravity (*ibid.*, p. 75).

NEWTONIAN FORCES AND LOCKEAN POWERS

ferent way. It is not proportional to the total quantity of matter, but is more intense the smaller the particle. Hence, the increase of force with the decrease of particle size is not merely a consequence of the inverse proportionality with distance. Thus the impulsive action of the aether as a function of its elasticity and density is an apparent, not real, mode of action. Therefore with respect to its microcharacteristics the aether offered in terms of its repulsive mode of action an economy of explanation. Moreover, such action is clearly an active principle, a cause of the gross properties of the aether to which it gives rise, properties such as elasticity and differential density. That it could be considered as an active substance with respect to its own properties by eighteenth-century thinkers is also clear from Newton's claim that the "elastick force" of this aethereal medium is higher in proportion to its density than is air and other elastic substances. It was Newton's theory of the microstructure of the aether as the embodiment of repulsive forces that was to enable a number of eighteenth-century thinkers to transform his concept of "active principle" into that of "active substance."

It is clear that Newton made an ontological distinction between the ultimate primordial particles and perceptible bodies. Indeed, his doctrine of the vacuity of matter was intimately associated with the view that light would be "stifled and lost"[20] within vacuities, so that the ultimate primordials could not interact with light, and so would be beyond experience. Nevertheless, by his third Rule of Philosophizing he was concerned to stress that certain characteristics of macrobodies—the essential qualities—could be transferred to the primordial particles. Without going into the difficulties surrounding Newton's doctrine of essential qualities or the justificatory principles he adumbrated to sanction inferences from what is observable to what is in principle unobservable, it must be emphasized that for Newton it was the essential qualities of hardness, impenetrability, mobility, and inertia which were common to all matter, whether

---

20. Newton, *Opticks,* p. 340. Newton's belief that the smallest particles of matter are in principle physically impossible to see—"it seems impossible to see the more secret and noble Works of Nature within the Corpuscles by reason of their transparency" (*ibid.,* p. 262)—hinges on the conception that matter is almost vacuous; because of the smallness of the corpuscles and this vacuity, the primordials will not reflect light. The primordials are beyond observation, and contextually in Newton's writings they have a different physical status from other levels of matter.

245

I

perceptible or imperceptible. Indeed, for Newton the essential qualities of matter are a reflection of God's immutability. In rejecting Newton's doctrine of essential qualities, eighteenth-century thinkers such as James Hutton were to reject Newton's view that the insensible primordials had properties in common with those of sensible bodies. For these thinkers such an explanation of the nature of matter was inappropriate: to explain the properties of gross bodies by ascribing similar properties to the constituent primordials was merely to explain one unknown by another. For Newton, however, such an argument was sanctioned by the "analogy of Nature"; the gap between bodies and their constituents was bridged by the postulation of a chain of bodies between the macro- and microworlds. Newton transformed the doctrine of the chain of being into that of the *scala naturae* so as to unify matter by the analogy of nature, and to bridge the ontological gap between bodies and their constituent particles.[21]

II

A central feature of seventeenth-century discussions of matter was the doctrine of primary and secondary qualities. Without going into the well-known epistemological difficulties surrounding this doctrine,[22] it can be stated that natural philosophers like Gassendi, Descartes, Charleton, and Boyle were concerned to establish the essential or primary characteristics of matter, which they held to exist independently of human perception. Qualities such as sensation of color, on the other hand, were held to arise as a result of a relation between the perceiving mind and the primary qualities of matter which provided their causal nexus. For ontological and epistemological reasons they accepted the distinction between absolute qualities (i.e., primary qualities) and relational qualities. Many leading eighteenth-century thinkers, we shall see, were to reject the validity of this distinction with respect to theories of matter, and with it the validity of the theory of primary and secondary qualities and related

---

21. See McGuire, "Atoms and the 'Analogy of Nature': Newton's Third Rule of Philosophizing," *Studies in History and Philosophy of Science, 1* (1970), 3-58.
22. For an interesting discussion of this question, see J. Bennett, "Substance, Reality and Primary Qualities," *Am. Phil. Quart., 2* (1965), 1-17.

NEWTONIAN FORCES AND LOCKEAN POWERS

doctrines. For them the essential characteristics of matter were entirely to be found in the seventeenth-century domain of secondary qualities, or as they saw it, in the realm of mind-dependent and relational properties.

The seeds of this fundamental shift in the presuppositions associated with theories of matter are to be found in the writings of many seventeenth-century *virtuosi* both in England and on the Continent. For example, though it was held that conceptions of matter are to be based on sensory experience, it was nevertheless contended that the essential qualities of microparticles, which were beyond such experience, could be known in principle.[23] As has been indicated, such arguments were fundamental to Newton's theory of matter; and we will argue that such epistemological ambivalence was to be mitigated in certain respects during the course of the eighteenth century. Nevertheless, even seventeenth-century thinkers were led to an implicit awareness of the eighteenth-century view that the characteristics of matter could only be established by means of the *ways* in which it aroused our sensations.

In his *Origine of Formes and Qualities* (1666) Robert Boyle explicitly states the view that ordinary material agents, ontologically speaking, are no more than the totality of their constituent particles which are known through their disposition to produce certain effects:

> I do not deny, but that Bodies may be said, in a very favourable sense, to have those Qualities we call Sensible, though there were no Animals in the World: for a Body in that case may differ from those Bodies, which now are quite devoid of Quality, in its having such a disposition of its constituent Corpuscles, that in case it were duely apply'd to the Sensory of an Animal, it would produce such a sensible Quality ... so if there were no Sensitive Beings those Bodies that are now the Objects of our Senses, would be but *dispositively*, if I may so speak, endow'd with Colours, Tasts and the like, and *actually* but onely with those more Catholick Affections of Bodies, Figure, Motion, Texture, etc.[24]

---

23. See McGuire, *op. cit.* (Note 21).
24. Robert Boyle, *The Origine of Formes and Qualities, according to the Corpuscular Philosophy* (Oxford, 1666), pp. 47 ff. Boyle also states that "if there were no animals in the world, there would be no pain, yet a pin may upon account of its figure be fitted to cause pain" (Boyle, *ibid.*, p. 47). This last sentence is revealing of Boyle's view of dispositions. In considering the "power" that

I

Though Boyle's discussion is within the framework of primary and secondary qualities, he connects the latter with the primary qualities as associated dispositional properties. Since bodies merely have a disposition to produce sensations of colors and tastes under certain conditions of perception, there is nothing actually in them which corresponds to our ideas of these secondary qualities. Moreover, his view of dispositional properties is relational in character: they are not substantive, essential entities inherent in bodies.

In his *Essay Concerning Human Understanding* (1690), Locke developed this line of reasoning. Chapters 8 and 21 of Book II are concerned with an analysis of the idea, implicit in the "New Science," that objects have the disposition to produce sensations in the mind which do not correspond to anything in the object itself. Thus, besides having "original" or primary properties defining their essence, Locke held that material objects and particles possessed "imputed" and relational properties called "powers": "For the power in fire to produce a new colour, or consistency, in *wax* or *clay*—by its primary qualities, is as much a quality in fire, as the power it has to produce in *me* a new idea or sensation of warmth or burning, which I felt not before—by the same primary qualities, viz. the bulk, texture, and motion of its insensible parts."[25] Since secondary qualities "are powers barely, and nothing but powers, relating to several other bodies, and resulting from the different modifications of the original qualities,"[26] Locke not only designates secondary qualities as relational properties, but also tends to construe them as exemplifying an undefined notion of causation. In the *Essay* the discussion of causation is separated from that of power, perhaps because Locke wished more closely to associate the latter

---

a key has to open a door Boyle points out that there is nothing in the key over and above its shape and size and the fact that it fits a particular lock. This shows three things about Boyle's conception of power: (1) that it is *relational*, (2) that powers are *not* entities distinct from the primary qualities nor are they inherent properties in objects, and (3) that they are distinct from the effects objects have on one another by means of their inherent qualities.

25. John Locke, *An Essay Concerning Human Understanding*, ed. A. C. Fraser, 2 vols. ([Dover edition], New York, 1959), *1,* 171.

26. *Ibid.*, p. 179. Though there are passages to the contrary, Locke's basic view of powers is relational. Like Boyle he holds that dispositional powers like malleability, solubility, and fragility must be analyzed in relation to other objects. Both thinkers were also aware that the primary/secondary-qualities distinction does not do full justice to the nature of such predicates.

I

NEWTONIAN FORCES AND LOCKEAN POWERS

with change in any given substance rather than with interaction between substances as in his analysis of causation. And though he relates power to the persistence of, and consistent changes in, our ideas either of sensation or reflection, the term nevertheless is employed contextually in an "active" causal sense. For Locke, the mind looks for the agent of change: with secondary qualities this is the efficacy of powers inherent in physical objects. According to this conception the primary or original qualities give rise to causal powers either actually efficacious or able so to act. To say of matter that it possesses the property of being red is the same as to say it is capable of producing under suitable conditions an idea of redness in our awareness. Thus, a chair does not have the color red as well as the power to produce the idea in the mind. To have a causal power is not the same as to have a property like red. With respect to primary qualities, however, Locke holds that they exist absolutely and categorically in the object and also have the "power" to produce ideas of primary qualities which in the mind "resemble" those qualities themselves. From the epistemological point of view it seems that Locke must deny the coherence of the ordinary idea of material objects being colored, for neither they nor their interstitial parts are colored, having only the disposition to produce such sensations. Since, however, we see bodies as colored surfaces, experience still allows the formulation of the everyday conception of objects, and Locke's account analyzes how the corpuscular hypothesis explains our impression that objects are colored in terms of "theoretical" matter possessed only of primary qualities.[27]

The notion of "power" is of crucial importance in eighteenth-century natural philosophy, and it seems clear that Locke's discussion of this problem was influential. Though Locke tends to use the term "natural powers" contextually in close association with the notion of causal efficacy, he does deny, however, that powers inherent in physical objects are active. Drawing on the traditional distinction between "active" and "passive," Locke states:

> A body at rest affords us no idea of any active power to move; and when it is set in motion itself, that motion is rather a passion than an action in it. For, when the ball obeys the motion of a billiard-stick,

---

27. See also John W. Yolton, *Locke and the Compass of Human Understanding: A Selective Commentary on the 'Essay'* (Cambridge, 1970), pp. 21 ff.

it is not any action of the ball, but bare passion. Also when by impulse it sets another ball in motion that lay in its way, it only communicates the motion it had received from another, and loses in itself so much as the other received: which gives us but a very obscure idea of an *active* power of moving in body, whilst we observe it only to *transfer,* but not *produce* any motion.

Thus, strictly speaking, bodies are not ontologically causative in nature, and it seems to Locke that "we have, from the observation of the operation of bodies by our senses, but a very imperfect obscure idea of *active* power; since they afford us not any idea in themselves of the power to begin any action, either motion or thought."[28] Nevertheless, if anyone claims that he has a clear idea of active power from the observation of bodies, Locke is not willing to reject this on epistemological grounds.[29] In the final analysis, however, the clearest idea of this notion comes from two related sources: a "consideration of God and spirits,"[30] and the mind "from reflection on its own operations."[31] Though Locke is somewhat uneasy about such concepts as "action," "change," and "power" and about their relationships, especially as they apply to physical objects, he never doubted that it was possible to have, though

---

28. Locke, *op. cit.* (Note 25), *1,* 312. There are numerous passages in his *Principles of Philosophy* where Descartes seemed to recognize the difference between powers and qualities. Of the secondary qualities he states that they are "nihil aliud esse . . . quam dispositiones quasdam in magnitudine, figura & motu consistentes," *Oeuvres de Descartes,* ed. Charles Adam and Paul Tannery, 12 vols. (Paris, 1897-1905), *8,* cxcix, 323. Also: "non etiam a nobis animadverti, ea, quae in objectis externis, luminis, coloris, odoris, saporis, soni, caloris, frigoris & aliarum tactilium qualitatum, vel etiam formarum substantialium, nominibus indigitamus, quicquam aliud esse quam istorum objectorum varias dispositiones, quae efficiunt ut nervos nostros variis modis movere possint" (*ibid.,* cxviii, p. 322). This is similar to Boyle's position.

It is interesting also that in his *De Corpore* Hobbes associates the notion of "power" with that of causal efficacy, arguing that the *power of the agent* and the *efficient cause* are the same thing, and goes on to argue that "these powers . . . are but conditional, namely, *the agent has power, if it be applied to a patient; and the patient has power if it be applied to an agent;* otherwise neither of them have power, nor can the accidents, which are in them severally, be properly called powers." (*The Metaphysical System of Hobbes in Twelve Chapters From Elements of Philosophy Concerning the Body,* selected by Mary Whiton Calkins, 2nd ed. [LaSalle, Illinois, 1963], pp. 76 ff.) Hobbes, like Descartes, thus denies that bodies are ontologically causative in nature, that the powers are inherently active in bodies. They exist only insofar as bodies are related in certain specifiable ways.

29. Locke, *op. cit.* (Note 25), *1,* 313.
30. *Ibid.,* p. 310.
31. *Ibid.,* p. 313.

imperfectly, a "simple" idea of natural power. And on the whole he tends to conceive powers in the relational sense, though passages such as those cited could be construed, and were by eighteenth-century thinkers, as supporting a substantive conception of powers.

It remained for Berkeley, Hume, and Reid to contest the Lockean analysis. Working from different points of view, they isolated a central difficulty which has a twofold aspect. Can there be any clear and distinct idea of power from sensory experience? Even granted an affirmative answer to this, there is seemingly no warrant in terms of Locke's doctrine of primary and secondary qualities for ascribing the notion of powers to insensible particles of matter. Both these problems were fundamental to natural philosophers like Hutton and Priestley.

III

Newton's theory of forces and Locke's doctrine of powers were to have a profound but diverse influence on eighteenth-century thought. Two thinkers early in the eighteenth century who developed these ideas were the New England divine Jonathan Edwards and the Cambridge theologian and natural philosopher Robert Greene. Edwards' natural philosophy was primarily an extension of ideas implicit in the Queries to Newton's *Opticks,* and a reformulation of the theory of primary and secondary qualities (probably influenced by Locke and Berkeley).[32] Thinking within a generalized Newtonian framework about matter and force, Edwards concluded that the essence of matter was resisting power. This theory, though not always derived from the same presuppositions, was to be advanced many times in the course of the eighteenth century.

Theological in orientation and following in the tradition of the Cambridge Platonists, Edwards closely identifies space with God, arguing that "Space is this necessary, eternal, infinite, and omnipresent being."[33] Since Edwards identifies being in general with

---

32. See George Rupp, "The 'Idealism' of Jonathan Edwards," *Harvard Theological Review,* 62 (1969), 209-226.
33. Harvey G. Townsend, ed., *The Philosophy of Jonathan Edwards from His Private Notebooks* (Eugene, Oregon, 1955), p. 2.
Although Edwards' ideas as expressed in his notebooks were very likely not widely known, similar views regarding matter and space are apparent in his influ-

God, all things are from God, and through Him subsist their characteristics and mutual relationships. Thus it is not so much *that* the reality of all things is *in* God which interests Edwards, but *how* that reality is *comprehended* in God. Accordingly his identification of being in general with divine presence does not result in pantheism.[34] Crucial in the thought of Edwards, as in that of Newton, is the relationship of space with God. Though he identifies being in general with consciousness, believing it inconceivable that anything exist and nothing be conscious of it,[35] Edwards does not wish to affirm Berkeley's conclusion that for a finite "material" entity *esse* is *percipi*. Thus the real and necessary existence of absolute space shows *how* all things are comprehended in God. But Edwards repudiates Berkeley's conclusion that space is relative, since for Berkeley it is the case "either that real space is God, or else that there is something besides God which is eternal, uncreated, infinite, indivisible, immutable."[36] For this reason alone, Edwards is not a "subjective idealist" but more an empiricist holding that entities and their relations dynamically projected in time through space manifest an objective order which Newton's natural philosophy describes and explains.[37]

Edwards' view of matter follows directly from his conception of the total dependence of all existence on God. In a non-Lockean move Edwards argues that all primary qualities are merely manifestations of one and the same thing; i.e., solidity, impenetrability, and indi-

---

ential *Freedom of the Will* ed. Paul Ramsey (New Haven, 1957), pp. 384-396. In this work Edwards developed doctrines of causation and determinism which not only shaped his views on moral responsibility, but also set the framework for his philosophy of nature. Edwards' views on free will and causation were widely known in Scotland, as he commented on the determinism advocated by Lord Kames. (*Ibid.*, pp. 453-479.) Priestley held a high opinion of the New England divine, whose ideas on divine necessity he considered in association with Kames, Hartley, Collins, and Hume. (*Works, 3,* 449-540 [Note 84, below].)

34. Though Edwards holds that nature is an expression of God's attributes he does not contend that it is identical with God. On the contrary, he is at pains to stress that there is a reality separate from human perception which God created as the object of knowledge.

35. Edwards' view that it is absurd to suppose anything exists and nothing be aware of it basically characterizes the ubiquity of God. In Edwards' view the creation of anything presupposes a consciousness of it.

36. *The Works of George Berkeley, Bishop of Cloyne*, ed. A. A. Luce and T. E. Jessop, 9 vols. (London, 1948-1957), *2,* 94.

37. Rupp, *op. cit.* (Note 32), and Priestley, *op. cit.* (Note 6).

NEWTONIAN FORCES AND LOCKEAN POWERS

visibility are similar phenomena, since "bodies resist division and penetration only as they obstinately persever to be."[38] They remain in being, however, since

> resistance or solidity are by the immediate exercise of divine power, it follows that the certain unknown substance which philosophers used to think subsisted by itself and stood underneath and kept up solidity and all other properties (which they used to say it was impossible for a man to have an idea of) is nothing at all distinct from solidity itself. Or, if they must needs apply that word to something else that does really and properly subsist by itself and support all properties, they must apply it to the divine being or power itself. And here, I believe, all those philosophers would apply it if they knew what they meant themselves. So that this substance of bodies at last becomes either "nothing" or nothing but the Deity acting in that particular manner in those parts of space where he thinks fit. So that speaking most strictly there is no proper substance but God himself.[39]

There are a number of interesting points arising from this passage. Here and elsewhere Edwards rejects by implication the need for intermediary entities like an aether or fluids of various sorts; his close connection between God, space, and power obviates the need for such mediating principles. Thus, solidity, the essence of matter at the level of sensory experience, "results from the immediate exercise of God's power causing there to be indefinite resistance in that place where it is."[40] With matter thus reduced to a resisting power—a resistance to being annihilated—there is no epistemological and ontological need for the existence of an unknown substratum: atoms and visible bodies are fundamentally characterized as focal points of divine energy.[41]

This line of reasoning can be illuminated by further considering Edwards' view of the distinction between primary and secondary

---

38. Townsend, *op. cit.* (Note 33), p. 13.
39. *Ibid.*, p. 17.
40. *Ibid.*, p. 16.
41. It is fascinating to observe that Edwards' conception of parts of empty space becoming by divine fiat centers of resisting power is similar to Newton's doctrine, as expressed in an unpublished manuscript *De Gravitatione* (see A. Rupert Hall and Marie Boas Hall, eds., *Unpublished Papers of Isaac Newton* [Cambridge, 1962], pp. 90-156), of spatial loci manifesting through divine power "imperviousness" to penetration. It may be that Edwards used hints scattered throughout Newton's published writings in developing his own position.

qualities. The only true substance is God, according to Edwards, and since all reality is comprehended in God, space is the "Deity acting," and the nature of this action is the law of space and gravity. From the epistemological point of view, Edwards, in denying the existence of a substratum, can hold that ideas of primary qualities do not relate to qualities inherent in such an entity. Thus, they and secondary qualities in principle can be known, since the primary qualities are not in a privileged ontological position in the sense of inhering in an unknowable substratum. Theologically speaking, given that primary qualities reduce to solidity or resistance and that the latter is a direct expression of divine activity, no qualities attributable to such a phenomenon will be in a privileged epistemological position. Reasoning in this manner, Edwards reached an interesting conclusion which unites Newton's theory of forces with the idea of matter as a collection of resisting powers. Space being the most general condition of existence, the manifestation of the dynamics of God's action, and all things by its mediation being comprehended in divine nature, Edwards' general view of reality is fundamentally relational. Gravitation is merely a means of characterizing centers of resisting power with respect to general relations like motion, just as sensory qualities are a means of characterizing divine power as it shows itself in parts of space by making these impenetrable. Thus solidity, in Edwards' sense, and gravitation are two faces of the same reality, for the "laws of nature" were "the stated methods of God's acting with respect to bodies and the stated conditions of the alteration of the manner of His acting."[42] These laws of the manifestation of divine power, Newton's laws, could only be known through sensory experience as solidity or resistance.

While Edwards reasoned within a Newtonian framework and developed a theological argument to demonstrate that the essence of matter was resisting power, Greene rejected Newton's corpuscularian philosophy of homogeneous matter and the void and developed a philosophical argument to show that matter was resisting power. Thus, Greene, along with Berkeley, was one of the first English natural philosophers to attempt to overthrow the fundamental principles of the new science, though he accepted in principle the

42. Townsend, *op. cit.* (Note 33), p. 19.

I

NEWTONIAN FORCES AND LOCKEAN POWERS

theory of universal gravitation. We have already noted the close association of force and void space in Newton's thought, and it is significant that while Priestley was to develop a concept of matter as powers by extending Newton's theory of the paucity of matter and the primacy of force, Greene was led to a similar conclusion by rejecting Newton's doctrine of the void, but nevertheless basing his argument on a theory of active forces. In his *Principles of the Philosophy of the Expansive and Contractive Forces* (1727) he argues that the doctrine of the void was not confirmed by sensory experience. After examining Newton's ideas regarding the porosity of matter, he concludes:

> And now I ask could any Authority, besides that of the present Philosophy, ever support so absurd an assertion as this, that Gold and consequently all other dense Substances here mention'd have more Pores than solid Parts? Why, we must bid adieu to our Senses, and to all our Notices communicated from thence, if we must acknowledge this for a Truth, and affirm that Solidity, Plain, Visible, and palpable Solidity is nothing but mere Space.[43]

Greene thus holds the concept of void space to be gratuitous. A similar epistemological view was to be developed by Kant in a more sophisticated way, for Kant was to maintain that empty space is not a possible object of direct experience.[44] With Greene it is clear that

---

43. Robert Greene, *The Principles of the Philosophy of the Expansive and Contractive Forces or An Inquiry into the Principles of Modern Philosophy: that is, into the Several Chief Rational Sciences, which are Extant* (Cambridge, 1727), p. 5. For somewhat different treatments of Greene's thought see Schofield, *op. cit.* (Note 3), pp. 117-121, and Thackray, *op. cit.*, (Note 11), pp. 126-134, who fail to delineate the philosophical argument that was fundamental to Greene's conception of nature. Schofield's failure to do this leads him to regard Greene as a "materialist" (supposedly believing causes to inhere in substances), whereas Greene's notion that the essence of matter is action or force would seem to indicate that Greene should be regarded as a "mechanist" (in the emphasis on forces), to use Schofield's terms. In our view Schofield's categories of "mechanism" and "materialism" are simply inadequate here. See Note 3 above.

44. In itself there is nothing remarkable about this claim: probably no one has ever claimed that empty space was an object of experience. Kant, however, was the first to take this seriously in his consideration of the foundations of Newtonian science. When we explain densities in terms of comparative ratios of void intensities to solid particles composing bodies, as do the Newtonians, the explanation turns on something that is not directly experienced. This is essentially Greene's point. Of course Greene had nothing like the Kantian critical philosophy at his disposal, but both in respect to being a plenist and in his view of force he is close to Kant in spirit. In the *Metaphysical Foundations of*

his critique of the new science was founded on a more empirical view of knowledge which itself, ironically enough, more nearly satisfied the ideology of seventeenth-century science.

In place of the theory of void space, Greene held that there was a plenum in nature. He stated that there are four possible positions which can be held regarding the conception of matter: matter could be "Similar or Dissimilar, and there must be a Plenum or a Vacuum; a Plenum and a Vacuum it is Evident cannot Subsist together, nor a Similar and Dissimilar Matter; consequently there are only Four Cases Remaining, and therefore there are only Four Possible Hypotheses, which Philosophers can Espouse, or Maintain."[45] After characterizing the possible combinations of similar and dissimilar matter, a plenum, and a vacuum, Greene asserts that he will maintain and defend the conception of "Dissimilar Matter and a Plenum"

Natural Science, trans. James Ellington (New York, 1970), Kant tells us: "The familiar question as to the admissibility of empty spaces in the world. For space is required for all forces of matter; and since space also contains the conditions of the laws of the diffusion of these forces, it is necessarily presupposed before all matter," and he adds: "For all experience gives us only comparatively empty spaces to cognize; these can be perfectly explicated from matter's property of filling its space by an expansive force greater or progressively smaller to infinity, in all possible degrees without requiring empty spaces" (p. 94). Thus, space is necessarily posited before matter. In the *Critique of Pure Reason* [A:24] we are told that we can never represent to ourselves the absence of space though we can think it empty of objects. Space for Kant is a form of pure intuition. As Gerd Buchdahl has pointed out in a private communication, space as pure formal intuition should not be confused with empty intuition. However, in the *Critique* [A:166-170; B:208-212] Kant tells us that in an epistemological context "Every reality therefore in a phenomenon has intensive quantity, that is, a degree." And [A:170-174; B:212-216] "if therefore all reality in perception has a certain degree, between which and negation there is an infinite succession of ever smaller degrees, and if every sense must have a definite degree of receptivity of sensations, it follows that no perception, and therefore no experience is possible, that could prove—the complete absence of all reality in a phenomenon. We see therefore that experience can never supply a proof of empty space—because the total absence of reality in a sensuous intuition can itself never be perceived." Again, in the third analogy of experience Kant puts his position on void space: "Empty space may exist where perception cannot reach, and where therefore no empirical knowledge of coexistence takes place, but, in that case, *it is no object for any possible experience*," *Critique* [A:212-216; B:259-263]. Italics supplied. In the *Metaphysical Foundations*, Kant argues against the mechanical mode of explaining phenomena. He conceives reality as filled with the intensive forces of repulsion and attraction. Though both are ontologically the same, repulsion with respect to experience is epistemologically prior. (*Ibid.*, pp. 57-58.)

45. Greene, *op. cit.* (Note 43), p. 934.

I

NEWTONIAN FORCES AND LOCKEAN POWERS

which hitherto has had no advocates. Greene thus rejected both Newton's doctrine of void space and his theory of the homogeneity of matter, and the crux of his acceptance of a plenum was his rejection of "Similar Matter and a Vacuum."[46] In addition, he rejected Newton's doctrine of essential qualities, those qualities which did not intend and remit of degrees. Speaking of motion, Greene argues that the postulation of a vacuum is not necessary, since the plenum will not offer "infinite Resistance" to bodies:

> if all Matter was the same, there would indeed be an infinite Resistance in a Plenum; but if it is not, and there are various kinds of Matter, and of differing Forces, and Aether should be suppos'd to have an infinitely small Resistance, such an Objection will be of no Validity against a Plenum, and consequently no Argument in Favour of a Vacuum; nor can it be said, if the world was full of the minutest Resistance, that taken together such a Resistance would be Infinite, and consequently Motion impossible; since the Quantity of Resistance cannot be estimated from the Quantity of Matter which resists, but from the Degree of Resistance, which belongs to any greater or less portion of it . . . for the intrinsick Nature of the Fluid is to be consider'd (and not the Quantity) to determine its Quality and Force.[47]

Hence by means of his theory that matter manifests various gradations and intensities, the plenum—its "intrinsick Nature"—is something that can be intended and remitted. This is a very important argument. According to Newton, objects can only fill or occupy space in an absolute sense;[48] in order to explain why of any two bodies one is heavier than the other, we must suppose that it is more tightly packed with solid particles and consequently contains less pores or empty space.[49] In rejecting the Newtonian doctrine of void space, Greene offers an alternative to Newton's argument.

---

46. *Ibid.*, pp. 934 f. Greene also argued that the concept of a plenum in nature was in consonance with divine power (*ibid.*, p. 652).

47. Robert Greene, *The Principles of Natural Philosophy, In which is shown the Insufficiency of the Present Systems, to give us any Just Account of that Science: And the Necessity there is of some New Principles, In order to furnish us with a True and Real Knowledge of Nature* (Cambridge, 1712), pp. 117 f.

48. See McGuire, *op. cit.* (Note 5).

49. For interesting discussions of this conception of matter and Kant's alternative view, see Jonathan Bennett, *Kant's Analytic* (Cambridge, 1966), pp. 170-176, and Patrick Suppes, "Some Extensions of Randall's Interpretation of Kant's Philosophy of Science," *Naturalism and Historical Understanding* (New York, 1967), pp. 109-120.

He rejected the Newtonian theory of intention and remission as applied only to *qualities,* and argued that two bodies may be of the *same size,* take up exactly the same volume, while having different degrees of hardness or rigidity. Thus the way in which these two volumes could contain two different amounts of "stuff" would not depend on the ratio of particles to void space. Thus every space can be thought of both as full and yet as filled in varying degrees. That is, for Greene, "bodies" can intend and remit of degrees, and the distinction between material bodies and the plenum is merely one of degree of intensity. Material bodies present more "intense" degrees of resistance in nature than does the plenum, and can be conceived to pass through a celestial plenum having "minutest Resistance." Thus, by viewing forces as manifestations of a plenum with degrees of intensity in its action on the senses, Greene, as Kant later, could bypass the question of the nature of the centers to and from which these forces act. It was not necessary to ask to what these forces were to be ascribed. The novelty of Greene's thought is partially obscured by the fact that he is still using the traditional distinction between substance and attribute. Moreover, it is not that Greene saw himself as providing a *Principia* containing a set of scientific techniques, but as outlining the possibility of a physics based on different principles from those of the corpuscularian philosophy.

This interpretation of a universal plenum is borne out by his conception of "dissimilar matter"; for in the context of rejecting atoms and the void he says:

> I have also shewn that such a Similar and Homogeneous Matter is a mere Hypothesis of the Mind, and wholly Incapable of solving any one Appearance we can name, or any one Quality of that Matter, which is assum'd and taken to account for; on the contrary, we propose from these Intrinsick forces in Matter, and from an Universal Action in all Nature . . . to Explain, the Various Phenomenons which occur to us and which we are fully satisfied may be better and more Rationally done than from fanciful and humorous Abstractions of a void Space, of a mere Length, Breadth, and Thickness, and of an Hypothetick, Extended, Solid, Divisible and Moveable Matter, without one Real Force belonging to it.[50]

50. Greene, *op. cit.* (Note 43), p. 62.

NEWTONIAN FORCES AND LOCKEAN POWERS

We could find no more uncompromising repudiation of Newtonian principles than this. The traditional primary qualities are for Greene merely "Abstracted" ideas,[51] and thus matter as generally conceived is merely a hypothetical construct having no existence in reality.

According to Greene's theory of matter, however, dissimilarity in physical objects and the differential intensities of the universal plenum are to be explained by the ratio of two different kinds of force. Matter is an active substance and is thus known through its action which "we have also said is distinguished into the Expansive and Contractive Forces, which, and the Different Combinations of them, are the occasion of those Diversities of Matter we Feel and See to Exist in Like and Equal Portions of Space."[52] For Greene, "Nature is active, and . . . matter itself is so,"[53] and he argues that "Action or Force in General is the Essence or Substratum of Matter."[54] It is merely a prejudice of the "Corpuscular Way" that philosophers have argued that "Action is Inconceivable without some Solid Substance to support such Action, and in which it should Inhere."[55] Thus, the active substratum is expansive and contractive forces, and Greene is quite explicitly stating two related theses which are found in later writers. First, the essence of matter is resistance or action, and second, matter is merely a set of active powers, not adhering in a substratum and capable of resisting by impulse. Moreover, Greene holds that the abstracted ideas of primary qualities themselves arise from resistance, since we could not see or feel extension, impenetrability, or solidity unless bodies were "Endued with some Force or Action."[56] Greene is therefore groping his way toward the notion that resistance *qua* active force is epistemologically *prior* to the idea of solidity as a mode of contact between material bodies conceived as filling regions of space.

Greene did not develop his novel ideas with clarity or rigor, and they lay buried in his rambling and diffuse writings. It is likely that Greene generalized the line of reasoning of Boyle and Locke analyzed above, for though Greene could not accept Locke's ontology

51. Greene, *op. cit.* (Note 47), p. 120.
52. Greene, *op. cit.* (Note 43), p. 409.
53. Greene, *op. cit.* (Note 47), p. 391.
54. Greene, *op. cit.* (Note 43), p. 286.
55. *Ibid.*, p. 409.
56. *Ibid.*, p. 287.

or epistemology—and he devotes an entire book of his major treatise to the philosophy of Locke's *Essay*—it is probable that his own theory of matter arose from Locke's analysis of secondary qualities arising from causal powers. For in his examination of Locke's account of the simple ideas of color, taste, and smell, Greene concludes:

> Lastly as to Peculiar, Extensions of Bodies by which they Appear in such a Certain Manner to Fill the Eye with a Greater or Less Constipation of their Parts, and to our Feeling to have a certain Degree of Roughness or Smoothness, of Solidity or Fluidness, of Rarer or Denser, and of all the Tangible Qualities of Bodies, by which they are Infinitely Diversify'd to us; They seem to arise from the Filling of their Dimensional Spaces with Infinitely Different kinds of Matter, that is, with Different Sorts of Actions, Communicated to our Senses. . . . All which theory of Matter only proceeds upon this One Plain Axiom, that it is Impossible for us to have any Sensations from Matter, but by some Kind of Action, or Other, Impressed upon our Minds from it; And that, it is Impossible, we should have Different Sensations but by such Different Impressions or Actions.[57]

Thus, for Greene, a material object is no more than a set of active powers able to produce visual and tactile experience, and Locke's powers are assimilated into the realm of mind-related experience from the invisible realm of particles. Thus such Lockean occult qualities as substance and subtratum are avoided, as indeed is the Newtonian category of forces as causes, and Greene's conception of matter is squarely based on sensory evidence. As we shall see, Robert Young in his *Essay on the Powers and Mechanism of Nature* (1788) was to indicate that his conception of matter as active powers was derived from Locke, linking these causal powers to an active substance, an immaterial entity possessed of inherent activity. It seems clear that Greene viewed the content of sensations as varying not only in kind but in intensity, and he conceived matter as a counterpart comprising varying combinations of moving force impinging on the senses as action or resistance. Thus, apart from the intrinsic difficulties which Greene associates with the atomic hypothesis, he could well have been led to the

---

57. *Ibid.*, p. 659.

NEWTONIAN FORCES AND LOCKEAN POWERS

theory that matter and the plenum manifest differential intensities arising from active powers by a theory of knowledge based directly on the character of the contents of sensation. Though this conception of matter would not have satisfied Hume, it does have striking parallels with the more sophisticated views of Kant. Nevertheless, it is significant that Greene developed his conception of matter in terms of the categories of the Newtonian theories of force, space, and essential qualities (which he rejected) and of the Lockean doctrine of powers (which he implicitly extended to the realm of mind-related experience). Both Edwards and Greene developed theories of matter which are best understood in terms of their relation to Newtonian forces and Lockean powers.

IV

The problems of Locke's analysis of matter and of his discussions of causal powers and the relation between primary and secondary qualities were to receive a sustained analysis in the work of Berkeley and Hume. Both were concerned to reduce primary qualities to the perceptible domain of the secondary, and both held that the idea of power was not established either from direct sensory experience or from reflection. These arguments were to be reflected in the epistemology of natural philosophers like Priestley and Hutton, who were to make the realm of seventeenth-century secondary qualities the basis for doctrines regarding the essential characteristics of matter. At the same time these natural philosophers did not accept the views of Berkeley and Hume on the ontological status of power, regarding the essence of matter as being constituted of "powers." However, the legitimacy of the concept of power was defended by Thomas Reid, and the interpretation of Berkeley's and Hume's arguments is essential to an understanding of the thought of Priestley and Hutton.

On the basis of his critique of abstract ideas and a nominalistic ontology of unrelated particulars,[58] Berkeley rejects the view that

58. In discussing the possibility that ideas represent objects, Berkeley emphasizes that "an idea can be like nothing but an idea" (*op. cit.* [Note 36], 2, 44). Thus, ideas can only represent other ideas, because they only resemble one another in being ideas. For Locke, however, ideas resemble objects, and he appeals to God for certainty that our ideas resemble things.

power or activity is inherent in physical objects. In the *Principles of Human Knowledge* (1710) he opposed Locke's doctrine of abstract general terms (held to correspond to abstract ideas), rejecting the Lockean distinction between things and ideas. Analogous to this was his rejection of a substratum of invisible particles, which the new philosophy held was responsible both for the properties of physical objects and for the mind's sensations and ideas. For Berkeley, all that is known of external reality is what is perceivable, and *qua* ideas these are concrete and unrelated particulars, not a spurious realm of invisible particles. Hence the corpuscles of the new science exist only as reified concepts.[59] In the same way he rejects the distinction between primary and secondary qualities: "For my own part, I see evidently that it is not in my power to frame an idea of a body extended and moved, but I must withal give it some colour or other sensible quality which is acknowledged to exist only in the mind. In short, extension, figure, and motion, abstracted from all other qualities, are inconceivable. Where therefore the other sensible qualities are, there must these be also, to wit, in the mind and no where else."[60] Thus both sorts of quality are on the same ontological footing; both are mind-dependent, and he applies the same argument to Lockean powers: "All our ideas, sensations, or the things which we perceive, by whatsoever names they may be distinguished, are visibly inactive, there is nothing of power or agency included in them . . . since they [ideas] and every part of them exist only in the mind, it follows that there is nothing in them but what is perceived. But whoever shall attend to his ideas, whether of sense or reflexion, will not perceive in them any power or activity; there is therefore no such thing contained in them."[61] Thus, Berkeley concludes that an idea of power cannot be obtained from experience; ideas are passive and can reveal neither activity nor power. It follows that the primary qualities can neither be the cause of sensations nor "the effects of powers" resulting from the configuration of corpuscles. For Berkeley, agency

59. For an interesting and rather different view of Berkeley's treatment of abstract general ideas and the substratum of invisible particles see Gerd Buchdahl, *Metaphysics and the Philosophy of Science; The Classical Origins: Descartes to Kant* (Oxford, 1970), pp. 279 ff, 309.
60. Berkeley, *op. cit.* (Note 36), 2, 45.
61. *Ibid.*, p. 51.

NEWTONIAN FORCES AND LOCKEAN POWERS

and change are to be located "in an incorporeal active substance or spirit"[62] to accord with his conception of divine causation. Not only did Hume criticize doctrines of causation apparent in seventeenth-century thinkers, but he also rejected the theological view of agency found in the writings of Berkeley, and with that the view of Malebranche and the Cartesians.[63]

In the work of Hume there is a sustained *philosophical* analysis of the concept of power, with the consequence that theological and many natural philosophical presuppositions are rejected as being without meaning for such concepts as change and cause. In the *Treatise of Human Nature* (1739) Hume presents a devastating attack on the principles of the new science, especially those relating to the theory of primary qualities.[64] Having accepted that secondary qualities have no real independent existence, Hume argues further that we have no idea of solidity and therefore none of matter, so the primary qualities do not afford us a distinct idea of body:

> The idea of solidity is that of two objects, which being impell'd by the utmost force, cannot penetrate each other; but still maintain a separate and distinct existence. Solidity, therefore, is perfectly incomprehensible alone, and without the conception of some bodies, which are solid, and maintain this separate and distinct existence. Now what idea have we of these bodies? The ideas of colours, sounds, and other secondary qualities are excluded. The idea of motion depends on that of extension, and the idea of extension on that of solidity. 'Tis impossible, therefore, that the idea of solidity can depend on either of them. For that wou'd be to run in a circle, and make one idea depend on another, while at the same time the latter depends on the former. Our modern philosophy, therefore, leaves us no just nor satisfactory idea of solidity; nor consequently of matter.[65]

---

62. *Ibid*, p. 52.

63. See Richard H. Popkin, "Berkeley and Pyrrhonism," *Review of Metaphysics*, 5 (1951), 223-246; *id.*, "David Hume and the Pyrrhonian Controversy," *ibid.*, 6 (1952), 65-81; A. A. Luce, *The Dialectic of Immaterialism: An Account of the Making of Berkeley's Principles* (London, 1963); and Richard A. Watson, *The Downfall of Cartesianism 1673-1712: A Study of Epistemological Issues in Late 17th Century Cartesianism* (The Hague, 1966).

64. Hume argues not only that we only know "impressions" and "ideas," but that only impressions and ideas exist; thus "The idea of a substance as well as that of a mode, is nothing but a collection of simple ideas, that are united by the imagination, and have a particular name assigned to them." (David Hume, *A Treatise of Human Nature*, ed. L. A. Selby-Bigge [Oxford, 1888], p. 16.)

65. Hume, *op. cit.* (Note 64), pp. 228 f.

I

Therefore there "remains nothing, which can afford us a just and consistent idea of body."[66]

Drawing on his argument that activity is not a necessary characteristic of a physical thing's continuing existence, Hume rejects the view that we have an idea of power, force, or efficacy. Instances of power in bodies are not observed under any specifiable conditions: "All ideas are deriv'd from, and represent impressions. We never have any impression, that contains any power or efficacy. We never therefore have any idea of power."[67] He also criticizes natural philosophers who attribute power to the activity of God: "For if every idea be deriv'd from an impression, the idea of a deity proceeds from the same origin; and if no impression, either of sensation or reflection, implies any force or efficacy, 'tis equally impossible to discover or even imagine any such active principle in the deity."[68] Hence, even if force or power did exist as an independent entity, it could not be a characteristic of, or a substitute for, matter, the existence of which, as described by the new science, Hume also doubted. With this went the rejection of Lockean powers as attributable to invisible particles. Though the natural philosophers of the eighteenth century could accept the reduction of primary qualities to the perceptible domain of the secondary, they could not accept Hume's uncompromisingly skeptical conclusion:

> When we reason from cause and effect, we conclude, that neither colour, sound, taste, nor smell have a continu's and independent existence. When we exclude these sensible qualities there remains nothing in the universe, which has such an existence.[69]

In denying the reality of the external world, Berkeley and Hume clearly went too far for natural philosophers such as Priestley and Hutton, for though the natural philosophers wished to interpret nature in terms of principles squarely related to experience and though they rejected the invisible realm of seventeenth-century thought, the principles of these philosophers threatened the very possibility of a realist view of scientific knowledge. In addition, the natural philosophers related their work, in one sense or another, to

66. *Ibid.*, p. 229.
67. *Ibid.*, p. 161.
68. *Ibid.*, p. 160.
69. *Ibid.*, p. 231.

I

NEWTONIAN FORCES AND LOCKEAN POWERS

that of Newton, whereas Berkeley and Hume showed little or no interest in discussing Newton's methodology or philosophy of science.[70] The Scottish Common-Sense school of philosophy was in marked contrast to this; not only did Thomas Reid attempt a repudiation of what he characterized as Hume's uncompromising skepticism, but he also undertook the first systematic analysis of Newton's methodology and philosophical principles, having interests both in natural philosophy and metaphysics.[71] For these reasons, Reid's philosophy was an important element of the general intellectual climate to which many natural philosophers were indebted.[72]

Reid's appeal to common sense appears very clearly in his examination of the concept "power" in the thought of Locke, Hume, and, by implication, Berkeley. In the *Essay on the Active Powers of the Human Mind* (1788), Reid considers terms like "agency," "efficacy," "action," "cause," and "change," which in everyday language are closely associated with power.[73] He argues that the idea of power cannot be derived from experience, and though he agrees with Hume that we have no idea of power either from sense or reflection, he holds, nevertheless, that we have such a concept and moreover that it is meaningful, clear, and distinct.[74] For Reid, the idea of power arises mainly from the operations of the mind:

> The only distinct conception I can form of active power is, that it is an attribute in a being by which he can do certain things if he wills. This, after all, is only a relative conception. It is relative to the effect,

---

70. The British empiricists did not, of course, ignore Newton: Berkeley's *De Motu*, for example, continued a critique of Newton's concepts of absolute space and time; but these philosophers paid little attention to Newton's methodological writings.

71. See L. L. Laudan, "Thomas Reid and the Newtonian Turn of British Methodological Thought," *The Methodological Heritage of Newton,* ed. Butts and Davis (Oxford, 1970), pp. 103-131; G. E. Davie, "Hume and the Origins of the Common Sense School," *Revue Internationale de Philosophie, 6* (1952), 213-221; and Ernest C. Mossner, *Life of David Hume* (Austin, 1954).

72. The natural philosophy of the Scottish Enlightenment has received scant attention by historians. For common-sense philosophy see Andrew Seth, *Scottish Philosophy* (Edinburgh and London, 1885); S. A. Grave, *The Scottish Philosophy of Common Sense* (Oxford, 1960); and also George Elder Davie, *The Democratic Intellect: Scotland and Her Universities in the Nineteenth Century* (Edinburgh, 1961).

73. Thomas Reid, *Essays on the Active Powers of the Human Mind,* introduction by Baruch Brody (Cambridge, Mass., 1969), p. 28.

74. *Ibid.,* p. 39.

and to the will of producing it. Take away these, and the conception vanishes.[75]

Active power is thus known only relative to its effects. Reid denies that we can know power in the Lockean sense of arising from collocations of primary qualities, but argues that we derive the idea of power from an instinctive disposition to see nature as uniform with respect to change and from attention to the operations of the mind, though "we neither perceive the agent nor the power, but the change only."[76] Thus though the concept of power is not found in sensory experience, it, like causation and the uniformity of nature, anticipates and structures our experience. Accordingly, Reid provided a justification of the concept of power, since the genesis of the idea is located in an area of human nature not treated explicitly by Hume's philosophical principles. This is clearly stated in the following passage from Reid's most mature writing:

> It is not easy to say where we first get the notion or idea of power. It is neither an object of sense nor of consciousness. We all see events one succeeding another; but we see not the power by which they are produced. We are conscious of the operations of our minds; but power is not an operation of mind. If we had no notions but such as are furnished by the extreme senses and by consciousness, it seems to be impossible that we should ever have any conception of power. Accordingly Mr. Hume, who has reasoned the most accurately upon this hypothesis denies that we have any idea of power, and clearly refutes the account given by Mr. Locke of the origin of this idea.
>
> But it is in vain to reason from an hypothesis against a fact, the truth of which every man may see by attending to his own thoughts. It is evident that all men, very early in life, not only have an idea of power, but a conviction that they have some degree in themselves, . . . without which no man can act the part of a reasonable being.[77]

Nevertheless, Reid's analysis failed to meet Hume's doubts regarding the origin of the notion, if it were claimed to arise from general experience.[78]

75. *Ibid.*, pp. 38 f.
76. *Ibid.*, p. 33.
77. Thomas Reid, *Essays on the Intellectual Powers of Man* [1785], ed. A. D. Woozley (London, 1941), pp. 382 f.
78. For a discussion of the differences between Hume and Reid on the notion of causality, see Laudan, *op. cit.* (Note 71), pp. 127 ff.

I

NEWTONIAN FORCES AND LOCKEAN POWERS

Reid went on to discuss "those active powers which Philosophers teach us to ascribe to matter,"[79] and he argued that for Newton, science was restricted to establishing laws connecting antecedent and consequent conditions, so that a law becomes a cause.[80] For this reason, it is not the concern of natural philosophy to discover causes having dispositional powers, and so natural philosophers can avoid the ambiguities inherent in terms like *"cause, agency,"* and *"active power."*[81] The notion of active power is meaningful, and efficient causes actually exist in reality even though the mind can never know "what their nature, their number, and their different offices may be."[82] Nevertheless Reid held that bodies could be conceived as sets of active powers: "I conclude, then, that colour is not a sensation, but a secondary quality of bodies, in the sense we have already explained; that it is a certain power or virtue in bodies, that in fair daylight exhibits to the eye an appearance, which is very familiar to us, although it hath no name."[83]

The similarity to Locke's analysis of causal powers giving rise to secondary qualities is apparent, and it is possible that Reid is indebted to the former for his dispositional theory of material objects. In this way, Reid can be seen to have provided a justification for the ascription of powers to matter; and it was this doctrine that was fundamental to the thought of Priestley and Hutton. Both, however, were critical of Reid. Priestley, though he tends to misrepresent Reid's position, criticizes his doctrine of instinctive principles of the mind by arguing that they can be reduced to Hartley's principle of association,[84] itself derived from Locke. In general, Priestley defends Locke's doctrines of ideas and sensation and his view of existence of the external world against Reid. Hutton, on the other hand, simply rejects Reid's claim that knowledge is to

---

79. Reid, *op. cit.* (Note 73), p. 41.
80. *Ibid.*, pp. 45 ff.
81. *Ibid.*, p. 41.
82. *Ibid.*, p. 47.
83. Thomas Reid, *An Inquiry into the Human Mind on the Principles of Common Sense* [1764], ed. T. Duggan (London, 1970), p. 101.
84. Priestley's "Introductory Essays" to his *Hartley's Theory of the Human Mind, on the Principle of the Association of Ideas; with Introductory Essays Relating to the Subject of It* (London, 1775), in *The Theological and Miscellaneous Works of Joseph Priestley*, ed. J. T. Rutt, 25 vols. (London, 1817-1831), *3*, 183 ff.

be found directly in sensation. Such crude empiricism, as Hutton saw it, went against a rationalistic approach to natural knowledge. Neither thinker, however, rejected Reid's notion that it was meaningful to speak of powers existing in matter.

V

A full understanding of Priestley's thought regarding matter demands an appreciation of a number of intellectual movements, which can only be indicated here. Of importance is the early reaction to Berkeley's *Principles,* for Berkeley was seen as a skeptic and immaterialist and was considered in many quarters, both in Britain and the Continent, as an atheist in consequence of his denial of the existence of matter.[85] As Berkeley denied the existence of matter according to the common-sense conception of a brute, irreducible entity, so his thought endangered the traditional theological dichotomy between the soul and matter. In his *Enquiry into the Nature of the Human Soul* (1733), Andrew Baxter developed the first sustained and serious critique of Berkeley's *Principles,*[86] with the avowed aim of defending the metaphysics of Christianity. Using the Newtonian idea of forces as the manifestation of God's power—gravity being "the virtue and power of an immaterial cause, or being, constantly impressed"[87] upon matter—Baxter sought to reassert the importance of the distinction between mind and matter, and thus to combat the alleged atheistic consequences of Berkeley's ideas. Baxter's work was well known to the Scottish Common-Sense school; and Priestley was aware both of Baxter's writings and of the reaction of philosophers like Reid to the skepticism of Berkeley and Hume. Priestley's response was an attempt to combat the immaterialism and skepticism of Berkeley, but—ironically—his materialism gave rise to the same fears as had Berkeley's immaterialism; for Priestley's philosophy also denied the traditional mind and matter dichotomy, though in a very different way than Berkeley's did. Priestley argued that "matter" was the only ontological reality, whereas for Berkeley it

85. See Harry M. Bracken, *The Early Reception of Berkeley's Immaterialism 1710-1733,* rev. ed. (The Hague, 1965).
86. *Ibid.,* pp. 59-81.
87. Andrew Baxter, *An Enquiry into the Nature of the Human Soul* (London, 1733), p. 15.

was "spirit." In the wider context both thinkers were against the dualist doctrine of man in traditional Christianity. Their monist viewpoint was not so much concerned with concepts of matter as with differing views regarding the nature of spirit as distinct from matter, and of the relationship between the two.

Finally, the extent to which Priestley's thought was indebted to his examination of academic philosophers such as Reid, Beattie, Oswald, and Hume has not been sufficiently appreciated. Priestley accepted the general philosophical framework of Locke and especially his doctrine of ideas. Moreover he upheld Hartley's theory of the mind, itself derived from Locke, in which all mental operations were held to be subject to the law of the association of ideas.[88] Thus, in terms of the empirical philosophy of Locke and Hartley, Priestley rejected many of the doctrines of the Common-Sense school of philosophy: their criticisms of Lockean ideas, their avowal of instinctive principles of the mind, and their analysis of sensation. In rejecting Hume's doctrine of causation and his general philosophical position, Priestley defended Locke's doctrines of power and causation.[89] Priestley's *Examination of Dr. Reid's Inquiry into the Human Mind* was written in 1774, before Priestley's mature statement of his philosophy of nature and theology in the *Disquisitions Relating to Matter and Spirit* (1777). His critical reactions to the Scottish philosophers—there are many references to Hume in the *Examination*—almost certainly helped to form his views on the nature of matter. Priestley's thought admirably illustrates the widespread interaction between academic philosophy and natural philosophy, evident during the course of the eighteenth century.

The system of thought developed by Priestley in the *Disquisitions Relating to Matter and Spirit* can be characterized as a philosophical monism. Basing his thought on a close examination of sensory experience he propounded a philosophy which purported to reinterpret the relationship between nature and man, and which he held to be in accordance with the pristine sense of Scripture. His principal object was:

88. See Joseph Priestley, *Examination of Dr. Reid's Inquiry into the Human Mind on the Principles of Common Sense* (London, 1774).
89. See Priestley's *Letters to a Philosophical Unbeliever* (London, 1780), in *Works* (Note 84), *4*, 398.

I

> to prove the uniform composition of man, or that what we call *mind,* or the principle of perception and thought, is not a substance distinct from the body, but the result of corporeal organization, ... for whatever matter be, I think I have sufficiently proved that the human mind is nothing more than a modification of it.[90]

His view of mind as a modification of matter, his denial of the preexistence of souls, his rejection of free will by his conception of philosophical necessity are the central doctrines of what Priestley called materialism. These and "that which is commonly called *Socinianism*" formed one system of thought based on nature and Scripture. He asserts that "whoever shall duly consider their *connection* and *dependence on one another,* will find no sufficient consistency in any general scheme of principles, that does not comprehend them all."[91] Though in general conditioned by his theological and religious outlook, Priestley's conception of matter is nevertheless important for his general philosophy of nature and man.[92] While he maintains that there are close links between the doctrines of materialism, Socinianism, and necessity, each was capable of separate demonstration; as scriptural exegesis led to Socinianism, the systematic and rational use of Newton's first two rules of philosophizing supported materialism. With a strict adherence to a theory of knowledge related to the contents of sensory experience, Priestley rejects the traditional theories of matter with their insistence on the absolute existence of primary qualities like solidity, arguing that "*resistance,* on which alone our opinion concerning the solidity or impenetrability of matter is founded, is never occasioned by *solid matter,* but by something of a very different nature, viz. a *power of repulsion* always acting at a real, and in general, an assignable distance from what we call the body itself."[93] Thus all that can be truly gathered about external reality is that "all resistance can differ only in degree, this circumstance ... [leading] to the supposition of a greater or less repulsive power, but never to the supposition of a cause of resistance entirely different from such a power."[94]

90. Joseph Priestley, *Disquisitions Relating to Matter and Spirit,* 2nd edition, 2 vols. (Birmingham, 1782), *1,* iv, in *Works* (Note 84), *3,* 220.
91. Priestley, *Works, 3,* 221.
92. For a different view of Priestley see Schofield, *op. cit.* (Note 3), pp. 261 ff.
93. Priestley, *Disquisitions,* in *Works* (Note 84), *3,* 223.
94. *Ibid.,* p. 227.

NEWTONIAN FORCES AND LOCKEAN POWERS

Newton's third Rule of Philosophizing is implicitly denied, since an invisible realm beyond the experience of senses, though it may exist, is not a possible object of knowledge.

This conception of matter, Priestley is keen to assert, is not incompatible with the characteristics of the mind. On his view, matter, being "destitute of what has hitherto been called *solidity*," is "no more incompatible with sensation and thought, than that substance, which, without knowing any thing farther about it, we have been used to call *immaterial*."[95] Employing this type of reasoning, Priestley concludes: "Man, according to this system, is no more than what we now see of him. His being commences at the time of his conception, or perhaps at an earlier period. The corporeal and mental faculties, inhering in the same substance, grow, ripen, and decay together; and whenever the system is dissolved, it continues in a state of dissolution, till it shall please that Almighty Being who called it into existence to restore it to life again."[96] Hence in Priestley's theory of matter, nature and man formed a coherent unity, and the skeptical challenge is thus abated: there is no need to posit the existence of a soul beyond experience, no need to entertain such theological doctrines as the preexistence of souls, and no need to ponder how the immaterial can act on the material. In knowing matter, manifested by varying degrees of intensity in relation to the content of immediate experience, we know the wisdom of God in creating a reality that can be utilized for human ends. And in knowing reality we comprehend all that is necessary for an understanding of human nature. As he rejected the absolute nature of primary qualities traditionally conceived as inhering in an invisible substratum, he rejected an immaterial and invisible soul. In this way not only does the mind avoid the extravagances of vain imagining, but it propounds an interpretation of nature that is consistent with the primitive sense of Scripture.

We must now give a more complete analysis of Priestley's arguments in relation to his natural philosophy. As has been noted, in his *Disquisitions Relating to Matter and Spirit* (1777) he wished to abolish the separate categories of matter and spirit, denying that "there are *two distinct kinds of substance . . . matter* and *spirit*."

95. *Ibid.*, p. 230.
96. *Ibid.*, pp. 256 f.

I

In Priestley's view matter had "been said to be possessed of the property of *extension* . . . and also of *solidity* or *impenetrability*, but it is said to be naturally destitute of all powers whatever," while spirit had been defined as "a substance entirely *destitute of all extension,* or *relation to space,* so as to have no property in common with matter; and therefore to be properly *immaterial,* but to be possessed of the powers of *perception, intelligence,* and *self-motion*." Moreover, he denies that two substances could be "capable of *intimate connection* and *mutual action*" unless they had common properties, and argues that "matter is not that *inert* substance that it has been supposed to be; that powers of *attraction* or *repulsion* are necessary to its very being, and that no part of it appears to be impenetrable to other parts."[97] In abolishing the dichotomy between matter and spirit Priestley argues that matter could not be defined as separate from its powers of attraction and repulsion:

> I therefore, define it [matter] to be a substance possessed of the property of *extension,* and of *powers of attraction or repulsion*. And since it has never yet been asserted, that the powers of *sensation* and *thought* are incompatible with these (*solidity,* or *impenetrability* only, having been thought to be repugnant to them) I therefore maintain, that we have no reason to suppose that there are in man two substances so distinct from each other, as have been represented.[98]

The essence of matter was therefore extension together with inherent powers of attraction and repulsion conceived to exist in a substantive sense and not merely relationally or dispositionally as in seventeenth-century thought. Appealing to Newton's first two Rules of Philosophizing, he went on to argue that the apparent impenetrability and solidity of matter were not essential properties of matter. Resistance was not due to the impenetrability and solidity of matter but to a power of repulsion; it was the powers which were "essential to the *actual existence* of all matter."[99] By denying that solidity and impenetrability were essential properties of matter, he concludes that solidity and impenetrability were due to the powers: "The reason why *solid extent* has been thought to be a complete definition of matter, is because it was imagined that we could separate from

97. *Ibid.,* pp. 218 ff.
98. *Ibid.,* p. 219.
99. *Ibid.,* p. 223.

NEWTONIAN FORCES AND LOCKEAN POWERS

our idea of it every thing else belonging to it, and leave these two properties independent of the rest, and subsisting by themselves. But it was not considered, that, in consequence of taking away *attraction,* which is a *power, solidity* itself vanishes."[100] Rejecting Locke's argument that solidity constituted the "essence of matter" he argues that the powers are essential to the existence of matter:

> I by no means suppose that these powers, which I make to be essential to the being of matter, and without which it cannot exist as a material substance at all, are *self-existent* in it. All that my argument amounts to, is, that from whatever source these powers are derived, or by whatever being they are communicated, matter cannot exist without them. . . . Whatever *solidity* any body has, it is possessed of it only in consequence of being endued with certain *powers.*[101]

Thus, solidity and substance were the mere effects of the powers, and all that was known of matter was powers and extension. He argues that "we know nothing more of the nature of substance than it is something which supports properties."[102] He supposes that the powers are essential to matter: "take away attraction and repulsion, and matter vanishes."[103] Priestley made a number of moves here. Not only did he argue that matter was known only through its powers, but he advanced an ontological statement that matter was known this way because it possessed extension and powers of attraction and repulsion. Without these powers it would be nothing except vacuous extension. Thus powers, rather than impenetrability or solidity, made matter what it was.

It is important to realize that Priestley did not explain the way in which powers could *"inhere in"* or *"belong to"*[104] matter and that he regarded the powers of attraction and repulsion as dispositional properties which by their action gave the appearance of impenetrability and solidity to matter. Thus, in effect Priestley was arguing that matter was a set of powers with respect to extension, not merely collapsing the traditional primary and secondary qualities distinction into the world of appearances, but abolishing it all together. It is

---

100. *Ibid.,* p. 224.
101. *Ibid.,* pp. 224 f.
102. *Ibid.,* p. 233.
103. *Ibid.,* p. 238.
104. *Ibid.*

little wonder that his critics failed to understand him, since like Berkeley's his thought lay essentially outside the traditional logic of substance and attribute.

This notion of matter as a set of powers and the denial of solidity as constituting the essence of matter can be found in Robert Young's *Essay on the Powers and Mechanism of Nature* (1788), a work in which Priestley's influence was acknowledged explicitly. Young argues that "Body . . . may be said to contain, or consist of, all its primary qualities, extension, solidity, figure, inactivity, and mobility, together with a power to produce certain effects."[105] He continues by emphasizing that "it appears to me as little justifiable to say solidity is in body, as to say heat is in the fire,"[106] arguing that "We can only conceive of solidity as being a resistance of the parts of any body, to a power which endeavours to separate them, or to bring them nearer together," denying that "bodies are in any sense solid, [other] than as having a power to resist."[107] The solidity of bodies is therefore held to be the result of the resisting powers of bodies, and Young goes on to maintain that "all which is real, positive, and peculiar to body, are certain active powers."[108] His position with respect to the content of sensations in relation to matter is similar to that of Greene. Young argues that "Our ideas of the differences of densities in bodies, is that of different fulnesses," and he goes on to emphasize that "Fulness is an idea capable of intention and remission; the same extension may be filled with different quantities of the filling substance; it may be more or less full, in all possible degrees."[109] Young, like his contemporary Kant and his predecessor Greene, is denying the corpuscularian hypothesis that the differences in densities of bodies is to be explained by varying ratios of pores to solid parts; rather, the hypothesis of varying intensity of "filling substance" satisfies the evidence of the senses and does not turn on the gratuitous assumption of empty space.

105. Robert Young, *An Essay on the Powers and Mechanism of Nature, intended By a Deeper Analysis of Physical Principles, To extend, improve, and more firmly establish, The Grand Superstructure of the Newtonian System* (London, 1788), pp. 11 f.
106. *Ibid.*, p. 15.
107. *Ibid.*, p. 17.
108. *Ibid.*, p. 20.
109. *Ibid.*, p. 34. Young explicitly applies the notion of intension and remission to bodies in a very similar way to Greene: see Greene, *loc. cit.* (Note 47).

I

NEWTONIAN FORCES AND LOCKEAN POWERS

In regarding matter as a complex of intensive powers capable of producing effects—a set of dispositional properties—Young also advanced ideas similar to Priestley's, to which he referred with approval, accepting Priestley's argument "inasmuch as it denies solidity."[110] Young indicated that his conception of matter as a set of active powers was derived from Locke's discussion of powers, explicitly referring to Locke's discussion of "powers in the bodies,"[111] and he explicitly rejected Berkeley's argument that "there was no intermediate agency between our minds and the supreme mind."[112]

Priestley's theory of matter as powers in conjunction with extension, his denial of solidity, and his supposition of the *"mutual penetrability of matter"*[113] were extremely influential. Priestley's arguments were taken up almost immediately by William Nicholson in his *Introduction to Natural Philosophy* (1782), where Nicholson states that "Matter is known to us only by its properties . . . we are totally ignorant of the substance in which these properties are united."[114] For Nicholson these properties are powers rather than qualities such as impenetrability. He goes on to argue that all the effects of impenetrability could be ascribed to the action of a repulsive force, noting that all bodies "exert a repulsive force on each other, and that the common effects which are attributed to contact and collision are produced by this repulsion: and, if so, why not attribute all the effects of the same nature to this cause, which we know exists, instead of supposing an impenetrability that can never be proved? If the force of repulsion be sufficiently great, it may not be in the power of any natural agent to overcome it; and, consequently, all the effects of a real impenetrability will take place, though the substance of matter itself may not be impenetrable, or even extended,"[115] Nicholson goes farther than Priestley in admitting the possibility of nonextended matter. In interpreting contact and collision in terms of repulsive action, Nicholson was advancing a

---

110. Robert Young, *op. cit.* (Note 105), p. 65.
111. *Ibid.*, p. 11n.
112. *Ibid.*, p. 64.
113. Priestley, *Works* (Note 84), *3*, 232.
114. William Nicholson, *An Introduction to Natural Philosophy*, 4th ed., 2 vols. (London, 1796), *1*, 7.
115. *Ibid.*, p. 15.

mode of analysis which was, as we shall see, treated more fully by John Leslie, John Robison, and Dugald Stewart in their rejection of contact action. With respect to micromatter, Nicholson's position was equally radical: "If by the first rule of philosophizing we are to admit no more causes of natural things than are sufficient to explain the phenomenon, then we know that a sphere of repulsion exists as the proximate cause of our ideas of impenetrability and extension, why should we add to this an extended atom existing in the centre of the sphere of repulsion?"[116] With his rejection of the necessity of extended atoms or centers of force, Nicholson goes beyond Boscovich and hints at a possibility not realized until the nineteenth century of a truly dynamical model of force entailing the denial of microparticles conceived as centers of force.

It is significant that Priestley develops his theory of matter as a set of powers in terms of the Newtonian theory of the primacy of force and the paucity of matter in the world. In arguing that the powers and forces in nature were all that constituted matter he refers to the Newtonian doctrine that space contained very little solid matter:

> The principles of the Newtonian philosophy were no sooner known, than it was seen how few, in comparison, of the phenomena of nature were owing to *solid matter,* and how much to *powers,* which were only supposed to accompany and surround the solid parts of matter. It has been asserted . . . that all the solid matter in the solar system might be contained within a nut-shell, there is so great a proportion of *void space* within the substance of the most solid bodies. Now, when solidity had apparently so very little to do in the system, it is really a wonder that it did not occur to philosophers sooner, that perhaps there might be nothing for it to do at all, and that there might be no such thing in nature.[117]

Thus, Priestley explicitly connects his denial of solidity and his theory that matter was a set of powers with the Newtonian doctrine of the paucity of matter and vacuity of the universe; powers and forces thus became the primary agents in nature. Priestley extended the Newtonian theory of the paucity of matter and propounded a

---

116. *Ibid.,* pp. 16 f.
117. Priestley, *Works* (Note 84), *3,* 230.

theory of Newtonian forces in the context of his interpretation of the Lockean doctrine of causal powers.

The implications of Priestley's denial of solidity and his emphasis on the forces in nature have been noted for chemical theories in the eighteenth century.[118] It has not, however, been sufficiently realized that Priestley developed his ideas in the context of optical theory. This is extremely significant, in that one of Newton's most important statements of the porosity of matter was propounded—as we have noted—in relation to the penetration of bodies by light, light being "stifled and lost" within the vacuities. Priestley denied the solidity and impenetrability of matter, and he argued that if one supposed the *"penetrability of matter"*[119] then one could explain the penetration of bodies by light, for "the particles of light are never found to impinge upon . . . or to be obstructed by"[120] dense bodies. Priestley stated that his theory of the penetrability of matter was also that of John Michell. Michell regarded light particles as ponderable entities, and his theory of the *"mutual penetration of matter"*[121] enabled him to explain the penetration of bodies by these particles.[122] Priestley also claimed that this theory of the penetrability of matter was similar to that of Boscovich.[123] Though Boscovich did not, in fact, replace matter by powers, since he maintained nonextended centers from which repulsion and attraction operated, nor did he argue for the penetrability of matter, nevertheless Priestley's connection of his own views with those of Boscovich shows the relation of his

---

118. Arnold Thackray, " 'Matter in a Nut-shell': Newton's *Opticks* and Eighteenth-century Chemistry," *Ambix, 15* (1968), 29-53; see also Thackray, *op. cit.* (Note 11).

119. Priestley, *Works* (Note 84), *3*, 231.

120. *Ibid.*, p. 228.

121. *Ibid.*, p. 232.

122. Joseph Priestley, *The History and Present State of Discoveries relating to Vision, Light, and Colours* (London, 1772), p. 391. Regarding light particles as ponderable entities he attempted to "ascertain the momentum of light" (*ibid.*, p. 387); he also calculated the short-range force between light and matter (*ibid.*, pp. 790 f.), and the gravitational retardation of the sun's light (*ibid.*, pp. 787-790). See also Russell McCormmach, "John Michell and Henry Cavendish: Weighing the Stars," *Brit. J. Hist. Sci., 4* (1968), 126-155. Though generally regarding the attraction of light by bodies as analogous to gravitational attraction, he also speculated that "it is just also possible, that light (and perhaps too the electric fluid, which seems to be in some degree allied to it, etc.) may not be so much affected by gravity, in proportion to their vis inertia, as other bodies" (Michell to Cavendish, 20 April 1784, Cavendish MSS., Chatsworth).

123. Priestley, *op. cit.* (Note 122), pp. 391 f.

theory of powers to the Newtonian tradition of forces operating in an almost matterless universe. The basis of Boscovich's system was a force law operating between mathematical points.[124] This law involved alternating zones of attractive and repulsive forces, undoubtedly an extension of Newton's notion of atoms as surrounded by envelopes of attractive and repulsive forces.[125] In arguing that light particles did not impinge on dense bodies, Priestley was using Newton's idea that a ray of light is reflected at a distance by an envelope of repulsive power surrounding a body. These arguments, as we will see, were important for a number of writers in the tradition of Newtonian forces.

Priestley's account of this theory of the penetration of bodies by light was taken up by William Herschel, whose unpublished speculations on the nature of matter date from about 1780 and were prompted by Priestley's *Disquisitions*. Herschel rejected the theory of the mutual penetrability of matter and the system of alternating spheres of attracting and repelling forces postulated by Boscovich, arguing that each particle of matter was endowed with a system of central forces and that phenomena were produced by the joint effect of the different forces. The innermost sphere (attraction of cohesion) "would effectively stop every particle that comes within its compass," and this would explain the absorption of light by bodies.[126]

Thomas Young referred to the theory "that matter itself is penetrable, that is, immaterial"[127] in his *Lectures on Natural Philosophy*

---

124. For a discussion of Boscovich's system see J. Brookes Spencer, "Boscovich's Theory and its Relation to Faraday's Researches: An Analytic Approach," *Arch. Hist. Exact Sciences, 4* (1967), 187-194.

125. Boscovich's system is also based on the Leibnizian "Law of Continuity" which he "considered as existing in Nature," *A Theory of Natural Philosophy*, trans. J. M. Child (London, 1922), p. 45.

126. William Herschel, "Observations on Dr. Priestley's Optical Desideratum— 'What becomes of light?'" [unpublished paper, 1780], *The Scientific Papers of Sir William Herschel*, ed. J. L. E. Dreyer, 2 vols. (London, 1912), *1*, lxx. Herschel relates his argument quite explicitly to Newton, Boscovich, and Michell:

> Sir Isaac Newton says that reflexion and refraction may be caused by the powers of *repulsion and attraction* belonging to bodies and extending to certain distances beyond their surfaces.
>
> Mr. Boscovich goes a little farther and maintains that matter consists of physical points only, endowed with powers of attraction and repulsion taking place at different distances; that is, surrounded with various spheres of attraction and repulsion, in the same manner as solid matter is supposed to be. And that it acts upon light by these powers. Mr. Michell, also, is of this latter opinion (*ibid.*, lxix).

127. Thomas Young, *A Course of Lectures on Natural Philosophy and the Mechanical Arts*, 2 vols. (London, 1807), *1*, 458.

NEWTONIAN FORCES AND LOCKEAN POWERS

(1807). He argued that this theory supposed that the particles of light could "penetrate the ultimate atoms of other matter,"[128] but he did not regard this notion with favor. He pointed out that the wave theory of light avoided the necessity of explaining the penetration of bodies by light by a theory which required such an "astonishing degree of porosity"[129] of matter, for this was what was implied by the emission theory of light. Thus, matter theory was again related to optical problems. While Michell and Priestley used the problem of the transmission of light through bodies to support their theory of the penetrability of matter, Young regarded such a theory of matter with disfavor. Starting from different conceptual presuppositions, Young considered it "probable that the particles of matter are absolutely impenetrable to each other,"[130] and for this reason he could well regard the emission theory of light as decidedly inferior to the wave theory.

Priestley's theory that the essence of matter was not to be found in its solidity and impenetrability, but in extension and its powers, in its disposition to give the effects of solidity and impenetrability, was developed within the framework of a Newtonian theory of forces and of the porosity of matter. With respect to his theory of powers he could extend the Newtonian theory of the material vacuity of nature and argue that there was no such thing as solidity in nature, only powers. Though Priestley in general is critical of Reid's philosophy, his view of the origin of the concept "power" was similar. In his *Introductory Essays* to *Hartley's Theory of the Human Mind* (1775), Priestley states:

> the idea of *power* seems at first sight to be a very simple one; but it is in fact exceedingly complex. A child pushes at an obstacle, it gives away . . . in like manner he practises a variety of other bodily and mental exercises, in which he finds that it only *depends upon himself* whether he performs them or not; and at length he calls that general feeling, which is the result of a thousand different impressions, by the name of *power*. . . . Even inanimate things have certain invariable *effects,* when applied in a particular manner. Thus a rope sustains a

---

128. *Ibid.*, p. 607.
129. *Ibid.*, p. 458.
130. *Ibid.*, p. 611. For Young the essential properties of matter include extension, impenetrability, and inertia (*ibid.,* 607).

weight, a magnet attracts iron, a charged electrical jar gives a shock, &c. From these and other similar observations, we get the idea of *power, universally and abstractedly considered;* so that in fact, the idea of power is acquired by the very same mental process by which we acquire the idea of any other property belonging to a number of bodies, viz. by leaving out what is peculiar to each, and appropriating the term to that particular circumstance or appearance, in which they all agree."[131]

Priestley goes on to claim that "the idea of *solidity*, or *impenetrability* [is] what could not be deduced from *sense*, but must have its origin in the understanding."[132] He concludes in support of his position that "we see in the case of Father Boscovich, and Mr. Michell that the very idea of the proper impenetrability of matter may be disputed."[133] In his *Letters to a Philosophical Unbeliever* (1780) he observes in a critical discussion of Hume's doctrine of causation that "I think I have sufficiently shown in the third of the *Essays* prefixed to my edition of *Hartley's Theory of the Mind* that there is nothing in the idea of *power* or *causation* (which is only the same idea differently modified) that is not derived from the impressions to which we are subject, this being to be ranked in the class of *abstract ideas*, where it does not appear that Mr. Hume ever thought of looking for it."[134] The influence of Locke is evident. Moreover, Priestley is not willing to grant that Hume's rejection of the term power has any validity for scientific thought. In 1778 Price raised the following query: "Since experiments, do not furnish us with the ideas of *causation*, and *productive power*, how come we by these ideas, and how does Dr. Priestley know they have any existence? How, in particular, does he avoid the sceptical system which Mr. Hume has advanced?"[135] Priestley answered: "my idea of *causation*, and of its *origin* in the mind is . . . the very same with that of other persons; but we all distinguish between *primary* and *secondary* causes, though speaking strictly and philosophically, we call secondary causes mere effects, and confine the term *cause* to the primary

---

131. Priestley, *Works* (Note 84), *3*, 191.
132. *Ibid.*, p. 191.
133. *Ibid.*, p. 192.
134. *Ibid., 4*, 398.
135. *Ibid.*, p. 106, in Joseph Priestley, *A Free Discussion of the Doctrines of Materialism and Philosophical Necessity, in a Correspondence between Dr. Price and Dr. Priestley* (London, 1778).

cause."[136] For Priestley this is the deity, "the same first cause from which the powers of the magnet, and all the powers of nature are derived."[137] Thus action in nature is in reality divine power. In this respect Priestley differs from deists like Hutton by denying that nature is a self-regulating system. In any event, the two traditions of Newtonian forces and Lockean epistemology of powers merge in Priestley's theory of matter, as they did—in different ways—in the thought of Edwards and Greene. Priestley did more than formulate a philosophical foundation for the description of the essence of matter: he also developed a theory of matter such as to account for a major problem in the theory of optics.

VI

With James Hutton the Lockean doctrine of power was developed in a somewhat similar way—from the philosophical point of view— as in Priestley's *Disquisitions*. The striking differences between their arguments result from the very different theories of nature and matter in the work of these two natural philosophers. With Hutton the basis for interpreting nature must begin from metaphysical first principles which provide the general framework within which specific disciplines can be developed. Thus for him the business of natural philosophy is "to investigate the powers or laws of action."[138] These, however, can only be investigated when we have a theory of matter based on established principles of knowledge. Hutton, more explicitly than Priestley, recognized that the basic properties of material things cannot be established by observation alone. Moreover, he also realized that any particular scientific theory of matter presupposed the problem at issue, which concerns the conceptual status of the terms employed. Thus it is necessary that a theory of knowledge illuminate the relationships between concepts like impenetrability, solidity, and resistance. Both the terms *body* and *matter* have been abstracted from "our compound natural perceptions." Body is "the thing conceived as subsisting independent of our

---

136. Priestley, *Works* (Note 84), *4*, 106.
137. *Ibid.*, p. 107.
138. James Hutton, *Dissertations on Different Subjects in Natural Philosophy* (Edinburgh, 1792), p. ix.

thinking principle"; "*body* is made of matter," and matter as opposed to body does not "signify anything that may be immediately examined, but denotes something inferred, or judged of, from things which appear."[139] In his *Dissertations on Different Subjects in Natural Philosophy* (1792), Hutton begins his analysis of matter and body by establishing what he takes to be the principles necessary for knowing their existence and properties. Thus he makes a consistent distinction between sensible and perceptible qualities, the first arising from the immediate effect of sensation, and the second carrying an existential import by the action of the mind; he goes on to distinguish these qualities from judged or inferred qualities which "proceed in reason from those sensible and perceptible qualities."[140] It is from these judged qualities that our knowledge of matter must arise, for sensible and perceptible qualities only characterize gross bodies which are themselves made up of "matter." Thus Hutton makes a clear distinction, in terms of his division of qualities, between matter and body; as we shall see, this is a point of crucial significance. Again, sensible and perceptible qualities cover those distinguished by the traditional primary and secondary qualities dichotomy, an ontology which Hutton rejects, since he cannot accept the doctrine of absolute and independent qualities that it entails.[141] Qualities in bodies such as extension and impenetrability are only "conditional," depending on the state of contraction or dilation of the resisting powers from which they arise:

> instead then of saying that matter, of which natural bodies are composed, is perfectly hard and impenetrable, which is the received opinion of philosophers, we would affirm, that there were no permanent properties of this kind in a material thing: but that there were certain resisting powers in bodies, by which their volume and figures are presented to us in the actual information, which powers, however, might be overcome. . . . [Thus] the extension of the most solid body, would be considered only as a conditional thing.[142]

Hence properties like extension and resistance do not "arise from the absolute nature of the thing"[143] since intrinsic powers of bodies

139. *Ibid.*, pp. 278 f.
140. *Ibid.*, p. 281.
141. *Ibid.*, pp. 290-292.
142. *Ibid.*, p. 290.
143. *Ibid.*, p. 292.

NEWTONIAN FORCES AND LOCKEAN POWERS

can be modified or even annihilated. Thus knowledge of bodies and matter is relational, that is, relative to conditions obtaining in the powers external to the mind. Intrinsically powers and the sensible properties to which they give rise are conditional. The absolute and relational quality distinction has no place in the thought of Hutton. All properties ontologically speaking are relational. Because he holds this view, he is in clear disagreement with the metaphysics of seventeenth-century science.

Hutton holds that the idea of motion is derived from attending to changes in the content of sensation. We can have no concept of motion without that of moving things which denote external action; this necessarily involves ideas of magnitude, figure, space, situation, and time. The mind is "informed by means of observed motion, of design; for when a regular order is observed in those changing things, whereby a certain end is always attained, there is necessarily inferred an operation somewhere, an operation similar to that of our mind, which often premediates the exertion of a power and is conscious of design."[144] The teleological cast of Hutton's thought is apparent, and it is fundamental to his philosophy of nature in general. For Hutton "the proper purpose of philosophy is to see the general order that is established among the different species of events, by which the whole of nature, and the wisdom of the system, is to be perceived."[145] Hutton denies that final causes cannot be discovered, asserting that they are "the proper object of our knowledge." It is only when final causes are discovered that "we may be said to understand those things, when we see the end for which they are intended in the system of this world, and perceive the means by which, in the wisdom of nature, the end is certainly effected."[146] With respect to Hutton's theory of knowledge and of matter, this teleological approach is of special importance. Hutton draws an analogy between the intentions of the mind and the ends of external change through the motion of things. Thus there is a *de facto* harmony between things and powers without us "actuated by design"[147] and the anticipations of the mind which is intensely

144. *Ibid.*, p. 285.
145. *Ibid.*, p. 262.
146. *Ibid.*, p. 624.
147. *Ibid.*, p. 286.

conscious of them. Thus the order and design constitutive of the mind is reflected in the structure of nature teleologically oriented, such that the operations of powers producing the sensible qualities of bodies can be premediated in judgment. In the *Investigation of the Principles of Knowledge* (1794) Hutton agrees with Locke and Berkeley that ideas are not innate,[148] and with Berkeley that primary and secondary qualities are on the same ontological level.[149] He does not agree, however, with Berkeley that we can only know our ideas,[150] the reliability of which depends on God, or with Hume's skeptical view that since causation is no more than belief associated with present impressions, the knowledge of external reality is custom based on constant conjunction. Nor does he agree with Reid that the truth lies in things and that sensory knowledge is certain as a matter of fact. Rather, scientific knowledge is gained through a slow process of mental operations, which organize, order, and structure sensory impressions and subsequent conceptualizing into a systematic and consistent representation of reality; for "Truth is not a thing and truth is not a fact."[151] He goes on to argue that "truth and falsehood are things which cannot properly be said to exist in nature, being only distinctions which take place with regard to the mind of man."[152] Thus Hutton's view of truth and knowledge is one of internal consistency, the organizing power of an active mind structuring reality. Accordingly, he believes that the mind can premediate nature's operation and that the principle of economy is reflected by the economy of forces in nature. There is no doubt that Hutton is an *a priorist* rather than an inductive thinker: "Order is in thought not thing."[153] His position closely approaches the view that the *esse* of material things is *concipi*.

148. James Hutton, *An Investigation of the Principles of Knowledge, and of the Progress of Reason, from Sense to Science and Philosophy*, 3 vols. (Edinburgh, 1794), *1*, 86 ff.
149. *Ibid.*, *1*, 132.
150. *Ibid.*, *1*, 359.
151. *Ibid.*, *2*, 258.
152. *Ibid.*, *2*, 279.
153. *Ibid.*, *2*, 106. The annotations in his own copy of Volume I of Hutton's *Investigation,* now in the British Museum, show that Samuel Coleridge linked Hutton with the philosophical approach of Kant: "There's a great metaphysical talent displayed in it; and the writer had made an important step beyond Locke, Berkeley and Hartley, and was clearly on the precincts of the Critical Philosophy with which and the previous treatises of Kant he appears to have had no acquaintance."

I

NEWTONIAN FORCES AND LOCKEAN POWERS

Hutton's theory of knowledge is more sophisticated than that of Greene, who also based his theory on the content of experience to formulate his concept of matter. But where Greene holds that primary and other qualities, being "abstracted" ideas and hence having no external reality, are irrelevant to the conception of matter, Hutton uses them as characteristics of body to infer the nature of invisible matter manifested to the senses as power. This, for him, is the proper object of our knowledge, since "material things exist not in the form which we ourselves imagine; but . . . they exist in power and energy; and . . . the effect of that external power and action is passion and knowledge in our mind."[154]

The notion of "power" is fundamental to Hutton's theory of matter. In the *Investigation* he emphasizes that "when it relates to effects which are known not to have been in consequence of our action, then, power properly denotes a thing, a real existence; for, this is all that is known of the external cause";[155] indeed, with respect to experience, "power, the cause of our sensation, is to be considered as a first cause."[156] He goes on to point out that when power is exerted there must be "a substance existing, in which that power should reside."[157] Arguing that the term "substance" requires explanation, he examines the doctrine of essential qualities, that is, the Newtonian view that certain qualities cannot be intended and remitted of degree. Thus, he argues that

> according to the philosophy which is now considered, or the principles generally adopted by philosophers, the substance of a body is that thing which, however it may be divided or changed in its figure, always preserves its volume; and therefore, in this philosophy, it is believed, that every material substance has necessarily a certain volume, which fundamentally is unalterable. Therefore, solidity, as opposed to vacuity, must appear to be the proper idea of substance in that philosophy.[158]

This is Newton's view that bodies fill or occupy space in an absolute sense, and it is this doctrine which Hutton rejects as untenable. He states that "magnitude and figure have no other existence than in the conceiving faculty of our mind, and that these qualities are truly

---

154. *Ibid., 3,* 49.
155. *Ibid., 2,* 385 f.
156. *Ibid., 2,* 387.
157. *Ibid.,* p. 389.
158. *Ibid.,* p. 392.

ideas formed upon certain occasions and according to established rules, then, this philosophical idea of substance falls to the ground, and, together with it, all the material system built thereon." Thus, like Priestley, Hutton denied that solidity was the essence of substance, and it was power which was "the cause of our knowledge ... subsisting externally in relation to our mind or thought." Nevertheless, power was "to be considered as a term implying an unknown thing in action."[159]

It is here that Hutton's distinction between matter and body is important, for it was *body* which possessed extension and figure, while *matter*—which constituted body—"is considered as the substance, essence, or principles of external things,"[160] and as having neither magnitude, figure, nor inactivity. Emphasizing that "the term substance comes to be, in some respects, equivalent to that of matter,"[161] he concludes that "Matter, in this view, will appear to be a thing absolutely different from that external thing which is perceived by our mind; and the proper attribute of matter will be, the having power to affect our mind in making us to know. This is all that matter has in relation to our mind or knowledge; and this is the proper metaphysical idea of matter."[162] On the level of experience, "power and matter are found to mean the same thing, matter being properly the thing, and power the attribute thereof."[163] Thus, with respect to experience, power is to be considered as the first cause and to denote existing things.

It is here that Hutton makes an important distinction between the "physical and metaphysical ideas of matter."[164] The physical idea of matter was derived from the idea of power, while the metaphysical idea of matter was to be distinguished from our perceptions of external things. This distinction relates to his distinction between matter and body, and to his emphasis on the fact that to assume that matter was composed of extended solid particles—inert, hard atoms— was to assume as the principles of bodies "nothing but bodies

159. *Ibid.*, p. 393.
160. *Ibid.*, p. 399.
161. *Ibid.*, p. 394. He goes on to say that "the term matter is general to the whole of external things; the term substance is the matter of a particular body or class of bodies."
162. *Ibid.*, p. 407.
163. *Ibid.*, p. 403.
164. *Ibid.*, p. 407.

NEWTONIAN FORCES AND LOCKEAN POWERS

themselves under the pedantic designation of atoms or corpuscles."[165] This argument was based on an implicit denial of Newton's third Rule of Philosophizing, for Hutton argued that the principles of bodies must be different from the bodies themselves. With Hutton, as with other contemporary thinkers, Newton's third Rule was an ill-conceived attempt at disguising the fallacy of composition. Nevertheless, a physical conception of matter must be founded on properties "by which perceived things are made known to us."[166] He argues that though we cannot literally ascribe sensible qualities to invisible matter, as the third Rule prescribes, there being no absolutes in reality, it is from these sensible qualities that we are to infer the characteristics of powers and the unobservable substratum: "nothing is to be allowed, as belonging to matter, that is not authorized in the strictest examination of actual things. For science, at least that of physics, consists not of imagining what may be; but in the investigation of what is actually found in nature."[167]

Hutton's theory of material existence would appear to have three distinct levels: body, matter in its physical aspect (that is, matter as manifested by powers), and matter in its metaphysical aspect (matter as a nonspatial substance, powers being its attribute). It is at this third level, which is only indirectly manifested through the action of powers (which, with respect to experience, are held to constitute the first cause), that the qualities of matter as a substratum can only be characterized negatively: "But whatever matter is of itself, it must be considered as the cause of motion and resistance in natural bodies; and this is all that we are permitted to judge of in the science of physics. We never shall learn to know what matter is in itself; nor have we any occasion for that knowledge. . . . But though we know not what matter truly is, we certainly may know what it is not."[168] Thus *qua* substratum, matter is destitute of bodily form, cannot change place in space, is nonsolid, nonspatial, and incessantly active. Its mode of action, therefore, can only be likened to a metamorphosis in time, not a geometrical translation through space. Though its ontological status is somewhat unclear, it seems in the final analysis

---

165. Hutton, *op. cit.* (Note 138), p. 669.
166. Hutton, *op. cit.* (Note 148), 2, 406.
167. Hutton, *op. cit.* (Note 138), p. 300.
168. *Ibid.*, p. 315.

that for Hutton the substratum is nonmaterial in nature. That there is a harmony between the constitution of the mind and the processes of nature assures us that we may have some idea of matter in itself through the design of its operations manifested by powers.

With reference to the third Rule, Robert Young made a distinction similar to Hutton's between compounds and simples. In his *Essay on the Powers and Mechanism of Nature* (1788), he argues that "the separate elements of matter . . . cannot answer to the definition of matter,"[169] for "the elements of matter are not of the nature of matter";[170] his term "matter" corresponds to Hutton's term "body" and his phrase "elements of matter" to Hutton's term "matter." More clearly than Hutton, Young identified the substratum with an immaterial entity, an "active substance" which was "possessed of active power."[171] Also like Hutton, with respect to the substratum Young attempted to adumbrate a level of existence which is neither mental nor physical. This he could only do negatively. For Young, "Matter is a being, as a whole quiescent, and inactive, but constituted of active parts"; on the other hand, "Mind is a substance which thinks." Young concludes: "A being which should answer to neither of these definitions would be neither matter nor mind, but an immaterial, and, if I may so say, an *immental* substance. Such is the active substance."[172] This active substance was the substratum, the elements of matter, and so was of a different nature from matter. In constituting matter it "puts on . . . the form of matter, and becomes material, solid, and inert."[173] For Hutton, too, the contrast between inactive, passive body (to use his term) and active matter was fundamental; he emphasized that the law of inertia applied only to bodies, for "there is not any evidence of *inertia* being proper to the matter,"[174] again implicitly rejecting Newton's third Rule as applying to the totally different category of Huttonian "matter."

169. Robert Young, *op. cit.* (Note 105), p. 154.
170. *Ibid.,* p. 156.
171. *Ibid.,* p. 1.
172. *Ibid.,* pp. 84 f.
173. *Ibid.,* p. 150.
174. Hutton, *op. cit.* (Note 138), p. 297. He emphasizes that "it is not in the *matter,* which constitutes natural bodies, that the law of *inertia* has been investigated, but in the *bodies* themselves." Hutton thus again emphasizes the distinction between the macro- and microworlds. In his *Dissertation upon the Philosophy of Light, Heat and Fire* (Edinburgh, 1794), p. 262, Hutton argues

I

NEWTONIAN FORCES AND LOCKEAN POWERS

There are a number of traditions merging in Hutton's natural philosophy. The first is the notion of power, which probably derives from Locke, since Hutton devotes considerable space to his writings in the *Investigation*. Hutton's use of the concept of power is strikingly original, but his argument that power was to be construed as a first cause, as regards experience, was characteristic of the tradition which we have been discussing. Hutton also develops the Newtonian theory of forces in an interesting and complex way, and we will now turn to this problem in his thought. Here his argument that "When a power is found to be exerted, it is commonly thought that there must be a substance existing, in which that power should reside"[175] is crucial, for his concept of force was intimately connected with his view of the nature of this substance, that is, of matter. Hutton supposed two kinds of matter: gravitational matter which acted by the principle of attraction, and matter emanating from the sun—the "solar substance"—which acted by the principle of repulsion. The hardness and cohesion of a body was due to the gravitating matter, which acted on the principle of attraction, while heat, for example, was "a power in bodies by which the uniting principle perceived in cohesion, gravitation, and hardness, is opposed and resisted" by a principle of repulsion. Gravitational matter could not be separated from a body, while the solar substance could be considered as having existence apart from a body in one or other of its modifications. For Hutton, light, heat, and electricity were different modifications of the solar substance:

> Thus light, heat, and electricity, appear to be three different modifications of the same matter. Light is considered as being perfectly disconnected with the body from whence it moves; and, the moment it is again connected with a body, so as to lose its proper motion, it ceases to be light. Heat, on the contrary, is perfectly connected with a body, and forms part of its substance; heat being removed from this internal connection of bodies, ceases to be heat. Electricity is a modification that will appear to be a medium between light and heat, considered as

---

that bodies "acquire inertia in the balance of those opposite powers" of attraction and repulsion. See Note 19 above for Newton's discussion of a noninertial aether.

175. Hutton, *op. cit.* (Note 148), 2, 389.

extremes; for neither is it unconnected with bodies, nor internally connected with their substance.[176]

Phlogiston was explained in terms of a union of the matter of light and heat with some of the chemical substances of bodies; the destruction of phlogistic matter when bodies burn was balanced by its regeneration in plants, for it was in plants that "the combination of the solar substance is made for the production of phlogistic matter."[177] This, for Hutton, was an example of "a system of things which seem all to be connected together by design," illustrating the "admirable contrivance of the system in which we are placed."[178] Thus he stressed the notion of natural cycles, especially the great cycle of the organic and the inorganic. This contained heat, light, water, earth, and fixed air, supporting the plants which in their turn would produce vital air and phlogiston to maintain animal life. When in turn animal life decayed, it sufficiently renewed the stocks of fixed air, water, heat, earth, and light for the great cycle to begin anew. The great cycles of nature were themselves manifestations of the "attractive and repulsive powers" of the gravitational and solar substances opposing and balancing one another, thus securing a dynamic tension in nature.[179] When the gravitational power is supposed to prevail, bodies would form an inert mass, and when the power of heat prevails bodies are dispersed throughout the universe; but "by a just combination of those two different powers, we find moveable and moving bodies properly disposed in a great and connected system of things."[180]

Thus for Hutton, the processes and balance of nature were due to the operation of two kinds of material entity, one associated with attractive and the other with repulsive power. As we have shown, matter for Hutton was an active substratum, and his theory of "acting powers"[181] as attributes of a substratum can be seen to have relation to Newton's conception of the aether in the 1717 *Opticks*. As we pointed out above, Newton regarded the microstructure of the aether as the embodiment of repulsive forces acting between van-

176. Hutton, *op. cit.* (Note 138), pp. 505 f.
177. *Ibid.*, p. 229.
178. *Ibid.*, p. 233.
179. *Ibid.*, p. 265.
180. *Ibid.*, p. 263.
181. *Ibid.*, p. 501.

NEWTONIAN FORCES AND LOCKEAN POWERS

ishingly small particles, and for Hutton, too, his nonspatial, noninertial, effectively immaterial substratum could be considered only in terms of attractive and repulsive powers. While Newton's concept of active principle was used to explain the ontological problem of the causation of force in terms of the causation of divine agency in the natural world, for Hutton the balance of nature was secured by the operations of the attractive and repulsive powers alone. Though God is "the author of nature," God must be distinguished from nature, for the system of nature comprises all powers and relations in the universe (though "nature" itself is a figurative term):

> We do not necessarily ascribe this power of the universe to God, as the immediate cause; for, we consider every person as possessed of a certain power and influence in this system of moving things, being able at will to move and resist to a certain degree, however limited. Reasoning, therefore, by analogy, we consider a certain being interposed between the superintending mind, or first cause, and those effects of power which we perceive; and, this imaginary Being is called Nature. Hence, every thing that is observed either to act or suffer, is said to be a natural thing; and nature is always employed in every change that happens to those things. Now, as a thing cannot be known except by either acting or resisting, in both of which cases there is power; so, everything that is known, is considered as belonging to nature; and, every action that takes place, is considered as being performed by this power, which is, in relation to human art, supreme.[182]

---

182. Hutton, *op. cit.* (Note 148), 2, 415. Hutton's deistic emphasis on nature as a self-contained system must be sharply distinguished from the Hutchinsonians' rejection of Newton's conception of nature. For the Hutchinsonians, Newton had employed divine action in explaining the processes and operations of nature as an "occult cause." Regarding nature as a mechanism, they rejected all "occult causes" for physical phenomena. Nevertheless, nature was ultimately totally subordinate to God: "If God, instead of framing the universe into so curious a piece of perpetual motion, had designed to transact all by his own immediate presence, there had been no use for . . . such regular laws"; the "perspicuity and perfection" of nature manifests God's power, so there was no need for God "to work by occult qualities." (*An Abstract from the Works of John Hutchinson, Esq. being a Summary of his Discovery in Philosophy and Divinity,* 2nd ed. [London, 1775], p. 142.) Hutchinson argues that occult qualities detract from "the essential attributes of JEHOVAH ALEIM" (*ibid.,* p. 155).

As William Jones puts it, the Hutchinsonians maintained "an agency of material and secondary causes, under the direction of God, the moral governor of the world, and the Supreme cause of all things" (*op. cit.* [Note 19], p. 55). For Hutton, the order of nature manifests the wisdom of its creator; for the Hutchinsonians, nature was subject to the direct agency of spiritual causes. For

I

Nature was thus a self-contained system comprising the totality of effects in the universe, these effects being produced by attractive and repulsive powers, that is, by the active substratum. Unlike Newton, who conceived forces as acting dynamically *between* particles, and Priestley, who saw the essence of matter as power *and* extension, in Hutton's view matter is fully dynamic in the sense that it is neither predicated on point centers conceived atomically nor on nonextended Boscovichean entities. Nor is extension a necessary condition of its existence. Newton's conception of active principle as a cause of the forces operating in nature has here been conflated into the concept of powers which are themselves held to manifest activity. Hutton, therefore, transformed Newton's theory of forces, with respect to his theory of powers, into a conception of nature as a self-contained, active system, which in its structure manifested the wisdom and design of God. But the system of nature was to be explained purely in terms of the operations and balance of the attractive and repulsive powers, and its operations were not subject to the providential intervention of God. On the contrary, because he was a rational deist believing profoundly in a religion of nature, its self-sufficiency operated by chains of unbroken laws, which were not, for Hutton, to be abrogated by any form of divine intervention. Since nature as created is sufficient for divine ends, the powers implanted in it are adequate for the production of design. And if nature represents the perfection of God, its present state indicates that the forces now at work do so with the same intensity as they did during the earlier history of physical processes. Hutton's uniformitarianism is thus conditioned by his deism and the belief that should nature have ever been different from its present state it would be an imperfect

---

a discussion of the Hutchinsonians see Albert J. Kuhn, "Glory or Gravity: Hutchinson vs. Newton," *J.H.I.*, 22 (1961), 303-322.

It is interesting to observe that the Scot John Robison in his *Proofs of a Conspiracy against all the Religions and Governments of Europe* (Philadelphia, 1798), contends that Priestley's materialist system goes against the Newtonian philosophy which is the best support for traditional religion. For Robison, Newtonianism affords the best basis of arguments for God's existence in that it posits immaterial forces acting in nature on passive and contingent matter. In the supplement to the third edition of the *Encyclopædia Britannica* he links also Priestley with the atheistic and subversive thought which led to the excesses of the French Revolution. By implication Hutton is associated with the subversive trends undermining Christian mankind in a nonutopian society.

NEWTONIAN FORCES AND LOCKEAN POWERS

system. Thus nature was a system of organic processes, manifesting cycles among cycles arising from the resultant tension of repulsive and attractive power producing a state of equilibrium. These are the fundamental principles constitutive of Hutton's system. And his view of uniformitarianism and the doctrine of economy of geological forces are, for Hutton, closely linked to these principles.

This conception of nature provided the framework for Hutton's analysis of geological processes as developed in his *Theory of the Earth* (1795). The subterranean heat of the earth is the central agent of Hutton's theory.[183] It is the compensating mechanism which regenerates land for the preservation of organic life and which balances the gradual degenerative process of denudation. Not only does heat fuse rocks in the bowels of the earth, but it is the means whereby the new strata are elevated out of the sea. This view was supported, Hutton argued, by signs of elevation on existing rocks—folding, fractures, contortions, faults—which indicated that heat was responsible for their elevation. On the principle of the economy of forces, earthquakes, volcanoes, and mineral and metallic veins also were caused by the action of heat. This agent was identical with the expansive, active operations of repulsive power, and was balanced by the contractive power of gravitation.[184]

Hutton's conception of matter as powers was widely known in Scotland in the late eighteenth century. Indeed, in his *Philosophical Essays* (1794) Dugald Stewart supports Hutton's theory by arguing that Locke had implicitly conceived the essence of matter in terms of repulsive powers. Stewart gives a clear statement in support of the conception of matter advanced by Priestley and Hutton: "The effects ... which are vulgarly ascribed to actual contact, are all produced by repulsive forces, occupying those parts of space where *bodies* are perceived by our senses; and, therefore, the correct idea that we ought to annex to *matter,* considered as an object of percep-

---

183. See John Playfair, *Illustrations of the Huttonian Theory of the Earth* (Edinburgh, 1802), pp. 181 f, 187, for the association of Newton's Query 11 of the *Opticks* with Hutton's theory of heat.
184. James Hutton, *Theory of the Earth with Proofs and Illustrations* (Edinburgh, 1795), pp. 3-32; and Hutton, "Theory of the Earth; or an Investigation of the Laws Observable in the Composition, Dissolution, and Restoration of Land Upon the Globe," *Trans. Roy. Soc. Edinb., 1* (1788), 269 ff. For Hutton's deism see R. Hooykaas, *The Principle of Uniformity in Geology, Biology, and Theology* (Leiden, 1963).

tion, is merely that of *a power of resistance,* sufficient to counteract the compressing power which our physical strength enables us to exert."[185] Referring to Book II, Chapter IV of Locke's *Essay* ("Of Solidity"), Stewart maintains that Locke, in analyzing cohesion and compressibility, implicitly held that the essence of matter could be conceived in terms of repulsive powers. Thus Stewart is consciously connecting Locke's theory of powers with the conceptions of matter of Priestley and Hutton. Stewart concludes that the views of Boscovich, Priestley, and Hutton "with respect to *matter,* so far as hardness or relative incompressibility is concerned, offer no violence to the common judgments of mankind, but aim only at a more correct and scientific statement of *the fact* than is apt to occur to our first hasty apprehensions."[186]

The view that the essence of matter is power led, in Scotland, to a critique of contact action. The argument is clearly put by John Playfair in his "Biographical Account of James Hutton":

> But if this be granted, and if it be true that in the material world every phenomenon can be explained by the existence of power, the supposition of extended particles as a *substratum* or residence for such power, is a mere hypothesis, without any countenance from the matter of fact. For if these solid particles are never in contact with one another, what part can they have in the production of natural appearances, or in what sense can they be called the residence of a force which never acts at the point where they are present? Such particles, therefore, ought to be entirely discarded from any theory that proposes to explain the phenomena of the material world.
>
> Thus, it appears, that power is the essence of matter, and that none of our perceptions warrant us in considering even body as involving anything more than force, subjected to various laws and combinations.[187]

185. Dugald Stewart, *Philosophical Essays,* 3rd ed. (Edinburgh, 1818), p. 123.
186. *Ibid.,* p. 133.
187. Playfair, "Biographical Account of James Hutton, M.D.," *The Works of John Playfair,* 4 vols. (Edinburgh, 1822), *4,* 85. It is interesting to observe that the Scottish writers on contact action, unlike Maupertius and Boscovich, do not, with the exception of John Leslie, argue explicitly that such action violates continuity in nature. Nevertheless, in general the view that matter is essentially powers manifesting degrees was related to the continuity of action and reaction. The Scottish concern with power, cause, and continuity in nature can be traced from the time of Rankenian Club in the early eighteenth century. These problems were discussed by Lord Kames and David Hume. See Mossner, *op. cit.* (Note 71).

NEWTONIAN FORCES AND LOCKEAN POWERS

Playfair goes on to state that matter conceived in this way was "indefinitely extended" through all space as "is proved by the universality of gravitation." Playfair's views on contact action were also held by Dugald Stewart, John Robison, and John Leslie. While affirming that action at a distance was unintelligible, these Scots also affirmed their belief in the nonintelligibility of contact action.[188] As the passage from Playfair shows, if interstitial particles can be conceived as being unable to come into contact, they serve no important role in explaining the properties of things, since these can be shown to arise from intrinsic powers. He made the point clearly with respect to gravitation. It is not "according to this system . . . the action of two distant bodies upon one another, but it is the action of certain powers, diffused through all space, which may be transmitted to any distance."[189] Thus conceiving the essence of matter as powers was seen to be not only incompatible with contact action but also with the theory of invisible particles.

Though Stewart, in his conception of matter, held that powers were more fundamental than solidity, like Hume he nevertheless denied that the former concept was derived from experience. In arguing that ideas of color can only "reside in a mind" he holds that "In the same way we are led to associate with inanimate matter, the ideas of *power, energy,* and *causation* which are all attributes of mind, and can exist in a mind only."[190] Also influenced by the Humean analysis of power was the Edinburgh physician James Gregory. In analyzing the work of Locke, Reid, and Priestley, Gregory constantly affirms that the term power can only be applied to inanimate things metaphorically,[191] for only agents which can deliberate have the volition to act toward a preconceived end. Stewart and Gregory both attest to the widespread use of the philosophical connotations of the term power, reflect also the Humean critique of the notion, and provide clear evidence that the notion was derived from Locke's *Essay*.

---

188. See Richard Olson, "The Reception of Boscovich's Ideas in Scotland," *Isis, 60* (1969), 91-103.

189. Playfair, *op. cit.* (Note 187), *4,* 86.

190. *The Collected Works of Dugald Stewart,* ed. Sir William Hamilton, 10 vols. (Edinburgh, 1854-1858), *2,* 98.

191. James Gregory, *Philosophical and Literary Essays,* 2 vols. (Edinburgh, 1792), *1,* x-cclxvi.

VII

Hutton's deistic philosophy of nature raises issues that extend beyond the limits circumscribed by the themes of this study, but his interpretation of nature in terms of the operation and balance of attractive and repulsive powers is of great significance for the traditions we have been discussing. We will now attempt to put Hutton's system of nature clearly in the tradition of Newtonian forces, by examining more fully the development of that tradition and Hutton's relation to it. Thus far we have been mainly concerned with the connections between the traditions of Newtonian forces and Lockean powers, but theories of force were not always explicitly developed in the context of a doctrine of powers. The significance of Hutton's system as a development of a Newtonian theory of forces can be seen by comparing his theory with an earlier work, Gowin Knight's *Attempt to Demonstrate, that all the Phaenomena in Nature may be Explained by Two Simple Active Principles, Attraction and Repulsion* (1748). Knight argues that the essential or primary qualities of matter are immutable and are universal properties of all bodies, their immutability being secured by the immediate will of God: "All immediate Causes, being the Effects of God's Will, must necessarily be constant, immutable and irresistible by any finite force. From hence appears the Truth of Sir *Isaac Newton's* third Rule." Thus the "Existence, Extension, Impenetrability, mobility, and *Vis Inertiae* of Matter, are apparently the immediate Effects of God's Will." The very existence of matter, as well as these general properties, was therefore held to be the direct effect of God's will, and so Knight followed Newton in regarding the essential qualities as an expression in nature of the perfection of God; the essential qualities were a reflection of God's immutability. Knight goes on to argue that the essential qualities are inactive and do not admit of intension and remission of degrees, and that motion, not being immutable, is not an essential property of matter. From this he concludes that there is in nature "some Active Principle, or Principles capable of producing and continuing Motion in the Universe."[192]

---

192. Gowin Knight, *An Attempt to Demonstrate, that all the Phaenomena in Nature may be Explained by Two Simple Active Principles, Attraction and Repulsion: wherein The Attraction of Cohesion, Gravity and Magnetism, are shown to be one and the same; and the Phaenomena of the latter are more particularly explained* (London, 1754), pp. 4 f.

I

NEWTONIAN FORCES AND LOCKEAN POWERS

These active principles are those of attraction and repulsion, and are themselves the manifestations of divine activity in nature.

Thus far Knight's conception of nature would seem to have little relation to that of Hutton. But despite their different theological ideas, they had many ideas in common; this appears clearly with Knight's association of the active principles of attraction and repulsion with material entities. In addition he goes on to conclude that "attraction and repulsion cannot both, at the same time, belong to the same individual substance, being contraries. . . . Therefore we must conclude, that there are in Nature two kinds of Matter, one attracting, the other repelling."[193] Though Knight's view of the nature of the attractive and repelling substrata is determined by his interpretation of the third Rule—and so his primary particles possess the essential qualities of matter—his theory of attractive and repelling substances has obvious affinities with Hutton's system.

Knight therefore uses the third Rule to argue for material substrata, one possessed of attractive and the other of repulsive force. The essential qualities of bodies—the immutable qualities to which the third Rule was held to apply—were insufficient to explain the activity of nature. The active principles of attraction and repulsion were required, and these principles were associated with two different substrata. His primary particles, which he holds to be "originally of the same Size, and all round,"[194] are of two types: those which attracted one another, and those which repelled each other but were attracted by the attracting particles. Light, heat, electricity, and magnetism are all explained in terms of the operations of this repellent matter. Thus he supposed light to be the propagation of a vibrational tremor through a series of repellent particles; and magnetism is explained in terms of a "perpetual Motion" of the repellent matter from one side of a body to the other, a "circulation of the repellent fluid"[195] which had no connection with the vibratory motion which was the cause of light. Fundamental to his system is

---

193. *Ibid.*, p. 10. Schofield, *op. cit.* (Note 3), pp. 176 ff, fails to emphasize sufficiently the relation of Knight's ideas to the tradition of Newtonian forces. As in his treatment of Greene (see Note 43) his dichotomy of "mechanism/materialism" has lead him to emphasize only one aspect of Knight's thought. On Knight see also Mary Hesse, *Forces and Fields* (London, 1961), p. 182, and Thackray, *op. cit.* (Note 11), pp. 141-147.
194. Knight, *op. cit.* (Note 192), p. 12.
195. *Ibid.*, pp. 66 f.

the argument that every particle of attracting matter was surrounded by "as many repellent particles as will just ballance its attracting force,"[196] and gravitational inverse square law forces were explained as arising from the superposition of attracting force (decreasing inversely with distance) and repelling force (decreasing with distance though no precise force law is given). The operations and balance of nature can be explained in terms of the attractive and repulsive forces. Here again there are obvious similarities with Hutton's system.

In developing theories in which nature was to be explained in terms of the action of active substrata of attractive and repulsive forces, Hutton and Knight were employing the imponderable fluid theories of eighteenth-century natural philosophy. It has long been established that these theories, in which electricity, for example, was explained in terms of the action of subtle, mutually repulsive electrical particles diffused through common matter, show the influence of Newton's theory of the aether as developed in the Queries to the *Opticks*.[197] The striking feature of the systems proposed by Hutton and Knight is the association of the principles of attraction and repulsion with substrata, these substrata being considered as "active" and regarded as entities forming the "matter" which underlies gross bodies. Significantly for the interpretation of the aether of the 1717 *Opticks* proposed in this study, both Hutton and Knight regarded the microstructure of their attractive and repulsive principles as merely the embodiment of attractive and repulsive forces. It was these attractive and repulsive forces which explained the operations and balance of nature, and accounted for the manifestation of various fluids. Just as the aether of the 1717 *Opticks* was, with respect to its microstructure, force embodied in space, the attractive and repulsive substrata supposed by Hutton and Knight were forces opposing and balancing one another.

It is therefore plain that Hutton and Knight were developing theories of the primacy of force. Hutton's "matter" and Knight's attractive and repellent particles were very different entities. Hut-

196. *Ibid.,* p. 19.
197. See I. Bernard Cohen, *Franklin and Newton: An Inquiry into Speculative Newtonian Science and Franklin's Work in Electricity as an Example Thereof* (Philadelphia, 1956); and also Schofield, *op. cit.* (Note 3), pp. 157-190.

NEWTONIAN FORCES AND LOCKEAN POWERS

ton's "matter" was nonspatial, noninertial, and effectively immaterial, while Knight's primary particles possessed the same essential qualities as gross matter. Nevertheless, they were both conceived as the embodiment of attractive and repulsive forces, being analogous to the aether of the 1717 *Opticks*. Again, though Hutton envisaged nature as a self-contained system (his "matter" being an active substance) and Knight supposed his active principles of attraction and repulsion to be the immediate effects of divine action in nature, in the works of both these theorists we see the conflation of the Newtonian categories of "force" and "active principles." Though Knight's active principles are the immediate effects of God's will, they are themselves the attractive and repulsive forces; and Hutton's attractive and repulsive powers could manifest activity in and of themselves. Despite their very different theological conceptions of nature, both Hutton and Knight rejected the hierarchical, Neoplatonic framework of Newton's thought. While Newton asserted the primacy of force and regarded matter as embodying the lowest degree of reality and perfection, for Knight and Hutton the concepts of "force" and "matter" were intimately associated with one another.

The association of principles of attraction and repulsion with different substances as a basis for a system of nature was not uncommon in eighteenth-century natural philosophy. Bryan Higgins proposed a similar system in his *Philosophical Essay Concerning Light* (1776). For Higgins, earth and water were forms of attractive matter, while electricity, light, and phlogiston were forms of repellent matter. Using Newton's third Rule, he argues for the immutability of atoms, and supposes the "powers [of attraction and repulsion] implanted in the atoms" as being "incessant and immutable," these powers being endowed by God.[198] The repellent matter is here considered nongravitational, and this notion is maintained by Patrick Dugud Leslie in his *Philosophical Inquiry into the Cause of Animal Heat* (1778).[199] The association of the two principles of attraction

---

198. Bryan Higgins, *A Philosophical Essay Concerning Light* (London, 1776), p. 23.

199. Patrick Dugud Leslie, *A Philosophical Inquiry into the Cause of Animal Heat: with Incidental Observations on Several Physiological and Chymical Questions, connected with the Subject* (London, 1778). For Leslie, "phlogiston is fire and light, or a certain subtile elastic fluid, upon the modifications of which the phenomena of heat and light depend." The sun communicates phlogiston to

and repulsion with different substances also appears in Robert Harrington's *New System on Fire and Planetary Life* (1796), the two principles being those of light and fire (the principle of motion) and of earth (the principle of inactivity), the former consisting of mutually repelling and the latter of mutually attracting particles. Again, the balance of nature was secured by the action of attractive and repulsive principles. Harrington is quite clear as to the implications of this idea, pointing out that whereas Newton had been "obliged to bring in the immediate hand of the Deity" to account for gravitation, his own theory did away with the necessity of supposing divine action.[200] He explained the gravitational action of the earth and the sun in terms of the circulation of fire (the repellent principle) between the earth and the sun and its attraction by the matter of the earth and sun. Similar ideas can be found in Adam Walker's *System of Familiar Philosophy* (1799), for Walker supposes that *"attraction and repulsion are the great acting principles of the universe,"*[201] light, fire, electricity, and phlogiston being "modifications of one and the same principle,"[202] the principle of repulsion. He emphasises that the operations of nature were "determined by a balance of those two powers"[203] of attraction and repulsion: "But of all opposing or antagonistic principles, none exhibit so general an enmity as fire and attraction. These two enemies are in a state of unceasing warfare: attraction drawing the particles of matter into a closer and closer union; while fire (or

---

bodies, "the same matter, which in a separate state constitutes fire and light, when modified in bodies is the cause of the inflammability" (*ibid.*, p. 104 f.). This matter is "the chief cause and principle of activity" in the universe (*ibid.*, p. 9), and is "exempted from the common laws of gravitation" (*ibid.*, p. 119). For Higgins on nongravitational matter, see his *A Syllabus of Chemical and Philosophical Enquiries* (London, [1775]), p. xlviii. The relation to Hutton's ideas is clear. Higgins, Leslie, and Hutton were all associated with Joseph Black: see J. R. Partington and D. McKie, "Historical Studies on the Phlogiston Theory. III. Light and Heat in Combustion," *Annals of Science, 3* (1938), 337-371. Cf. Michell, who regarded light particles as ponderable (Note 122, above).

200. Robert Harrington, *A New System on Fire and Planetary Life; shewing that the Sun and Planets are inhabited, and That They Enjoy the same Temperature as our Earth* (London, 1796), p. 18.

201. Adam Walker, *A System of Familiar Philosophy*, rev. ed., 2 vols. (London, 1802), *1*, 1.

202. *Ibid.*, p. 14.

203. *Ibid.*, p. 6. The idea of the balance of nature is itself a topic of investigation.

NEWTONIAN FORCES AND LOCKEAN POWERS

caloric, in the language of modern chemistry) is still striving to set those particles more and more at a distance."[204] The distance of the earth from the sun is determined by a balance of the power of gravity and the impulse of light from the sun, and Walker follows William Herschel in supposing the sun to be a planet surrounded by an atmosphere of fire.[205] The principles of attraction and repulsion were identified with material entities; by "matter" was meant "everything solid or fluid in nature, and we conceive this matter to be made up of particles . . . [which are] infinitely small."[206]

In the writings of these theorists we can see the influence of the Newtonian conception of the aether as the embodiment of force, and of the rejection of Newton's doctrine of active principles with its replacement by a conception of nature as a closed system, its operations secured by attractive and repulsive forces. In discussing the aether of the 1717 *Opticks* we pointed out that this aether—its microstructure embodying forces between vanishingly small particles—must be viewed in the context of Newton's theory of a nearly matterless universe regulated by forces. Indeed, his theory of force and paucity of matter and his theory of the "force-aether" were expressions of his concept of the primacy of force in the universe. Gowin Knight explicitly linked his theory of attractive and repulsive forces to the Newtonian doctrine of the paucity of matter in the universe, arguing that "All bodies whatsoever, whether solid or fluid, must contain more Pores than solid Parts. The Truth of this Proposition has been sufficiently proved by most of the Philosophers of this and the last Century, from Facts and Experience."[207] These theories, then, must be viewed in the context of the Newtonian

---

204. *Ibid.*, p. 18.
205. *Ibid.*, p. 12. See William Herschel, "On the Nature and Construction of the Sun and Fixed Stars," *Philosophical Transactions,* 85 (1795), 46-72; reprinted in Herschel, *Papers* (Note 126), *1*, 470-484. Herschel argues that the sun was a planet, sunspots being its "real solid body" which was covered by an atmosphere of "various elastic fluids" some of which are of "shining brilliancy" (*ibid.*, pp. 472 f.). See also Harrington, *op. cit.* (Note 200), p. 2.
206. Walker, *op. cit.* (Note 201), *1,* 37.
207. Knight, *op. cit.* (Note 192), p. 37. Cf. Walker: "the whole matter of the universe is supposed capable of being compressed into a walnut" (*op. cit.* [Note 201], *1*, 371); and also Higgins: "some authors suppose that the pores of [bodies] . . . may be much larger than their solid impenetrable parts; and the ingenious *Boscovich* finding this insufficient, supposes that matter is not impenetrable according to our conception of it" (*op. cit.* [Note 198], p. 246). Walker and Higgins clearly reflect Priestley's influence (*loc. cit.* [Note 117]).

tradition of the primacy of force. The influence of these ideas, developed in a different way than in Knight's theory, but nevertheless having relation to it, can be seen in John Rowning's *Compendious System of Natural Philosophy* (1738–1745). Like Knight, Rowning denies that the operations of inactive matter can be explained by a mechanical cause. They are "the Act of an *immaterial Cause,* in Virtue of which *inactive Matter* performs the offices for which it was designed,"[208] this cause being "the continued acting of God upon Matter, either mediately or immediately."[209] Like Knight, Rowning identifies the attractive and repulsive forces as "Powers or active Principles" which were not "essential to its Existence, but impressed upon it by the Author of its Being."[210] The influence of Newton is clear, though neither Rowning nor Knight maintained his relative distinction between force and active principles. Rowning attempted to explain a variety of phenomena using these principles, extending Newton's statement in Query 31 on envelopes of forces surrounding particles by supposing each particle to be surrounded by "three Spheres of Attraction and Repulsion, one within another."[211]

These ideas on spheres of force, to be extended by Boscovich and further developed by Priestley into a theory of the primacy of force, clearly have relation to the theories of attractive and repulsive powers developed by theorists such as Hutton and Knight. Despite the apparent differences, all these theories form part of a tradition of Newtonian forces. The eclecticism of these eighteenth-century theorists is paralleled by Newton's own varying views on the nature of force. Over and above their debt to Newton, these theorists also rejected much of his natural philosophy. This appears most clearly with respect to Newton's concept of active principles, for the activity of nature came to be regarded as being inherent in the natural realm. The concept of active substances provides a clear example of this; and the identification of a substratum with a principle of activity occurs in much of the natural philosophy we have discussed. A further example, which yet again emphasizes the relation of theories of this kind to the concept of power, can be

208. John Rowning, *A Compendious System of Natural Philosophy,* 4th ed. (London, 1745), Part 1, p. vi.
209. *Ibid.,* p. xxxix.
210. *Ibid.,* p. 12.
211. *Ibid.,* Part 2, p. 6n.

NEWTONIAN FORCES AND LOCKEAN POWERS

found in the work of Cadwallader Colden. In his *Explication of the First Causes of Action in Matter* (1748), Colden explained phenomena in terms of three kinds of powers—resisting, moving, and elastic powers—and he identified these powers as "agents or acting principles."[212] He considered that "We have no idea or conception of any thing other than of its power or force,"[213] for in the attempt to "describe matter without action, power, or force, the whole description must consist of negatives . . . it must be the description of *nothing*."[214] Colden regarded these "agents or acting principles" as "species of matter,"[215] for, as he put it in his *Principles of Action in Matter* (1751), action had to inhere in something: "motion is a property or quality, or more properly an action; we cannot then conceive it without supposing that it exists in something, which has in itself the power of moving." As he made clear, action not only existed in matter—or could be regarded as an attribute of matter—but was itself a substance, a species of matter. Indeed, matter as such could not be considered apart from action, power, or force. Colden quite explicitly associates his theory of motion as an action, existing in a material entity itself possessed of the power of moving, with a rejection of Newton's theory of bodies being maintained in motion by the continued action of the deity. For he stated that "It seems to be a very unphilosophical method of reasoning to suppose, that motion comes immediately from the Divine Being."[216] Once again, a theory of powers, forces, and active substances was conceived in terms of a conception of nature as a self-contained system.

A theory of a balance of powers can also be found in Thomas Exley's *Principles of Natural Philosophy* (1829). Arguing that matter is perceptible by means of its powers "which in themselves are in continual operation, and appear to constitute the very essence of matter,"[217] he affirms that the powers of attraction and repulsion

---

212. Cadwallader Colden, *An Explication of the First Causes of Action in Matter, and of the Cause of Gravitation* (London, 1746), p. 25.
213. *Ibid.*, p. 38.
214. *Ibid.*, p. 26.
215. *Ibid.*, p. 25.
216. Cadwallader Colden, *The Principles of Action in Matter, the Gravitation of Bodies and the Motion of the Planets explained from those Principles* (London, 1751), p. 73. For a rather different account of Colden see Schofield, *op. cit.* (Note 3), pp. 130-133.
217. Thomas Exley, *Principles of Natural Philosophy: or, a New Theory of Physics, founded on Gravitation, and applied in explaining the general proper-

secure a balance in nature: "These powers are denominated attraction and repulsion. Their nature is not known, but the laws of their operation have been at least partially developed: that both these belong to matter is incontrovertible: did attraction exist without repulsion, matter would be conglomerated into one body, and if there were repulsion only, all bodies would be universally dispersed."[218] Exley's theory of powers is based on his view that the powers constitute the essence of matter. Arguing that "we know nothing of *matter*, but by the forces which it exerts, and which doubtless constitute its nature,"[219] he goes on to state that all that could be known of an atom was

> a balance of forces on every side of a central point, and this is all we can understand of it . . . for it is nothing but mere hypothesis, the effect of imagination, and a vulgar notion, to judge, that there is a minute solid impenetrable mass necessary to constitute an atom of matter, on which forces act . . . we know nothing of such little solids, we have never seen them, nor felt them, nor perceived them by any one of the senses; if they do exist at all, we have not been affected by them but only by the forces of attraction and repulsion . . . the forces are considered as constituting the essence of matter.[220]

These arguments attest to the widespread use of the idea of a balance of attractive and repulsive forces, particularly in relation to the philosophical implications of the notion of power.

CONCLUSION

In this study we have attempted to delineate the relationships among a number of connected themes underlying eighteenth-century British natural philosophy; these themes were centered on the epistemological and ontological problems of matter theory. We have shown that many of the fundamental principles of late seventeenth-century natural philosophy—the primary and secondary qualities distinction and Newton's notion of essential qualities, the connection of unobservables to observables—were rejected by a significant group

---

ties of matter, the phenomena of Chemistry, Electricity, Galvanism, Magnetism, and Electro-Magnetism* (London, 1829), p. vi.
218. *Ibid.*, p. vii.
219. *Ibid.*, p. 470.
220. *Ibid.*, pp. 473 f. Unlike Hutton, Exley maintains that "matter exists continually by the power of its great Author" (*ibid.*, p. xxvii).

NEWTONIAN FORCES AND LOCKEAN POWERS

of eighteenth-century natural philosophers. This important shift in the foundations of scientific knowledge was intimately associated with the rise of new systems of science. In addition, Newton's hierarchical conception of nature and his notion of divine providence were rejected: nature came more to be seen as a self-contained system with activity ascribable to its intrinsic characteristics rather than to the operations of divine energy. In attempting to show how these ideas can be viewed in a tradition deriving from Newton and Locke we have sought to characterize a number of apparently diverse currents of thought, indicating common themes which were fundamental to the problems of scientific explanation. In tracing these ideas by no means have we sought to imply that these problems pervaded all of eighteenth-century British natural philosophy. However, in linking diverse systems of natural philosophy to the traditions of Newtonian forces and Lockean powers we have shown that these ideas appear in systems of nature which are characteristic of the natural philosophy of the period. For this reason alone, the conclusions of this study have wide implications for the history of natural philosophy in the post-Newtonian period.

The main theme of this study has been the doctrine that the essence of matter is constituted by powers. We have established the pervasive influence of this notion in eighteenth-century thought, and in conclusion we will indicate that this idea can be traced into the nineteenth century. Indeed, this notion was employed by Michael Faraday and was to underlie his development of the theory of the primacy of lines of force. Thus, one of the characteristic ideas of nineteenth-century field theory was developed from the view that matter consisted of powers and forces which extended continuously throughout space. Faraday argued that the hardness of matter was due to the *"force of repulsion* . . . in the particles,"* and "if we recognize matter by its *hardness*, what do we other than recognize by our sensations a force exerted by it."[221] Matter was known only by the forces it exerted, and Faraday considered that these forces constituted the essence of matter. Disinguishing between the particles of matter and the powers associated with these particles, Faraday defined "the particles of matter away from the powers a, and the system of powers or forces in and around it m," arguing that

---

221. Michael Faraday, MS on "Matter," quoted in T. H. Levere, "Faraday, Matter and Natural Theology," *Brit. J. Hist. Sci.,* 4 (1968), 105.

the properties of a substance belong to it "in consequence of the properties or forces of the *m*, not of the *a*, which, without the forces, is conceived of as having no powers. But then surely the *m* is the *matter.*" Faraday concluded that "the substance consists of the powers or *m*," and he went on to suppose that this notion of matter supposed "the mutual penetrability of matter."[222] For by virtue of its powers and forces—which constituted its essence—"matter" extended continuously throughout space, and interactions between material particles were conceived in terms of the interactions between forces diffused through space. From this notion of matter as powers and forces diffused through space Faraday was led to develop his theory of the ontological primacy of lines of force.[223] It was this theory of Faraday's that Maxwell was to adopt in his first attempt to develop Faraday's ideas in "Faraday's Lines of Force" (1856), and though the problem of Maxwell's adoption of concepts from Faraday is extremely complex, his use of Faraday's theory of lines of force—which treat "the distribution of forces in space as the primary phenomenon"[224]—was fundamental to his development of Faraday's work.[225] Seen in this way, the concept of the physical field can in part be traced through the speculative tradition in British thought discussed in this paper to Newton's emphasis on the role of forces in nature.

ACKNOWLEDGMENTS

We wish to thank Gerd Buchdahl and Laurens Laudan for comments, Jack Morrell for useful suggestions, Roy Porter for discussion on Hutton, Alan Shapiro for drawing our attention to a passage in Hobbes, and other colleagues for their kindness in reading the manuscript.

222. Michael Faraday, "A Speculation touching Electric Conduction and the Nature of Matter" (1844), *Experimental Researches in Electricity,* 3 vols. (London, 1839-1855), *2,* 290 ff.
223. The results of this study clearly challenge L. Pearce Williams' interpretation of Faraday in his *Michael Faraday* (London, 1965). For a critical analysis of Williams' views see J. B. Spencer, *op. cit.* (Note 124), pp. 184-202. For a different interpretation of Faraday to that of Williams see P. M. Heimann, "Faraday's Theories of Matter and Electricity," *Brit. J. Hist. Sci.,* 5 (1971), 235-257.
224. Draft MS on "Faraday's Lines of Force," University Library, Cambridge, Add. 7655. The paper was published in *Trans. Camb. Phil. Soc., 10* (1856), 27-83.
225. See P. M. Heimann, "Maxwell and the Modes of Consistent Representation," *Arch. Hist. Exact Sci.,* 6 (1970), 171-213.

II

"NATURE IS A PERPETUAL WORKER": NEWTON'S AETHER AND EIGHTEENTH-CENTURY NATURAL PHILOSOPHY

INTRODUCTION

THE historiography of eighteenth-century natural philosophy has been determined by the interpretation of seventeenth-century science as the "mechanical philosophy", as embodying a mechanical or mechanistic world-view. This approach received clear expression in Dijksterhuis' *Mechanization of the World-Picture* (1950). In this important study Dijksterhuis attempted to characterize the meaning of "mechanistic" in a manner adequate to its historical role: "With the appearance of Newton's *Principia* . . . natural scientists had been furnished with an aim which they were to pursue for two centuries as the only conceivable one." His conclusion was that this "mechanization of the world-picture . . . meant the introduction of a description of nature with the aid of the mathematical concepts of classical mechanics".[1] Historians of eighteenth-century science have tended to see the mathematical, mechanical programme of the *Principia* as crucial to the natural philosophy of the period. For example, in emphasizing that the speculative tradition deriving from Newton's *Opticks* was of great importance in eighteenth-century natural philosophy, I. B. Cohen regarded the *Opticks* as having provided a "mechanical basis for understanding the phenomena of matter".[2] It would be incorrect to deny the importance of Newton's clear implication that the models and methods of the *Principia* could be applied to the treatment of the interparticulate forces discussed in the *Opticks*. This ideal shaped much natural philosophy in the eighteenth century: the hope of a quantified science of interparticulate forces dominated significant areas of chemical thought in the period[3] and was crucial to a natural philosopher such as Henry Cavendish, who attempted to apply the mathematical, mechanical programme of the *Principia*, which he saw as providing a model of quantitative

---

* Department of History and Philosophy of Science, University of Cambridge, Whipple Museum, Cambridge CB2 3RH.

[1] E. J. Dijksterhuis, *The Mechanization of the World-Picture*, trans. C. Dikshoorn, Oxford, 1961, 495, 501.

[2] I. Bernard Cohen, *Franklin and Newton*, Philadelphia, 1956, 121.

[3] Arnold Thackray, *Atoms and Powers: An Essay on Newtonian Matter-Theory and the Development of Chemistry*, Cambridge, Mass., 1970.

II

science, to problems discussed in the *Opticks*.[4] However, in this paper I wish to emphasize the importance of another conception of nature in eighteenth-century British natural philosophy, and to relate this to Newton's speculative writings. It will become clear that for many eighteenth-century thinkers, as well as for Newton himself, vivifying principles which could not be subsumed under the laws of mechanics played a fundamental role in their conceptions of nature, and that these ideas had intimate relation to the use of chemical and aethereal principles.

The theme of this paper is the transformation of Newton's aethereal speculations in eighteenth-century British natural philosophy. Newton's aethereal speculations remain among the most puzzling features of his natural philosophy, and in this paper I shall not attempt to provide a full analysis of Newton's ideas on the aether, but will be concerned with his theories of the aether as they appear in his published writings, so as to give an account of his speculations as they were known to his successors, and to delineate the influence of these speculations on eighteenth-century natural philosophy. It will be shown that, after the mid-eighteenth century, natural philosophers rejected Newton's theory that the activity of nature was maintained by divine agency. For Newton, laws of nature were regarded as being imposed on nature by God, and "active principles" were the manifestations of divine agency in nature. However, many eighteenth-century natural philosophers rejected this conception of nature, and conceived the activity of nature as being intrinsic to the natural order (rather than being due to the operations of divine agency), and laws of nature were regarded as being immanent in the fabric of nature. In this paper I will be concerned with the ideas of those natural philosophers who regarded the aether as the source of activity in the cosmos. In conceiving the aether as an active substratum these thinkers transformed Newton's ideas, in a sense conflating Newton's concepts of the aether and active principles. I will suggest that these natural philosophers assimilated the concept of the aether as propounded in the Queries to the *Opticks* as a cause of gravity to Newton's aethereal ideas of the 1670s (which were not published until the mid-eighteenth century). In his aethereal speculations of the 1670s, Newton implied a conception of nature as self-sufficient, in that aether was conceived as an underlying substratum and as the source of activity in the cosmos, and this provided later natural philosophers with a model for a conception of

---

[4] Russell McCormmach, "Henry Cavendish: A Study of Rational Empiricism in Eighteenth Century Natural Philosophy", *Isis*, **60**, 293–306, 1969. In rejecting the aether and imponderable fluids Cavendish's approach to natural philosophy was almost unique in late eighteenth-century Britain: see McCormmach, "John Michell and Henry Cavendish: Weighing the Stars", *Brit. J. Hist. Sci.*, **4** 150 f., 1968.

nature as self-sufficient. For these natural philosophers the aether functioned as an active substratum maintaining the activity of nature.

Eighteenth-century scientists were especially interested in problems relating to optics, heat, electricity and chemistry, and the speculative systems discussed in this paper illustrate that interest. The physics of imponderable fluids, active substances and the aether, which was closely related to chemical principles, represents one of the main currents of speculation in natural philosophy in the second half of the eighteenth century. This tradition has relation to the view of nature which stressed the primacy of forces.[5] This can be seen from a consideration of the other main speculative tradition in late eighteenth-century British thought, that in which the essence of matter was defined as being constituted by attractive and repulsive forces,[6] for the theory of matter as forces and the concept of an active substratum conceived as the embodiment of forces appear clearly in the natural philosophy of James Hutton.[7]

I

For eighteenth-century thinkers, Newton's most familiar discussion of the aether was to be found in the Queries which he added to the second English edition of the *Opticks* in 1717. This aether was posited as an explanation of gravity, and it is possible that Newton published his idea in response to Leibniz's charge that he had employed gravity as an occult quality.[8] Newton argued that the aether consisted of extremely small particles endowed with repulsive forces of great intensity in relation to their size. The relation between smallness of size and greatness of force follows from Newton's theory of the porosity of matter and the primacy of force and he argued that "the smallest particles of Matter may cohere by the strongest Attractions".[9] In the *General*

---

[5] Cf. Robert E. Schofield, *Mechanism and Materialism: British Natural Philosophy in An Age of Reason*, Princeton, 1970. Schofield's distinction between force and aether theories in Newton and later theorists is disputed in this paper.

[6] P. M. Heimann and J. E. McGuire, "Newtonian Forces and Lockean Powers: Concepts of Matter in Eighteenth Century Thought", *Historical Studies in the Physical Sciences* (ed. R. McCormmach), **3**, 233–306, 1971.

[7] For a discussion of the impact of the aether on biological thought see Philip C. Ritterbush, *Overtures to Biology: The Speculations of Eighteenth Century Naturalists*, New Haven and London, 1964.

[8] "The Leibniz–Clarke Correspondence" in Leroy E. Loemker (ed.), *Gottfried Wilhelm Leibniz: Philosophical Papers and Letters*, new ed., Dordrecht, 1969, 716. For Leibniz, forces were either mechanical (and therefore natural) or a manifestation of God's will (and miraculous). For Newton, to be natural did not necessarily imply being mechanical: that forces could be subsumed under laws was sufficient to characterize them as being natural.

[9] Isaac Newton, *Opticks: or a Treatise of the Reflections, Refractions, Inflections & Colours of Light*, 4th ed., London, 1730 [reprinted 1952], 394.

Scholium to the second edition of the *Principia* (1713) he argued that gravity "must proceed from a cause that penetrates to the very centres of the sun and planets", and which "operates not according to the quantity of the surfaces of the particles upon which it acts (as mechanical causes are accustomed)".[10] Gravity cannot be explained by the impulsive action of an aethereal fluid, for the impulsive action of such a fluid is in proportion to the surfaces of the bodies. Since impulsive action is a necessary condition of a mechanical hypothesis, the 1717 aether cannot be mechanical. It is arguments of this kind that Newton adduces in Query 21 of the 1717 *Opticks* when speaking of the aether as the cause of gravity, stating that "gravity is greater in the surfaces of small Planets than in those of great ones in proportion to their bulk". Gravity is explained by the "exceeding smallness" of the particles of aether which "thereby make that medium . . . exceedingly more able to press upon gross bodies by endeavouring to expand itself".[11] Newton is clearly not supposing that the aether acts by mechanical pressure, and, given his statement of the relation between smallness of size of the aether particles and the greatness of force associated with those particles, by analogy the possibility is open that in the limit the dimensions of particles would be so contracted that space would contain forces grouped round foci.

This appears to be the implication of Newton's discussion of the aether, and this is not an explanation of gravity by a theory of "contact-action";[12] indeed the rejection of such mechanically acting media was fundamental to Newton's development of the *Principia*.[13] In the *Opticks* Newton attempted to reduce distance forces such as the gravitational force to the repulsive force of the aether. The aether was a substance which was dynamic in character in that it was the embodiment of interstitial forces which filled space and could not be explained in mechanical terms. The gross properties of the aethereal medium are thus phenomenal manifestations of a repulsive force.[14]

[10] Isaac Newton, *Principia*, ed. Motte–Cajori, London, 1934, 546.

[11] Newton, *op.cit.* (9), 352.

[12] I will argue below that the clear realization of this fundamental feature of the 1717 aether underlies much eighteenth-century natural philosophy. Bryan Robinson's *Dissertation on the Aether of Sir Isaac Newton*, Dublin, 1743, is not part of the tradition discussed here in that he developed a mechanical treatment of phenomena in terms of the sizes and motions of aether particles. This approach is not characteristic of British aether theorists.

[13] D. T. Whiteside, "Before the *Principia*: The Maturing of Newton's Thought on Dynamical Astronomy, 1664–1684", *Journal for the History of Astronomy*, **1**, 5–19, 1970.

[14] This interpretation is strengthened by his clear distinction between the aether and matter. In a manuscript on Hauksbee's experiments, intended for the 1717 *Opticks*, Newton wrote, concerning his "very subtile active substance or medium": "To distinguish this Medium from the air, I will hence forward call it Aether & by the word bodies I will understand the bodies which flote in it" (University library, Cambridge, Add. 3970.9, fol. 623ʳ). Newton argued that this aether is "a substance in which bodies move and flote

It is clear that the aether has a close relation to the central features of Newton's natural philosophy, for the notions of the primacy of force and the paucity of matter in the universe were fundamental to Newton's natural philosophy.[15] For Newton, immaterial "active principles", used as a general term to denote the cause of forces, were fundamental to the operations of nature. But Newton's commitment to active principles did not conflict with this theory of the aether; indeed the aether itself can be viewed as a type of active principle. It would be incorrect to suppose that Newton employed the concepts of the aether and of active principles interchangeably; the latter are not only of wider connotation but subsume the concept of the aether. However, it was Newton's theory of the micro-structure of the aether as the embodiment of repulsive forces that was to enable eighteenth-century thinkers to transform his concept of the aether into that of "active substances", by conflating his concepts of the aether and active principles.

Given this claim for the *implicit* connection between the aether and active principles in Newton's thought, some discussion of his concept of active principles is in order. J. E. McGuire has made a fundamental study of this problem[16] and my discussion of active principles is indebted to his analysis. As McGuire has amply demonstrated, Newton's discussion of "active principles" is bedevilled by ambiguities. His manuscripts show that his ideas on this and related concepts were in a state of flux throughout his intellectual development. My purpose here is to place the emphasis on Newton's published writings, though it should be noted that his manuscripts are compatible with his published writings, and to delineate the way in which his successors conflated concepts which for him were perhaps more clearly defined.

Newton's commitment to the void from the mid-1680s to the publication of the *Optice* (1706) was fundamental to his doctrine that there exists in nature a paucity of matter. Moreover, this was connected to his belief in the primacy of forces in nature, his tendency to stress the way in which forces arranged the constituents of matter. For Newton forces were not reducible to matter, and the problem of the causation of forces was fundamental to Newton's conception of force. For Newton this involved discussion of the mode of causation of divine agency in the natural world. In the Queries to the *Optice* (1706)— preserved, with modifications, in the 1717 *Opticks*—he employed the notion of active principles. Though God was the ultimate cause and sustainer of all entities and phenomena in the natural order, active principles referred to the

which therefore has no *vis inertiae*, but acts by other laws than those that are mechanical" (Add. 3968.17, fol. 357^r).

[15] J. E. McGuire, "Force, Active Principles and Newton's Invisible Realm", *Ambix*, **15**, 154–208, 1968.
[16] *Ibid.*

means by which the divine power was continually present in nature. Though some of his unpublished manuscripts, dating from the 1690s to the publication of the *Optice*, seem to indicate that Newton regarded God as the direct cause of gravity by means of active principles, the published Queries (of 1706 and 1717) imply that Newton regarded the notion of active principles more as a general term which he used to denote the causes of forces. Newton here regarded active principles as existing within the order of nature. He argued that these principles were "general Laws of Nature . . . Their Truth appearing to us by Phaenomena, though their Causes be not yet discover'd . . . For we meet with very little Motion in the World, besides what is owing to these active Principles."[17] Active principles were conceived as being the manifestations of divine agency in nature, but as operating within the natural order rather than functioning solely as divine interventions.

A crucial feature of these active principles is the way in which Newton links them to chemical phenomena. He contrasts the "passive Principle" of the *vis inertiae* which relates to matter in motion[18] with "a very potent Principle",[19] the active principle which gave rise to "vital Motions".[20] He contrasts the laws of the *Principia*, which refer to matter in motion, with active principles, with the "great and violent"[21] motions of fermentations "by which the Heart and Blood of Animals are kept in perpetual Motion and Heat; the inward Parts of the Earth are constantly warm'd, and in some places grow very hot; Bodies burn and shine, Mountains take fire, the Caverns of the Earth are blown up, and the Sun continues violently hot and lucid, and warms all things by his Light".[22] In these passages Newton is affirming that the activity of nature is due to active principles. As McGuire has emphasized, there were features in nature which could not be explained by the mechanical philosophy, by the laws of matter and motion.[23]

Newton's arguments here are distinctly ambiguous. The active principles are imprecisely defined, though it is clear that he believed that there was activity in nature which was inexplicable in terms of the categories of the mechanical philosophy. Perhaps the most crucial aspect of this concept of active principles was his argument that gravity could not be explained mechanically. In the *General Scholium* to the second edition of the *Principia* (1713) he argued that gravity cannot be explained by the impulsive action of an ae-

[17] Newton, *op.cit.* (9), 399ff.
[18] *Ibid.*, 397.
[19] *Ibid.*, 380.
[20] *Ibid.*, 340.
[21] *Ibid.*, 380.
[22] *Ibid.*, 3 9.
[23] McGuire, *op.cit.* (15).

thereal fluid.[24] Since impulsive action is a necessary condition of a mechanical hypothesis, the 1717 aether cannot be mechanical.[25] The concept of the aether makes the phenomenon of gravity intelligible, and gravity is explicitly defined as a non-mechanical agent. In the *Opticks* Newton argued that "active Principles . . . are the cause of Gravity".[26] Given that his concept of the aether is not "mechanical", that it is an active, dynamic "medium", it has affinities with the very "potent" active principles which Newton contrasts with mechanical, passive principles. Thus there is some reason to regard the aether as an active principle, though his discussion of active principles here clearly places them on a higher level as modes of explanation. Like the aether, active principles operate within the natural order. This interpretation is compatible with Newton's philosophy of nature and is consistent with his published remarks, and it is plausible to argue that later natural philosophers saw this as the implication of Newton's published speculations.

This connection is implicit in later natural philosophy, and is given further credence by Newton's remarks at the close of the *General Scholium*. Around 1707 Newton became interested in experiments carried out by Francis Hauksbee on electro-luminescence.[27] This interest is reflected in his allusions to an "electric and elastic spirit" as the possible cause of gravity in the *General Scholium* (1713).[28] The term "spirit" is ambiguous, but Newton's use of the term has relation to Henry More's use of the term "spirit".[29] Accepting a hierarchy between material and spiritual entities, More and Cudworth stressed the role of intermediaries in nature; and, though Newton distinguished his own ideas from their use of intermediaries as causative agents, he did not accept a strict dualism between the material and the immaterial. The electric spirit was a substance intermediate between passive matter and the higher spiritual entities. Through Hauksbee's experiments, Newton came to regard this electric spirit as a physical entity, a medium with properties perhaps closer to the material than to the higher immaterial entities. His remarks on the electric

[24] *Loc.cit.* (10).
[25] See above.
[26] *Ibid.*, 399.
[27] Henry Guerlac, "Francis Hauksbee, expérimentateur au profit de Newton", *Archives Int. d'hist. des Sciences*, **16**, 113–28, 1963.
[28] Newton, *op.cit.* (10), 547. Though the qualification of this spirit as "electric and elastic" does not appear in any Latin edition of the *Principia*, these words having been interpolated by Motte, these words agree with terms used by Newton in drafts. See A. R. Hall and Marie Boas Hall, *Unpublished Scientific Papers of Isaac Newton*, Cambridge, 1962, 208. The qualification of the spirit as electric and elastic also appears as a marginal note in Newton's own copy of the *Principia*. See A. Koyré and I. B. Cohen, "Newton's 'Electric and Elastic Spirit'," *Isis*, **51**, 337, 1960.
[29] See McGuire, *op.cit.* (15), 184ff.

spirit indicate that this spirit had some relation in its intrinsic characteristics to the aether of the 1717 *Opticks*. Chemical, electrical and aethereal spirits thus acted as active principles in nature.

This discussion of the aether and active principles, as developed in Newton's published writings, is insufficient to serve as a full analysis of his views, but indicates the notion of the aethereal medium as an active principle, the embodiment of forces in space, which was transmitted to Newton's successors. Newton was thus seen to have suggested an explanation of activity in nature in terms of the operations of an aethereal medium. Though Newton regarded second causes—such as an aether—as manifestations of divine agency in nature, arguing that God's will was the only causally efficacious agency in nature, natural philosophers in the eighteenth century saw in the aether a source of the activity in nature which obviated the necessity of having recourse to divine energy. The Queries to the *Opticks* provided a basis for this conception of nature, but its full realization incorporated ideas first proposed by Newton in the 1670s, though not published until the mid-eighteenth century.

In a letter to Oldenburg of 1675 Newton suggested that nature originated from the transmutations of aethereal spirits: *"The whole frame of nature may be nothing but aether condensed by a fermental principle* . . . may be nothing but various contextures of some certain aethereal spirits or vapours, condensed, as it were, by precipitation, much after the manner, that vapours are condensed into water, or exhalations into grosser substances . . . and after condensation wrought into various forms, at first by the immediate hand of the Creator, and ever since by the power of nature, who, by virtue of the command, *Increase and Multiply*, became a complete imitator of the copies set her by the Protoplast. Thus perhaps may all things be originated from aether."[30] This was first published in 1744, and here Newton is unmistakably connecting the aether to chemical principles; and, moreover, he suggests that once activated by God it is to be considered as acting "by the power of nature", that is, within the natural order. This letter was written to correct details of a paper of 1675 which was not published until 1756. In this paper Newton characterized the operations of the aether as a source of activity in nature:

> For nature is a perpetual worker, generating fluids out of solids, and solids out of fluids, fixed things out of volatile, and volatile out of fixed, subtle out of gross and gross out of subtle; some things to ascend, and make the upper terrestrial juices, rivers, and the atmosphere; and by consequence, others to descend for a requital to the former. And, as the earth, so perhaps may the sun imbibe this spirit copiously, to conserve his shining, and keep the planets from receding further from him. And they, that will, may also suppose, that this spirit affords or carries

[30] *The Works of the Honourable Robert Boyle*, 5 vols., London, 1744, vol. 1, 74.

with it thither the solary fewel and material principle of light: and that the vast aethereal spaces between us and the stars are for a sufficient repository for this food of the sun and planets.[31]

Thus, by "nature making a circulation"[32] the activity of the cosmos is conserved. This notion of the self-sufficiency of nature, the balance of nature, by the circulation of aethereal substances was to be of crucial significance in the thought of later eighteenth-century thinkers such as James Hutton. Of equal importance was the notion advanced by Newton here, that the aether was an underlying principle out of which all things originated, that other entities were modifications of the aether. For later thinkers the unity of nature was maintained by the transformations of an aethereal principle. The aether served the same function as active principles in maintaining the activity of nature,[33] and Newton was quite explicit here that the aether functioned within the natural order, "by the power of nature". Thus the connection between the aether and active principles was again implicit.

Newton's letter to Boyle of 1679, published together with the letter to Oldenburg in 1744,[34] certainly qualified the speculations about aethereal spirits, but the impression of the self-sufficiency of nature remained. Despite major differences of emphasis—both in the theory of the replenishing of nature and in the fact that the tails of comets rather than the aether were responsible for the balance of nature[35]—passages in the *Principia* also gave the impression that Newton regarded "vapours" and "spirits" as responsible for recruiting and sustaining activity in nature.[36] The relation to Newton's later speculations is apparent.

The sources for Newton's concepts of the aether and of active principles remain obscure. However, it is clear from Newton's discussion of transmutation in the 1670s that his concept of the aether at that time had strong chemical overtones. Moreover, the evidence here cited suggests that all these speculations, on the aether, on spiritous agencies and on active principles, are closely related.[37] The importance of chemical and organic processes is

---

[31] Thomas Birch, *The History of the Royal Society of London*, 4 vols., London, 1756–57, vol.3, 251. In his manuscript, Newton uses the phrase "nature is a perpetuall circulatory worker", *The Correspondence of Isaac Newton*, ed. H. W. Turnbull, Cambridge, 1959, vol.1, 366.

[32] Birch, *loc.cit.*

[33] David Kubrin, "Newton and the Cyclical Cosmos: Providence and the Mechanical Philosophy", *Journal of the History of Ideas*, **28**, 335, 1967; J. E. McGuire, "Transmutation and Immutability: Newton's Doctrine of Physical Qualities", *Ambix*, **14**, 85, 1967.

[34] *Op.cit.* (30), vol.1, 70 ff.

[35] Kubrin, *op.cit.* (33), 336 ff; McGuire, *op.cit.* (33), 86 f.

[36] Newton, *op.cit.* (10), 529 f, 542.

[37] See also Frank Manuel, *A Portrait of Isaac Newton*, Cambridge, Mass., 1968, 182.

stressed in the *Opticks* and in the speculations of the 1670s, and in the latter the emphasis on circulation in nature is made explicit.

[38] Newton's appeal to chemical principles as a key to unravel the fundamental problems of natural philosophy was a strong current in his thought, and suggests the continued influence of Paracelsian and Helmontian conceptions of a chemical philosophy of nature.[39] A full understanding of Newton's speculations on these matters is impossible without an analysis of the influence of these traditions on his thought, but his constant disjunction between active principles and the principles of motion, and his theories of the aether and of spiritous agencies in nature, demonstrate that many of his speculations lay outside the framework of the mechanical philosophy. In these speculations Newton was hinting at a chemical philosophy of nature, and it is the concern of this paper to consider the impact of this conception of nature on subsequent natural philosophy.

II

The concept of the aether was to take many forms in eighteenth-century natural philosophy: in its different modifications, the aether was held to be the principle of heat, electricity and chemistry; and the theory of an aethereal principle manifesting itself in different forms expressed the unity of nature. Given the chemical context of Newton's own ideas, it is hardly surprising that developments in chemical theory in the early eighteenth century were seen by subsequent thinkers to have relation to speculations on the explanation of activity in nature by an aethereal agent. Of paramount importance are Boerhaave's chemical writings. To demonstrate the transformation in the concept of the aether which occurred in the eighteenth century I will indicate the way in which these chemical speculations were assimilated to Newton's theory of the aether.

---

[38] For circular symbolism, see the fundamental works of Walter Pagel: "Giordano Bruno, the Philosophy of Circles, and the Circular Movement of the Blood", *J. Hist. Med.*, **6**, 116–24, 1951; "William Harvey and the Purpose of Circulation", *Isis*, **42**, 22–38, 1951; *William Harvey's Biological Ideas*, Basle, 1967.

[39] See Allen G. Debus, "Renaissance Chemistry and the Work of Robert Fludd", *Ambix*, **14**, 42–59, 1967; P. M. Rattansi, "The Helmontian-Galenist Controversy in Restoration England", *Ambix*, **12**, 1–23, 1964; C. Webster, "Water as the Ultimate Principle of Nature: the Background to Boyle's Sceptical Chymist", *Ambix*, **13**, 96–107, 1966. Though arguing that these aethereal speculations show Newton's adherence to a mechanical philosophy of nature, R. S. Westfall concedes that the aether of the 1670s "suggested the lingering presence in his thought of a tradition alien to the mechanical", *Force in Newton's Physics*, London, 1971, 369. I believe that this is an understatement.

The history of the various editions and translations of Boerhaave's *Elementa Chemiae* (1732) is confusing,[40] but Shaw's English translation of 1741 rapidly became the standard English version.[41] Boerhaave's intellectual sources have yet to be fully explored, but it is clear that his writings were seen as a synthesis of the ideals of Newtonian natural philosophy and the traditional chemical philosophies of nature. Though Boerhaave's doctrine of fire, the theoretical basis of his chemistry, shows similarities to Descartes' subtle fluid,[42] by the mid-eighteenth century it was rapidly assimilated to the Newtonian tradition, a process aided both by Shaw's presentation of ideas derived from Newton's *Opticks* in his extensive footnotes, and by the publication, shortly after the appearance of Shaw's translation, of Newton's letters to Boyle and Oldenberg. Boerhaave's book has been seen as an adumbration of a "corpuscular mechanics" interpreted by Shaw as following the "exact corpuscular philosophy of the *Opticks*",[43] for Boerhaave argued that "chemistry is employed in changing ... bodies ... and the change it produces in them is effected by means of motion alone".[44] However, the degree to which this idea of motion determined Boerhaave's philosophy of nature has been exaggerated. Moreover, it would seem that Shaw did not accept this as a viable programme for chemistry but wished to emphasize the peculiarly *chemical* features of chemical phenomena. Shaw added a long footnote to Boerhaave's statement, in which he pointed out that the laws of motion "will not reach to those more remote, intestine motions of the component particles ... Beside the common laws of sensible masses, the minute parts they are composed of, seem subject to some others, which have been but lately taken notice of, and are yet more than guessed at".[45] This is the power of attraction, and Shaw goes on to explain the way in which Newton and his followers had attempted to develop a quantitative science of interparticulate forces so as to explain chemical effects. Referring to this as a "New mechanics", Shaw's endorsement was less than enthusiastic. In the first place this violated his feeling that speculations of this kind were "too precipitate". This view is hardly surprising, for Shaw was also the translator of Stahl's *Fundamenta chymiae* (1723).[46] Shaw's statement, in his *Chemical*

---

[40] F. W. Gibbs, "Boerhaave's Chemical Writings", *Ambix*, **6**, 117–35, 1958.

[41] [Herman Boerhaave,] *A New Method of Chemistry: including the History, Theory and Practice of the Art: translated from the Original Latin of Dr Boerhaave's Elementa Chemiae*, trans. Peter Shaw, 2 vols., London, 1741.

[42] H. Metzger, *Newton, Stahl, Boerhaave et la doctrine chimique*, Paris, 1930, 221.

[43] Cohen, *op.cit.* (2), 224f.

[44] Boerhaave, *op.cit.* (41), 155.

[45] *Ibid.*, 155n.

[46] [G. E. Stahl,] *Philosophical Principles of Universal Chemistry*, trans. Peter Shaw, London, 1730.

II

Lectures (1734), that "genuine chemistry" preferred to leave to "other philosophers the sublimer disquisitions of primary corpuscles or atoms", that chemistry should avoid such "metaphysical speculations",[47] reflects Stahl's emphasis on chemical utility which governed his belief that the "mechanical philosophy" only "scratches the shell and surface of things and leaves the kernel untouched".[48] In his note appended to Boerhaave's remark on motion, Shaw went on to quote almost verbatim from Newton's remarks on active principles in Query 31, arguing that "all the phaenomena, all the changes in the universe, are the effects of motion. Accordingly, to have a succession of such changes, the author of nature has added to bodies certain active principles to be the sources of motion."[49] The implication was that the ultimate principles in nature, those which were within the province of chemistry, were not to be found in the study of the motions of particles but in Newton's active principles. Thus Newton's own emphasis on a chemical philosophy of nature is reflected in Shaw's notes.

The emphasis on a chemical philosophy of nature is an important feature both of Boerhaave's text and of Shaw's notes. As Shaw emphasized, it was "by means of chemistry, that Sir *Isaac Newton* has made a great part of his surprising discoveries in natural philosophy; and that curious set of queries, which we find at the end of his optics, are almost wholly chemical. Indeed chemistry, in its extent, is scarce less than the whole of natural philosophy."[50] Boerhaave's doctrine of fire "as the cause and principle of almost all the effects cognizable by our senses"[51] was a chemical agent, a kind of active principle. Emphasizing the "excessive minuteness of its constituent parts",[52] Boerhaave states that fire was an "active element"[53] which had the "property of penetrating all solid and fluid bodies" and which "exists always, and everywhere".[54] Fire was distributed through the universe, it was "perpetually present in all places, as well as in the fullest corporeal space, as in the most perfect vacuum" and was "equally distributed every where, so long as no particular cause arises to collect it, thus dispersed, in some determinate place".[55] An important feature of fire—crucial to many eighteenth-century natural philosophers—was that it was non-gravitational, for "it has no more tendency

---

[47] Peter Shaw, *Chemical Lectures publickly read at London*, London, 1734, 146.
[48] Quoted in J. R. Partington, *A History of Chemistry*, vol. 2, London, 1961, 665. See Thackray, *op.cit.* (3), 171–6.
[49] Boerhaave, *op.cit.* (41), 157n.
[50] *Ibid.*, 173n.
[51] *Ibid.*, 206.
[52] *Ibid.*, 208.
[53] *Ibid.*, 212.
[54] *Ibid.*, 236.
[55] *Ibid.*, 338.

II

to the centre of the earth than to any other point . . . it is present everywhere, unless hindered by some foreign cause, through the whole universe".[56] Fire consisted of subtle, immutable particles, and possessed the power of permeating the pores of bodies, and it was "the great changer of all things in the universe, while itself remaining unchanged".[57] The similarities of this space-pervading substance to Newton's aether of the 1717 *Opticks* is clear, and, moreover, Boerhaave regarded fire as an active principle responsible for change in the universe. The apparent affinity to Newton's speculations was strengthened by Shaw's footnotes, which provided a Newtonian commentary on the text.

III

The problem of Boerhaave's sources is a topic which lies beyond the limits of the present paper, which is concerned, rather, with his influence.[58] That influence appears very clearly in Berkeley's *Siris* (1744),[59] in which constant appeal is made to Stoic, Pythagorean, Hermetic, and Neoplatonic traditions to justify belief in a universal aether or invisible fire, a "diffused and active principle, which, at the same time that it shakes the earth and heavens, will enter, divide and dissolve the smallest, closest, and most compacted bodies", and which was "the spirit of the universe".[60] Moreover, the aethereal fire was "the seed of the generation of all things. . . [and the] Stoics also taught that all substance was originally fire, and should return to fire; that an active subtle fire was diffused or expanded throughout the whole universe, the several parts whereof were produced, sustained, and held together by its force".[61] Rejecting hypothetical causative agents, Berkeley rejects Newton's aether—

---

[56] *Ibid.*, 359.

[57] *Ibid.*, 362.

[58] Boerhaave's sources are clearly diverse, but I would suggest that his *Chemistry* shows Helmontian overtones. Indeed, Boerhaave refers to a dynamic principle in nature, a "certain *Aura* or spirit, peculiar to . . . [a] single body . . . called by the ancient chemists, who were deeply skilled in the nature of things, *Spiritus rector*, or presiding spirit . . . lodged by the creator in a tenacious durable matter . . . [It is] endued with an incredible power of generating a spirit like itself . . . hence they call it the vital spark, *Filius Solis*, the son of the sun, *Spiritus intus alens*, the internal nourishing spirit" (*ibid.*, 168f). These ideas exhibit certain similarities to Helmont's concept of the immanence of the dynamic principle in matter. Moreover, Boerhaave's emphasis on the activating power of fire shows certain analogies to Helmont's stress on fire as a dynamic principle in nature. For important insights see Walter Pagel, "The Religious and Philosophical Aspects of van Helmont's Science and Medicine", *Supplements to the Bulletin of the History of Medicine*, No. 2, Baltimore, 1944.

[59] See Jessop's introduction to his edition of *Siris* in *The Works of George Berkeley, Bishop of Cloyne*, ed. A. A. Luce and T. E. Jessop, vol. 5, London, 1953, 11f.

[60] *Ibid.*, sections 158–9.

[61] *Ibid.*, section 166.

proposed in the *Opticks* as a putative cause of gravitation—as a *cause* of gravity, light and fire, and argues for a single universal "subtle medium" which "according to its various quantities, motions, and determinations sheweth itself in different effects or appearances, and is aether, light or fire".[62] In arguing for a universal subtle medium which manifests itself in various modifications, Berkeley has thus assimilated Newton's concept of the aether to the universal active "aether" of fire developed by Boerhaave. Berkeley's statement that this medium could manifest itself as fire, light or aether in its different modifications was to be a fundamental feature of the natural philosophy of men such as James Hutton.

As I. B. Cohen has shown, Boerhaave's doctrine of fire was of great influence on electrical studies in the 1740s.[63] Men such as Benjamin Wilson, William Watson and Benjamin Franklin developed theories in which fire, aether and electricity were regarded as "different modifications of the same thing",[64] though Franklin came to distinguish more carefully between fire and electricity. By the 1740s natural philosophers were seeking to encompass electrical and chemical effects within a single conceptual scheme, and appealed to Newton's hypothesis of the aether, as developed in the *Opticks*, for justification. Schofield has argued that the proposal of the relation between the aether and electricity at this time was due to the revival of interest in Newton's aethereal ideas by Bryan Robinson's *Dissertation on the Aether of Sir Isaac Newton* (1743) which, however, followed an approach different from other works relating to the aether, and developed a mechanical treatment of phenomena in terms of the sizes and motions of aether particles, and to the publication of Newton's letters to Boyle and Oldenberg in 1744.[65] These electrical ideas have clear relation to those of Boerhaave, but the relation to Newton's aether is made explicit in Gowin Knight, *An Attempt to Demonstrate, that all the Phaenomena in Nature may be Explained by Two Simple Active Principles, Attraction and Repulsion* (1748). Knight argues that the essential qualities of matter are immutable, their immutability being secured by the immediate will of God, but that motion, not being immutable, was not an essential property of matter, so that there is in nature "some Active Principle or Principles capable of producing and continuing Motion in the Universe".[66] These active principles are those of attraction and repulsion, and are associated with two

[62] *Ibid.*, section 226.
[63] Cohen, *op.cit.* (2).
[64] I. B. Cohen, ed., *Benjamin Franklin's Experiments*, Cambridge, Mass., 1941, 210.
[65] Schofield, *op.cit.* (5), 106, 159.
[66] Gowin Knight, *An Attempt to Demonstrate, that all the Phaenomena in Nature may be Explained by Two Simple Active Principles, Attraction and Repulsion* (London, 1754), 4f. Knight was well known as a "magnetic philosopher" and as librarian of the British Museum.

different material entities, one attracting, the other repelling. Light, heat, electricity and magnetism are explained in terms of the operation of this repellent matter. Knight's attractive and repulsive substances were the embodiment of forces opposing and balancing one another, and he clearly identified these attractive and repulsive substances as active principles. The relation to the aether of the 1717 *Opticks* is apparent, for this aether was the embodiment of force diffused through space. Thus, by the mid-century, natural philosophers were developing conceptions of nature in which the aether of the 1717 *Opticks* was assimilated to concepts of fire and electricity, and regarded as an active principle in nature.

The concern with the activating power of electricity or fire was widespread in this period, often undoubtedly showing the influence of Boerhaave. Natural philosophers regarded fire as a dynamic principle in nature analogous to Newton's aether. Speculations of this kind dominate the writings of the Hutchinsonians, whose writings were influential in this period. John Hutchinson's works include *A Treatise of Power, Essential and Mechanical* (1732) and *Glory or Gravity* (1733), in which Newton's doctrine of active principles as the manifestation of divine agency in nature was rejected as an occult cause. Regarding nature as totally subordinate to God, he argued that "if God, instead of framing the universe into so curious a piece of perpetual motion, had designed to transact all by his own immediate presence, there had been no case for . . . natural laws". Emphasizing divine omniscience and the "perspicuity and perfection" of nature, he rejected the need for God "to work by occult qualities" such as active principles, and sought to develop a "mechanism" to explain the operations of nature.[67] The activity of nature was maintained by the circulation of light, the particles of light condensing into a spirit at the "circumference of our system", and this is "pressed inwards with great force, feeds the central fire [of the sun], and enables it to send forth perpetual streams of light without diminution".[68] Hutchinson asserted a perpetual circulation of light in the universe. The connection between these speculations and Newton's concept of the aether was made by one of Hutchinson's disciples, William Jones, whose concern with the active element of fire shows the influence of Boerhaave.[69] In his *Essay on the First Principles of Natural Philosophy* (1762)

---

[67] *An Abstract from the Works of John Hutchinson, Esq., being a Summary of his Discoveries in Philosophy and Divinity*, 2nd ed., London, 1755, 142. For a discussion of the Hutchinsonians and their influence see Albert J. Kuhn, "Glory or Gravity: Hutchinson vs. Newton", *J. History Ideas*, **22**, 303–22, 1961.

[68] *Op.cit.*, 150.

[69] Schofield, *op.cit.* (5), 127, suggests that the influence of Boerhaave on Jones can be attributed to the influence of Nathan Alcock, with whom Jones had studied and who had himself studied under Boerhaave. Jones was a prominent churchman and well-known author.

Jones argued that "God doth govern the natural world by a delegation of material instruments". Claiming that this was *"one* of the opinions of Sir Isaac",[70] Jones stated that the "frame of nature [is] . . . a perfect and well-ordered machine . . . the fluid aetherial matter of the heavens acts by impulse on the solid matter of the earth".[71] Thus the aether is employed to explain the activity of the natural world, and Jones agrees with Leibniz rather than Clarke in appealing to divine wisdom as justification of his view that God "rules the world by natural causes under the direction of himself the supreme cause".[72] Jones' views both of the nature of the aether and of the mode of its "impulsive" action are of great interest. Referring to Newton's argument in the *General Scholium* (see above) that gravity acts in proportion to the quantity of matter, not to the surfaces of planetary bodies, Jones argues that gravity is to be explained by aethereal matter passing in a "stream through the densest bodies, and can *penetrate the inmost substance of their solid matter*: the influence therefore of such a material cause will neither be confined to the surfaces, nor be proportional to them: and I am willing to think, that if *Sir Isaac* had lived . . . he would have enlarged his notions very much with regard to the natural power and extent of mechanism".[73] The aether does not act by "mechanical impulse", and Jones is thus claiming that the aether could be regarded as an agent which was dynamic in nature and which could penetrate material substances. This is Newton's theory of the aether. For Jones, aether was a form of fire, and electricity too was a form of fire which was diffused throughout the world as an active principle.[74] The influence of Boerhaave and the electrical theorists is apparent.

The concern with the aether as the source of activity in nature appears clearly in the writings of Cadwallader Colden. In his *Principles of Action in Matter* (1751) he states that it "seems . . . to be a very unphilosophical method of reasoning, to suppose that motion comes immediately from the Divine Being", and he emphasizes that motion cannot be conceived other than in that "it exists in something, which has in itself the power of moving".[75] He explained

---

[70] William Jones, *An Essay on the first Principles of Natural Philosophy: wherein the Use of Natural Means, or second Causes in the Oeconomy of the Material World, is demonstrated from Reason, Experiments of various kinds, and the Testimony of Antiquity*, London, 1762, 85.

[71] *Ibid.*, 7.

[72] *Ibid.*, 22.

[73] *Ibid.*, 26.

[74] William Jones, *Philosophical Disquisitions: or, Discourses on the Natural Philosophy of the Elements*, London, 1781, *passim.*

[75] Cadwallader Colden. *The Principles of Action in Matter, the Gravitation of Bodies and the Motion of the Planets explained from those Principles*, London, 1751, 73. Colden was a physician, natural philosopher and historian who was resident in the American Colonies and educated at Edinburgh University.

phenomena in terms of three powers which were "species of matter" and defined as "agents or acting principles".[76] These powers are a resisting power (which possesses *vis inertiae*), a moving power (light) and a third power, an "elastic or expansive force".[77] The aether, which is responsible for the communication of action in nature, is an elastic power and is identified with Newton's "elastic" spirit, and "gravitation is truly and really performed by pulsion, or more properly is the effect of the joint actions of the moving, resisting and elastic powers".[78] Thus the aether is regarded as a species of matter, defined as an active principle, and endued with an elastic force.

The impact of Newton's concept of the aether as a dynamic active medium appears clearly in the writings of these men, often assimilated to or associated with Boerhaave's doctrine of fire as an active principle in nature. By the mid-eighteenth century developments certainly justified John Rowning's statement in his influential *Compendious System of Natural Philosophy* (1737–43) that some philosophers admit *"elementary fire"* as a principle: "they consider fire as endowed with active Powers distinct from those of other Matter",[79] and the notion that fire, aether and electricity were all modifications of the same substance was widespread. The idea that the aether was an active principle was employed to explain the activity of nature. Though Newton regarded active principles as operating within the natural order, in the published Queries, he nevertheless regarded them as manifestations of divine power, for God's Will was the only causally efficacious agency in nature. Thus all activity was God's activity. For these later thinkers, the activity of nature was held to be intrinsic to nature itself; and the aether, as a dynamic active medium, functioned as the source of that activity.

IV

This conception of nature was fundamental to James Hutton's natural philosophy, which was first developed in the 1760s.[80] In his *Dissertations on Different Subjects in Natural Philosophy* (1792) and his *Investigation of the Principles of Knowledge* (1794) he proposed a natural philosophy firmly grounded on metaphysical first principles. For Hutton the substratum, which he called

---

[76] *Ibid.*, 27.

[77] Cadwallader Colden, *An Explication of the First Causes of Action in Matter, and of the Cause of Gravitation*, London, 1746, 22.

[78] *Ibid.*, 51. See Colden, *op.cit.* (75), 28 on Newton's elastic spirit.

[79] John Rowning, *A Compendious System of Natural Philosophy*, London, 1737–43, Preface (1743), iii.

[80] See John Playfair, "Biographical Account of James Hutton", *The Works of John Playfair*, Edinburgh, 1822, IV, 88. Hutton was, of course, famous as a geologist, and was an important figure in the Scottish Enlightenment.

"matter", was to be distinguished from its phenomenal manifestations, which he called "body". Qualities in bodies such as extension and impenetrability were relational, and did not "arise from the absolute nature of the thing". Rather "matter" was to be considered as "certain resisting powers in bodies, by which their volumes and figures are presented to us in the actual information".[81] Hutton denied that "matter" was comprised of atoms, for to characterize extended, solid "body" by means of atoms endowed with the same essential qualities was to assume as the principle of bodies "nothing but the bodies themselves under the pedantic designation of atoms or corpuscles".[82] Nevertheless the nature of the unobservable substratum was to be inferred from the sensible qualities which were characteristic of the bodies themselves, for "nothing is to be allowed, as belonging to matter, that is not authorized in the strictest examination of actual things. For science, at least that of physics, consists not in imagining what may be; but in the investigation of what is actually found in nature".[83] Hutton draws an analogy between the intentions of the mind and the order of nature, arguing that the order and design constitutive of the mind were reflected in the structure of nature, teleologically oriented. Thus, "when a regular order is observed in those changing things, whereby a certain end is always attained, there is necessarily inferred an operation somewhere, an operation similar to that of our mind, which often premediates the exertion of a power and is conscious of design".[84] This harmony between nature and the mind enabled the operations of the powers producing the sensible qualities to be inferred from the sensible qualities.[85] In its intrinsic nature "matter" was to be considered as a substratum, for "when a power is found to be exerted, it is commonly thought that there must be a substance existing, in which that power should reside".[86]

As a substratum "matter" is destitute of bodily form,[87] and he emphasized that "there is not any evidence of *inertia* being proper to the matter".[88] Matter is nonsolid, nonspatial and "possessing active powers".[89] Hutton thus supposes that the mode of action of "matter" cannot be characterized by the laws of mechanics, as matter is devoid of inertia, extension and solidity. Hutton

[81] James Hutton, *Dissertations on Different Subjects in Natural Philosophy*, Edinburgh, 1792, 290ff.
[82] *Ibid.*, 667.
[83] *Ibid.*, 300.
[84] *Ibid.*, 285.
[85] For further discussion of Hutton's epistemology see Heimann and McGuire, *op.cit.* (6).
[86] James Hutton, *An Investigation of the Principles of Knowledge, and of the Progress of Reason, from Sense to Science and Philosophy*, 3 vols., Edinburgh, 1794, II, 389.
[87] This follows from his rejection of Newton's doctrine of essential qualities.
[88] Hutton, *op.cit.* (81), 297.
[89] *Ibid.*, 237.

NATURE IS A PERPETUAL WORKER

considers "matter" as a substance whose nature is defined in terms of its intrinsic activity: "Matter may be thus considered as acting powers; and the several intentions, perceived as belonging to those acting powers, may be considered as modifications of matter."[90] This concept of the substratum as noninertial, its essence defined in relation to its intrinsic activity, its powers and forces, has analogies to Newton's conception of the aether in the 1717 *Opticks* as the embodiment of force. Despite his denial of Newton's theory of atoms as defined by the essential qualities of solidity, impenetrability and inertia, Hutton's theory of matter belongs to the Newtonian tradition in that he elaborated a theory of reality which is a development of Newton's theory of the primacy of forces in nature and which has clear relation to Newton's theory of the aether. Hutton regarded his "matter" as the embodiment of attractive and repulsive forces, and he followed Newton in this asserting the primacy of forces in nature. In a not dissimilar way Joseph Priestley rejected Newton's theory of essential qualities and proposed a theory of matter which was an extension of Newton's theory of the primacy of force.[91]

Hutton supposed two kinds of matter: gravitational matter which acted by the principle of attraction, and matter emanating from the sun which acted by the principle of repulsion. These two different powers are incessantly active, and the "opposite powers are continually balancing one another, or alternately prevailing". If the gravitational power were to prevail, then "gravitation ... would soon bring all the matter of this machine [the universe] to rest, and would lock up every body in a state of the most absolute inactivity". Thus the "emanation of matter from the sun"[92] is one of the prime movers of the machine and "by a just combination of those two different powers, we find moveable and moving bodies properly disposed in a great and connected system of things", so that "without the influence of the sun, this world would remain an useless mass of inert matter". Hutton speaks of this source of action as a "necessary cause of vital motion",[93] and he argues that light, heat and electricity are different modifications of the solar substance:

> Thus light, heat, and electricity, appear to be three different modifications of the same matter. Light is considered as being perfectly disconnected with the body from whence it moves; and the moment it is again connected with a body, so as to lose its proper motion, it ceases to be light. Heat, on the contrary, is perfectly connected with a body, and forms part of its substance; heat being removed from this internal connection of bodies ceases to be heat. Electricity is a modification that will appear to be a medium between light and heat, considered as extremes, for

[90] *Ibid.*, 501.
[91] See Heimann and McGuire, *op.cit.*, (6).
[92] Hutton, *op.cit.* (81), 246.
[93] *Ibid.*, 263.

neither is it unconnected with bodies, nor internally connected with their substance.[94]

Whereas gravitational matter is inseparable from a body, being a fixed principle, the solar substance could exist separate from a body. However, heat cannot be separated from a body without becoming connected to another body, and as *heat* it is always connected with gravitating matter. If heat is separated from a body, then it can no longer be considered as heat but is "the proper matter of heat, or that which was the principle of heat in bodies", and light is "considered as the matter of heat separated from bodies, and moving with extreme velocity". The only principle of action of this abstracted matter is motion, so motion is "proper to the matter of heat in its separated state" as light.[95] Electricity is situated on the surfaces of bodies, and by changing its location this modification of the solar substance might become either light or heat. The solar substance opposes and balances the gravitating matter, so that the weight of a body "is not the measure of its gravitating matter . . . the weight properly measures only the excess of . . . the gravitating above the repulsive power".[96]

The full implications of this theory of the balance of powers in nature appear in Hutton's account of phlogiston. For Hutton, after the life of animals and the growth of plants "the most wonderful and the most important operation of this earth is the burning of fire and the production of light".[97] These operations are explained in terms of the theory of phlogiston. Hutton asserts that "the doctrine of phlogiston may be considered as implying that a quantity of the matter of light and heat is occasionally contained in bodies as a part of their composition".[98] The union of the matter of light and heat with some of the chemical substances of bodies is termed a "phlogistic substance" which is continually being destroyed when bodies burn. Hutton concludes that there must be another operation by which the phlogistic substance may be regenerated, and argues that this "cannot be denied unless it should be alleged, that the general quantity of phlogistic matter upon the globe diminishes". Claiming that there is no evidence in nature for decay without renewal, he states that there "would also appear to be in the system of this globe, a reproductive power, by which the constitution of this world, necessarily decaying, is renewed".[99] Hutton argues that phlogiston is regenerated in plants: "plants compose phlogistic matter in growing, as animals in breathing decompose the same substance",[100] and he refers to Ingenhousz who demonstrated "the production

[94] *Ibid.*, 505f.
[95] *Ibid.*, 490ff.
[96] *Ibid.*, 528.
[97] *Ibid.*, vii.
[98] *Ibid.*, 173.
[99] *Ibid.*, 214.
[100] *Ibid.*, 218.

of vital air [oxygen] by growing plants".[101] Thus it is in plants that "the combination of the solar substance is made for the production of phlogistic matter".[102] The breathing of animals, the growth of plants, and the burning of fire were thus connected. Hutton's conception of nature has strong chemical overtones.

Hutton thus conceived nature as a system of processes and transformations manifesting cycles arising from the tension between attractive and repulsive powers. His theory of phlogiston and light as sources for the regeneration of nature, for the recruitment of activity in nature, shows analogies to Newton's aethereal speculations of the 1670s, published in the mid-eighteenth century. Hutton's theory of light as emanating from the sun and activating the universe, his theory of the circulation of phlogiston, and his emphasis on conservation in nature, show strong analogies to Newton's theory that the activity of nature was maintained by the circulation of the aethereal principle. Newton's idea that the aether was an underlying principle, that other entities were modifications of the aether, is paralleled by Hutton's theory of light, heat and electricity as different modifications of the solar substance. Moreover, Newton's statement that the aether functioned "by the power of nature"[103] is reflected in Hutton's insistence on the regeneration and conservation of nature. In supposing that "matter" could not be characterized by means of the essential qualities of extension, solidity and inertia, Hutton clearly held that though substances could be characterized by the laws of mechanics in their phenomenal manifestations (as "body"), this did not apply to the substratum. Hutton's emphasis on the role of phlogiston shows that he regarded chemical principles as applicable to the micro-realm. His theory of the solar substance manifesting itself in different forms illustrates his emphasis on the unity of nature. The chemical principles which determined the operations of Huttonian matter could not, by definition, be reduced to the laws of mechanics. As John Playfair put it, in his "Biographical Account of James Hutton", in Hutton's system "the chemist, indeed, is flattered more than anyone else with the hopes of discovering in what the essence of matter consists; and Nature, while she keeps the astronomer and the mechanician at a great distance, seems to admit him to more familiar converse, and to a more intimate acquaintance with her secrets".[104]

The conception of nature as a self-contained, self-activating system was fundamental to Hutton's natural philosophy., The system of nature manifested the wisdom and design of God, and the search for final causes was "the

---

[101] *Ibid.*, 220. See Jan Ingenhousz, *Experiments on Vegetables*, London, 1779.
[102] Hutton, *op.cit.* (81), 229.
[103] *Loc.cit.* (30).
[104] *Op.cit.* (80), 83.

II

proper object of our knowledge", for we can only "be said to understand those things, when we see the end for which they are intended in the system of this world, and perceive the means by which, in the wisdom of nature, the end is certainly effected".[105] Nature is a self-contained system, and its self-sufficiency is maintained by chains of unbroken laws which were not to be abrogated by divine action. Nature is defined as the totality of effects in the world, so that "everything that is observed either to act or suffer is said to be a natural thing", and the activity of the universe is not to be ascribed "to God as the immediate cause". Thus laws of nature are immanent in the fabric of nature and Hutton asserts that this is "no other than delegating the power of God".[106] This conception of nature contrasts sharply with Newton's conception of active principles, the cause of forces operating in nature, as the manifestation of divine agency in nature. The conception of nature as a self-regenerating system of active powers obviates the necessity of having recourse to divine energy as the source of activity in nature. The concept of active principles has been subsumed under that of active powers which are part of the fabric of nature and their agency is not conceived in relation to divine power, for God's powers have been delegated to nature. The basis of this conception of nature is to be found in Newton's own argument that active principles operated within the natural order rather than functioning solely as divine interventions. Thus Newton's different theories of the aether, as an active principle in nature, can be seen as fundamental to Hutton's conception of nature. Hutton therefore transformed Newton's theory of forces into a conception of nature as comprised of self-activating powers. For Hutton "nature is a perpetual worker".

Hutton's theory of the solar substance as an activating agency in nature has certain affinities with Boerhaave's doctrine of fire. Like Boerhaave's fire, Hutton's solar substance was an active agent which was non-gravitational, and this solar substance has obvious similarities to the concepts of fire and aether proposed by such men as Berkeley and Jones. Similar ideas can be found in the writings of other contemporary natural philosophers. In his *Philosophical Essay Concerning Light* (1776) Bryan Higgins supposed that light, phlogiston, fire and electricity were different modifications of a single repellent matter: "Fire is not to be considered as a homogeneal body different from light and phlogiston: and I am unwilling to admit the Electric Fluid as an element different from these."[107] However, though "light and gross bodies act on each other, and light is not totally exempt from the laws which govern each other

---

[105] *Op.cit.* (81), 624.
[106] *Op.cit.*, (86), II, 415f.
[107] Bryan Higgins, *A Philosophical Essay Concerning Light*, London, 1776, 13. Higgins was well known as a lecturer and chemist.

NATURE IS A PERPETUAL WORKER

matter",[108] light and gross matter are not interconvertible.[109] In his *Philosophical Inquiry into the Cause of Animal Heat* (1778) P. D. Leslie claims that "phlogiston is fire and light, or a certain subtle elastic fluid, upon the modification of which the phenomena of heat depend". The sun communicates phlogiston to bodies: "The same matter, which in a separate state constitutes fire and light, when modified in bodies is the cause of the inflammability."[110] This matter "is the chief cause and principle of activity" in the universe and is "exempted from the common laws of gravitation".[111] The similarity to Hutton's ideas is clear.[112] Similar ideas can be found in Robert Harrington's *New System on Fire and Planetary Life* (1796), in which light and fire circulate between the earth and sun and serve as active principles, and in Adam Walker's *System of Familiar Philosophy* (1799) in which it is supposed that *"attraction and repulsion are the great acting principles* of the universe",[113] light, fire, electricity and phlogiston being "modifications of one and the same principle", the principle of repulsion.[114] The operations of nature are "determined by a balance of those two powers" which are "opposing or antagonistic principles ... in a state of unceasing warfare".[115] For Walker electricity was the "genuine principle of light and fire" and "solar light ... [is] in a more elementary state in the character of the electric fluid, than it is in either ordinary fire or light".[116] Electricity from the sun is an "ethereal matter" and activated the universe, for it was "the soul of the material world".[117] These ideas attest to the widespread use of the theory of the aether in expressing the unity of nature: phlogiston, light, fire and electricity were modifications of the aethereal principle.

Conclusion

The ideas discussed in this paper can be traced into the nineteenth century. Humphry Davy emphasized that chemistry "relates not only to the minute

[108] *Ibid.*, 1.

[109] *Ibid.*, 43.

[110] Patrick Dugud Leslie, *A Philosophical Inquiry into the Cause of Animal Heat: with Incidental Observations on Several Physiological and Chymical Questions connected with the subject*, London, 1778, 104f. Leslie was a physician educated at Edinburgh.

[111] *Ibid.*, 119.

[112] For further discussion of the chemical theories of Higgins, Leslie and Hutton see also J. R. Partington and D. McKie, "Historical Studies in the Phlogiston Theory. III. Light and Heat in Combustion", *Annals of Science*, **3**, 338–71, 1938.

[113] Adam Walker, *A System of Familiar Philosophy*, rev. ed., 2 vols., London 1801, I, 1. Walker was well known as a lecturer.

[114] *Ibid.*, 14.

[115] *Ibid.*, 6, 18.

[116] *Ibid.*, II, 1, 10.

[117] *Ibid.*, 74.

alterations in the external world . . . but likewise to the great changes and convulsions in nature".[118] Chemistry would lay bare "the most profound secrets of nature",[119] and in an early work (of 1798) he remarked, echoing Hutton, that the various powers of nature—such as light and electricity— "appear to be continually mutually producing each other".[120] The eighteenth-century emphasis on the balance of nature and on transformations in nature underlies Grove's *Correlation of Physical Forces* (1846), with its emphasis on the interconversion of natural powers, and Faraday's remark, fundamental to his science, that "the various forms under which the forces of matter are made manifest have one common origin; or in other words, are so directly related and mutually dependent, that they are convertible, as it were, one into another".[121] The widespread emphasis on the balance and conservation of nature in late eighteenth-century natural philosophy can also be traced to Faraday's notion of the conservation of force as a *"conversion* of one form of power into another".[122]

The traditions discussed in this paper are fundamental to much eighteenth-century British natural philosophy, and relate to an important shift in scientific sensibility: the transition from the Newtonian conception of nature as a contingent artefact of divine omnipotence to the Huttonian view of nature as a system of self-regulating active powers whose self-sufficiency is not to be abrogated by divine action. For Newton, laws of nature were regarded as being imposed on nature by God, whereas for Hutton laws were immanent in the fabric of nature. The *way* in which this transformation in world-view was manifested in natural philosophy attests to the importance of the view eighteenth-century natural philosophers held as to Newton's concepts of the aether and active principles. A full understanding of this shift in sensibility demands an analysis of wider intellectual currents than those discussed here. Fundamental to this is the analysis of changing philosophical and theological views in relation to changing conceptions of law and nature in the period; and assessment of the importance of traditions other than those deriving from the Newtonian corpus is a crucial problem which awaits analysis. Here I have suggested that eighteenth-century natural philosophers associated Newton's

[118] *Collected Works of Sir Humphry Davy*, ed. J. Davy, London, 1839, II, 311.
[119] *Ibid.*, 320.
[120] *Ibid.*, 28.
[121] Michael Faraday, *Experimental Researches in Electricity*, London, 1839–55, III, par. 2146.
[122] Michael Faraday, "On the Conservation of Force", *Experimental Researches in Chemistry and Physics*, London, 1857, 455. For a discussion of the influence of the eighteenth-century conception of matter as powers on Faraday's theory of the physical field, see P. M. Heimann, "Faraday's Theories of Matter and Electricity", *Brit. J. Hist. Sci.*, **5** 235–57, 1971.

concepts of the aether and active principles with Boerhaave's theory of the activating power of fire. However, it is likely that earlier theories of light and fire as active principles distinct from ordinary matter[123] continued to have influence in the post-Newtonian period, and the influence of chemical traditions on natural philosophy in this period clearly warrants further analysis. Nevertheless, given Newton's importance and the richness and complexity of the Newtonian tradition, the analysis of that tradition serves to illuminate many features of eighteenth-century science.

Acknowledgements

I wish to express my thanks to J. E. McGuire for comments and for many helpful discussions on problems relating to the theme of this paper, to A. W. Thackray for helpful discussions and comments, and to G. Buchdahl, P. M. Rattansi, and P. Strømholm for useful comments.

[123] See note 58 above, and R. Love, "Some sources of Herman Boerhaave's concept of Fire", *Ambix*, **19**, 157–74, 1972.

III

Ether and imponderables

The physics of active, ethereal imponderable fluids represented the main current of speculation among British natural philosophers in the second half of the eighteenth century. These 'fluids' were envisaged as being composed of particles that mutually repelled each other, this property being referred to as 'elasticity'. The 'elastic fluids' were conceived as being 'subtle' (being able to penetrate the empty spaces between the particles of ordinary matter in bodies), as being weightless (or at least with no measurable weight), and as being attracted by the particles of ordinary matter. Frequently postulated to explain the phenomena of electricity, magnetism, optics, heat, and chemistry, the operations of the repellent particles of the imponderable fluids were thus traced to interparticulate forces of attraction and repulsion. These characteristic features of the imponderable fluids suggest that their articulation was influenced by Newton's concept of ether, postulated as a 'subtle', 'elastic', particulate substance in the queries appended to the second English edition of the *Opticks* (1717), and by Newton's theory of interparticulate forces of attraction and repulsion, especially as explicated in query 31 of the 1717 *Opticks* (Cohen, 1956; Schofield, 1970; Heimann and McGuire, 1971; Heimann, 1973).

The extent to which the theory of ethereal substances proposed by eighteenth-century British natural philosophers can be analysed in relation to Newtonian categories has, however, been questioned (Home, 1977*a*). The theory of imponderable fluids may seem to echo the Cartesian doctrine of the all-pervading subtle ether that, though in decline in cosmology (Aiton, 1972:244–56), provided the model for the fluid theories of fire and magnetism advanced by Daniel Bernoulli and Euler in the 1740s. Nevertheless, there are important differences between the Cartesian and Newtonian ethers. The Cartesian ether was a plenum; its operations arose from the contact action of

III

its component particles. By contrast, the Newtonian ether was composed of particles that were separated by void space and that acted on gross bodies by means of their repulsive forces. The 'Newtonian' character of the elastic fluids postulated by British natural philosophers was explicit, and cannot be regarded as a Newtonian veneer disguising an essentially Cartesian vortex model. Nevertheless, the development of the imponderable fluid theories cannot be ascribed solely to the influence of the ether concept, though in attempting to clarify the diverse conceptual origins of the imponderable fluid theories this chapter emphasises the primary importance of the Newtonian concept of ether. An analysis of the development of Continental imponderable fluid theories would show different patterns of thought, with 'Newtonian' concepts exercising a less dominant influence; and although understanding imponderable fluid theories in eighteenth-century British natural philosophy in relation to Newton's theory of ether does not completely characterise their intellectual provenance, that theory does provide an illuminating context for historical analysis.

Newton's ether theory aroused little interest until the 1740s, and a central aim of this chapter is to analyse the reasons for its adoption at that time and to clarify the manner in which the concept of ether provided the paradigm for the imponderable fluid theories. Further, the incorporation of Boerhaave's 'fire' in theories of an ethereal 'electrical fire' and of Stahl's 'phlogiston' (the chemical principle of inflammability) as a modification of ether led to a broadening and transformation of the theory of ether. By the end of the century attempts were made to formulate a unified theory of ether, reducing the diversity of phenomena to the modifications of a single ethereal active substance. This chapter attempts, then, to clarify how Newton's theory of ether was transformed into the concept of an inherently active substance, a theory of nature that contradicted Newton's own doctrine of the intrinsic passivity of material entities, all activity being for him ultimately grounded in divine agency. For these later theorists, active powers were held to be intrinsic to some or even all material substances, and ether functioned as the source of the activity of nature. The transformation of Newton's theory of ether was associated with a blurring of the distinction between the categories of activity and passivity in Newton's natural philosophy, and a rejection of its theological implications.[1]

However, despite the dominance of the theory of ethereal fluids in late eighteenth-century British natural philosophy, alternative conceptual schemes continued to be canvassed. The speculative and qualitative cast of the theory of imponderable fluids was unacceptable to those natural philosophers interested in a mathematical theory of nature, to whom Newton's *Principia*

Ether and imponderables

(1687), with its stress on the role of the forces quantitatively determining natural phenomena, appeared a more appropriate paradigm for physical theory. The Scottish natural philosophers Robison and Playfair opposed the supposition of interstitial particles of ether to explain gravity and of imponderable 'ethers' to account for the phenomena of electricity and heat (Cantor, 1971; Olson, 1975:157–224). Cavendish attempted to develop Newton's theory of the unity of matter and the Newtonian programme of the quantification of the interparticulate forces; for Cavendish, the fluids of light, electricity, and phlogiston were ponderable, and heat was regarded as the motion of the particles of ordinary matter. Ether played no role in his theory of nature, and he rejected the supposition of imponderable fluids and anomalous forms of matter.[2]

The disjunction between the theory of imponderable fluids and the quantitative theory of interparticulate forces as alternative programmes for physical explanation does illuminate the aims of some eighteenth-century British natural philosophers. However, it has been argued by Schofield that there was a fundamental opposition in eighteenth-century British natural philosophy between (1) any theory of atoms and interparticulate forces and (2) any theory of an ether or of imponderable fluids. On Schofield's account, although these two lines of theorising both derived from Newton's natural philosophy, they employed quite distinct principles of physical explanation.[3] This interpretation imposes a distorting analytic framework, simplifying Newton's natural philosophy and the complexities of eighteenth-century interpretations of Newton's theory of nature. In Newton's natural philosophy the mode of action of ether was grounded on the agency of repulsive forces; and eighteenth-century ether theorists stressed the role of the repulsive forces associated with the ethereal imponderable fluids, arguing that there was a balance in nature between the attractive force associated with ordinary matter and the repulsive force of the ethereal fluids. To make a contrast between force and ether concepts the analytic framework for the interpretation of eighteenth-century British natural philosophy is to ignore the relation between Newton's ether and his concept of 'active principles', natural agents that he held to be distinct from the 'passive' principles that characterised the properties of matter. In this chapter it is argued that the status of ether as an active principle was fundamental to the development of theories of active, ethereal imponderable fluids. In place of a disjunction between 'force' and 'ether' concepts, it is suggested that a more appropriate analytic framework for characterising the 'Newtonian' origins of British imponderable fluid theories is to be found in the relations among the Newtonian concepts of forces, active principles, and ether. For Newton's speculations were ambiguous, and these categorial complexities were reflected in the conceptual structures of eighteenth-century ether theories, in which 'Newtonian' concepts of force, active principles, and ether were conflated in the theory of inherently active ethereal imponderables endowed with repulsive forces (Heimann and McGuire, 1971).

Newton's ether theory: the published sources

Newton provided several sources from which eighteenth-century natural philosophers could learn of his ether theory. His first published discussion of ether was his introduction of a subtle and elastic ether in the queries to the 1717 *Opticks* to explain optical reflection and refraction and to provide a causal explanation for gravity.[4] But his earliest speculations on ether, introduced in his 'Hypothesis explaining the properties of light' written in 1675 (though not published until 1757)[5] and in a letter to Oldenburg of 1676 correcting this paper (published in 1744),[6] placed these optical speculations in the context of a cosmology based on the circulation and transformation of ethereal spirits. Newton qualified this ethereal cosmology in a letter to Boyle written in 1679 (though not published until 1744),[7] where he expressed the possibility of an explanation of gravity in terms of the differential densities and sizes of ether particles. The problems of interpreting Newton's theory of ether derive both from the different emphases of these discussions and from the ambiguity of Newton's arguments.

Newton's ether was thus most familiar to the eighteenth-century natural philosophers in the account given in the 1717 *Opticks,* which introduced the physical model of ether as composed of mutually repelling particles. The most extended account of the mode of action of ether was given in query 21, where Newton argued that

> the exceeding smallness of its Particles may contribute to the greatness of the force by which those Particles may recede from one another, and thereby make that Medium exceedingly more rare and elastick than Air, and by consequence exceedingly less able to resist the motions of Projectiles, and exceedingly more able to press upon gross Bodies, by endeavouring to expand it self.[8]

In suggesting this model to explain the agency of gravity, Newton was not invoking the Cartesian concept of pressing or impact of contiguous particles constituting a plenum. In the *General scholium* to the second edition of *Principia* (1713) he had argued that gravity 'must proceed from a cause that penetrates to the very centres of the sun and planets' and that 'operates not according to the quantity of the surfaces of the particles upon which it acts (as mechanical causes are accustomed)'.[9] In referring to the 'pressing' of the ether, Newton was not suggesting the Cartesian impact model; nor was he

Ether and imponderables

envisaging a fluid medium acting by hydrostatic pressure. As he pointed out in query 28, at any point in a fluid the pressure acts equally in all directions, whereas 'Gravity tends downwards';[10] hence fluid pressure is irreconcilable with the directionality of gravity. Though Newton's ether has sometimes been viewed as providing some form of contact-action explanation of gravity, Newton's own statements emphasised the irreducibility of gravity to 'mechanical' or contact-action theories.[11]

Newton apparently envisaged ether acting by a differential density arising from the repulsive forces exerted by the minute particles of ether, while the great 'elastick force' of the ether, its tendency to 'expand it self', enabled it to 'press upon gross Bodies' and to cause planets to approach or recede. Arguing analogically, in query 21, Newton claimed that just as the small size of light corpuscles implied forces of great intensity in relation to size, the particles of ether, which were 'exceedingly smaller than those of Air, or even than those of Light', were endowed with the strongest forces with respect to their sizes. Ether was composed of 'Particles which endeavour to recede from one another', its agency manifested through the differential density of the ethereal 'medium'.[12] So Newton's gravitational ether did not act by contact action; its particles were separated by void space and acted on one another by their repulsive forces. It has been argued that in attempting to reduce the force of gravity to the repulsive forces of the ether particles, Newton's ether embodied the problem of action at a distance that it purported to explain (McGuire, 1968:187; Westfall, 1971:395). In questioning the intelligibility of ether as an explanation of gravity this interpretation ignores an important characteristic of the ether, its status as a Newtonian active principle.

Newton distinguished between gravity and those physical properties – hardness, extension, inertia – that he held to be intrinsic to the nature of matter. As he emphasised in a famous statement to Bentley (published in 1756), gravity was not to be considered as 'innate, inherent and essential to Matter'.[13] In query 31 of the 1717 *Opticks,* Newton contrasted passive principles such as *vis inertiae* (force of inertia) and the 'passive Laws of Motion as naturally result from that Force' with 'active Principles, such as that of Gravity'.[14] In Newton's natural philosophy active principles were agents that were not reducible to the passive principles of matter. As a putative explanation of gravity the ether of the 1717 *Opticks* was, by implication, an active principle establishing the intelligibility of the phenomenon of gravity (Heimann and McGuire, 1971:240–5). This interpretation is in consonance with the theological function of ether. One likely motive for Newton's inclusion of ether in the 1717 *Opticks* was to refute Leibniz's criticism of Newton's concept of gravity as a 'miracle', an 'occult quality' and a 'fiction'.[15] Arguing for a contact-action or 'mechanical' explanation of gravity, Leibniz expounded his views at length in his correspondence with Clarke in 1715–16. Newton conceived active principles as manifest in certain 'general Laws of Nature'. Regarded as the manifestation of God's lawful, causal agency in nature, they functioned as the cause of motion and gravity.[16] Rejecting the reducibility of gravity to a contact-action model, Newton conceived the ether of the 1717 *Opticks* as an active principle communicating God's causal agency and as a physical model (though not a contact-action model) establishing the intelligibility of the distance force of gravity.

This interpretation of ether as an active principle implies that ether had an ambiguous conceptual status in Newton's natural philosophy. Composed of particles of matter, ether would ostensibly appear to fall under the category of passive principles. However, Newton's manuscript references to ether between 1706 and 1717 show that he sought to distinguish between the passivity and inertia of *ordinary* matter and the active properties of ether.[17] Despite these reflections on the anomalous nature of ether particles, Newton did not characterise their properties in a systematic way, and his only published hints about these issues were in his discussion of the 'greatness' of the 'elastick force' of ether, and its implied status as an active principle. Nevertheless the conceptual status of ether as an active principle was to exercise considerable influence on the development of the imponderable fluid theories. In Newton's natural philosophy active principles were distinct from the passive properties of matter, and their activity was dependent on God's causal agency; but the ambiguous conceptual status of Newton's ether as both an active and a material principle led many eighteenth-century theorists to interpret ether as a substance endowed with inherent activity, conflating the active – passive dualism of Newton's natural philosophy.

In query 31 of the 1717 *Opticks,* Newton linked active principles with the 'great and violent' processes of chemistry, questioning the reducibility of chemistry to the 'passive Laws of Motion'.[18] Taking ether as an active principle, some eighteenth-century chemists assimilated 'fire' and 'phlogiston' to ether and emphasised the irreducibly chemical properties of ether. The association between ether and chemical active principles was heightened by the publication of Newton's 'Hypothesis on light' and his letter to Oldenburg, where the operations of ether were linked to chemical processes, and where ether served the same function as active principles in maintaining the activity of nature. Newton suggested that 'the whole frame of nature may be nothing but aether condensed by a fermental principle'. He supposed that nature

> may be nothing but various Contextures of some certaine aethereall Spirits or vapours condens'd as it were by precipitation, much after

Ether and imponderables 67

> the manner that vapours are condensed into water or exhalations into grosser Substances and after condensation wrought into various formes, at first by the immediate hand of the Creator, and ever since by the power of Nature . . . Thus perhaps may all things be originated from aether.

Newton added that 'nature is a perpetuall circulatory [the word *circulatory* was omitted from the published version] worker'; by the chemical transformation of ethereal spirits and by 'nature making a circulation', the activity of the cosmos was conserved.[19] In stressing that ether was an underlying first principle from which all things originated, in supposing that the activity of the cosmos was conserved by the circulation of ethereal spirits, in arguing for the generation of all things from ether; and in relating the operations of ether to chemical processes, Newton echoed seventeenth-century alchemical and neo-Platonist writers.[20] In a manner analogous to his disjunction between active principles and the passive principles of matter, this chemical, active ethereal cosmology lay outside the framework of the 'passive Laws of Motion'.[21]

The emergence of imponderable fluid theories

Newton's ether theory aroused little interest among natural philosophers until the 1740s. A contemporary assessment of the ether hypothesis of the 1717 *Opticks* as 'something new in the latest edition of his *Opticks* which has surprised his physical and theological disciples'[22] hinted at the reason for this lack of interest. Newton's discussion of the mode of action of ether in query 21 was far from clear, and Newtonian natural philosophers had been schooled to be wary of contact-action or 'mechanical' explanations of gravity. Natural philosophers such as John Keill and theologians like Clarke had taken up the cudgels in public defence of Newton's theory of the attractive force of gravity and his theological argument in explicating gravity as the effect of the divine will. Ether appeared to have a questionable status in this 'Newtonian' world view. Indeed, the review of the Latin edition of the 1717 *Opticks* in the *Acta eruditorum* regarded Newton's introduction of ether as providing a contact-action explanation of gravity, reflecting Leibnizian criticisms of the 'occult' nature of attractive forces.[23] In England, Robert Greene claimed, in his *Philosophy of the expansive and contractive forces* (1727), that Newton had proposed ether in the 1717 *Opticks* in response to the criticisms of Newton's theories of atoms, the void, and the passivity of material entities in Greene's *Principles of natural philosophy* (1712) (Heimann and McGuire, 1971:255–61). Despite these responses, Henry Pemberton, who had edited the third edition of *Principia* (1726) for Newton, mentioned Newton's 'subtle and elastic substance diffused through the universe' in his *View of Sir Isaac Newton's philosophy* (1728).[24] Nevertheless, until the 1740s, Newtonian popularisers avoided ether in favour of Newton's theory of short-range interparticulate forces as developed in the queries to the *Opticks* (Schofield, 1970:19–62; Thackray, 1970:8–82).

The new interest in Newton's theory of ether among British natural philosophers was related to the burgeoning enthusiasm for electrical studies. As Benjamin Martin noted in his *Philosophia Britannica* (1747), though Newton had discussed ether 'he seem'd not at all delighted with the thought, nor ever laid any stress upon it'; by contrast, contemporary theorists 'are arriv'd at great dexterity since Sir Isaac's time . . . [and] can now almost prove the existence of this aether by the phenomena of electricity'.[25] Four important developments in the period 1717–46 fostered this shift in opinion: an increasing stress on the role of repulsive forces and on the balance in nature between attractive and repulsive forces; the impact of Boerhaave's concept of 'fire'; the publication of Newton's early letters to Boyle and Oldenburg on ether, and of Bryan Robinson's *Dissertation on the aether of Sir Isaac Newton* (1743); and the interest in electrical effluvia (Cohen, 1956:205–362; Heimann, 1973:10–17). These four points will be discussed in turn.

The early Newtonians focused on the description of attractive forces, which was consonant with the gravitational paradigm for the theory of interparticulate forces, but in his *Vegetable staticks* (1727), Stephen Hales developed the implications of Newtonian repulsive forces. Hales was concerned to discuss the production of gases in chemical and biological processes and, following Newton, to explicate the properties of gases in terms of repulsive forces. In the *Opticks,* Newton had associated the 'repelling Power' of particles with the gaseous state: A 'true permanent Air' contained 'particles receding from one another with the greatest Force'. Moreover, Newton had argued that *'Aether* (like our Air) may contain Particles which endeavour to recede from one another', the 'elastick force' of the ether being traced to the 'exceeding smallness of its Particles' and hence the 'greatness of the force by which those particles may recede from one another'.[26] Hales considered that chemical processes were maintained by the production and absorption of gases by chemical substances, which he supposed brought about by attractive and repulsive forces. Associating 'air' with the alkali principle, he interpreted the interaction between acidic and alkaline substances in terms of the interaction of opposing forces. In expounding a theory of 'air' based on the Newtonian concept of repulsive forces, Hales developed the implications of Newton's theory of ether, postulating that the order of nature was dependent on a balance between attractive and repulsive forces. Nature would become 'one in-

Ether and imponderables

active cohering lump' if matter were 'only endued with a strongly attracting power'; so intermingled with 'attracting matter' there was 'a due proportion of strongly repelling elastic particles [air], which might enliven the whole mass, by the incessant action between them and the attracting particles'.[27]

Hales envisaged a fundamental balance of nature, a balance between attractive and repulsive forces. Associating attractive and repulsive forces with different material entities, an attracting matter and an 'elastic', ethereal repelling matter, he considered nature as inherently active, its activity maintained by the 'incessant action' of attractive and repulsive forces. Hales's two-substance theory of attractive ordinary matter and repulsive 'air' was to exercise considerable influence on the development of Benjamin Franklin's theory of electricity in the 1740s, which posited a dualism of ordinary matter and a repulsive, ethereal electric 'fluid'; the concept of a balance of powers between attractive matter and ethereal repelling 'fluids' was to be a characteristic feature of the theory of unified ethereal substances developed by James Hutton in the 1790s; and Hales's arguments were to have a significant influence on the development of the imponderable fluid theories.

Boerhaave's concept of 'fire', the theoretical kernel of his *Elementa chemiae* (1732; translated into English by Dallowe in 1735 and Peter Shaw in 1741), was a major influence on the development of Franklin's theory of electricity. For Boerhaave, fire was a physical instrument, the cause of chemical change and 'the instrumental cause of all motion', being 'the great changer of all things in the universe, while itself remaining unchanged'.[28] Boerhaave's 'active element' of fire was not an elastic fluid, and there is no evidence that Boerhaave's formulation of the concept owed anything to Newton's ether. Nevertheless, ether and fire did have some properties in common. Boerhaave stressed the 'excessive minuteness' of the particles of fire, and emphasised that fire was a space-pervading substance that was immutable and not subject to the laws of gravity. Fire had the 'property of penetrating all solid and fluid bodies'; it 'exists always and everywhere'. Fire maintained the activity of the universe, for through the agency of the 'active element' of fire the 'whole universe might continue in perpetual motion'.[29] These outward similarities between Boerhaave's space-pervading substance of fire and Newton's ether led natural philosophers to conflate the two concepts.

This affinity to Newton's speculations was emphasised in Shaw's footnote commentary to his translation. Shaw implied a relation between Boerhaave's quasi-material fire and Newton's active principles; as a substance possessing inherent activity, the source of the activity of nature, fire was interpreted as being analogous to Newton's ether, itself an active principle maintaining the activity of nature. The conflation of ether–fire as an inherently active substance was fostered by the ambiguous conceptual status of Newton's ether as both an active principle and a material substance. The dualism between ether–fire and ordinary matter posited by British natural philosophers in the 1740s can be traced to Boerhaave's view that fire 'has a power of expanding everything else', counteracting the contractive power of 'the remaining bodies which have a virtue implanted in them, whereby they constantly resist this separation of their elements'. Thus there were 'two principles' in nature, 'one of expansion, the other of attraction',[30] a dualism analogous to Hales's theory of attractive and repelling substances, which was explicitly linked to the Newtonian dualism between ordinary matter and ether. By the 1740s natural philosophers had developed dualistic theories in which *'elementary fire'* was considered to be an ethereal substance 'endowed with active Powers distinct from those of other Matter'.[31]

The publication of a systematic treatise on Newton's ether, Bryan Robinson's *Dissertation on the aether of Sir Isaac Newton* (1743), and the publication of Newton's letters to Oldenburg and Boyle in 1744 and of Robinson's pamphlet *Sir Isaac Newton's account of the ether* (1745), which included a reprint of the letter to Boyle and of extracts from the ether queries of the 1717 *Opticks,* brought Newton's theory of ether to the attention of natural philosophers. In his *Dissertation on the aether,* Robinson emphasised that Newton had considered ether to be composed of particles acting on each other at a distance by their repulsive forces. Although his quantitative treatment of optics, gravitation, and capillarity in terms of the sizes and forces of ether particles was not echoed in the writings of the imponderable fluid theorists, his espousal of the Newtonian ether had a considerable impact on the work of the electrical theorists of the 1740s. Benjamin Wilson's identification of ether with an electrical substance in his *Essay towards an explication of the phenomena of electricity deduced from the aether of Sir Isaac Newton* (1746) was made with an explicit acknowledgment to Robinson.

The interest in electrical studies in the late 1740s can be linked to the new concern with Newton's ether; it was supposed that investigations in electricity would enable natural philosophers to 'discover the nature of that subtile elastic and etherial medium, which Sir Isaac Newton queries on, at the end of his *Opticks*'.[32] Boerhaave's ethereal fire, Hales's dualism of ordinary matter surrounded by repelling ethereal air, and Newton's theory of the ethereal elastic fluid were to help shape the hypotheses of the electrical theorists, notably the work of Benjamin Franklin. Franklin had read the work of Hales, Boerhaave, and Wilson, as well as Newton's *Opticks,* and his theory of the electrical fluid brought the concept of material electrical 'effluvia', which electrical theorists had employed as an explanation of electrical phenomena, within the frame-

Ether and imponderables

work of the Newtonian concept of ether. The focus of Franklin's theory of electricity was to seek an explanation for the charging and discharging of bodies, especially the Leyden jar, a device capable of delivering electric shocks, which had been discovered shortly before he began his researches in 1747 (Cohen, 1956:285–478; Home, 1972). In Franklin's influential theory electrification was represented by the permeation of the electrical fluid through the interstitial pores of the electrified body. Franklin considered this 'electrical matter' to consist of 'particles [which were] extremely subtile', differing from 'common matter in this, that the parts of the latter mutually attract, those of the former mutually repel each other'. In Franklin's theory, 'though the particles of electrical matter do repel each other, they are strongly attracted by all other matter', by ordinary matter, that is; and he argued that surplus 'electrical matter' was held in place around electrified bodies as an 'electrical atmosphere' by an attraction between the particles of these bodies and those of the electric fluid.[33] In explicating a theory of electrification, Franklin posited a dualism of ordinary matter and the electric fluid, developing Hales's dualistic theory for the explanation of electrical phenomena. Boerhaave's influence can be seen in his reference to the electrical fluid as an 'electrical fire'. The electrical fluid was conceived as analogous to Newton's ether, being composed of mutually repelling particles. The electrical matter was envisaged as an electrical ether, and Franklin suggested that fire, ether, and electricity were 'different modifications of the same thing',[34] though he ultimately distinguished between the properties of fire and those of the electric fluid (Schofield, 1970:172).

Franklin was concerned to explain electrification rather than to formulate a systematic theory of nature, but his ideas illustrate the impact of the Newtonian ether, and the associated theories of Hales and Boerhaave, on the electrical imponderable fluid theories of the 1740s. A systematic treatment of the identification of Newton's ether with a repelling, active, material substance that was applied to explain a diversity of phenomena can be seen in Gowin Knight's *Attempt to demonstrate, that all the phaenomena in nature may be explained by two simple active principles, attraction and repulsion* (1748). Knight claimed that the activity of nature required the supposition of 'some Active Principle or Principles capable of producing and continuing Motion in the Universe', these active principles being the forces of attraction and repulsion.[35] Knight associated the forces or active principles with two different material entities, and he argued that 'attraction and repulsion cannot both, at the same time, belong to the same individual substance, being contraries', concluding that 'there are in Nature two kinds of Matter, one attracting the other repelling'. Echoing Hales's dualistic theory, Knight held that the repel-

III

lent ethereal matter clustered around the particles of attracting matter, and argued that the phenomena of light and magnetism could be reduced to the motions of the repellent matter. Light was explained as the propagation of a vibrational tremor along a chain of mutually repellent particles, and magnetism (Knight's major interest) was explained as a 'circulation of the repellent fluid' between magnetic poles.[36]

Although Knight's treatise illustrates the transformation of the Newtonian concepts of force, active principles, ether, and matter in the 1740s, he was careful to emphasise that the active principles of attraction and repulsion were not inherent in material substances but were themselves the manifestation of divine activity in nature. However, the further development of the imponderable fluid theories led some natural philosophers to the enunciation of a theory of nature in which matter was endowed with inherent activity. The transformation of the Newtonian dualism between active and passive principles into a dualism of ordinary attracting matter and an active, ethereal repelling substance, and the conflation of ether–fire as an inherently active substance, led to the conflation of the dualism between active and material or passive principles that was a seminal feature of Newton's natural philosophy. Ether functioned as an inherently active substance endowed with repulsive force, and ordinary matter was considered as possessing an inherent attractive force. This theory contradicted Newton's concept of the intrinsic passivity of material entities; activity was subsumed in the inherent powers of material substances. These arguments were fully articulated in James Hutton's theory of nature in the 1790s, but although many natural philosophers did not explicitly formulate the philosophical and theological implications of this position, an early statement of this argument in Cadwallader Colden's *Principles of action in matter* (1751) illustrates the conceptual transformation associated with the interpretation of ether as an inherently active substance. Asserting that it was 'unphilosophical' to ascribe activity to divine agency, Colden claimed that motion was inherent in matter: Motion 'exists in something, which has in itself the power of moving'. All material substances, including ordinary matter, were regarded as 'acting principles', as being endowed with inherent activity. Ether was a 'species of matter', an acting principle maintaining the activity of nature.[37]

The interpretation of ether as an inherently active substance threatened the theological foundations of Newton's philosophy of nature. For Newton ether was an active principle, a manifestation of God's causal agency in nature. Newton's view of ether was maintained by Colin Maclaurin in his *Account of Sir Isaac Newton's philosophical discoveries* (1748), which echoed Newton's voluntarist theology in pointing out that if gravity were 'produced by a

Ether and imponderables

rare and elastic *aethereal medium'*, then 'the whole efficacy of this medium must be resolved into his power and will, who is the supreme cause', for God is 'the source of all efficacy'. Maclaurin's interpretation of the theological status of ether was being called into question by the emergent view of ether as an inherently active substance endowed with repulsive force. This theory of nature was sustained by the view that the phenomena of nature could be reduced to the interaction of two material principles, attractive and repulsive, and that the diversity of phenomena could be explained in terms of a single ethereal substance: The 'terms *Fire, Electricity, electrical Aether, aetherial Spirit*' were 'synonymous'.[38] This interpretation of ether was to be fundamental to the development of the unified theory of ether in the second half of the eighteenth century.

Chemistry and the development of unified ether theories

In query 31 of the 1717 *Opticks*, Newton provided hints about his theory of chemistry. Despite his appeal to a programme of chemical explanation in terms of a quantified science of interparticulate forces (Thackray, 1970:18–42), he associated chemical phenomena with the operation of active principles, questioning the reducibility of chemistry to 'passive Laws of Motion'. The chemical connotations of ether and active principles were heightened by the strongly chemical ethereal speculations in Newton's 'Hypothesis explaining the properties of light' and his letter to Oldenburg. The revival of ether in the 1740s and the development of a dualistic natural philosophy of ordinary matter and ethereal fluids led some British chemists to invoke ether for the explanation of chemical processes, the chemical resonances of ether being strengthened by the assimilation of Boerhaave's concept of fire to the ether concept. The chemical theories that employed ether, and that were enunciated from the late 1740s on, proposed a dualism between ordinary matter and the irreducibly chemical properties of ether, with fire and phlogiston being assimilated to ether.[39] This expansion of the ether concept led to the emergence of unified ether theories in which the diversity of phenomena were reduced to the operations of an ethereal substance.

Peter Shaw's translations of Stahl's *Philosophical principles of universal chemistry* (1730) and of Boerhaave's *New method of chemistry* (1741) made an important contribution to these developments. Shaw followed Stahl in questioning the reducibility of chemistry to the mechanical philosophy, claiming, in his *Chemical lectures* (1734), that 'genuine chemistry' preferred to leave to 'other philosophers the sublimer disquisitions of primary corpuscles or atoms' and urging that chemistry should avoid such 'metaphysical specu-

III

lations'.[40] In commenting in his edition of Boerhaave's treatise on Boerhaave's assertion that chemical change 'is effected by means of motion alone', Shaw questioned the reducibility of chemical phenomena to the motion of corpuscles, pointing out that the 'common laws of sensible masses . . . will not reach to those more remote, intestine motions of the component particles'. Shaw claimed that 'besides the common laws of sensible masses, the minute parts they are composed of seem subject to some others, which have as yet been but lately taken notice of, and are yet more than guessed at'. He was here referring to the 'new mechanics' that Newton had based on the power of 'attraction', a quantified science of interparticulate forces 'not reducible to any of those in the great world'. Nevertheless, Shaw questioned the applicability even of this 'sublimer mechanics' to chemistry, going on to quote almost verbatim from Newton's remarks on active principles in query 31, and arguing that active principles were the fundamental agents in nature: 'The author of nature has added to bodies certain active principles to be the sources of motion'. For Shaw the ultimate principles in nature were irreducibly chemical, to be found in the study of the chemical role of active principles rather than in the motion of corpuscles:

> [It is] by means of chemistry that Sir *Isaac Newton* has made a great part of his surprising discoveries in natural philosophy; and that curious set of queries, which we find at the end of his optics, are almost wholly chemical. Indeed chemistry, in its extent, is scarce less than the whole of natural philosophy.[41]

These arguments helped to shape the chemical doctrines advanced by William Cullen in his chemical lectures at Glasgow in the late 1740s. Cullen was concerned to pinpoint the sources of chemical change, and he followed Newton and Hales in arguing that there were 'two great principles, the attractive & repulsive,' which were 'the source of motion and change'. In emphasising the importance of the theory of elective attractions, Cullen followed Newton's own stress on the quantification of interparticulate forces, but the influence of Hales, Boerhaave, and Shaw is apparent in Cullen's stress on repulsion, on the expansive force of fire as the source of repulsion, and hence on the irreducibility of chemistry to universal forces of attraction and repulsion. In Cullen's view 'fire pervades all bodies and keeps their parts asunder', and hence 'attraction & fire were to be considered as the primary causes of motion'. He associated fire with electricity and ether, reflecting contemporary work in natural philosophy: 'Fire [is] an elastic fluid . . . [we know there is] an aether in bodies from the reflexion &c of light, from electricity. The same with fire & present everywhere'. Cullen developed the dualistic theory of ordinary matter and ether to incorporate the chemical role of ether. Lecturing in 1757–8, he argued that 'there are only two elements, one of them gravitating matter, the

Ether and imponderables

other a subtile aether', going on to note that according to this hypothesis, 'its [*sic*] probable that light and all other phaenomena of Fire depend upon this Subtile Aether in all Bodies'. Cullen explained the crucial chemical phenomenon of combustion by supposing 'that inflammable bodies are of such a particular texture as to recover these particles of Aether' as 'phlogiston'.[42] Cullen's introduction of Stahl's principle of inflammability, phlogiston, to denote the chemical manifestation of ether broadened the conceptual framework of the theory of ethereal substances.

These ideas were further developed in the Edinburgh lectures of Cullen's student Joseph Black. In appealing to the theory of ether, Black was concerned to explain the combustion of chemical substances, ether serving to justify the intelligibility of the phlogiston concept. In a lecture in 1768, Black declared:

> Sir Isaac Newton is of the opinion that there is in nature a certain fluid of exceeding elasticity subtility and density, that pervades all nature, the different modifications of which produce the phenomena of Electricity, magnetism and Gravity and the cohesion of the smaller parts of bodies to each other . . . I am therefore of the opinion that this is the inflammable principle. [Talbot, 1967: ch. 13, 42]

Phlogiston was thus a 'modification' of ether, its supposition justified by appeal to the Newtonian pedigree. In a lecture delivered in the 1780s, Black argued that the principle of inflammability, 'phlogiston' or 'subtle aether', was a 'subtile & active fluid', and he affirmed the dualistic theory of nature in denying that this ether or phlogiston was a 'gravitating substance'; rather, 'this matter is exempted from the laws of gravitation'.[43] Questioning the unity of matter, Black stressed the chemical connotations of ether and the disjunction between chemical principles and the laws of ordinary matter. In Black's view, 'heat may be considered in nature as the great principle of chemical movement and life', and he supposed that phlogiston was a manifestation of heat: 'Heat or light are the principles of inflammability'.[44] In Black's theory of nature chemical and thermal phenomena were closely associated, and heat, light, and phlogiston were imponderable substances, modifications of ether and distinct from ordinary matter; chemical and ethereal principles were not reducible to the passive laws of ordinary matter.

Black's lectures expanded the theory of ether to include chemical, optical, and thermal phenomena, providing hints towards the formulation of a unified ether theory. The chemical role of ether, in its 'modifications' as heat, light, and phlogiston, was emphasised in several works published in the 1770s, often reflecting Black's influence.[45] In his *Philosophical inquiry into the causes of animal heat* (1778) the Edinburgh-educated physician P. D. Leslie

III

followed Black in arguing that 'phlogiston is fire and light, or a certain subtle elastic fluid, upon the modifications of which the phenomena of heat and light depend'. This ethereal substance 'is the chief cause and principle of activity in the universe' and is 'exempted from the common laws of gravitation'. Leslie explicitly identified phlogiston with the *'Newtonian* ether, the electrical *aura, materia subtilis,* fire and light'.[46] Similar ideas were proposed by Bryan Higgins in his *Philosophical essay concerning light* (1776). Higgins supposed that light, phlogiston, fire, and electricity were different modifications of ether: 'Fire is not considered as a homogeneal body different from light and phlogiston; and I am unwilling to admit the Electric Fluid as an element different from these'.[47]

The phlogiston concept thus played a central role in eighteenth-century British natural philosophy. However, many chemists considered phlogiston an ordinary chemical substance rather than an ethereal imponderable. British chemists who adopted this interpretation included Kirwan, Cavendish, and – for a time – Priestley, all of whom equated phlogiston with some form of 'inflammable air [hydrogen]'. Nevertheless the view of phlogiston as an ethereal active substance represents an important British chemical tradition: Phlogiston was identified with or viewed as a 'modification' of fire, light, electricity, and ether.[48] This unified ether theory stressed the unity and activity of nature; avoiding a superfluity of diverse imponderable fluids, these theorists reduced the operations of nature to a dualism of gravitative matter and ether.

The systematic *Dissertations on different subjects in natural philosophy* (1792) by Black's associate James Hutton provided a full statement of this unified ether theory, with an emphasis on its philosophical and theological implications. Hutton supposed a dualism of gravitational (attractive) matter and the 'emanation of [repelling] matter from the sun';[49] these two kinds of matter maintained the operations of nature, 'the opposite powers . . . continually balancing one another, or alternately prevailing'. If the gravitational matter were to prevail then 'gravitation would soon bring all the matter of this machine [the universe] to rest, and would lock up every body in a state of the most absolute inactivity'. The emanation of matter from the sun was thus a 'necessary cause of vital motion', for 'without the influence of the sun this world would remain an useless mass of inert matter'. This solar substance was envisaged as an active principle embracing all the imponderable fluids: 'Light, heat and electricity appear to be three different modifications of the same matter'.[50] In explicating this theory of the unified ether or solar substance, Hutton appealed to a wide variety of phenomena. He was especially concerned to explain the interrelationships among heat, light, electricity, and chemistry. The relationship between light and heat, the association of a loss of heat with the emission of light, was explained by arguing that light and heat were different 'modifications' of the repulsive solar substance. Phosphorescence was explained by the claim that light is 'arrested and detained in a certain modification' within bodies forming a 'phlogistic substance'; this matter may be emitted from its connection with a body and 'resume its former character of light'. The phlogiston theory thus implied 'the union of the matter of light and heat with some of the chemical substances of bodies' to form a 'phlogistic substance'. Combustion involved the loss of light and heat and the decomposition of phlogistic substances.[51] Hutton regarded electricity as related to light and thought heat a modification of the solar substance, and he claimed that heat and light would affect the conduction of electricity by bodies. Biological and chemical processes were also connected in Hutton's scheme, and he contended that 'plants compose phlogistic matter in growing', for there was no evidence for decay without renewal: 'There would also appear to be in the system of this globe, a reproductive power, by which the constitution of this world, necessarily decaying, is renewed'.[52] Nature was thus conceived as a system of processes and transformations, different modifications of the ethereal solar substance serving as sources for the regeneration of nature.

In Hutton's system light emanated from the sun and was contained in bodies as phlogiston, an idea probably acquired from Black and Macquer;[53] and the operations of nature were maintained by the circulation and conservation of phlogiston. Hutton's conception of nature has analogies with Newton's theory of the 1670s, in which ether was an underlying principle maintaining the activity of nature by its circulation, though Hutton's theory reflected the transformation in the Newtonian concepts of ether and active principles in the eighteenth century. Hutton rejected Newton's dichotomy between active principles and passive matter. Rejecting Newton's atomism and theory of the passivity of material entities, Hutton distinguished between the phenomenal manifestations of substances, which he termed 'body', and the underlying substratum, or 'matter'. This substratum was defined in terms of its intrinsic activity: 'Matter may thus be considered as acting powers'.[54] In Hutton's dualistic theory the ethereal solar substance functioned as an inherently active substance endowed with repulsive force, balancing the inherent attractive force of gravitative matter. On the theological level this conception of nature contrasted with Newton's stress on divine sustenance by means of active principles, for activity was subsumed in the acting powers constituting material substances. Nature was thus a self-regenerating system of active powers, its self-sufficiency maintained by the inherent activity of material substances.

III

Ether functioned as an active substance immanent in the fabric of nature, conserving and recruiting activity by its transformations and circulation: 'Nature is a perpetual circulatory worker'.

Hutton's emphasis on the role of phlogiston suggests that he considered chemical principles applicable to the powers that characterised the invisible realm of matter. Devoid of solidity, extension, and inertia, Huttonian matter could not be characterised by the passive laws of motion.[55] As John Playfair expressed it, in Hutton's system 'the chemist . . . is flattered more than anyone else with the hopes of discovering in what the essence of matter consists; and Nature, while she keeps the astronomer and mechanician at a great distance, seems to admit him to a more familiar converse, and to a more intimate acquaintance with her secrets'.[56] Hutton thus suggested a cosmology determined by irreducibly chemical principles.

Adam Walker's textbook *A system of familiar philosophy* (1799) provided a full exposition of the unified ether theory. Walker asserted the identity of fire, light, electricity, and phlogiston as 'modifications of one and the same principle', the ethereal repelling substance. The operations of nature were determined by a 'balance' of the two 'powers' of attraction and repulsion, which were 'opposing or antagonistic principles . . . in a state of unceasing warfare'. Electricity was the 'genuine principle of light and fire', and the emanation of the 'ethereal matter' of electricity from the sun activated the universe, for electricity was 'the soul of the material world'.[57]

The stress on the unity of natural phenomena thus led to enunciations of a dualistic world view, in which the transformations of an ethereal, active repellent substance balanced the attractive power of gravitating matter, providing a coherent scheme for the systematisation of a diversity of phenomena and the interactions between natural agents. In his *Mathematical and philosophical dictionary* (1795–6), a reliable guide to contemporary attitudes, Charles Hutton reported that 'there was such a strong affinity between the elements of fire, light and electricity, that we may not only assert their identity upon the most probable grounds, but lay it down as a position against which at present no argument of any weight has an existence'.[58]

The influence of unified ether theories

Between 1798 and 1806 there were several new developments in British natural philosophy that initiated the decline of the imponderable fluid theories. In 1798, Rumford rejected the imponderable fluid theory of heat, arguing that the theory could not explain the generation of heat by friction. The invention of the battery and the discovery of electrolysis in 1800 led to Humphry Davy's theory of electrochemistry; in a full statement of his theory in 1806, Davy explained electricity by the forces of chemical affinity, abandoning the theory of the electric fluid. Thomas Young's advocacy of an undulatory theory of light in papers written between 1799 and 1804 led him to reject the concept of light as an ethereal elastic fluid analogous to fire, as well as Newton's 'emission' theory of light as the projection of 'rays' of discrete corpuscles.[59] Although these developments illustrate the decline of imponderable fluid theories in the early nineteenth century, the conceptions of nature explicated by Rumford, Davy, and Young demonstrate the continued influence of the theory of unified ethereal substances on the development of natural philosophy.

The impact of the unified ether on the ideas of Rumford, Young, and Davy can be seen by a brief survey of their theories of nature. Rumford rejected the theory of heat as an imponderable fluid in favour of a theory in which the effects of heat were held to be the result of the interaction between the motion of the particles of ordinary matter and the vibrations of an ambient ethereal medium. Supposing a dualism of ordinary matter and ether, he asserted that the vibrations of the 'atmospheres composed of aether' surrounding the particles of ordinary matter were communicated to the surrounding ether and finally to other particles of ordinary matter.[60] This theory of the transmission of heat was reminiscent of Gowin Knight's account of the propagation of light based on a dualistic theory of matter and ether. Rumford echoed concepts characteristic of eighteenth-century ether theories in maintaining that *'motion is an essential quality of matter'*; matter was inherently active and hence 'rest is nowhere to be found in the universe'.[61]

The theory of ethereal atmospheres was also adopted by Young in his early discussions of the mode of action of ether. He supposed a universal ethereal substance that 'may possibly be the ground work of all the phenomena of nature', speculating that 'light, heat, cohesion and repulsion' may 'depend on some modification of the actions of the medium [the ether]', which was 'connected with the electric fluid'. Although he abandoned this programme of a unified natural philosophy grounded on the concept of ether, probably because he could not satisfactorily explain cohesion and repulsion through the theory of ethereal atmospheres, the theory of the unified ether shaped the development of Young's natural philosophy, and the concept of a luminiferous ether as the vehicle of light and radiant heat became the central feature of his theory of optics (Cantor, 1970).

In an early essay, Davy argued that 'the electric fluid is probably light in a condensed state . . . its chemical activity upon bodies is similar to that of light'; he claimed that 'the different species [of matter] are continually changing into each other'. Davy referred to James Hutton, and this commitment to

III

the unity and interconversion of natural powers was characteristic of Hutton's unified ether theory. This conception of nature was of fundamental importance for Davy's formulation of his electrical theory of chemical affinity. Davy argued that the electrical and chemical powers were so interconnected that it was likely that the electrical and chemical forces were 'identical'. Although he abandoned the theory of the electric fluid, his emphasis on the unity of natural powers echoed the unified ether theory. Davy continued to maintain a dualistic natural philosophy in which an 'etherial matter' endowed with repulsive force was conceived as the *'antagonist* power to the attraction of cohesion',[62] a concept characteristic of the unified ether theory.

Davy's theory of nature exemplifies the manner in which the unified ether theory continued to shape the commitments of natural philosophers, even though the supposition of imponderable fluids – to explain the phenomena of heat, repulsion, and electricity – was increasingly being called into question. The unified ether theory emphasised the balance of forces, the unity and interconversion of natural phenomena, and the self-sufficiency of nature, contending that the activity of nature was maintained by forces of attraction and repulsion. These ideas, ultimately divorced from imponderable fluid theories, had a continued and significant influence on the development of British natural philosophy in the nineteenth century. The concepts of the balance of forces and the self-sufficiency of nature were developed by Faraday and Joule in the 1830s and 1840s into the theory of the convertibility and indestructibility of natural powers, one of the strands that, transformed, became explicated as the 'conservation of energy' by about 1850.[63] The theory of the unified ether thus had an enduring impact on the history of natural philosophy.

Notes

1 Heimann (1973); P. M. Heimann, 'Voluntarism and immanence: conceptions of nature in eighteenth-century thought', *Journal of the History of Ideas 39* (1978), 271–83.
2 R. McCormmach, 'John Michell and Henry Cavendish: weighing the stars', *British Journal for the History of Science 4* (1968), 150; R. McCormmach, 'Henry Cavendish: a study of rational empiricism in eighteenth-century natural philosophy', *Isis 60* (1969), 293–306.
3 Schofield (1970), 15, asserts a rigid dichotomy between 'mechanists' who sought 'the causation for all phenomena of nature . . . [in] the primary particles of an indifferentiable matter . . . and the forces of attraction and repulsion between them', and 'materialists' who believed that 'the causes of phenomena inhere in unique substances'. These categories are derived from a distinction between force and ether theories in Newton's natural philosophy. Cf. P. M. Heimann, 'Newtonian natural philosophy and the scientific revolution', *History of Science 11* (1973), 1–7.
4 I. Newton, *Opticks; or, a treatise on the reflections, refractions, inflections and colours of light,* 4th ed., 1730 (reprinted, London, 1952), 347–70.

Ether and imponderables

5 I. Newton, 'An hypothesis explaining the properties of light', in T. Birch, *The history of the Royal Society at London*, 4 vols. (London, 1756–7), 3:247–305; reprinted in *Isaac Newton's papers and letters on natural philosophy*, ed. I. B. Cohen (Cambridge, 1958), 177–235; text in I. Newton, *The Correspondence of Isaac Newton*, ed. H. W. Turnbull, J. F. Scott, A. R. Hall, and L. Tilling, 7 vols. (Cambridge, 1959–77), 1:362–86.
6 Newton to Oldenburg, 25 Jan. 1675/6, in R. Boyle, *The Works of the Honourable Robert Boyle*, ed. T. Birch, 5 vols. (London, 1744), 1:74; reprinted in Cohen, *Papers and letters*, 254. See Newton, *Correspondence*, 1:413–14.
7 Newton to Boyle, 28 Feb. 1678/9, in Boyle, *Works*, 1:70–3; reprinted in Cohen, *Papers and letters*, 250–3; text in Newton, *Correspondence*, 2:288–95. See also I. Newton, 'De aere et aethere', in *Unpublished scientific papers of Isaac Newton*, eds. A. R. Hall and M. B. Hall (Cambridge, 1962), 214–20. On the date of this manuscript of the 1670s cf. Hall and Hall, *Unpublished papers*, 187; Westfall (1971), 373, 409–10.
8 Newton, *Opticks*, 352.
9 I. Newton, *Mathematical principles of natural philosophy*, trans. A. Motte, rev. F. Cajori (London, 1934), 546. Hereafter *Principia*. On Newton's rejection of Cartesian vortices see Whiteside (1964, 1970).
10 Newton, *Opticks*, 362. On Newton's concept of pressure see A. E. Shapiro, 'Light, pressure and rectilinear propagation: Descartes' celestial optics and Newton's hydrostatics', *Studies in History and Philosophy of Science 5* (1974), 273–6.
11 A classic statement of the interpretation of Newton's ether as a 'mechanical' medium is in Maxwell's 1878 article 'Ether', in J. C. Maxwell, *The Scientific Papers of James Clerk Maxwell*, 2 vols. (Cambridge, 1890), 2:763–75. Commentators who adopt this interpretation take different attitudes to the significance of the ether. Rosenfeld (1965) views Newton's 'mechanical' ether as his preferred position; whereas Hall and Hall (1967) view the 'mechanical' ether as unimportant in Newton's natural philosophy, as it contradicts the methodology of *Principia*. Both these accounts begin from a mistaken premise: that Newton's ether was a quasi-Cartesian 'mechanical' medium.
12 Newton, *Opticks*, 351–2. Cf. Bechler (1974).
13 *Four letters from Sir Isaac Newton to Doctor Bentley containing some arguments in proof of a Deity* (London, 1756), 25; reprinted in Cohen, *Papers and letters*, 302.
14 Newton, *Opticks*, 401.
15 Draft letter from Newton to the editor of *Memoirs of Literature* (written some time after 5 May 1712) in reply to a letter of Leibniz's, in Newton, *Correspondence*, 5:298–300.
16 Newton, *Opticks*, 401. Cf. McGuire (1968), 187–208.
17 In drafts he referred to a 'subtile Aether or Aetherial elastic spirit' (quoted in Guerlac [1967], 48); this was reflected in his allusion to a 'subtle spirit' in the *General Scholium* to the 2nd ed. of *Principia* (1713). This was qualified as an 'electric and elastic' spirit in a marginal note in Newton's own copy of *Principia* and in Motte's 1729 English translation. See Newton, *Principia*, 547. On Newton's use of the phrase 'electric and elastic' see A. R. Hall and M. B. Hall, 'Newton's electric spirit: four oddities', *Isis 50* (1959), 473–6; A. Koyré and I. B. Cohen, 'Newton's "electric and elastic spirit" ', *Isis 51* (1960), 337. In a draft reply to Leibniz (see n. 15), Newton argued that gravity could be explained 'by a power seated in a substance in wch bodies move & flote without resistance & wch has therefore no *vis inertiae* but acts by other laws than those that are mechanical'. Newton, *Correspondence*, 5:300.
18 Newton, *Opticks*, 380, 401. Cf. McGuire (1968), 164–74.
19 Newton, *Correspondence*, 1:364–6.

20 B. J. T. Dobbs, *The foundations of Newton's alchemy or 'the hunting of the Greene Lyon'* (Cambridge, 1975), 204–6. The tentative suggestion by Walker (1972) that Newton's ether is to be identified with the neo-Platonic *spiritus mundi* is mistaken. Cf. McGuire (1977), 107–9.
21 Newton, *Opticks*, 401. Cf. McGuire (1967), 85; Heimann (1973), 8–10.
22 Quoted in R. Kargon, *Atomism in England from Hariot to Newton* (Oxford, 1966), 138.
23 *Acta eruditorum* (1720), 185–8.
24 R. Greene, *The principles of the philosophy of the expansive and contractive forces; or, an inquiry into the principles of the modern philosophy: that is, into the several chief rational sciences, which are extant* (Cambridge, 1727), 1–2; H. Pemberton, *A view of Sir Isaac Newton's philosophy* (London, 1728), 377. See also B. Worster, *A compendious and methodical account of the principles of natural philosophy*, 2nd ed. (London, 1730), 28.
25 B. Martin, *Philosophia Britannica; or, a new and comprehensive system of the Newtonian philosophy*, 2 vols. (Reading, 1747), quoted in Thackray (1970), 135.
26 Newton, *Opticks*, 351, 352, 396.
27 S. Hales, *Vegetable staticks; or, an account of some statical experiments on the sap in vegetables* (London, 1727), 178.
28 [H. Boerhaave] *A new method of chemistry: including the history, theory and practice of the art: translated from the original Latin of Dr. Boerhaave's Elementa chemiae*, trans. P. Shaw, 2 vols. (London, 1741), 1:220, 236.
29 Ibid., 1:208, 223, 359, 362.
30 Ibid., 246–7.
31 J. Rowning, *A compendious system of natural philosophy* (London, 1737–43), iii.
32 Peter Collinson to Cadwallader Colden, March 1745, quoted in Cohen (1956), 435.
33 I. B. Cohen (ed.), *Benjamin Franklin's experiments* (Cambridge, Mass., 1941), 213–14.
34 Ibid., 233, 210.
35 G. Knight, *An attempt to demonstrate, that all the phaenomena in nature may be explained by two simple active principles, attraction and repulsion* (London, 1754), 4–5.
36 Ibid., 10, 66–7. Home (1977a), 262, considers Knight a Cartesian. This view fails to acknowledge the distinctive Newtonian framework of Knight's theory: cf. Heimann and McGuire, (1971), 296–9.
37 C. Colden, *The principles of action in matter, the gravitation of bodies and the motion of the planets explained from those principles* (London, 1751), 27, 28, 73. Cf. Schofield (1970), 130–3; Heimann and McGuire (1971), 303.
38 C. Maclaurin, *An account of Sir Isaac Newton's philosophical discoveries* (London, 1748), 381–9. See Heimann, 'Voluntarism and immanence', 275; R. Lovett, *The subtil medium prov'd* (London, 1756), n.p., preface.
39 Heimann (1973). For a survey of eighteenth-century chemical writings on this topic see Ziemacki's discussion (1974) of phlogiston and ethereal agents in eighteenth-century British chemistry. This work supplements the study of 'Newtonian' chemistry by Thackray (1970), who ignores the development of imponderable fluid theories in chemistry.
40 P. Shaw, *Chemical lectures publickly read at London* (London, 1734), 146.
41 Boerhaave, *Chemistry*, 155–7, 173.
42 A. L. Donovan, *Philosophical chemistry in the Scottish Englightenment: the doctrines of William Cullen and Joseph Black* (Edinburgh, 1975), 141–51.
43 Quoted in D. McKie, 'On some Ms. copies of Black's chemical lectures', *Annals of Science 21* (1965), 223.
44 Quoted, respectively, in Donovan, *Philosophical chemistry*, 229, and in T. Coch-

rane, *Notes from Doctor Black's lectures on chemistry 1767/8*, ed. D. McKie (Wilmslow, Cheshire, 1966), 83. On Black and theories of heat, see D. McKie and N. H. de V. Heathcote, *The discovery of specific and latent heats* (London, 1935); Fox (1971), 6–67; Donovan, *Philosophical chemistry*, 222–77; Talbot (1967).

45 J. R. Partington and D. McKie, 'Historical studies in the phlogiston theory: III, Light and heat in combustion', *Annals of Science 3* (1938), 338–71.

46 P. D. Leslie, *A philosophical inquiry into the causes of animal heat: with incidental observations on several physiological and chymical questions connected with the subject* (London, 1778), 104, 119, 124.

47 B. Higgins, *A philosophical essay concerning light* (London, 1776), 13.

48 Ziemacki (1974) distinguishes between theories in which phlogiston was considered to be a universal active medium and theories in which phlogiston was identified with an ordinary ponderable substance. A parallel development occurred in France in the 1760s: Rouelle, Macquer, and Venel equated phlogiston, Stahl's inflammable principle, with Boerhaave's fire, thus transforming both concepts. For Boerhaave fire was a physical instrument, the source of chemical change while itself remaining unchanged; for Stahl phlogiston was one of the chemical 'principles' that formed the basis of chemical substances. In identifying Stahl's phlogiston with Boerhaave's fire, Rouelle emphasised that fire was a chemical constituent of bodies, like phlogiston. See M. Fichman, 'French Stahlism and chemical studies of air, 1750–1770', *Ambix 18* (1971), 94–122; H. Metzger, *Newton, Stahl, Boerhaave et la doctrine chimique* (Paris, 1930), 209–45; R. Rappaport, 'Rouelle and Stahl – the phlogistic revolution in France', *Chymia 7* (1961), 73–102; Love (1974).

49 J. Hutton, *Dissertations on different subjects in natural philosophy* (Edinburgh, 1792), 246. On Hutton's natural philosophy cf. Heimann and McGuire (1971), 281–95.

50 Hutton, *Dissertations*, 263, 505.

51 Ibid., 175, 517, 519.

52 Ibid., 214, 218.

53 McKie, 'Black's chemical lectures', 215; P. J. Macquer, *Dictionnaire de chymie*, 2nd ed. 4 vols. (Paris, 1778), 3:144.

54 Hutton, *Dissertations*, 501.

55 Ibid., 257. See Heimann (1973), 19–21, on Hutton's theory of chemistry.

56 J. Playfair, 'Biographical account of James Hutton', in J. Playfair, *The works of John Playfair*, 4 vols. (Edinburgh, 1822), 4:83.

57 A. Walker, *A system of familiar philosophy*, rev. ed., 2 vols. (London, 1802), 1:6, 14, 18, and 2:1, 74.

58 C. Hutton, *A mathematical and philosophical dictionary*, 2 vols. (London, 1795–6), 1:473.

59 Fox (1971), 99–103; P. M. Heimann, 'Conversion of forces and the conservation of energy', *Centaurus 18* (1974), 152–3; Cantor (1970).

60 B. Rumford, *The complete works of Count Rumford*, 4 vols. (Boston, 1870–5), 2:172.

61 Ibid., 2:104. Goldfarb (1977) argues convincingly that Rumford's work has been wrongly interpreted as a precursor of the kinetic theory of heat, and stresses the role of the ether in Rumford's natural philosophy. However, in pointing to Boerhaave as Rumford's probable source, Goldfarb ignores the tradition of natural philosophy discussed in the present chapter. Another possible source of Rumford's ether is Lambert's *Pyrometrie* (Berlin, 1779), sections of which Rumford translated for Fourier. See Fox (1979).

62 H. Davy, *Collected works of Humphry Davy*, 9 vols. (London 1839), 2:28, 35; 4:44, 56, and 5:40.

63 Heimann, 'Conversion of forces', 147–61.

Bibliography

Aiton, E.J. 1972. *The Vortex Theory of Planetary Motions*. London.
Bechler, Z. 1974. 'Newton's law of forces which are inversely as the mass'. *Centaurus 18*: 184–222.
Cantor, G.N. 1970. 'The changing role of Young's ether'. *British Journal for the History of Science 5*: 44–62.
— 1971. 'Henry Brougham and the Scottish methodological tradition'. *Studies in History and Philosophy of Science 2*: 69–89.
Cohen, I.B. 1956. *Franklin and Newton: an inquiry into speculative Newtonian experimental science and Franklin's work in electricity as an example thereof*. Philadelphia.
Fox, R. 1971. *The Caloric Theory of Gases from Lavoisier to Regnault*. Oxford.
— 1979. 'The science of fire: J.H. Lambert and the study of heat'. In *Université de Haute Alsace: colloque international et indisciplinaire Jean-Henri Lambert. Mulhouse, 26–30 Septembre 1977*, pp. 325–42. Paris.
Goldfarb, S. 1977. 'Rumford's theory of heat: a reassessment'. *British Journal for the History of Science 10*: 25–36.
Guerlac, H. 1967. 'Newton's optical ether: his draft of a proposed addition to his *Opticks*'. *Notes and Records of the Royal Society of London 22*: 45–57.
Hall, A.R. and Hall, M.B. 1967. 'Newton and the theory of matter'. *Texas Quarterly 10*: 54–68.
Heimann, P.M. 1973. ' "Nature is a perpetual worker": Newton's aether and eighteenth-century natural philosophy'. *Ambix 20*: 1–25. This volume: Essay II.
Heimann, P.M. and McGuire, J.E. 1971. 'Newtonian forces and Lockean powers: concepts of matter in eighteenth-century thought'. *Historical Studies in the Physical Sciences 3*: 233–306. This volume: Essay I.
Home, R.W. 1972. 'Franklin's electrical atmospheres'. *British Journal for the History of Science 6*: 131–51.
— 1977. ' "Newtonianism" and the theory of the magnet'. *History of Science 15*: 252–66.
Love, R. 1974. 'Hermann Boerhaave and the element-instrument concept of fire'. *Annals of Science 31*: 547–69.
McGuire, J.E. 1967. 'Transmutation and immutability: Newton's doctrine of physical qualities'. *Ambix 14*: 69–95.
— 1968. 'Force, active principles, and Newton's invisible realm'. *Ambix 15*: 154–208.
— 1977. 'Neoplatonism, active principles and the *Corpus Hermeticum*'. In R.S. Westman and J.E. McGuire, *Hermeticism and the Scientific Revolution*. Los Angeles.
Olson, R. 1975. *Scottish Philosophy and British Physics*. Princeton, N.J.
Rosenfeld, L. 1965. 'Newton and the law of gravitation'. *Archive for History of Exact Sciences 2*: 365–85.
Schofield, R.E. 1970. *Mechanism and Materialism: British Natural Philosophy in an Age of Reason*. Princeton, N.J.
Talbot, G.R. 1967. 'Origins and solutions of some problems of heat in the eighteenth century'. Unpublished doctoral dissertation, University of Manchester.

BIBLIOGRAPHY

Thackray, A.W. 1970. *Atoms and Powers: an Essay on Newtonian Matter-theory and the Development of Chemistry*. Cambridge, Mass.

Walker, D.P. 1972. *The Ancient Theology*. London.

Westfall, R.S. 1971. *Force in Newton's Physics: the Science of Dynamics in the Seventeenth Century*. London.

Whiteside, D.T. 1964. 'Newton's early thoughts on planetary motion: a fresh look'. *British Journal for the History of Science 2*: 117–37.

— 1970. 'Before the *Principia*: the maturing of Newton's thoughts on dynamical astronomy, 1664–1684'. *Journal for the History of Astronomy 1*: 5–19.

Ziemacki, R.L. 1974. 'Humphry Davy and the conflict of traditions in early nineteenth-century British chemistry'. Unpublished doctoral dissertation, University of Cambridge.

IV

VOLUNTARISM AND IMMANENCE: CONCEPTIONS OF NATURE IN EIGHTEENTH-CENTURY THOUGHT

The traditional historiography of science has supposed that the metaphysical reorientation fundamental to the "scientific revolution" in the seventeenth century established the conceptual framework of eighteenth-century scientific thought.[1] This characterization of eighteenth-century ideas has been sustained by an interpretation of seventeenth-century thought that has placed emphasis on the modernity of the conceptual revolution associated with the establishment of the mechanical philosophy.[2] According to this interpretation, the mechanical philosophy conceived nature as a self-contained, law-governed system, in which God's relation to nature was viewed merely as a first efficient cause, and the appeal by natural philosophers to second causes (laws of nature) established knowledge of nature as independent of divine providence. Thus it is maintained that doctrines of providence declined in importance in the period, and the establishment of the mechanical philosophy is viewed in terms of the secularization of knowledge in the seventeenth century.[3] Newton and Boyle are regarded as having "prepared the ground for the deists of the Enlightenment"; for "deism, the religion of reason, steps full grown from the writings of the Christian virtuosi."[4]

This historiography is doubly misleading: in its account of doctrines of providence in the thought of Boyle and Newton, and of the consequent characterization of eighteenth-century intellectual history. Recent

---

* An early version of this paper was read as a lecture to The Society for the Humanities, Cornell University on 17 October, 1972. I am grateful to Professor Henry Guerlac for his kind invitation and for his comments on the paper. I am also grateful to Gerd Buchdahl, Ralph Grant, and J. E. McGuire for discussions on the themes of this paper.

[1] The following studies are representative: E. A. Burtt, *The Metaphysical Foundations of Modern Physical Science* (2nd ed., London, 1932); E. J. Dijksterhuis, *The Mechanization of the World-Picture* (Oxford, 1961). These studies and the works referred to in footnotes (2) to (4) below are cited here for their merits as important statements of the traditional historiography.

[2] M. Boas, "The establishment of the mechanical philosophy," *Osiris*, 10(1952), 412-541.

[3] Richard S. Westfall, *Science and Religion in Seventeenth-Century England* (New Haven, 1958); Paul Hazard, *The European Mind 1680-1715* (London, 1953).

[4] Westfall, *op. cit.*, 219.

scholarship has questioned the traditional view that doctrines of providence declined in importance in late seventeenth-century natural philosophy. Stressing the influence of the voluntarist tradition of theology on Descartes, Boyle, and Newton, it has been argued that these men regarded God's will as the only causally efficacious agency in nature. To conceive nature as subject to laws did not obviate divine providence, for in regarding nature as a contingent artifact of divine omnipotence laws of nature were considered as being imposed on nature by God, having their source in the efficacy of the divine will. Laws and the abrogations of laws were both manifestations of divine providence.[5] The implications of this reconsideration of the theological dimension of seventeenth-century science are of considerable importance for an understanding of eighteenth-century thought. The assumption that Enlightenment skepticism was "already present in embryo among [the virtuosi]"[6] is clearly to be questioned. The current revaluation of seventeenth-century attitudes suggests that the transition from the natural theology of the virtuosi to the religion of reason of the eighteenth century involved a more complex shift in theological sensibility than has generally been supposed.

In this paper I am concerned to characterize the shift in theological sensibility associated with the emergence of new conceptions of nature in eighteenth-century British thought. The transition from the Newtonian view that the activity of the natural order was to be ascribed to the continued sustenance of passive matter by God's will to the theories of nature proposed in the late eighteenth century by Joseph Priestley and James Hutton which supposed—though in different ways—that activity was intrinsic to matter and immanent in the natural order, was associated with the rejection of Newton's voluntarist theory of nature which supposed that God's will "sustains the world in its minutest details." These eighteenth-century natural philosophers emphasized divine omniscience and rejected divine abrogation of the laws of nature as impugning divine foresight, rejecting the voluntarist conception of nature which stressed that God "gives order as well as deviation from order," a view that "diminishes the gap between the natural and the supernatural."[7] This was an important development in theological attitude towards the natural world, but these natural philosophers did not limit God's relation to nature as a first efficient cause, supposing a mechanical universe run by immutable natural laws established by

---

[5] Francis Oakley, "Christian Theology and the Newtonian Science: the rise of the concept of the laws of nature," *Church History*, 30(1961), 433-57; J. E. McGuire, "Force, Active Principles and Newton's Invisible Realm," *Ambix*, 15 (1968), 187-208; *id.*, "Boyle's Conception of Nature," *JHI*, 33(1972), 523-42.

[6] Westfall, *op. cit.*, 219.

[7] R. Hooykaas, *The Principle of Uniformity in Geology, Biology and Theology: Natural Law and Law and Divine Miracle* (Leiden, 1963), 170f. Hooykaas terms this view of God's relation to nature the "Biblical" view.

God, which then maintained the operations of nature independently of divine energy, but supposed—though with different emphasis—that divine causality was manifested in the active powers[8] which were immanent in the fabric of nature. This shift in theological sensibility involved a change in attitude towards the causality of God and the relationship between God and nature.

I. The theological dimension of Newton's natural philosophy was familiar to eighteenth-century thinkers from his *Principia* and *Opticks* and also from the distinctively Newtonian cast of the writings of the Boyle lecturers, notably Samuel Clarke.[9] In the *Opticks* Newton emphasized that his conception of nature affirmed the voluntarist doctrine of divine omnipotence: everything in the world, he argued, is "subordinate to him, and subservient to his Will." As God's will was the only causally efficacious agency in nature, Newton declared that God "may vary the Laws of Nature, and make worlds of several sorts in several parts of the universe."[10] Newton distinguished between the role of active and passive principles in natural processes, maintaining that the laws of motion and the essential qualities of material substances—extension, impenetrability, inertia—were passive principles by which "there never could have been any motion in the world."[11] Newton concluded that the principles of the mechanical philosophy were limited in their comprehension of nature. As Hume later noted, "while Newton seemed to draw off the veil from some of the mysteries of nature, he showed at the same time the imperfections of the mechanical philosophy."[12] Newton argued that "some other principle [than the passive principles of matter and motion] was necessary for putting bodies into motion; and now they are in motion some other principle is necessary for conserving the motion." The passive laws of motion could neither originate nor sustain motion, and Newton concluded that a different category of causal agent, active principles, were responsible for "conserving and recruiting" activity and motion in nature, these active principles being "such as are the cause of gravity." In denying that the activity of nature was intrinsic to the natural order, Newton emphasized the role of active principles, which were defined in relation to divine omni-

---

[8] For an analysis of the significance of the concept of "power" in eighteenth-century British natural philosophy: P. M. Heimann and J. E. McGuire, "Newtonian Forces and Lockean Powers: Concepts of Matter in Eighteenth-Century Thought," *Historical Studies in the Physical Sciences*, 3(1971), 233-306; also Philip P. Wiener, "James Gregory: "On Power," *JHI*, 20(1959), 241-68.

[9] On the Newtonian cast of the Boyle Lectures: Henry Guerlac and M. C. Jacob, "Bentley, Newton and Providence," *JHI*, 30(1969), 307-18; M. C. Jacob, "The Church and the Formulation of the Newtonian World View," *Journal of European Studies*, 1(1971), 128-48.

[10] Isaac Newton, *Opticks* (4th ed., rpt., London, 1952), 403f   [11] *Ibid.*, 397.

[12] David Hume, in his *History of England*, as quoted in Norman Kemp Smith, *The Philosophy of David Hume* (London, 1941), 58.

potence and conceived as the manifestations of God's causal agency in nature. Functioning as the cause of motion and gravity, active principles were regarded as "general Laws of Nature" rather than as divine abrogations of the laws of nature.[13] There was no conflict between Newton's stress on the lawlike function of active principles and their construal as manifestations of providence, for Newton argued that while all natural phenomena were constrained by God's will, nevertheless God also worked through second causes by divine concurrence with the order of nature that He had established. In terms of this voluntarist theology, the laws of nature as well as divine abrogations of law are expressions of divine providence. Newton bridged the dichotomy between natural laws and divine interventions, arguing that "miracles are so called not because they are the works of God but because they happen seldom and for that reason create wonder."[14] Newton did not publish this remark, but his ideas were echoed by Samuel Clarke in his famous correspondence with Leibniz.[15] Clarke declared that "*natural* and *supernatural* are nothing at all different with regard to God, but distinctions merely in our conceptions of things."[16] All of nature is subject to God's will, and whether we call an event a natural and lawlike phenomenon or an abrogation of law and a miracle lies "merely in the unusualness of God's doing it," for "with regard to God, no one possible thing is more miraculous than another."[17] In his *Discourse Concerning the Being and Attributes of God* (1705-06) Clarke stressed Newton's view that the activity of nature was dependent on an "Immaterial Power . . . *perpetually and actually* exerting itself every moment in every part of the world,"[18] for matter and motion were "arbitrary and dependent things."[19]

The import of Newton's concept of active principles is apparent in his theory of the aether developed in the 1717 edition of his *Opticks*.

---

[13] Newton, *Opticks*, 397-401; McGuire, "Force, Active Principles . . ." *op. cit.*, 154-208.

[14] Newton MS quoted in Guerlac and Jacob, *op. cit.*, 309n.

[15] On Newton's role in the Leibniz-Clarke correspondence cf. A. Koyré and I. B. Cohen, "Newton and the Leibniz-Clarke Correspondence," *Arch. int. d'hist. sci.*, 15(1962), 63-126; also F. E. L. Priestley, "The Clarke-Leibniz Controversy," *The Methodological Heritage of Newton*, ed. R. Butts and J. W. Davis (Oxford, 1970), 34-56.

[16] H. G. Alexander, ed. *The Leibniz-Clarke Correspondence* (Manchester, 1956), 24.

[17] *Ibid.*, 114.

[18] Samuel Clarke, *Discourse Concerning the Being and Attributes of God*, 2 vols. (4th ed., London, 1716), II, 17. Clarke's Boyle Lectures were first published as: *A Demonstration of the Being and Attributes of God* (London, 1705) and *A Discourse Concerning the Unchangeable Obligations of Natural Religion* (London, 1706).

[19] Clarke, *op. cit.*, I, 23.

The aether was employed as an explanation of gravity, and Newton was careful to imply that the aether functioned as an active principle, not as a passive or mechanical principle of matter and motion analogous to the Cartesian celestial vortices. In the General Scholium to the second edition of *Principia* in 1713, Newton had denied that gravity could be explained by "mechanical causes," and Newton implied that the aether, as a possible cause of gravity, was an active principle subordinate to God's will.[20] Newton's concept of the aether was echoed by Colin MacLaurin in his *Account of Sir Isaac Newton's Philosophical Discoveries* (1748). MacLaurin stressed that Newton was "particularly careful" to represent God as a "free agent . . . equally active and present everywhere,"[21] and in noting that gravity "seems to surpass mere mechanism" he pointed out that if gravity were "produced by a rare and elastic *aethereal medium,* as Sir *Isaac Newton* conjectured," then "the whole efficacy of this medium must be resolved into his power and will, who is the supreme cause." MacLaurin followed Newton in supposing that the aether was contingent on God's will; hence the supposition of an aether did not "derogate from the government and influence of the Deity" for God "is the source of all efficacy." MacLaurin thus affirmed Newton's voluntarism, viewing second causes as manifestations of the "power and will" of the Deity.[22]

However, by the 1740s natural philosophers were developing conceptions of nature in which the aether was considered as an active principle which was immanent in the fabric of nature, and which functioned as the source of the activity of nature. This transformation in thought involved a blurring of the distinctive categories of Newton's natural philosophy and a rejection of its theological overtones. Newton's natural philosophy was dualistic: a dualism of matter and force, attractive and repulsive forces, atoms and void space, and active and passive principles. By the middle of the eighteenth century conceptions of nature were being proposed in which there was a bridging of the dualism of these Newtonian categories. The emergence of a theory of nature in which activity was considered as immanent in the structure of nature led to a rejection of Newton's doctrine that all causal activity in nature was imposed by God's power and will.

The theory that nature was endowed with intrinsic active forces or powers had been proposed earlier in the century in opposition to the

---

[20] Isaac Newton, *Mathematical Principles of Natural Philosophy,* trans. and ed. A. Motte and F. Cajori (Berkeley, 1934), 546; *id., Opticks,* 349-54; Clarke, *op. cit.,* II, 16-19. On the background to Newton's aether: Henry Guerlac, "Newton's Optical Aether," *Notes and Records of the Royal Society of London,* 22(1967), 45-57.

[21] Colin MacLaurin, *An Account of Sir Isaac Newton's Philosophical Discoveries* (London, 1748), 381f.

[22] *Ibid.,* 387-89.

Newtonian world view, but these ideas had been rejected by Newton and Clarke. In his *Specimen Dynamicum* Leibniz had rejected the view that extension and motion were the defining characteristics of substance, arguing that force constituted the inmost nature of material substance,[23] and this rejection of the theory of the passivity of material entities had its counterpart in his hostility to Newton's voluntarism. As he later affirmed to Clarke, the Newtonians "acknowledge power, but not sufficient wisdom, in the principle or cause of all things." The inherent activity of matter did "not exclude God's providence, or his government of the world: on the contrary, it makes it perfect," for a "true providence of God requires a perfect foresight." Leibniz emphasized that the rejection of Newton's voluntarism did not restrict divine providence, denying that the world was a "machine," and affirming that "the creation wants to be continually influenc'd by its creator."[24] Nevertheless, Leibniz's opposition to a voluntarist conception of divine sustenance led to Clarke's vehement opposition to his natural philosophy. Clarke also dismissed the theory of a dynamic, inherently active universe proposed by John Toland in his *Letters to Serena* (1704). Asserting that the universe displayed constant activity, Toland claimed that "motion is essential to matter,"[25] but Clarke argued that matter could not be endowed with a self-existent principle of motion because "self-existence is necessary existence" and the existence of matter was contingent on God's will.[26]

From the early eighteenth century the concept of matter as an inherently active substance was developed explicitly in opposition to the Newtonian concept of nature. One of Newton's earliest English critics, Robert Greene, maintained that "nature is active . . . [and] matter itself is so,"[27] and in rejecting the Newtonian theory of atoms argued that "Action or Force in general is the Essence or Substratum of Matter."[28] Greene did not suppose that the active forces constituting material substance were self-existent, arguing that if matter were self-existent it would have a "necessary, certain and unvaried principle of existing"; however, natural phenomena were not unvaried but were diverse, and

---

[23] G. W. Leibniz, "Specimen Dynamicum," *Acta Eruditorum*, 14(1695), 145-57. On Newton's reaction to this work, cf. J. E. McGuire, "Body and Void and Newton's *De Mundi Systemate*," *Arch. Hist. Exact Sci.*, 3(1966), 237.

[24] Alexander, *op. cit.*, 18f.

[25] John Toland, *Letters to Serena* (London, 1704), 158. On Toland's relation to Newton, cf. M. C. Jacob, "John Toland and the Newtonian Ideology," *J. Warburg and Courtauld Institutes*, 32(1969), 307-31; also Rosalie L. Colie, "Spinoza and the Early English Deists," *JHI*, 20(1959), 23-46.

[26] Clarke, *op. cit.*, I, 49.

[27] Robert Greene, *The Principles of Natural Philosophy* (Cambridge, 1712), 391. On Greene's concept of force, cf. Heimann and McGuire. *op. cit.* 254-61.

[28] Robert Greene, *The Principles of the Philosophy of the Expansive and Contractive Forces* (Cambridge, 1727), 286.

"all Nature consists of an infinite number of actions different in their forces and contrary in their directions." Greene thus concluded that activity "cannot be self-existent," contending that the diversity of forces "must necessarily lead us to some Agent."[29] The immanent powers were not self-existent in nature but were dependent on divine agency for their activity.

The theory of activity as immanent in nature was a common assumption in the conceptions of nature developed in the 1740s, in which the aether was assimilated to Boerhaave's "active element" of fire[30] which was considered to be an active principle permeating the universe: "fire [was considered] as endowed with active Powers different from those of other Matter."[31] Electricity and fire were considered to be different modifications of the aether,[32] and the Newtonian notion that "motion comes immediately from the Divine Being" was rejected as "unphilosophical" in favor of supposing that activity was inherent in the aether, the aether being regarded as an active principle.[33] Newton's theory of the aether was transformed, so the aether was viewed as an active principle immanent in nature.

The implication of these developments in natural philosophy for Newton's doctrine of efficient causation as contingent on God's will is apparent in Hume's discussion of causation and the aether in his *Enquiry into the Human Understanding* (1748). Hume rejected the Newtonian doctrine of passive matter, the view—as he put it in his *Treatise of Human Nature* (1739)—that "the essence of matter . . . is endow'd with no efficacy," that because matter "is in itself entirely unactive, and depriv'd of any power" hence "the power . . . must lie in the DEITY." Hume thus opposed the notion that "the deity . . . is the prime mover of the universe, and who not only first created matter, and gave it its original impulse, but likewise by a continu'd exertion of omnipotence, supports its existence."[34] In his *Enquiry* Hume appealed to divine omniscience in rejecting the Newtonian doctrine that "nothing exists but by [God's]will," echoing Leibniz's arguments against Clarke in stating that the "purposes of providence" are manifested in the "perfect foresight"

---

[29] *Ibid.,* 108ff.

[30] Herman Boerhaave, *A New Method of Chemistry,* trans. P. Shaw (London, 1741), 212. On the impact of Newton's theory of the aether and Boerhaave's concept of fire on eighteenth-century natural philosophy, cf. P. M. Heimann, " 'Nature is a perpetual worker': Newton's aether and eighteenth-century natural philosophy," *Ambix,* **20**(1973), 1-25.

[31] John Rowning, *A Compendious System of Natural Philosophy* (London, 1737-43), iii.

[32] I. B. Cohen ed., *Benjamin Franklin's Experiments* (Cambridge, Mass., 1941), 210.

[33] C. Colden, *The Principles of Action in Matter* (London, 1751), 73.

[34] David Hume, *A Treatise of Human Nature* [1739-40], ed. L. A. Selby-Bigge (Oxford, 1888), 159.

IV

by which the "fabric of the world" was contrived, for "it argues surely more power in the Deity to delegate a certain degree of power . . . than to produce every thing by his own immediate volition." This latter view was in the realm of "fairy land."[35] Hume attributed the theory that all agency in nature was derived from divine volition to Malebranche, and ascribed the view that "matter has a real, though subordinate and derived [active] power" to the Newtonians. As an instance of the active powers of matter which he claimed were supposed by Newton, Hume appealed to Newton's "recourse to an etherial active fluid to explain his [theory of] universal attraction," denying that Newton attributed gravity to divine volition.[36] Hume maintained that the notion that matter has a real power and energy can be made intelligible if this power can be shown to be an instance of causal activity. Hence, subsuming the phenomena of gravity under the action of an "etherial active fluid" renders the power of gravity intelligible. Causal agency is thus seen as only being intelligible in relation to physical explanation, in relation to the laws of nature between material entities.[37]

In restricting the intelligibility of causal explanation to the formulation of laws of nature Hume rejected the notion of the efficient causality of God, of divine efficacy sustaining the natural world. Hume's restriction of the causal principle to the formulation of physical explanations rendered the notion of divine sustenance unintelligible, and this implication of Hume's arguments was resisted. The Scottish philosopher Thomas Reid attempted a systematic refutation of Humean principles, and in his *Essays on the Active Powers of the Human Mind* (1788) provided a full account of his theory of causality. Reid distinguished between causation in the sense of the formulation of laws of nature, which was the concern of science (and which Hume accepted), and "efficient causation," as in divine sustenance of the laws of nature, and sought to justify the supposition of efficient causes. Reid pointed out that natural philosophers were only concerned with the "cause of any phenomenon of nature" in the sense of a "law of nature of which that phenomenon is a necessary consequence." The laws of nature were merely "the rules according to which the effects are produced," but science was not concerned with the postulation of the "efficient cause" of phenomena, the supposition of a causal relation between an active agent and matter. However, it was meaningful to suppose an efficient cause of phenomena: "Upon the theatre of nature we see innumerable effects, which require an agent endowed with active power; but the agent is behind the scene. Whether it be the Supreme Cause alone, or a subordinate cause or causes; and if subordinate causes be employed by the Almighty, what

---

[35] David Hume, *An Enquiry into the Human Understanding* [1748], ed. L. A. Selby-Bigge (2nd ed., Oxford, 1902), 71f.   [36] *Ibid.*, 73n.

[37] Gerd Buchdahl, *Metaphysics and the Philosophy of Science. The Classical Origins: Descartes to Kant* (Oxford, 1969), 325-87.

their nature, their number, and their different offices may be are things hid, for wise reasons without doubt, from the human eye."[38] Reid thus sought to justify efficient causation, the supposition that the activity of nature was a consequence of the causality of God, whether activity was imposed on nature by divine volition or was maintained by immanent active powers dependent on divine energy for their efficacy. In distinguishing between laws of nature and efficient causes Reid sought to anaesthetize the thrust of the Humean critique. Nevertheless in making this distinction his argument reflects Hume's critique of Newtonian voluntarism. In seeking to validate the notion of divine sustenance without stressing divine volition as the cause of phenomena, Reid's argument attests to the shift in theological sensibility consequent on the rejection of Newton's theory that active principles were imposed by divine volition on passive matter, and on the development of theories of natural philosophy which employed the concept of the aether as an active principle immanent in nature.

II. These intellectual developments are apparent in the writings of Joseph Priestley and James Hutton, two scientists active in the latter part of the eighteenth century whose importance can be seen not only in their notable contributions to chemistry and geology, respectively, but also in their attempts to construct systematic systems of natural philosophy.

Priestley rejected the Newtonian duality of active and passive principles because of the difficulty in explaining God's causal relation to nature entailed by supposing that God "has no property whatever in common with matter." This would imply that "the divine being is necessarily cut off from all communication with, and all action and influence upon, his own creation."[39] Priestley resolved the problem of the interaction between matter and the immaterial deity by positing a monistic theory of nature, denying the Newtonian dualism of matter and force by defining matter as "a substance possessed of the property of extension and of powers of attraction or repulsion,"[40] thus asserting the "immateriality of matter"[41] and denying that "there are . . . two substances as distinct from each other" as matter and spirit.[42] If matter was considered as defined by the properties of extension and inherent

---

[38] Thomas Reid, *Essays on the Active Powers of the Human Mind* [1788], ed. B. Brody (Cambridge, Mass., 1969), 46f.

[39] Joseph Priestley, *Disquisitions Relating to Matter and Spirit* (London, 1777; 2nd ed., 2 vols., Birmingham, 1782), in *The Theological and Miscellaneous Works of Joseph Priestley*, ed. J. T. Rutt, 25 vols. (London, 1817-31), III, 298 (2nd ed. quoted); hereafter Priestley, *Disquisitions*.

[40] Priestley, *Disquisitions* in *Works*, III, 219. For an analysis of Priestley's theory of matter, cf. Heimann and McGuire, *op. cit.*, 268-81.

[41] Joseph Priestley, *The History and Present State of Discoveries Relating to Vision, Light and Colours* (London, 1772), 392.

[42] Priestley, *Disquisitions* in *Works*, III, 223.

powers of attraction and repulsion, then the nature of matter was compatible with "that substance which . . . we have been used to call immaterial."⁴³ Priestley rejected the Newtonian concept of passive matter together with Newton's doctrine of the causal relation between God and nature, claiming that the Newtonian theory of matter supposed "something to be *independent of the divine power*" in postulating "two original independent principles."⁴⁴ Priestley argued that his monistic theory was thus consonant to the notion of God's "filling all in all."⁴⁵

Priestley did not suppose that the powers which constituted matter were "self-existent in it"⁴⁶ but maintained that the activity of matter was sustained by divine agency, asserting that "the Deity not only attends to everything, but must be capable of either *producing* or *annihilating* anything."⁴⁷ Thus God's "power is the very life and soul of everything that exists . . . without him, we are, as well as can do, nothing,"⁴⁸ and without divine sustenance "substance ceases to exist, or is annihilated."⁴⁹ Priestley nevertheless rejected Newton's voluntarism, arguing that God acts by necessity not volition: God's causality "could not but have acted from all eternity."⁵⁰ He argued that the activity of nature was sustained by divine energy and that causal connections in nature were a necessary consequence of divine power, for God "was the same first cause from which all the powers of nature are derived"⁵¹ and "all the *powers of nature* . . . can only be the effect of the Divine energy perpetually acting,"⁵² concluding that causal connections in nature were "necessary" because there must be "some sufficient reason" for them.⁵³

There are Leibnizian resonances in these statements, and Priestley, like Leibniz, viewed nature as being "influenced" by God while rejecting the voluntarist doctrine of divine causality; as Leibniz expressed it,

---

⁴³ *Ibid.*, 230.   ⁴⁴ *Ibid.*, 241.   ⁴⁵ *Ibid.*, 301.   ⁴⁶ *Ibid.*, 224.

⁴⁷ *Ibid.*, 297. With reference to this and other statements of Priestley's, cf. J. G. McEvoy and J. E. McGuire, "God and Nature: Priestley's Way of Rational Dissent," *Historical Studies in the Physical Sciences*, 6(1975), 332f, argue that Priestley's thought developed from voluntarist to rationalist theism after the publication of the first edition of his *Disquisitions* in 1777. This is possible, though Priestley's writings are ambiguous; as they note, this statement of Priestley's in the first edition of the *Disquisitions* is not an overt statement of a voluntarist position.

⁴⁸ Priestley, *Disquisitions*, in *Works*, III, 241.   ⁴⁹ *Ibid.*, 224.

⁵⁰ Joseph Priestley, *Letters to a Philosophical Unbeliever* (London, 1780), in *Works*, IV, 343; hereafter Priestley, *Philosophical Unbeliever*.

⁵¹ Joseph Priestley, *A Free Discussion of the Doctrines of Materialism and Philosophical Necessity, in a Correspondence between Dr. Price and Dr. Priestley* (London, 1778), in *Works*, IV, 107.

⁵² Joseph Priestley, *Institutes of Natural and Revealed Religion*, 2 vols., 2nd ed. (Birmingham, 1782), in *Works*, II, 15.

⁵³ Priestley, *Philosophical Unbeliever*, in *Works*, IV, 403.

God was "the efficient and exemplary cause" of all phenomena.[54] For Priestley the laws of nature and the active powers were the effect of divine energy permeating nature, and—given his monism and his theory of divine causality—the laws of nature and active powers constituting nature were regarded as being immanent in the fabric of nature, not imposed by divine volition. In conceiving the structure and activity of nature as arising necessarily from divine energy, Priestley's ideas have a slight affinity—which was seized on by Coleridge[55]—to Spinoza's conception of divine causality. Priestley, however, was concerned to disavow any suspicion of such a similarity. Incorrectly interpreting Spinoza as denying any conceptual distinction between God and the aggregate totality of all things,[56] Priestley repudiated the suggestion that his own conception of nature, which supposed "the Deity to *be* as well as to *do* everything," was "anything like the opinion of Spinoza," for Priestley claimed that he distinguished (as Spinoza did not) between "infinite power" and "inferior beings" and hence, between God and nature.[57] While there is quite possibly a substantive relation between Priestley's ideas and Leibniz's arguments, the influence of Spinoza is doubtful,[58] but whatever Priestley's links to these thinkers, it is apparent that his rejection of Newtonian dualism and voluntarism and his supposition of a monistic theory of nature and concept of active powers as immanent in nature is grounded on a doctrine of divine causality that considers nature as dependent for its existence on divine sustenance.

In his *Dissertations on Different Subjects in Natural Philosophy* (1792) and *Investigation of the Principles of Knowledge* (1794), Hutton firmly opposed the Newtonian doctrine that "bodies are composed of atoms which are absolutely inert . . . infinitely hard, and perfectly incompressible,"[59] arguing that this "received opinion of philosophers"[60] merely supposed as the defining principles of gross bodies "nothing but the bodies themselves under the pedantic designation of atoms."[61] Hutton claimed that "magnitude and figure [the defining characteristics of atoms] have no other existence than in the conceiving faculty of our mind,"[62] and that sensory experience—far from providing

---

[54] Alexander, *op. cit.*, 84.

[55] Thomas McFarland, *Coleridge and the Pantheist Tradition* (Oxford, 1969), 170, 175.

[56] H. A. Wolfson, *The Philosophy of Spinoza*, 2 vols. (Cambridge, Mass., 1934), I, 324f.   [57] Priestley, *Disquisitions*, in *Works*, III, 241.

[58] *Cf.* McEvoy and McGuire, *op. cit.*, 332, for a different view of Priestley's relation to Spinoza.

[59] James Hutton, *Dissertations on Different Subjects in Natural Philosophy* (Edinburgh, 1792), 669; hereafter Hutton, *Dissertations*.

[60] *Ibid.*, 292.   [61] *Ibid.*, 669.

[62] James Hutton, *An Investigation of the Principles of Knowledge, and of the Progress of Reason, from Sense to Science and Philosophy*, 3 vols. (Edinburgh, 1794), II, 393; hereafter Hutton, *Investigation*.

knowledge of passive, hard atoms—only gave us evidence of "resisting powers in bodies, by which their volume and figure are presented to us."[63] Thus "power, the cause of our sensation, is to be considered as a first cause."[64] Hutton considered that activity was an essential property of substances, asserting that "instead of considering matter as a thing inert, and only passive in its nature . . . we find it necessary to conceive power of action to exist in external things," and concluding that "matter [is] thus conceived as having power or efficacy."[65] Activity was immanent in matter, and in rejecting the Newtonian theory of passive matter he dismissed Newton's doctrine that the active powers of matter were maintained by God's will, the view that the activity of nature was to be ascribed "to God as the immediate cause."[66]

In discussing God's relation to nature, Hutton emphasized teleology and divine wisdom. In his opinion, "the proper purpose of philosophy is to see the general order that is established among the different species of events, by which the whole of nature, and the wisdom of the system, is to be perceived."[67] Final causes were "the proper object of our knowledge"[68] in pursuing the "science of physics," and only when final causes were discovered could "the law of nature [be] investigated." Laws of nature could be known only in relation to final causes, and the design of the universe was manifested in the lawlike structure of nature: "in every law of nature there is system or design . . . it is then that in the system of nature we perceive wisdom, in seeing the purpose of those laws of nature."[69] In comprehending final causes the natural philosopher understands divine wisdom.

Hutton thus supposed that matter was active, and in stressing divine omniscience he claimed that the laws of nature could not be abrogated by divine action; in his view "we must deny the possibility of anything happening preternaturally or contrary to the common course of things."[70] In rejecting divine intervention in natural phenomena Hutton echoed Leibniz's statement to Clarke that "when God works miracles, he does not do it in order to supply the wants of nature, but those of grace,"[71] arguing that although the abrogation of the natural order would impugn the wisdom and foresight of God, this did not exclude God's supernatural intervention in cases where, as Hutton put it, "truths . . . [were] not to be discovered by natural means."[72] Echoing Leibniz in stressing divine wisdom and foresight, Hutton affirmed that the "laws of nature . . . [were] the decrees of God" and demonstrated "the existence of a superintending Being, who has conceived every thing in wisdom."[73]

---

[63] Hutton, *Dissertations*, 290. [64] Hutton, *Investigation*, II, 387.
[65] *Ibid.*, 404. For an account of Hutton's theory of matter and natural philosophy, cf. Heimann and McGuire, *op. cit.*, 281-93.. [66] Hutton, *Investigation*, II, 415.
[67] Hutton, *Dissertations*, 262. [68] *Ibid.*, 624. [69] *Ibid.*, 666.
[70] Hutton, *Investigation*, II, 309. [71] Alexander, *op. cit.*, 12.
[72] Hutton, *Investigation*, II, 309n. [73] *Ibid., II*, 310.

Hutton's theory of nature supposed a system of active powers whose self-sufficiency was not to be abrogated by divine intervention, but in regarding the active powers as immanent in nature he did not subsume God's agency under the laws of nature. Hutton pointed out that the term "nature" was figurative, corresponding to our structuring of experience, being a "creature of [our] fancy." The term "nature" applied to the "known part of the wise design, and powerful conduct of that infinite Being of whom we cannot form an adequate idea." Nature was "subordinate to God, who is the author of nature," and in formulating scientific explanations it was inappropriate to "ascribe this power of the universe to God, as the immediate cause." Because it was inappropriate for the natural philosopher to be "employing the term *God* in place of nature," the formulation of laws of "nature" could be regarded as "delegating the power of God, for the purposes that are perceived in natural things." Nevertheless, these statements were figurative, for God and divine power could not be regarded as being contained in or equivalent to "nature." Nature was "limited and changing" but God "is a Being which we cannot limit"; God is "infinite and unchangeable." Whereas "nature" is comprehended in terms of space and time it was absurd to suppose that "He who gave us the ideas of time and space can be limited by either of these," and Hutton dismissed the suggestion that "the author of nature was limited by natural things." God was transcendent over the order of nature, and "every existence is to be resolved . . . to that infinite Being and superintending mind."[74] The active powers immanent in the fabric of nature were thus grounded on divine agency.

The theories of the relationship between God and nature formulated by Priestley and Hutton attest to the shift in theological sensibility corresponding to the rejection of Newtonian principles in eighteenth-century British natural philosophy. In emphasizing divine omniscience rather than omnipotence, the foresight rather than the will of God, their ideas can be represented as a "religion of reason," but for these natural philosophers divine causality in nature was not to be subsumed under the concept of laws of nature.

University of Lancaster, England.

[74] *Ibid.*, II, 415-17.

V

Conversion of Forces and the Conservation of Energy

I

In his important paper on the origins of energy conservation Thomas Kuhn pointed to three factors which, he claimed, were of specific and decisive relevance to the "simultaneous discovery" of the principle of the conservation of energy in the years 1830 to 1850: the availability of conversion processes, the concern with engines and the influence of *Naturphilosophie*.[1] In this paper I wish to discuss the validity of regarding one of these factors—the availability of conversion processes—as a "triggerfactor"[2] which was specific and decisive to the period which Kuhn regards as that of simultaneous discovery, 1830 to 1850. Kuhn claims that only at this time and not earlier was this concept "close to the surface of scientific consciousness".[3] To this end I will discuss the group of British natural philosophers, Faraday, Grove and Joule, whom Kuhn includes in his list of "pioneers" of energy conservation and whose writings provided him with the bulk of his evidence for his stress on the role of conversion processes. By conversion processes Kuhn meant the early nineteenth century discoveries of the interconnexions of heat, electricity, light, magnetism and chemistry; and he claimed that "in the eighteenth century [such conversions] were isolated phenomena [and] few seemed of central importance to scientific research ... only after 1830 ... did they begin to look like conversion processes at all".[4] This view of the role of conversion processes is central to Kuhn's approach to the problem of the "simultaneous discovery" of energy conservation; however, I shall here suggest that the emphasis on the interconversion of the forces of nature in the writings of Faraday, Grove and Joule, which Kuhn ascribes to the influence of early nineteenth century experimental studies of conversion processes, is part of a clearly-articulated tradition in British natural philosophy and cannot be regarded as specific to the period 1830 to 1850. The belief in the interconversion of

© 1974 Munksgaard International Publishers Ltd., Copenhagen, Denmark.

natural powers and the unity of nature, grounded on an awareness of the relationships and connexions between the phenomena of heat, light, electricity and chemistry, was common in British natural philosophy by the late eighteenth century.

The notion of the universal convertibility of natural powers must be distinguished from that of the conservation of energy; yet this distinction seemed to be an insignificant one to Faraday and Joule. In 1853 Rankine published a paper *On the General Law of the Transformation of Energy* in which "the term *energy* is used to comprehend every affection of substances which constitutes or is commensurable with a power of producing change in opposition to resistance, and includes ordinary motion and mechanical power, chemical action, heat, light, electricity, magnetism and all other powers, known or unknown, which are convertible or commensurable with these".[5] The use of the term "energy" to mean "activity" was not uncommon (as in the usage by Davy cited below), so that his statement in the previous year that "all the different kinds of physical energy in the universe are *mutually* convertible"[6] could be understood as being no more than a restatement of the familiar doctrine of the interconversion of "forces"; but in the 1853 paper Rankine went on to state "the law of the conservation of energy" which held that "the sum of the actual [kinetic] and potential energies in the universe is constant".[7] This statement cannot be regarded as equivalent to Joule's doctrine of the indestructibility and convertibility of natural powers, yet Joule found nothing surprising or remarkable in the content and generality of this statement, merely noting, in a letter to William Thomson, that the "term energy employed ... seems admirably suited as the expression of any thing which might ultimately by proper transformation be exhibited in the form of, say, heat". The law of the conservation of energy as stated by Rankine seemed to Joule to express the way "light may be transformed into heat and the heat is transformed to be given out as chemical force."[8] Joule viewed the law as a statement of the interconversion of "forces". In a similar way, when Faraday stated the principle of the indestructibility of forces as the "Conservation of Force" in 1857, Maxwell objected that "we should keep our words for distinct things more distinct" because "energy is the power a thing has of doing work" while "force is the tendency of a body to pass from one place to another",[9] an objection later repeated by Rankine.[10] Faraday saw the difference between his term "force" and the term "energy" as being merely verbal; he explained his meaning by assuring Maxwell that by the term "force" he meant the "*source* or *sources* of all possible actions of the particles or materials of the universe; these being often called the *powers* of nature".[11] He defended his use of the expression "conservation of force" in an addendum to the paper which was published in 1859, distinguishing between "mechanical force" (that is, "force" in Maxwell's sense of the term) and his own use of the term "force" as the "*cause* of a physical action".[12] Given the meaning of "energy" (as used in Rankine's "law of the conservation of energy"), Faraday's concept of the "conservation of force" expressed something quite different from the "conservation of energy", for Faraday's doctrine expressed the conversion and indestructibility of natural powers; yet to Faraday the difference seemed minimal or even nonexistent. To Faraday and Joule the enunciation of the conservation of energy seemed to be a restatement of the concept of the convertibility and indestructibility of natural powers. This attests to the pervasive influence of the latter doctrine in early nineteenth century British natural philosophy. This conception of nature was grounded on the belief that, as Faraday expressed it in 1857, the "*annihilation* of force" would be "an effect equal in its affinity and its consequence with *creation*, and only within the power of Him who has created".[13] Joule emphasized that the indestructibility and conversion of forces expressed the self-sufficiency of nature, so that "we have reason to believe that the manifestations of living force [*vis viva*] on our globe are, at the present time, as extensive as those which have existed at any time since its creation, or, at any rate, since the deluge".[14] Once God had established the framework of natural forces these forces would remain constant in their total effect, a conception of nature which can be contrasted with Newton's view that "the variety of Motion which we find in the World is always decreasing",[15] thus necessitating continued divine sustenance of nature. The doctrine of the indestructibility of forces thus expressed a clearly-articulated theology of nature, in which divine providence was seen to be manifested in the wisdom and foresight by which God had established cosmic order in the indestructibility of forces. The importance of this doctrine in early nineteenth century British natural philosophy can be seen by an examination of the different ways in which it functioned in the thought of different natural philosophers. For Faraday it provided a framework for research; for Grove it was a fundamental doctrine which he wished to explicate and popularize; while for Joule it provided a framework for the interpretation of his experimental discoveries.

The basis of the doctrine, however, lay in late eighteenth century natural philosophy.

II

By the late eighteenth century the conception of nature as a selfcontained system, its activity maintained by a balance of opposing forces of attraction and repulsion, was widespread in British natural philosophy. These attractive and repulsive forces were frequently associated with different material entities, a view that is systematically presented in James Hutton's *Dissertations on Different Subjects in Natural Philosophy* (1792). Hutton considers the substratum (or "matter") underlying phenomenal entities (or "bodies") as a substance whose nature is defined in terms of intrinsic activity, so that "matter" is "considered as acting powers".[16] Hutton defined the essence of "matter" as being constituted by attractive and repulsive forces, supposing two kinds of "matter": gravitational matter which acted by the principle of attraction and matter emanating from the sun which acted by the principle of repulsion. The conservation of nature is maintained by "a just combination of those two different powers"[17] so that the "opposite powers are continually balancing one another". The "emanation of matter from the sun"[18] thus opposes and balances gravitational matter, and this solar substance is the principle of heat, light and electricity, these being "different modifications of the same matter".[19] Light and heat are considered as "active principles",[20] and his theory of the solar substance as a source for the regeneration of nature was probably derived from the Newtonian theory of the aether as an active principle and from Boerhaave's doctrine of fire as an activating agency in nature.[21] Nature is thus conceived as a self-regenerating system of active powers. This conception of nature can be contrasted with Newton's emphasis on the passivity of material entities, the activity of the natural order arising from divine sustenance.[22] Nevertheless Hutton's theory belongs to the Newtonian tradition in that he elaborated a theory of reality which is a development of Newton's theory of the primacy of forces in nature and which also displays the influence of Newton's conception of the aether as an active agent.[23]

The import of the theory emerges in Hutton's account of the theory of phlogiston. Arguing that there is no evidence in nature for decay without renewal he argues that the union of the matter of light and heat with chemical substances, "phlogistic matter", which is destroyed in combustion is regenerated by plants, for there "would also appear to be in the system of this globe, a reproductive power, by which the constitution of this world, necessarily decaying, is renewed".[24] Hutton stresses that the conservation of nature was an illustration of the "admirable contrivance of the system in which we are placed",[25] emphasizing that the balance and self-sufficiency of nature is maintained by chains of laws which were not to be abrogated by divine action. The selfsufficiency of nature manifests the wisdom of its creator. The unity of nature is maintained by the transformations of an aethereal principle whose essence is defined in terms of its intrinsic activity, its "powers" or "forces".

Hutton's conception of the unity of nature and of the interconversion of natural powers was a crucial feature of his system of natural philosophy, and he attempted to employ it so as to explain a wide variety of natural phenomena. He was especially concerned to explain the inter-relationships between the phenomena of heat, light, electricity and chemistry. The relationship between light and heat—for example, the fact that the emission of light is associated with a loss of heat—was readily explained by the fact that light and heat are modifications of the same repulsive "matter".[26] Phosphorescence was explained by the fact that light is "arrested and detained in a certain modification" within bodies, forming a "phlogistic substance"; this matter may be emitted from its connexion with a body and "resume its former character of light".[27] The production of light during chemical combustion was explained in terms of a loss of the matter of light from the combustible body.[28] Electricity was regarded as being related to light and heat in that it was yet a third modification of the solar substance, so that Hutton can argue that heat and light will affect the conduction of electricity by bodies. Thus "heat appears to dispose bodies for the conducting of electricity" so that "no solid substance appears to be proper for conducting electricity except such as contain phlogistic matter".[29]

Hutton's writings provide a full statement of a general position which was common in the period; Adam Walker's popular lectures, the *System of Familiar Philosophy* (1799) provides a different kind of example. Here light, fire and electricity are regarded as "modifications of one and the same principle", the principle of repulsion,[30] while the tendency of atoms to attract one another is supposed to be counteracted by the repulsive principle so that the operations of nature were maintained by "a balance of these two powers"³¹ of attraction and repulsion which are "opposing or antagonistic principles".³² The general Newtonian emphasis on attractive and repulsive forces provides the basis of a theory of the self-sufficiency of nature, viewed as arising from the balance between the attractive and repulsive principles.

Doctrines of this kind are expounded in Humphry Davy's *Essay on Heat, Light and the Combinations of Light* (1799). Here he argued that "the electric fluid is probably light in a condensed state ... its chemical action upon bodies is similar to that of light, and when supplied with repulsive motion by friction ... it takes the repulsive projectile form, and becomes perceptible as light".³³ Davy went on to argue that "no more sublime idea can be formed of the motion of matter than to conceive that the different species are continually changing into each other ... [so that] the gravitative, the mechanical, and the repulsive motions appear to be continually mutually producing each other".³⁴ This emphasis on the unity, transformations and interconversions of natural phenomena clearly echoes the ideas discussed above, and Davy in fact refers to Hutton's work when discussing the emission of light from combustible bodies in burning.³⁵ Like Hutton, he argued that phosphorescence was to be explained as arising from the union of light with bodies in a "state of loose combination".³⁶

Davy's ideas here are not, of course, to be equated with Hutton's. For example, Davy attacked imponderable fluid theories of heat with some severity, arguing that "heat has been proved to be a peculiar repulsive motion of the particles of bodies".³⁷ Nevertheless, certain features of this early paper are suggestive of the ideas discussed above, and of these the emphasis on the interconversions of forces was to be of fundamental importance for his electrical theory of chemical affinity. In his Bakerian lecture on *Some Chemical Agencies of Electricity* (1806) he claimed that the "attractive and repulsive forces [of electricity] are sufficiently energetic to destroy or suspend the actual operation of chemical affinity",³⁸ and he went on to argue that the electrical and chemical powers were so interconnected that it was likely that the electrical forces were "identical" with the forces of chemical affinity.³⁹ As in his "Essay on Heat and Light" he noted that the electrical and chemical powers were closely related to those of heat and light: "whenever bodies brought by artificial means into a high state of opposite electricities are made to restore the equilibrium, heat and light are the common consequences ... heat and light are like-

V

Conversion of Forces and the Conservation of Energy

wise the result of all intense chemical action".[40] Though Davy did not continue to maintain many of the physical concepts of his 1799 "Essay on Heat and Light" he did remain committed to perhaps the major feature of its basic worldview, that of the unity and interconversion of the different powers of nature. These ideas were restated in Davy's *Elements of Chemical Philosophy* (1812) where, like Adam Walker, he argued that "heat, or the power of repulsion may be considered as the *antagonist* power to the attraction of cohesion, the one tending to separate, the other to unite the parts of bodies".[41] He again drew attention to the relations between the phenomena of heat, light and chemistry, noting that "the heat and light produced in combustion seem to be merely indications of the strength of attraction of the acting substances",[42] that is their forces of chemical affinity.

Whether or not the works of Hutton and other eighteenth century natural philosophers were familiar to men such as Faraday, Grove and Joule, many of the seminal ideas developed by these earlier natural philosophers were expounded, though necessarily in a different context, in the writings of Humphry Davy, one of the most significant and influential of early nineteenth century scientists. There thus seems good reason to suppose that the late eighteenth century emphasis on the unity of nature and the conversions of natural powers would be familiar to natural philosophers working in the 1830s and 1840s. These ideas provided a conceptual framework into which the new experimental discoveries of conversion phenomena, particularly those of the 1820s by Oersted (relations between an electric current and magnetism), Seebeck (electrical effect of heat), and Melloni (the identification of light with radiant heat), could readily be incorporated. There seems little reason therefore to suppose that these experimental discoveries in themselves led to an awareness of the interrelationships among natural phenomena by natural philosophers; rather they reinforced and heightened that awareness.

III

The emphasis on the unity and conversion of forces was fundamental to the scope and direction of Faraday's experimental researches. Like Davy, Faraday was concerned to unravel the relationships between chemistry and electricity, and his experimental work on electrochemistry was undertaken as a means of investigating these relationships. He remarked in the course of a series of such experiments in 1834 that the chemical effects of electricity indicated that "the electric current is only another form of the forces of chemical affinity ... in other words, *the forces termed chemical affinity and electricity are one and the same*".[43] He drew attention to the implications of such interconnexions in a lecture on the "Relations of Chemical Affinity, Electricity, Heat, Magnetism and other powers of Matter" in the same year, where he suggested that "we cannot say that any one [of these powers] is the cause of the others, but only that all are connected and due to one common cause", and he gave demonstrations of "the production of any one [power] from another ... the conversion of one into another".[44] The unity of forces implied their interconversion. In 1840 he concluded his *Seventeenth Series of Experimental Researches* by emphasizing that natural powers could not be created from nothing, because "in no case ... [of the] *conversion* of one into another ... is there a pure creation of force; a production of power without corresponding exhaustion of something to supply it", and quoted a statement by P. M. Roget in support of this.[45] The concept of the unity and conversion of forces was thus closely linked to the doctrine of the indestructibility of powers. The belief in the conversion of forces was a pervasive feature of Faraday's physical thought, and it was therefore entirely to be expected that he should introduce his 1845 experimental paper on the action of magnetism on light with the statement that "the various forms under which the forces of matter are made manifest have one common origin; or in other words, are so directly related and mutually dependent, that they are convertible, as it were, one into another".[46] Faraday further developed the implications of this view in his *Thoughts on Ray-vibrations* of 1846. Here he argued that magnetism was to be explained in terms of the theory of lines of force and that he considered "radiation as a high species of vibration in the lines of force".[47] The relations of light and magnetism were thus explained in terms of lines of force diffused through space. In a similar way, Faraday had a continued interest in the relations between gravity and electricity, writing to Whewell in 1836 of his "notion ... that Universal Gravitation is a mere residual phenomenon of Electrical attraction and repulsion".[48] He made attempts to demonstrate this by experiment, though forced, in 1850, to conclude an attempt with the words: "here end my trials for the present ... [though] the results are negative ... [these experiments] do not shake my strong feeling of the existence of a

Conversion of Forces and the Conservation of Energy

relation between gravity and electricity, though they give no proof that such a relation exists".[49] For Faraday the belief in such conversions and interconnexions of forces was closely related to the notion of the indestructibility of forces, and this appears clearly in his 1857 paper *On the Conservation of Force* in which he attempted to demonstrate that "there is no apparent desire to loosen the force of the principle of conservation, even in those cases where the appearance and disappearance of force may seem most evident and striking" for here one found "the *conversion* of one form of power into another".[50] The doctrine of the conservation of force thus expressed the conversion and indestructibility of natural powers, and it is clear that this idea was central to Faraday's physical worldview, serving not only to provide a conceptual framework which would serve to make his discoveries intelligible but also to define the nature of his experimental investigations.

Grove's *Correlation of Physical Forces* (1846) is a work which manifestly belongs to the genre of popular science. P. G. Tait later felt "the impression of humbug" on reading the book, finding Grove "woefully loose and unscientific".[51] If one is expecting to find an account of the conservation of energy in the book, such a reaction is understandable, but Grove's purpose was to explicate the implications of conversion phenomena. In so doing he demonstrates the way such phenomena were seen to exemplify the balance of forces and the selfsufficiency of nature. Grove stated his purpose as being the desire to demonstrate that "the various imponderable agencies, or the affections of matter ... Heat, Light, Electricity, Magnetism, Chemical Affinity, and Motion are all Correlative, or have a reciprocal dependence ... [and] may, as a force, produce or be convertible into the other[s]".[52] The basis of Grove's argument for the convertibility of natural powers was his rejection of the belief that "the proper object of physical science [was] ... a search after essential causes",[53] for "an essential cause is unattainable—Causation is the will, Creation, the act, of GOD".[54] The purpose of physical science was not therefore to show which force was the "cause" of the others but to display the "facts and relations" persisting among different forces, for though "the word Cause may be used in a secondary and concrete sense, as meaning antecedent forces, yet in an abstract sense it is totally inapplicable".[55] Science is thus to be regarded as a search for secondary causes, that is antecedent forces, and the convertibility of forces follows from the fact that no force can ultimately be regarded as the "cause" of the others: all the forces of nature must be connected and interconvertible because "no force can strictly speaking be initial ... [so] there must be some anterior force which produced it". It therefore follows that "we cannot create force or motion any more than we can create matter".[56] The convertibility of forces is thus grounded on the self-sufficiency of nature, and Grove's account illustrates the way in which the concept of the convertibility and indestructibility of natural powers was linked to an explicit commitment to the belief in the self-sufficiency of nature.

Joule's experimental researches provide a further example of the influence of the notion of the conversion of forces in this period. Kuhn seems to me to be correct in arguing that the sequence of Joule's researches does not indicate any theoretical presuppositions relating to the connexions between different natural powers. Only as Joule's work proceeded did his theory begin to trace the "connective tissue" between conversion processes.[57] Though Joule did not undertake his experimental investigations as a programme to illustrate conversion phenomena, nor was he primarily concerned to develop the implications of such phenomena, nevertheless Joule was able to interpret his work as falling within the scope of the doctrine of the unity and conversion of forces. For Joule this doctrine was part of an accepted scientific worldview so that his experimental discoveries were readily incorporated within an already clearly-articulated framework of ideas. As he told William Thomson in an early letter of their correspondence, his work had provided "a proof of the convertibility of heat into power", that is, he had shown "the possibility of *converting heat into mechanical effect*",[58] and Joule himself never claimed the formulation of a general conservation principle in his papers. During the priority quarrel with Mayer he only claimed that he had provided support for the dynamical theory of heat and that he had measured the mechanical equivalent of heat. It was for this reason that "Mayer's paper [of 1842] was merely a speculation [while] mine [of 1843] was a research".[59] The existing framework of the conversion and indestructibility of natural powers, grounded on the argument that only God could destroy the agents of nature, was employed by Joule as a framework for the theoretical interpretation and explication of his experimental discoveries.

This is borne out by Joule's conclusion to his seminal paper *On the Calorific Effects of Magneto-Electricity and on the Mechanical Value of Heat* (1843), in which he measured the conversion of heat into mechanical effect, that "the grand agents of nature are, by the Creator's fiat, indestructible ... wherever mechanical force is expended an exact equivalent of heat is *always* obtained".[60] He made a similar remark in an 1845 paper which was concerned with the measurement of the mechanical equivalent of heat, remarking that "believing that the power to destroy belongs to the Creator alone, I entirely coincide with Roget and Faraday in the opinion that any theory which when carried out, demands the annihilation of force, is necessarily erroneous".[61] Joule was here referring to Faraday's 1840 paper mentioned above, and he clearly viewed his work as falling under the doctrine of the convertibility and indestructibility of forces. This commitment was supported by William Thomson who told Joule in 1848 how much he valued this paper "agreeing as I do with you when you say that you coincide with Faraday and Roget".[62] Joule amplified these ideas in his 1847 lecture on "Matter, Living Force and Heat". Here he argued that "we might reason, *a priori*, that ... absolute destruction of living force [*vis viva*] cannot possibly take place, because it is manifestly absurd to suppose that the powers with which God has endowed matter can be destroyed any more than that they can be created by man's agency."[63] It was by means of the conversion of forces that "order is maintained in the universe ... the entire machinery, complicated as it is, works smoothly and harmoniously".[64] The conversion and indestructibility of forces thus demonstrated the self-sufficiency of nature and "the wisdom and beneficence of the Great Architect of Nature".[65] These remarks should not be interpreted as expressing principles which were directly regulative of his research, but rather illustrate the intellectual context into which he could readily incorporate the results of his experimental work. Viewed in this way, Joule's work further attests to the importance of the doctrine of the self-sufficiency of nature and the conversion of forces in the period.

IV

In pointing to three factors which, he claimed, were of specific and decisive relevance to the "simultaneous discovery" of energy conservation in the years 1830 to 1850, Kuhn emphasized that viewing the phenomenon as being one of "simultaneous discovery" barred questions as to who discovered energy conservation first or whether any of the "pioneers" of energy conservation he included in his list really grasped the concept of the conservation of energy as such. Moreover, he made it clear that these pioneers do not all communicate the same thing, neither to one another nor to the historian, so that "only in view of what happened later can we say that all these partial statements [by the 'pioneers of energy conservation'] even deal with the same aspect of nature".[66] The fact that "pioneers" as different as, say, Joule and Mayer were in fact concerned with widely-differing problems, and the fact that only in retrospect do their views appear to be clear statements of the conservation of energy, does not at all weaken Kuhn's argument that the problem is one of "simultaneous discovery", for Kuhn was concerned to point to common factors which determined the direction and content of these different researches.[67] Kuhn's intention was to delineate common factors required for a "full statement of energy conservation" which, in the years 1830 to 1850 and not at an earlier period, were "close to the surface of scientific consciousness".[68] Kuhn was thus concerned to direct attention away from the "prerequisites" to the discovery of energy conservation towards the "trigger-factors" responsible for simultaneous discovery. Concepts and experimental procedures which were available for some years before the period 1830 to 1850 could not have provided immediate stimuli though they were clearly prerequisite for discovery.[69] In Kuhn's view, conversion phenomena were only of significance in the decade after 1830 and thus are regarded as trigger-factors.

The evidence presented in the present paper indicates that belief in the interconversion of forces was of significance, at least in Britain (and it was the British group whose writings provided Kuhn with the bulk of his evidence for his emphasis on conversion processes), much earlier than Kuhn would allow. The discovery of the new conversion processes is surely relevant to an understanding of the development of the concept of energy conservation, but the concern with conversion phenomena does not have the specificity to the period 1830 to 1850 which Kuhn claimed for it. Once the *specificity* of one of his factors to the period 1830 to 1850 is called into question Kuhn's analysis of "simultaneous discovery" is of course weakened, and his approach can only be maintained by pointing to different "trigger-factors". I would suggest—and the evidence presented in this paper supports this view—that Kuhn's formulation of the problem, as a "scientific revolution" occurring in the years 1830 to 1850, which is to be explained by trigger-factors specific to that period, is inadequate. The context of natural philosophy which is obscured when the problem is seen in

Conversion of Forces and the Conservation of Energy

terms of trigger-factors which explain simultaneous discovery is thus of crucial significance. Though Kuhn's formulation of the problem has the merit of conceptual clarity, it seems clear that the attempt to isolate certain "trigger-factors" from "prerequisites" cannot be maintained; and though it may still be possible to attach some meaning to the notion of "simultaneous discovery" in terms of retrospective awareness of a transformation of thought which became explicit and clearly articulated as the "conservation of energy" by around 1850, the analysis of the problem requires careful study of the context of natural philosophy.

NOTES

1. Thomas S. Kuhn: "Energy Conservation as an example of Simultaneous Discovery", *Critical Problems in the History of Science*, (ed) M. Clagett, Madison, 1959, pp. 321–56.
2. *Ibid.*, p. 345.
3. *Ibid.*, p. 323.
4. *Ibid.*, p. 324.
5. W. J. M. Rankine: "On the General Law of the Transformation of Energy", Philosophical Magazine 1853: 5: p. 106.
6. W. J. M. Rankine: "On the Reconcentration of Mechanical Energy in the Universe", Phil. Mag. 1852: 4: p. 358.
7. Rankine: *loc. cit.*, note 5.
8. J. P. Joule to W. Thomson, 3 February 1853. Letter J135, Kelvin collection, Cambridge University Library.
9. J. C. Maxwell to M. Faraday, 9 November 1857. L. Pearce Williams (ed.): *The Selected Correspondence of Michael Faraday*, Cambridge, 1971, vol. 2, p. 881.
10. W. J. M. Rankine: "On the Conservation of Energy", Phil. Mag. 1859: 17: 250–3.
11. Faraday to Maxwell, 13 November 1857. See Williams: *op. cit.*, p. 884.
12. M. Faraday: "On the Conservation of Force", *Experimental Researches in Chemistry and Physics*, London, 1859, p. 460. Published in Phil. Mag. 1859: 17: 166–9.
13. M. Faraday: "On the Conservation of Force", *Experimental Researches in Chemistry and Physics*, London, 1859, p. 447. The paper was published in Phil. Mag. 1857: 13: 225–39.
14. J. P. Joule: "On Matter, Living Force and Heat" [1847], *The Scientific Papers of James Prescott Joule*, London, 1884, p. 269.
15. Isaac Newton: *Opticks*, 4 edn, London, 1730, p. 399.
16. James Hutton: *Dissertations on Different Subjects in Natural Philosophy*, Edinburgh, 1792, p. 501.
17. *Ibid.*, p. 263.
18. *Ibid.*, p. 246.
19. *Ibid.*, p. 505.
20. James Hutton: *Dissertation upon the Philosophy of Light, Heat and Fire*, Edinburgh, 1794, p. 90.

21. P. M. Heimann: "'Nature is a perpetual worker': Newton's Aether and Eighteenth Century Natural Philosophy", Ambix 1973: 20: 1–25.
22. J. E. McGuire: "Force, Active Principles and Newton's Invisible Realm", Ambix 1968: 15: 154–208.
23. P. M. Heimann and J. E. McGuire, "Newtonian Forces and Lockean Powers: Concepts of Matter in Eighteenth Century Thought," Historical Studies in the Physical Sciences 1971: 3: 233–306.
24. Hutton: *op. cit.*, note 16, p. 214.
25. *Ibid.*, p. 233.
26. *Ibid.*, pp. 493ff.
27. *Ibid.*, pp. 517ff.
28. *Ibid.*, p. 176.
29. *Ibid.*, pp. 556f.
30. Adam Walker, *A System of Familiar Philosophy*, new edn., 2 vols., London, 1802, vol. 1, p. 14.
31. *Ibid.*, 6.
32. *Ibid.*, 18.
33. Humphry Davy: "An Essay on Heat, Light and the Combinations of Light" [in Thomas Beddoes: *Contributions to Physical and Medical Knowledge*, Bristol, 1799], *Collected Works of Humphry Davy*, 9 vols., London, 1839, vol. 2, p. 28.
34. *Ibid.*, p. 28n.
35. *Ibid.*, p. 39.
36. *Ibid.*, p. 32.
37. *Ibid.*, p. 26.
38. Humphry Davy: "On Some Chemical Agencies of Electricity" [1806], *Works*, vol. 5, p. 29.
39. *Ibid.*, p. 40.
40. *Ibid.*, p. 43.
41. Humphry Davy: *Elements of Chemical Philosophy*, 1812, in *Works*, vol. 4, p. 56.
42. *Ibid.*, p. 141.
43. Michael Faraday: *Experimental Researches in Electricity*, 3 vols., London, 1839–55, vol. 1, para. 918.
44. H. Bence Jones: *The Life and Letters of Faraday*, 2 vols., London, 1870, vol. 2, p. 47.
45. Faraday: *op. cit.*, note 43, vol. 2, para. 2071.
46. *Ibid.*, vol. 3, para. 2146.
47. *Ibid.*, p. 451.
48. Faraday to W. Whewell, 13 December 1836, printed in Williams: *op. cit.*, vol. 1, p. 306.
49. Faraday: *op. cit.*, note 43, vol. 3, para. 2717.
50. Faraday: "On the Conservation of Force", *Experimental Researches in Chemistry and Physics*, London, 1859 p. 455. On other aspects of Faraday's relation to earlier natural philosophy see P. M. Heimann: "Faraday's Theories of Matter and Electricity", Brit. J. Hist. Sci. 1971: 5: 235–57.
51. P. G. Tait to W. Thomson, 2 December 1862. Letter in Glasgow University Library.
52. W. R. Grove: *The Correlation of Physical Forces*, London, 1846, pp. 7f.
53. *Ibid.*, p. 5.

54. *Ibid.*, p. 50.
55. *Ibid.*, p. 5.
56. *Ibid.*, p. 48.
57. Kuhn: *op. cit.*, p. 326.
58. J. P. Joule to W. Thomson, 6 October 1848. Letter J61 in the Kelvin collection, Cambridge University Library.
59. J. P. Joule to P. G. Tait, 25 July 1863. Letter quoted in J. T. Lloyd: "Background to the Joule-Mayer Controversy", Notes and Records of the Royal Society 1970: 25: pp. 219f.
60. J. P. Joule: "On the Calorific Effects of Magneto-Electricity and on the Mechanical Value of Heat" [1843] *The Scientific Papers of James Prescott Joule*, London, 1884, p. 158.
61. J. P. Joule: "The Rarefaction and Condensation of Air" [1845], *ibid.*, p. 189.
62. W. Thomson to J. P. Joule, 27 October 1848. Letter J62 in the Kelvin collection, Cambridge University Library.
63. J. P. Joule: "Matter, Living Force and Heat" [1847], *op. cit.*, pp. 268ff.
64. *Ibid.*, p. 277.
65. *Ibid.*, p. 272.
66. Kuhn: *op. cit.*, p. 322.
67. The failure to perceive this vitiates the thesis of a paper by Y. Elkana: "The conservation of energy: a case of simultaneous discovery?", Arch. int. d'histoire des sciences 1970: numéro 90–91: 30–60. Elkana's point that the different "pioneers" discovered different things because they asked different questions, and that energy conservation is therefore not a case of simultaneous discovery, does not meet Kuhn's approach to the problem of "simultaneous discovery" here.
68. Kuhn, *op. cit.*, p. 323.
69. *Ibid.*, p. 345.

VI

FARADAY'S THEORIES OF MATTER AND ELECTRICITY

I

IN recent years a number of scholars have argued that Faraday's theories of matter and force were founded on concepts which were derived from Boscovich's *Theoria Philosophiae Naturalis* (1758).[1] The notion that Faraday's ideas display Boscovichean tendencies is not a new one: it was proposed by several of Faraday's immediate successors[2] and has been noted by more recent commentators.[3] Statements of this kind are not implausible as assertions of a general correspondence between Faraday's views on matter, as expressed in the "Speculation touching Electric Conduction and the Nature of Matter" of 1844,[4] and Boscovich's theory of point atomism, but Professor L. Pearce Williams has made much stronger claims for the dependence of Faraday's ideas on Boscovich's theory of matter.[5] Williams' interpretation has been questioned by recent scholarship,[6] and in this paper I wish to advance an alternative interpretation of Faraday's ideas on electricity and the nature of matter.

I will argue that Faraday's thought prior to the "Speculation" of 1844 does not show any correspondence to the Boscovichean theory of point atoms. In this period Faraday was developing a theory of electricity in terms of a particulate theory of matter which is perfectly comprehensible without employing Williams' assumption that "Faraday worked within . . . [the Boscovichean] framework from his earliest productive years".[7]

---

* Acknowledgement: I wish to express my gratitude to J. E. McGuire of the University of Leeds for his advice and helpful suggestions during the preparation of this paper.

[1] R. J. Boscovich, *Theoria Philosophiae Naturalis* (Vienna, 1758). The Venetian edition of 1763 was translated by J. M. Child: *A Theory of Natural Philosophy* (London, 1922). References will be to this Latin-English edition.

[2] See [Balfour Stewart and P. G. Tait,] *The Unseen Universe; or Physical Speculations on a Future State* (3rd edn., London, 1875), 102; J. H. Poynting, "The Growth of the Modern Doctrine of Energy" [1884], *Collected Scientific Papers* (Cambridge, 1920), 569 f., and "Atomic Theory (Medieval and Modern)" [1909], *ibid.*, 729. See also J. B. Stallo, *The Concepts and Theories of Modern Physics* (Cambridge, Mass., 1960), 179 ff. (republication of the 3rd, 1888 edn.).

[3] For example, see Emile Meyerson, *Identity and Reality* (trans.) Kate Loewenberg (London, 1930), 79; E. T. Whittaker, *A History of the Theories of Aether and Electricity* (2 vols., London, 1951-53), i, 193; Max Jammer, *Concepts of Force, a Study in the Foundations of Dynamics* (Harper edn., New York, 1962), 184.

[4] Michael Faraday, *Experimental Researches in Electricity* (3 vols., London, 1839-55), ii, 284-293. I will refer to this work as *Electricity*, followed by a volume number, and, where appropriate, Faraday's paragraph number, as in the following example: *Electricity*, ii, par. 2146. Otherwise page numbers will be given, for example: *Electricity*, ii, 284. *Faraday's Diary, Being the Various Philosophical Notes of Experimental Investigation made by Michael Faraday, D.C.L., F.R.S. during the Years 1820-1862* (London, 1932-36) contains little material relevant to this paper which is not in the *Electricity*.

[5] L. Pearce Williams, *Michael Faraday* (London, 1965).

[6] See J. Brookes Spencer, "Boscovich's Theory and its Relation to Faraday's Researches: An Analytic Approach", *Arch. Hist. Exact Sci.*, iv (1967), 184-202.

[7] Williams, *op. cit.* (5), 78. Williams nowhere provides evidence for this assumption. See Brookes Spencer, *op. cit.* (6).

The origins of this theory of Faraday's—which displays affinities with the dualistic theory of Berzelius—will not be discussed in this paper. I shall argue that an intellectual crisis can be delineated in Faraday's thought in the early 1840's, a crisis which arose as a result of the criticisms of Robert Hare. My account of Hare's critique and Faraday's response differs from that given by Williams in that Williams interprets the argument between Faraday and Hare in terms of Faraday's supposed adherence to Boscovich's theory of point atoms.[8] If my interpretation of Faraday's thought is adopted, it becomes clear that the "Speculation" was not a statement of concepts which Faraday had employed for years but never made explicit (as Williams suggests), but was proposed as a result of an intellectual crisis in which Faraday engaged in a critical examination of his fundamental assumptions.

I shall argue that Faraday's theory in the "Speculation" cannot be equated with ideas advanced by Boscovich in the *Theoria*, but is much more characteristic of a native British tradition in natural philosophy.[9] Faraday indicated that his ideas in the "Speculation" were in agreement with those of Boscovich,[10] and in view of the fact that Boscovich's ideas were well known in early nineteenth-century Britain[11]—indeed, Faraday certainly knew of Boscovich by the 1830's, if not earlier[12]—it is significant that Faraday's ideas in the "Speculation" differ so markedly from those of Boscovich. I shall suggest that Faraday's major source for the key ideas of the "Speculation" was Priestley's *Disquisitions Relating to Matter and Spirit* (1777), and I will demonstrate the similarity between ideas and expressions employed by Faraday and those used by Priestley. It is interesting that Priestley, like Faraday, gave the somewhat erroneous impression that the ideas he proposed were essentially the same as those of Boscovich. Priestley's statement that his ideas were like those of Boscovich could well have led Faraday to indicate that the theory of the "Speculation" resembled Boscovich's theory. References to Boscovich in this period must be regarded with caution, for the phrase "Boscovich's theory" was used in a misleadingly embracing sense. Though I shall indicate a link between Faraday's interests in the period around 1840 and

---

[8] *Ibid.*, 306 ff. Thus, Williams states that "Faraday's use of the theory of point atoms was here so basic that the presentation of his own ideas suffered seriously from his failure to make his debt to this theory explicit" (*ibid.*, 309).

[9] For a full discussion of this tradition, see P. M. Heimann and J. E. McGuire, "Newtonian Forces and Lockean Powers: Concepts of Matter in Eighteenth-Century Thought", *Historical Studies in the Physical Sciences*, iii (1971).

[10] Faraday, *Electricity*, ii, 290.

[11] Boscovich's ideas were much more widely known in early nineteenth-century Britain than Williams indicates; in fact, accounts of Boscovich's *Theoria* can be found, for example, in John Robison, *A System of Mechanical Philosophy* (4 vols., Edinburgh, 1822), i, 267-368; and in the article "Boscovich", *Encyclopaedia Britannica, Supplement to the Third Edition* (Edinburgh, 1803), i, 96-110. See also Richard Olson, "The Reception of Boscovich's Ideas in Scotland", *Isis*, lx (1969), 91-103.

[12] See R. P. Graves, *Life of Sir William Rowan Hamilton* (3 vols., Dublin and London, 1882-89), ii, 95, and also *ibid.*, i, 593.

Faraday's Theories of Matter and Electricity

the *possibility* of his interest being aroused in the *Disquisitions* and other works which could have served as an inspiration for the ideas in the "Speculation", it is likely that he came across these ideas prior to this period though such notions first appear in his work in the "Speculation".

My interpretation differs from that advanced by Williams in that I do not admit the influence of Boscovich on Faraday prior to 1840 and in that I consider that Williams too readily assimilates Faraday's position in the "Speculation" to that of Boscovich. I consider that the ideas in the "Speculation" were derived from a native British tradition exemplified by Priestley, and that although Boscovich's theory was apparently adopted by Priestley the distinguishing features of the "Speculation" are not to be found in Boscovich. Priestley incorporated aspects of Boscovich's theory into his argument and these ideas can be traced to Faraday, and so Faraday's views in the "Speculation" can be described as "Boscovichean" only in this sense. I distinguish a conceptual dichotomy in Faraday's thought between his early theories which were founded on the concept of particulate polarization, and his later work which was founded on the concept of the primacy of lines of force.[13] By evaluating Faraday's reasons for developing the arguments in the "Speculation" his theoretical ideas can be delineated and his contribution to the origins of field theory can be estimated.[14]

II

As a result of his discovery of electromagnetic induction in 1831[15] Faraday was led to explain the induction of an electric current between two coils of wire wound round an iron ring in terms of the creation of a "peculiar state"[16] or "peculiar condition"[17] in the ring. He called this "electrical condition of matter" the "*electrotonic* state",[18] regarding it as a "state of tension"[19] in the "particles" of the ring.[20] Faraday considered

---

[13] Williams seems to argue that in Faraday's later thought the supposed "Boscovicheanism" of the "Speculation" was abandoned, for if lines of forces were "the key to the unity of force phenomena" (Williams, *op. cit.* (5), 435), then Boscovich's theory of point atoms would cease to be necessary, for Williams states that in his later thought Faraday "had two types of polarity to work with; one was associated with the particles of matter and followed directly from the theory of point atoms ... The other involved the lines of force" (*ibid.*, 391). In this paper it is emphasized that the theory of the primacy of lines of force followed from the ideas in the "Speculation", for the significant feature of the "Speculation" was the notion of "matter" as "forces" diffused through space, as distinct from a Boscovichean theory of point atoms.

For a different interpretation of Faraday from that of Williams, one more in agreement with that advanced in the present paper, see Mary B. Hesse, *Forces and Fields: The Concept of Action at a Distance in the History of Physics* (London, 1961), 199-201.

[14] For an account of the relation between Faraday and Maxwell, see P. M. Heimann, "Maxwell and the Modes of Consistent Representation", *Arch. Hist. Exact Sci.*, vi (1970), 171-213.

[15] For a convincing reconstruction of Faraday's discovery, in which Boscovicheanism is not assigned a role, see Williams, *op. cit.* (5), 169-183, 191-202.

[16] *Electricity*, i, par. 60.
[17] *Ibid.*, par. 61.
[18] *Ibid.*, par. 60.
[19] *Ibid.*, par. 71.
[20] *Ibid.*, par. 73.

that when the current passed through the primary coil it caused a tension in the particles of the ring, leading to the creation of the electrotonic state. The electrotonic state caused the induction of the current in the secondary circuit, "the current . . . being as it were a contingency due to the existence of conducting power, and the momentary propulsive force exerted by the particles during their arrangement".[21] Thus, an electric current was considered as the creation and dissolution of the electrotonic state.

There are two important features of Faraday's argument. The first is that Faraday did not give any definition or description of the nature of this electrical condition, and the second is that whatever the nature of the electrotonic state, it was associated with the particles of matter. Faraday, then, was here adopting a particulate theory of matter, and the concept of electric action as a tension of the particles was to dominate his thought until 1844. A more explicit account of what was meant by the electrotonic state can be inferred from his discussion, in 1834, of problems in electrochemistry. His theory of electrochemistry was based on the view "of the *quantity* of electricity [being] associated with the particles of matter".[22] With characteristic caution he made it clear that he was not proposing an atomic theory as such, for he was "jealous of the term *atom*; for though it is very easy to talk of atoms, it is very difficult to form a clear idea of their nature".[23] Nevertheless, to speak of the particles of matter was rather different—the term "particle" does not imply indivisibility, for example—and he argued that "Although we know nothing of what an atom is, yet we cannot resist forming some idea of a small particle, which represents it to the mind",[24] and he was later to use the term "molecule". What Faraday was trying to do was to distinguish between the proposal of a theory of matter and a theory of the propagation of electrical action. The experimental facts indicated that electricity was associated with particles of matter, but he held back from developing a fully-fledged atomic theory of matter.[25]

The point I wish to emphasize is Faraday's extreme caution in committing himself explicitly to an atomic theory of matter. However, despite his attempt to side-step the problem by speaking merely of "particles", his view at this time (1834) was undeniably atomistic. Shortly afterwards he returned to the problem of the mode of electric action, and argued that electrochemical action involved "a peculiar state of tension

---

[21] *Ibid.*
[22] *Ibid.*, par. 870. Faraday explicitly refers to Berzelius here.
[23] *Ibid.*, par. 869.
[24] *Ibid.*, par. 852.
[25] This same caution can be seen in Faraday's reference to Boscovich in the 1844 "Speculation", as having supposed the atomic theory which involved the fewest assumptions (*Electricity*, ii, 289 f.). His only other citation of Boscovich, in the 1846 "Thoughts on Ray-vibrations", was for an even more limited purpose (*Electricity*, iii, 448).

Faraday's Theories of Matter and Electricity

or polarity".[26] Thus, he now introduced a term "polarity", which he associated with the "state of tension", and in 1837 he explained what he meant by the term: "With respect to the term *polarity* . . . I mean at present only a disposition of force by which the same molecule acquires opposite powers on different parts,"[27] clearly associating his state of tension with the polarity of molecules. Faraday was therefore advancing a physical view of the electrotonic state in which he envisaged matter being subjected to electrical tension, leading to a state of polarity in the molecules, and by polarity he meant opposite electrical states on different parts of the molecules. This theory is in accordance with a particulate theory of matter which is perfectly comprehensible without recourse to Boscovichean point atomism, and given his concern with clarity of exposition and his care over terminology, there seems little reason to suppose the influence of Boscovich.

It is important to note that shortly after the formulation of the electrotonic state Faraday temporarily abandoned the concept in favour of a theory of "lines of force". He found that if a magnet was placed in a jar of mercury and the mercury connected by wires to a galvanometer, rotating the magnet caused no difference on the effect the magnet had on the needle of the galvanometer,[28] and he concluded that there was a "*singular independence* of the magnetism and the bar in which it resides".[29] He therefore considered magnetism in terms of magnetic curves or lines, and he conceived the lines of force as entities which, though associated with the particles of matter, were also, in a sense, independent of them. Whereas he had at first suggested that electromagnetic induction was due to a tension of the particles of matter, the electrotonic state, he now suggested abandoning this concept in favour of a theory of lines of force, arguing that electromagnetic effects could be explained in terms of the action of magnetic curves or lines.[30] Thus, "the reasons which induce me to suppose a particular state [the electrotonic state] . . . have disappeared".[31] Already at this early stage in the development of his thought there was the suggestion that lines of force were entities independent of the particles of matter. These two modes of representation, lines of force and molecular polarization, were to dominate Faraday's thought, and were conceived as alternatives. As he later emphasized, the "*electrotonic state* . . . would coincide and become identified with that which would then constitute the physical lines of magnetic force".[32] The idea of particulate polarization was not renounced for long, however, and in his early

---

[26] *Electricity*, i, par. 949.
[27] *Ibid.*, par. 1304.
[28] *Ibid.*, par. 218-219.
[29] *Ibid.*, par. 220.
[30] *Ibid.*, par. 231, 238.
[31] *Ibid.*, par. 242.
[32] *Electricity*, iii, par. 3269.

thought the lines of force tended to be conceived as imaginary entities denoting the disposition of the individual particles as a result of electric tension being transmitted from particle to particle. In the very same paragraph in the 1837 paper "On Induction" in which he explained the meaning he attached to the term polarity, he pointed out that he had

> "used the phrases *lines of inductive force* and *curved lines* of force ... in a general sense only, just as we speak of the lines of magnetic force. The lines are imaginary, and the force in any part of them is of course the resultant of compound forces, every molecule being related to every other molecule in *all* directions by the tension and reaction of those which are contiguous."[33]

The particulate theory he was adopting was here quite explicitly stated in relation to the lines of force, and he made it quite clear that he used, as he put it, "the term *line of inductive force* merely as a temporary conventional mode of expressing the direction of the power".[34]

In his early thought it was the electrotonic state rather than lines of force which was the fundamental concept, and the notion of electrotonic state was connected to a particulate theory of matter. He spoke of induction as being "an action of the contiguous particles of the dielectric, which ... [are] thrown into a state of polarity and tension".[35] It is clear that at this stage the idea of a tension of matter described an existential condition of matter, whereas line of force merely expressed the direction in which the condition was manifested, a line of contiguous particles under strain.

Faraday's work on electrostatic induction was continued in further papers in 1838, and in all these papers he was quite emphatic that electrostatic action was not produced by action at a distance but by "an action of contiguous particles"[36] of matter. The particles were said to be polarized, and again he was quite clear what he meant by this, stating that "induction appears to consist in a certain polarized state of the particles, into which they are thrown by the electrified body sustaining the action, the particles assuming positive and negative points or parts, which are symmetrically arranged with respect to each other",[37] and he referred to the particles when polarized as being in a "forced" state.[38] Thus, electrostatic action occurred by means of the polarization of the particles of the dielectric medium, and he again returned to the concept of the electrotonic state to describe the action of the particles,[39] writing that "the intervening particles" assumed "a peculiar condition, which ... I have several times expressed by the term *electrotonic state*".[40]

[33] *Electricity*, i, par. 1304.
[34] *Ibid.*, par. 1231.
[35] *Ibid.*, par. 1224.
[36] *Ibid.*, par. 1295.
[37] *Ibid.*, par. 1298.
[38] *Ibid.*, par. 1298, 1671.
[39] *Ibid.*, par. 1661, 1729, 1733.
[40] *Ibid.*, par. 1729.

VI

Faraday's Theories of Matter and Electricity

It was in his account of electrostatic induction, however, that a problem implicit in the particular model he was employing was to cause Faraday great difficulty. This was his explanation of the mode of transmission of the electric tension from one polarized particle to another. He argued that the tension was transmitted not by action at a distance, but that "the first effect of an [electrically] excited body upon neighbouring matters" was "the production of a polarized state of their particles, which constitutes *induction*; and this arises from its action upon the particles in immediate contact with it, which again act upon those contiguous to them, and thus the forces are transferred to a distance".[41] His theory assumed that all the particles, whether of insulating or conducting matter, were "as wholes conductors", and were capable of being polarized by the influence of neighbouring charged particles.[42] The difference between conduction and insulation was not one of the mode of communication of force but in the rate of communication of force from particle to particle. When forces were readily communicated between contiguous particles, conduction occurred, and when communication of the forces was difficult, insulation occurred.[43] An important feature of his theory was his discovery that induction took place along curved rather than straight lines, and it was this fact which led him to speak of the alignment of the contiguous polarized particles as being represented by the "line of inductive force", a "temporary conventional mode" of representation.[44]

The crucial problem here is not what Faraday meant by particulate polarization—for even if his concept was not formulated mathematically it was clearly expressed[45]—but what he meant by contiguity. He argued that by contiguous particles he did not mean particles which touched one another, but merely neighbouring particles. As he put it, "I mean by contiguous particles those which are next to each other, not that there is *no* space between them."[46] He admitted that "the word *contiguous* is perhaps not the best that might have been used . . . for as particles do not touch each other it is not strictly correct",[47] but whatever ambiguities were implied by the use of the word, he was quite clear as to the meaning he attached to it. Faraday, then, did not represent the particles as being

---

[41] *Ibid.*, par. 1338.
[42] *Ibid.*, par. 1669, 1670.
[43] *Ibid.*, par. 1675.
[44] *Ibid.*, par. 1231.
[45] His concept of particulate polarization was expressed clearly enough for Maxwell to find it satisfactory in the *Treatise on Electricity and Magnetism* (Oxford, 1873), where he remarked that Faraday's induction "is a polarized state of the particles of the dielectric, each particle being positive on one side and negative on the other" (§ 54). The evidence does not support Williams' contention, with respect to this theory of polarization, that Faraday did not suppose a separation of charge, but that Faraday supposed the particles were "distorted", and that "this distortion seems to be what Faraday meant by polarization . . . There was not, in short, a *separation* of the forces so that equal quantities of positive and negative force were concentrated at each end of the particle" (Williams, *op. cit.* (5), 307).
[46] *Electricity*, i, par. 1665n; see also par. 1615, 1164n.
[47] *Ibid.*, par. 1164n.

VI

polarized as a result of mutual contact. He argued that if particles were separated by a vacuum

"it does not follow from this theory, that the particles on opposite sides of such a vacuum could not act on each other . . . nothing in my present views forbids that the particle should act at the distance of half an inch on all the particles forming the inner superfices of the bounding sphere, and with a force consistent with the well known law of the squares of the distance."[48]

Thus, despite abandoning action at a distance in favour of a theory of action between "contiguous" particles, Faraday was here obliged to admit, implicitly, short-range distance forces between the polarized "contiguous" particles. If a particulate theory was adopted and action by contact not maintained, this was implicit. Faraday argued that "I believe ordinary induction in all cases to be an action of contiguous particles consisting in a species of polarity, instead of being. an action of either particles or masses at sensible distances",[49] here denying action at "sensible distances", but in discussing action across a vacuum he recognized the action of forces across distances of "half an inch".

There was an undoubted difficulty in Faraday's reasoning here, which was immediately taken up by Robert Hare of Pennsylvania. Hare reminded Faraday that "you believe induction to be an action of *contiguous* particles, consisting of a species of polarity, instead of being an action of either particles or masses at '*sensible distances*' ",[50] and went on to ask Faraday: "if induction be not 'an action either of particles or masses at *sensible* distances', how can a particle, situated as above described, '*act at the distance of half an inch on all the particles forming the disk of the inner superficies of the bounding sphere?*' What is a sensible distance, if half an inch is not?"[51]

In his reply to Hare, Faraday stated that he had considered "*ordinary* induction" to be "an action of contiguous particles, being particles at insensible distances", and though induction across a vacuum was not an ordinary instance, "yet I do not perceive that it cannot come under the same principles of action".[52] Faraday argued that induction at insensible distances ("an ordinary instance") was similar to induction at sensible distances, the same principles of action being held to apply in each situation. This statement was of great significance, for it exposed the crucial difficulty in Faraday's theory of action between "contiguous"

---

[48] *Ibid.*, par. 1616.
[49] *Ibid.*, par. 1165.
[50] R. Hare, "A Letter to Prof. Faraday, on certain Theoretical Opinions", *Phil. Mag.*, xvii (1840), 44; *Electricity*, ii, 251. Though at this time, as he later conceded, Hare appears to have been somewhat confused by the meaning Faraday attached to "contiguity" (see R. Hare, "Second Letter to Prof. Faraday", *Phil. Mag.*, xvii (1841), 465-477), this did not affect the validity of this point here, for Hare was questioning Faraday's denial of action at "sensible distances" at the same time as supposing action at "the distance of half an inch".
[51] *Electricity*, ii, 252.
[52] *Ibid.*, 267.

Faraday's Theories of Matter and Electricity

particles, the fact that no account of the nature of this action had been proposed.

In his reply to Hare, Faraday suggested that the problem of accounting for action at sensible distances was identical to that of accounting for action at insensible distances, for he claimed that there was an analogy between the two situations. Thus, it did not matter if the distances between contiguous particles was sensible or insensible, for short-range forces would still have to be supposed as acting across the insensible distances, but if action at a distance was denied the mode of action of these forces would remain undefined. The difficulty raised by Hare was not answered, for Faraday had admitted, implicitly, that if there was a problem in accounting for action at sensible distances if action at a distance was denied—the difficulty raised by Hare—then the *same* problem applied to action at insensible distances; and having denied action at a distance, Faraday could as little account for one as for the other.

Whether or not Faraday thought of the problem in quite these terms, there can be little doubt that he was not satisfied with his reply to Hare, and sought to overcome the problem of explaining action across insensible distances. His response, though delayed, was a fundamental reconsideration of his basic concepts.

III

Faraday's response was the "Speculation touching Electric Conduction and the Nature of Matter", dated 25 January 1844,[53] and the delay was no doubt due, in part, to the crucial nature of Hare's intervention and the significance of the change in view engendered. In the "Speculation" he began by considering the particulate theory of matter and difficulties which followed from the adoption of such a theory and the denial of distance forces. He now would not admit the possibility of forces acting across insensible distances, and he ascribed a role to the void between particles to account for the communication of electric action. The theory of the action between "contiguous" particles across insensible distances was abandoned. He pointed out that according to the atomic theory as usually conceived, material atoms would not be in contact with one another, and therefore the interatomic void in bodies "must be taken as the only continuous part". This led to further difficulties, because the difference between conducting and non-conducting bodies would then be due to the void between the particles. In 1838 he had supposed that all the particles were "as wholes conductors", the difference between conduction and insulation being in the rate of communication of electric action between particles. But if action between "contiguous" particles across insensible distances was now abandoned in favour of ascribing

[53] *Ibid.*, 284.

a role to the void between particles, then the explanation of the difference between conducting and non-conducting bodies in terms of the interatomic void was an absurdity, for "space may be proved to be a non-conductor in non-conducting bodies and a conductor in conducting bodies".[54] For Faraday, space could not have causal or dispositional properties, and he was later to emphasize that "Mere space cannot act as matter acts."[55]

Hare's critique had led Faraday to abandon his theory of the action of "contiguous" particles across insensible distances, and to assign a role to the void within bodies in the propagation of electric action. Despite the absurdity resulting from the adoption of the atomic theory, Faraday continued, nevertheless "the mind is most powerfully drawn . . . to the acknowledgement of centres of force",[56] and he concluded that the safest theory to adopt was that of Boscovich, for this contained the fewest assumptions. However, as I have already indicated, Faraday's reference to Boscovich here must be regarded with some caution.

Faraday then attempted to avoid the contradictions arising from the adoption of a particulate theory, and his answer to the problem was the denial of a particulate theory of matter. He went on to distinguish between the particles of matter and the powers associated with these particles, defining "the particles of matter away from the powers a, and the system of powers or forces in and around it m", and argued that the properties of a substance "in regard to light, or magnetism, or solidity, or hardness, or specific gravity, must belong to it, in consequence of the properties or forces of the m, not those of the a, which, without the forces, is conceived of as having no powers. But then surely the m is the *matter*".[57] Faraday identified the system of powers and forces as the matter, claiming that "the a or nucleus vanishes, and the substance consists of the powers or m; and indeed what notion can we form of the nucleus independent of its powers?"[58] He went on to suggest that all knowledge of the atom was limited to the ideas of its powers, and that there was no "philosophical necessity"[59] to assume the existence of matter independent of the powers.

These views were re-stated, in a slightly different form, in a manuscript on "Matter" written shortly after the "Speculation".[60] Here Faraday argued that the hardness of matter was due to the "*force of repulsion* . . . in the particles", and "if we recognize matter by its *hardness*, what do we other than recognize by our sensations a force exerted by it?" Thus, matter was known only by the powers it exerted, the properties

---

[54] *Ibid.*, 286f.
[55] *Electricity*, iii, par. 2787.
[56] *Electricity*, ii, 289.
[57] *Ibid.*, 290.
[58] *Ibid.*
[59] *Ibid.*, 291.
[60] This manuscript, which is at the Institution of Electrical Engineers, London, and dated 19 February 1844, has been published: see T. H. Levere, "Faraday, Matter, and Natural Theology—Reflections on an Unpublished Manuscript", *Brit. J. Hist. Sci.*, iv (1968-69), 96-107.

Faraday's Theories of Matter and Electricity

of matter were dependent on forces, and there was no experience of the supposed material nuclei. For this reason, since a nucleus could not be conceived away from its forces, there was no reason "for supposing that there is any such nucleus in a particle of matter". Faraday went on to give further justification for his view by arguing that God's omnipotence could as easily arrange nature in this way as in any other: "Is the lingering notion which remains in the minds of some, really a thought, that God could not just as easily by his word speak power into existence around centres, as he could first create nuclei & then clothe them with power?"[61]

Thus far his argument has little relation to Boscovich's theory, for according to Boscovich matter consisted of "perfectly divisible & nonextended points",[62] round which alternating concentric spheres of attracting and repelling forces were grouped. An attempt to separate the "matter" from the point centres was quite contrary to Boscovich's system, for according to Boscovich the point centres of force *constituted* the matter, though Faraday was confused about Boscovich's view here.[63] For Boscovich, the mathematical points had "an attribute ... an inherent propensity to remain in the same state of rest, or of uniform motion in a straight line ... This propensity is the origin of what we call the 'force of inertia'",[64] and he spoke of the points as being "endowed with a force of inertia".[65]

The latter part of the "Speculation" must now be considered. Faraday went on to make it clear that in his view the centres of force were always in contact, for "matter will be *continuous* throughout, and in considering a mass of it we have not to suppose a distinction between its atoms and any intervening space".[66] Therefore the contradiction which

---

[61] In my view this remark of Faraday's does not justify the inference Levere draws from it, that Faraday adhered to "force atomism" because "it fitted in with the world picture imposed by his religion" (Levere, *op. cit.* (60), 101). Faraday clearly had a religious approach to nature, but his remark in the "Matter" MS. indicates his belief in God's omnipotence over the order of nature, not that his religious views determined his adoption of any *particular* theory of matter, or that "force atomism" more readily displayed the action of divine power over nature. The theological implications of Faraday's theory of matter warrants further examination.

[62] Boscovich, *Theory of Natural Philosophy* (London, 1922), § 7.

[63] Faraday erroneously connected the notion of separating the matter from the atoms with Boscovich, for he remarked that "in Boscovich's theory *a* [the particles of matter away from the powers] disappears" (*Electricity*, ii, 290). If as I shall suggest, Faraday derived these arguments from Priestley, he could well have gained the impression that this was Boscovich's view from Priestley. Priestley identified Boscovich's ideas with those of John Michell, and in expounding these ideas stated that "take away attraction and repulsion and matter vanishes" (*Disquisitions Relating to Matter and Spirit* (2nd edn., 2 vols., Birmingham, 1782), i, 36).

[64] Boscovich, *op. cit.* (62), § 8.

[65] *Ibid.*, § 516. As Maxwell pointed out, speaking of atoms as "centres of force without attributing to them any finite extension ... would be quite legitimate, provided centre of force is admitted to have mass" (draft MS.

University Library, Cambridge, Add. MSS. 7655). Maxwell noted that Boscovich "did not forget, however, to endow his mathematical points with inertia" (J. C. Maxwell, "Action at a Distance", *Scientific Papers*, ed. W. D. Niven (2 vols., Cambridge, 1890), ii, 317). William Whewell remarked that a "collection of mere centers of force can have no inertia" (*Philosophy of the Inductive Sciences*, 2nd edn., 2 vols., London, 1847), i, 433n, using this as an argument against Boscovich. I am grateful to Dr D. M. Knight for drawing my attention to this note, which does not appear in the first edition.

[66] *Electricity*, ii, 291.

Faraday claimed was implicit in the atomic theory as usually conceived, that space would have to be both an insulator and a conductor, disappeared if matter was supposed continuous and filling all space. Not only this, but he supposed "the mutual penetrability of matter", for if two atoms were centres of power they would "mutually penetrate to the very centres", though it did not necessarily follow "that the centres shall always coincide; that will depend on the relative disposition of the powers of each atom".[67]

He concluded that this fitted very harmoniously "with the old adage, 'matter cannot act where it is not'".[68] This overcame the problem raised by Hare, for now he considered the atoms, or centres of power, as mutually penetrable; the atoms would penetrate to "the very centres", for by virtue of the forces, which constituted the matter, the atoms extended continuously throughout space, and interactions between material particles were due to interactions between their forces conceived in this way. As he put it, "each atom extends, so to say, throughout the whole of the solar system, yet always retaining its own centre of force".[69] The particulate theory of matter was abandoned, and the contradictions which followed from the adoption of such a theory and the denial of distance forces were avoided.

This theory of the mutual penetrability of matter is quite different from Boscovich's theory, where impenetrability was an important property of the atoms. According to Boscovich "repulsive forces act at very small distances, & these forces increase indefinitely as the mutual distances decrease",[70] and the two point centres would never touch.

Faraday re-stated these views, and somewhat modified them, in the "Thoughts on Ray-vibrations"[71] written in 1846, where he again discussed the problem of the relation between the point centres and the properties of matter. He pointed out that gravitation and solidity were not due to "the weight and contact of the abstract nuclei", but that "the one is the consequence of an *attractive* force, which can act at distances as great as the mind of man can estimate or conceive; and the other is the consequence of a *repulsive* force, which forbids for ever the contact of any two nuclei".[72] It should be noted that Faraday was here asserting the impenetrability of the point centres, contradicting his earlier statement in the "Speculation". Once again, it is clear that Faraday's theory of forces has little connection with Boscovich's force law, for Faraday did not even hint at the system of alternating zones of attractive and repulsive forces which was fundamental to Boscovich's theory.

Though it is clear that this theory cannot be equated with Boscovich's

[67] *Ibid.*, 292 f.
[68] *Ibid.*, 293.
[69] *Ibid.*
[70] Boscovich, *op. cit.* (62), § 360.
[71] *Electricity*, iii, 447-452.
[72] *Ibid.*, 449.

Faraday's Theories of Matter and Electricity

system, and that it displays only a very loose resemblance to Boscovich's ideas, it does show correspondences with a tradition of British natural philosophy. The arguments that matter was only known by its powers and forces, and that the powers constituted the essence of matter,[73] was used, for example, by Robert Greene in *The Principles of the Philosophy of the Expansive and Contractive Forces* (1727), by Joseph Priestley in the *Disquisitions Relating to Matter and Spirit* (1777), by James Hutton in the *Dissertations on Different Subjects in Natural Philosophy* (1792), and by Thomas Exley in the *Principles of Natural Philosophy* (1829).[74] The penetrability of matter was asserted by John Michell, approvingly reported by Priestley in *The History and Present State of Discoveries relating to Vision, Light, and Colours* (1772) and in the *Disquisitions*. Faraday's further argument that the powers of matter were due to repulsive and attractive forces was a commonplace by Faraday's time, deriving from Newton's statement in the *Opticks* that the "attractive Force [of particles] can reach but to a small distance from them . . . where attraction ceases, there a repulsive Virtue ought to succeed",[75] which was a characteristic notion of the early Newtonians.[76] In the early nineteenth century statements similar to the one made by Faraday in the "Thoughts on Ray-vibrations" were made, for example, in John Robison's *System of Mechanical Philosophy* (1822),[77] Thomas Young's *Course of Lectures on Natural Philosophy* (1807),[78] Exley's *Principles of Natural Philosophy*, and—significantly for Faraday—in O. F. Mossotti's paper "On the Forces which regulate the Internal Constitution of Bodies".[79]

Though Faraday did not indicate his sources, nevertheless Faraday's views in these two speculative papers exhibit a striking similarity to ideas expressed in some of the works I have mentioned, and it is possible to suggest a direct link between Faraday's interests and likely reading and the possibility of his interest being aroused in Priestley's *Disquisitions* and

---

[73] A similar argument was used by Kant in the *Metaphysische Anfangsgründe der Naturwissenschaft* (Riga, 1786). Thus, Kant argued that "Matter fills space, not by its mere *existence*, but by a *special moving force*", Kant's *Prolegomena and Metaphysical Foundations of Natural Science*, trans. E. B. Bax (London, 1883), 170, the only forces of matter which could be conceived being the attractive and repulsive forces (*ibid.*, 171).

[74] See also James Hutton, *An Investigation of the Principles of Knowledge, and of the Progress of Reason, from Sense to Science and Philosophy* (3 vols., Edinburgh, 1794), ii, 383 ff., for a discussion of the "powers" of matter. A full analysis of the significance of the term "power"—which was derived from Locke—in Hutton and Priestley will be given in P. M. Heimann and J. E. McGuire, *op. cit.* (9). Faraday's idea that matter consisted of its powers was later followed by James Croll, "On the Nature of Heat Vibrations", *Phil. Mag.*, xxvii (1864), 346 f.; "On Certain Hypothetical Elements in the Theory of Gravitation", *ibid.*, xxxiv (1867), 449-460.

[75] Isaac Newton, *Opticks* (4th edn., Dover reprint, London, 1952), 395.

[76] See J. T. Desaguliers, *A Course of Experimental Philosophy* (3rd edn., 2 vols., London, 1763), ii, 337; Robert Smith, *A Compleat System of Opticks* (London, 1738), 88 f.; John Rowning, *A Compendious System of Natural Philosophy* (4th edn., London, 1745), part 2, 6.

[77] John Robison, *op. cit.* (11), i, 253 ff.

[78] Thomas Young, *A Course of Lectures on Natural Philosophy and the Mechanical Arts* (2 vols., London, 1807), i, 618.

[79] R. Taylor (ed.), *Scientific Memoirs*, i (London, 1837), 448-469.

Exley's *Principles*, in which discussions of the mutual penetrability of matter and the notion that matter consisted of its forces can be found. I will first sketch out the possible link between Faraday's interests and these works, and then briefly consider passages in them which show a marked similarity to Faraday's speculations. However, it must be emphasized that there is no concrete evidence that Faraday read Exley or Priestley; and, indeed, he might have read them quite independently of the link I will suggest.

In December 1836 Faraday received the paper mentioned above from Mossotti, which he forwarded to Richard Taylor for publication in the *Scientific Memoirs*. Faraday's enthusiasm for the paper can be seen from a letter he wrote to Whewell,[80] from the fact that he lectured on Mossotti's theory at the Royal Institution,[81] and from his mention of Mossotti's theory both in the "Speculation"[82] and in the "Thoughts on Ray-vibrations".[83] His interest in the paper was in connection with Mossotti's attempt to show that all the forces in nature had one common origin. Mossotti's theory was one in which two kinds of fundamental particles, atoms of matter and atoms of ether, were supposed to be endowed with attractive and repulsive forces. Mossotti began by arguing that the resistance opposed by bodies to compression increased indefinitely, and because "their molecules have not come into contact with each other, it shows that the force which they exercise is repulsive at the least distances",[84] and he went on to suggest that at greater distances the force would become attractive. Atoms of matter were said to be surrounded by atoms of ether; like atoms were mutually repulsive, but atoms of matter were attracted by atoms of ether.[85]

Mossotti's ideas were reported in the *Philosophical Magazine*,[86] which led to a response in that journal by Thomas Exley, who pointed out[87] the resemblance between Mossotti's theory and his own views as proposed in the *Principles of Natural Philosophy* (1829). Exley noted that he too had proposed two kinds of fundamental atom, and had argued that both

---

[80] Williams, *op. cit.* (5), 295.
[81] *Phil. Mag.*, x (1837), 317.
[82] *Electricity*, ii, 293.
[83] *Electricity*, iii, 450.
[84] Mossotti, *op. cit.* (79), 448.
[85] Gravitation was explained, because as "the repulsion of the molecules of matter is a little less than their attraction of the atoms of the aether, or than the mutual repulsion of the atoms themselves, this will be sufficient to leave an excess of attraction which ... would exactly represent the universal attraction" (*ibid.*, 450). It was this which interested Faraday, for, as he told Whewell, it agreed with "my notion which I think I mentioned to you that Universal Gravitation is a mere residual phenomenon of Electrical Attraction and Repulsion" (Williams, *op. cit.* (5), 295). Faraday made attempts to demonstrate this by experiment, though forced, in 1850, to conclude his first attempt with the words: "Here end my trials for the present. The results are negative. They do not shake my strong feeling of the existence of a relation between gravity and electricity, though they give no proof that such a relation exists" (*Electricity*, iii, par. 2717).
[86] *Phil. Mag.*, x (1837), 320 f.
[87] Thomas Exley, "Remarks on Mr. Mossotti's Theory of Physics", *ibid.*, 496-504.

Faraday's Theories of Matter and Electricity

kinds of atom consisted of "an indefinite sphere of force", a repulsive force acting in a "small concentric sphere" from the centre being succeeded by an attractive force.[88] Thus, Exley and Mossotti did not identify one type of atom with one force and the other type of atom with the other force.[89]

Given Faraday's knowledge of Mossotti's theory and his interest in the theory, it is likely that he read Exley's paper, published in a journal which he read and of which he was a distinguished contributor. In both Exley's and Mossotti's papers there were statements on attractive and repulsive forces which correspond to Faraday's remark in the "Thoughts on Ray-vibrations". However, thus far there has been no suggestion of ideas similar to the theory in the "Speculation", for the remarks on attractive and repulsive forces so far considered do not correspond to the theory proposed in the "Speculation". The origins of the theory in the "Speculation" is the intriguing problem, and any attempt to answer it must be conjectural. However, it is clearly possible that Faraday might have followed up Exley's paper by referring to the *Principles of Natural Philosophy*. In addition to the paper in the *Philosophical Magazine* in 1837, Exley had read a paper to the British Association in 1836, and would do so again in 1838,[90] these papers being extensions of his ideas on matter. Exley's ideas were being publicized at this time and Faraday might well have considered them of interest, particularly given his concern with Mossotti's theory.

The editors of the *Philosophical Magazine* clearly regarded the correspondence over Mossotti's ideas of interest, and "referred those who are interested in the philosophy of molecular action, to the account of the theories of Father Boscovich and Mr. Michell, in Dr. Priestley's Disquisitions on Matter and Spirit".[91] In view of Faraday's interest in Mossotti, and his later concern with Hare's critique, in which he had to face problems arising from forces acting across insensible distances (that is, molecular forces), it is possible that Faraday did refer to Priestley. Certainly his habit, when faced with difficulties, was to read up on all aspects of the problems, and if he did respond to the difficulties raised by

---

[88] *Ibid.*, 497.

[89] In this they differed from theorists who identified the forces of attraction and repulsion with two kinds of matter. See Gowin Knight, *An Attempt to Demonstrate, that all the Phaenomena in Nature, May be explained by Two Simple Active Principles, Attraction and Repulsion* (London, 1748); Bryan Higgins, *A Philosophical Essay Concerning Light* (London, 1776); James Hutton, *Dissertations on Different Subjects in Natural Philosophy* (Edinburgh, 1792) and *A Dissertation upon the Philosophy of Light, Heat, and Fire* (Edinburgh, 1794); Robert Harrington, *A New System on Fire and Planetary Life* (London, 1796); Adam Walker, *A System of Familiar Philosophy* (new edn., 2 vols., London, 1802). See Heimann and McGuire, *op. cit.* (9).

[90] *Report of the British Association for the Advancement of Science, 1836* (London, 1837), "Notes and Abstracts of Communications", 30; *Report of the British Association . . . 1838* (London, 1839), "Notes and Abstracts of Communications", 68.

[91] *Phil. Mag.*, x (1837), 357. This note by the editors followed a short paper advancing a theory somewhat similar to those of Mossotti and Exley: Paul Cooper, "Notice of a Theory of Molecular Action", *ibid.*, 355-357.

Hare by reading Exley and Priestley, he would have found some interesting passages, statements, in fact, which he could well have written himself.

In the *Principles of Natural Philosophy* Exley pointed out that the nature of the powers of attraction and repulsion was not known, and that "an atom consists of an indefinite small sphere of repulsion which is the central part of an indefinitely extended concentric sphere of attraction".[92] He emphasized that "the central points . . . will be utterly impenetrable to each other, since the repulsion there is infinite",[93] and distinguished his theory from that of Boscovich, for "the first sphere of repulsion, and the extreme sphere of attraction of that philosopher are retained; but the intermediate alternate spheres of attraction and repulsion are rejected".[94] This statement has affinities with the "Thoughts on Ray-vibrations", but remarks more in accordance with the "Speculation" were made in the "Concluding Remarks" to Exley's book. Here Exley argued that "we know nothing of *matter*, but by the forces which it exerts, and which doubtless constitute its nature",[95] and in a "Note" following these "Remarks" he elaborated on this, stating that all that can be understood of an atom is

"a balance of forces on every side of a central point, and this is all we can understand of it, whatever substratum we may imagine to exist; for it is nothing but mere hypothesis, the effect of imagination, and a vulgar notion, to judge, that there is a minute solid impenetrable mass necessary to constitute an atom of matter, on which forces act . . . we know nothing of such little solids, we have never seen them, nor felt them, nor perceived them by any one of the senses; if they do exist at all, we have not been affected by them but only by the forces of attraction and repulsion . . . the forces are considered as constituting the essence of matter".[96]

The relation between these remarks and Faraday's argument in the "Speculation" and the manuscript on "Matter" is clear, and it is interesting that Faraday's point in the "Matter" manuscript, that God could have created the world in any way he chose, was also made by Exley, who remarked that just as God could create solid atoms, He could also arrange powers to "constitute an atom having all the properties which we observe in the elements of matter", for God could act in an "infinity of ways".[97]

Turning now to Priestley's *Disquisitions*, there was a striking passage in which Priestley wrote that

"The principles of the Newtonian philosophy were no sooner known, than it was seen how few, in comparison, of the phenomena of nature, were owing

---

[92] Thomas Exley, *Principles of Natural Philosophy: or, a New Theory of Physics, founded on Gravitation and applied in explaining the general properties of matter, the phaenomena of Chemistry, Electricity, Galvanism, Magnetism, and Electro-Magnetism* (London, 1829), 3.
[93] Ibid., xx.
[94] Ibid., xxi.
[95] Ibid., 470.
[96] Ibid., 473.
[97] Ibid., xxvii.

Faraday's Theories of Matter and Electricity

to *solid matter*, and how much to *powers* . . . It has been asserted . . . that . . . all the solid matter in the solar system might be contained within a nut-shell . . . Now, when solidity had apparently so very little to do in the system, it is really a wonder that it did not occur to philosophers sooner . . . that there might be no such thing in nature."[98]

Priestley was here alluding to the Newtonian view that there was a paucity of matter in the world; as McGuire has shown, the notion of an almost matterless universe regulated by immaterial forces was strongly rooted in Newtonian natural philosophy.[99] Priestley extended the view of nature which attached more importance to force than to matter, and, moreover, he argued that matter was such in that it possessed powers. He stated that John Michell had maintained this view which he represented as being essentially the same as that of Boscovich, though Boscovich did not in fact separate "matter" from the point centres.[100] Priestley argued that "we know nothing more of the nature of *substance*, than that it is something which supports properties",[101] but he did not only maintain that matter was only known through its powers but went on to advance an ontological statement that the essence of matter was its extension and powers. He defined matter as a "substance possessed of the property of *extension*, and of *powers of attraction or repulsion*".[102] He supposed that the powers were "essential to the *actual existence* of all matter",[103] arguing that "take away attraction and repulsion and matter vanishes".[104] Priestley regarded solidity and substance as the mere effects of the powers, and supposed the "*mutual penetration of matter*",[105] for whatever solidity a body had "it is possessed of it only in consequence of being endued with certain *powers*".[106] Solidity and impenetrability were merely the effects of the powers, and it was the powers, rather than solidity, which made matter

---

[98] Joseph Priestley, *Disquisitions Relating to Matter and Spirit* (2nd edn., 2 vols., Birmingham, 1782), i, 22.

[99] J. E. McGuire, "Body and Void and Newton's *De Mundi Systemate*: some new sources", *Arch. Hist. Exact Sci.*, iii (1966), 206-248. See also Arnold Thackray, " 'Matter in a Nut-shell': Newton's *Opticks* and Eighteenth-century Chemistry", *Ambix*, xv (1968), 29-53. The notion of the paucity of matter in the universe in eighteenth-century natural philosophy will be discussed further in the paper referred to in note (9). Examples of such statements include: Adam Walker, *A System of Familiar Philosophy* (new edn., 2 vols., London, 1802), i, 38, where Priestley's language was followed: "the whole matter of the universe is supposed capable of being compressed into the size of a walnut".

[100] Boscovich did not replace "matter" by its forces (see above (63-65)). It should be noted that Priestley's account of Michell's ideas is our only source for knowledge of his theory of matter. Priestley emphasized that Michell's theory explained the penetrability of bodies to light (Priestley, *op. cit.* (98), i, 24). See also Bryan Higgins, *A Philosophical Essay Concerning Light* (London, 1776), 246. It was this requirement of the extreme porosity of matter—to explain the penetrability of bodies to light—that Thomas Young opposed in arguing against the particulate theory of light, for the wave theory of light "does not require the disproportion [between matter and void] to be by any means so great" (*op. cit.* (78), i, 459).

[101] Priestley, *op. cit.* (98), i, 27.
[102] *Ibid.*, ii.
[103] *Ibid.*, 11.
[104] *Ibid.*, 36.
[105] *Ibid.*, 26.
[106] *Ibid.*, 13.

what it was. Thus, the essence of matter was its extension and inherent powers of attraction and repulsion. Priestley's statements on the nature of matter show a clear relation to Faraday's arguments in the "Speculation"; like Faraday, Priestley used the phrase "the mutual penetrability of matter".[107] The similarity between Priestley's theory of matter and Faraday's ideas in the "Speculation" is so striking that it seems reasonable to suggest that Faraday knew of Priestley's work, but there is no documentary evidence that Faraday did draw on Priestley's *Disquisitions*. Whether or not Faraday did read Priestley and Exley, in the years around 1840 or at any other time, cannot be known, but enough has been said to show that Faraday's ideas in the "Speculation" show a much greater resemblance to the views of Priestley and Exley than to those of Boscovich. I do not wish to over-stress the possibility of making clear connections, particularly as Faraday's speculations, if deriving at all from Priestley and Exley, show an eclectic use of ideas found in the earlier writers.

It is important to note that Priestley's *Disquisitions* was widely discussed; indeed Exley's work drew some comment.[108] Though neither Exley's *Principles* nor Priestley's *Disquisitions* were in the library of the Royal Institution, Priestley's *History and Present State of Discoveries relating to Vision, Light, and Colours* (1772), which contained an account of the theory of the mutual penetrability of matter, was in the library.[109] In addition, well-known works by Charles Hutton and Thomas Young which contained discussions of theories of the penetrability of matter were also in the library.[110] Thus, a possible source for an account of Priestley's *Disquisitions* was the article on "Matter" in Charles Hutton's *Mathematical and Philosophical Dictionary* (1795/6) where Priestley was reported as arguing that matter was "a substance, possessed of the property of extension, and of powers of attraction or repulsion, which are not distinct from matter . . . but absolutely essential to its very nature and being; so that when bodies are divested of these powers, they become nothing at all", and of asserting the "penetrability of matter".[111] Boscovich, too, was held to suppose that matter was not impenetrable, and though Hutton did not accept these ideas his discussion of them could well have been familiar to Faraday. These ideas were also discussed by Thomas Young in his *Course of Lectures on Natural Philosophy* (1807). Young maintained that extension could scarcely be considered as separate from impenetrability "unless we conceive that it cannot occupy space, without

[107] *Ibid.*, 25.
[108] See Exley's reply to his critics in his *Physical Optics; or the Phaenomena of Optics explained according to Mechanical Science; and on the known principles of gravitation* (London, 1834), 204 f.
[109] B. Vincent, *A New Classified Catalogue of the Library of the Royal Institution* (London, 1857), 198. See Joseph Priestley, *The History and Present State of Discoveries relating to Vision, Light, and Colours* (London, 1772), 390-394. This passage was quoted in the *Disquisitions*, i, 24-28.
[110] See Vincent, *op. cit.* (109), 191, 228.
[111] Charles Hutton, *A Mathematical and Philosophical Dictionary* (London, 1795-96), ii, 83.

excluding other bodies from it. This opinion has indeed been maintained by some philosophers" who considered "each particle of matter as a sphere of repulsion, extended without being impenetrable".[112] Young explicitly associated the notion "that matter itself is penetrable, that is, immaterial" with Boscovich,[113] but he also referred to Priestley in this connection,[114] and like Hutton he did not accept these ideas.

Another statement of the penetrability of matter and of the argument that matter was known only by its properties was to be found in another well-known work, William Nicholson's *Introduction to Natural Philosophy* (1782), which was also in the library of the Royal Institution.[115] Nicholson stated that "Matter is known to us only by its properties . . . we are totally ignorant of the substance in which these properties are united",[116] and he went on to argue that all the effects of impenetrability could be ascribed to the action of a repulsive force and asked: "why not attribute all effects of the same nature to this cause, which we know exists, instead of assuming an impenetrability that can never be proved?"[117] Nicholson's remarks clearly reflect the influence of Priestley and provide another possible source for Faraday's speculations.

Despite the difficulty of establishing Faraday's sources, nevertheless I think one point is clear: that Faraday's ideas must be seen as part of a native British tradition of natural philosophy, a tradition which, in nineteenth-century Britain, went under the label of "Boscovich's theory". One possible reason for the stress on Boscovich's role is that Priestley developed his theory of matter in accordance with his religious ideas[118] which were widely regarded as atheistic, and which achieved for their author an unwelcome notoriety. Priestley's own explicit statement of the similarity between his views and those of Boscovich clearly provided later writers with a justification for ascribing ideas more properly characteristic of Priestley's *Disquisitions* to Boscovich's *Theoria*, but an unwillingness to be associated with Priestley's theological doctrines may have led Faraday to suppress Priestley's role.[119]

[112] Young, *op. cit.* (78), i, 607.
[113] *Ibid.*, i, 458.
[114] *Ibid.*, ii, 323.
[115] The first edition (1782) was in the library (see Vincent, *op. cit.* (109), 190), as was the first volume of the fourth edition (which will be quoted here).
[116] William Nicholson, *An Introduction to Natural Philosophy* (4 edn., 2 vols., London, 1796), i, 7.
[117] *Ibid.*, 15.
[118] Priestley made it clear (*op. cit.* (98), i, 26) that he denied the (Newtonian) notion of passive, inert matter found in Andrew Baxter, *An Enquiry into the Nature of the Human Soul* (London, 1733). Baxter emphasized that "passivity, and want of power in a substance" was "necessary in the universe" (*ibid.*, 28), for by denying activity as inherent in matter he was able to maintain the "necessity of an immaterial Mover in all spontaneous motions" (*ibid.*, 36), that is, a distinction between matter and spirit. By denying the notion of passive, solid matter, Priestley was able to deny the matter-spirit duality. For a discussion of Newton's theory of active principles see J. E. McGuire, "Force, Active Principles, and Newton's Invisible Realm", *Ambix*, xv (1968), 154-208.
[119] In the absence of knowledge of Faraday's theological views, little more can be said on this question. See (61). His membership of the Sandemanian Church is clearly relevant.

IV

The change in viewpoint which followed his speculations on matter as consisting of centres of force was announced almost immediately by Faraday in the "Thoughts on Ray-vibrations" in 1846. His view was that "the particle indeed is supposed to exist only by those forces and where they are it is", and he stated that "the consideration of matter under this view gradually led me to look at lines of force as being perhaps the seat of the vibrations of radiant phenomena",[120] and of electric and magnetic actions. In conceiving matter as diffused through space as forces he had abandoned his particulate theory of matter, and he began to think of explaining electric action in terms of the interaction of such forces. In the years following 1846 he was to return to the lines of force view, which he assimilated to his new theory of matter; the lines of force theory in turn was transformed, for he began to conceive the lines as possessing real physical existence in space. In the "Thoughts on Ray-vibrations" he went on to speak of the lines of force as being "known to connect particles",[121] and by "particles" here he meant centres of force. Thus, in the "Thoughts on Ray-vibrations" the lines of force were associated with the centres of force. As Williams has pointed out,[122] his discoveries in the years following 1846 were gradually to convince him that the lines of force themselves were the primary entities. The theory of action as propagated by the polarization of the particles of matter was replaced by a theory of the interaction of forces, his ideas being developed in terms of the primacy of lines of force; he began to conceive the lines of force as being entities independent of the particles of matter. However, this change in physical outlook stemmed from the "Speculation", as Faraday made quite clear in the "Thoughts on Ray-vibrations".

The first example of this can be seen in his explanation of the action of magnets on crystals, the magnecrystallic force, where he explained the effect in terms of the crystal placing itself along the lines of magnetic force.[123] Significantly, this led him to doubt the existence of a state of polarity in the crystal, for he found that a crystal which would align itself along the magnetic lines of force would continue to do so even if turned through 180°, and from this it was clear that "either end of the mass or of its molecules, is, to all intents and purposes . . . like the other end; and in many cases, therefore, the words *axial* and *axiality* would seem more expressive than the words *polar* and *polarity*".[124]

The problem of the polarity of crystals subjected to a magnetic force was carried over to Faraday's work on diamagnetism. Though he had at first concluded that under the influence of a magnetic force the particles

---

[120] *Electricity*, iii, 447.
[121] *Ibid.*, 451.
[122] Williams, *op. cit.* (5), 381.
[123] *Electricity*, iii, par. 2479.
[124] *Ibid.*, par. 2472.

Faraday's Theories of Matter and Electricity

of magnetic and diamagnetic substances would be polarized in opposite directions, under the same conditions of action, arguing that "an explanation of the movements of the diamagnetic bodies, and all the dynamic phenomena consequent upon the actions of magnets on them, might be offered in the supposition that magnetic induction caused in them a contrary state to that which it produced in magnetic matter",[125] later experiments led him to the conclusion that diamagnetics were not polarized.[126] This led to a new emphasis in his ideas, for prior to this the lines of force had been used to distinguish the direction of a chain of molecules subjected to tension, the particles being supposed to be polarized, but he now began to abandon the concept of the polarization of the particles in favour of the primacy of the lines of force. His failure to detect the polarity of diamagnetics had the consequence that the molecules of diamagnetics were not polarized, but merely interacted with the lines of force.

The polarity of molecules was an essential feature of Wilhelm Weber's theory of diamagnetism,[127] and this theory was therefore rejected by Faraday. His new view of the fundamental importance of the lines of force as entities distinct from the particles of matter can be seen in his explanation of paramagnetism and diamagnetism in terms of the relative magnetic conductibility of the bodies and the surrounding medium, that is, in terms of the propensity of lines of force to pass through the bodies.[128]

Thus, the effects were no longer explained in terms of the polarization of molecules, and in a paper of 1852, "On the Physical Character of the Lines of Force",[129] he argued that electric and magnetic lines of force had a real physical existence, stating that the forces "can only have relation to each other by *curved* lines of force through the surrounding space; and I cannot conceive curved lines of force without the conditions of a physical existence in that intermediate space".[130] The lines of force were the primary entities possessing a real physical existence, though

---

[125] *Ibid.*, par. 2429.
[126] *Ibid.*, par. 2640-2701.
[127] Wilhelm Weber argued that there was a difference between the molecules of paramagnetic and diamagnetic substances, and his theory was based on Ampère's theory that a magnet consisted of molecules within each of which electric currents circulated. Weber suggested that the molecules of diamagnetic substances did not have any electric currents circulating within them, but such currents were induced by a magnet. He assumed that "in the single molecules, or around them, closed paths exist in which the ... [electrical] fluids can move without resistance" (Weber, "On the Connexion of Diamagnetism with Magnetism and Electricity", Tyndall and Francis (eds.), *Scientific Memoirs, Natural Philosophy* (London, 1853), 166). Thus, according to Weber, currents circulated within the molecules of paramagnetic bodies, but not within the molecules of diamagnetic bodies, and he argued that paramagnetic and diamagnetic bodies would exhibit opposite polarities, under the same conditions of excitation, as the currents in the magnetic molecules circulated in the opposite direction to the induced currents in diamagnetic molecules. See W. Weber, "On the Excitation and Action of Diamagnetism according to the Laws of Induced Currents", Taylor, *Scientific Memoirs*, v (London, 1852), 477-488 (*Wilhelm Webers Werke* (6 vols., Berlin 1892-94) iii 255-268).
[128] *Electricity*, iii, par. 2806-2835.
[129] *Ibid.*, par. 3243-3299.
[130] *Ibid.*, par. 3258.

their nature remained unclear, whereas he had earlier considered them as mere conventional symbols for expressing the direction of polarized particles. In replacing the tension and polarization of the particles of matter by the primacy of the lines of force Faraday was arguing that polarity did not exist as a *state of matter*. However, he continued to use the *term* "polarity", speaking of "the polarity of each line of force",[131] but he now used the term to represent the direction of the lines of force, not the polarization of particles. As he said, "My view of polarity is founded upon the character in direction of the force itself."[132] Again, he pointed out that electrostatic lines of force would terminate on charges, opposite charges being at opposite ends of each line, but as he emphasized, "no condition of *quality* or *polarity* has as yet been discovered"[133] in the lines of electrostatic force. Thus, even though electrostatic lines of force had charged ends there was no condition of polarization *within* the lines. This was quite at variance with his abandoned theory of molecular polarization where the lines of force represented a line of polarized particles.

V

It is clear that the viewpoint formulated in the "Speculation" had a critical effect on Faraday's representation of electric and magnetic action. From the view that matter extended continuously throughout space by its forces, he was led to return to the notion of lines of force to represent these actions. The ontological status of the lines of force changed, being regarded as real, not imaginary, entities in his later thought. The physical reality of the lines of force and the theory of polarity as merely a directional term, enabled the older theory, based on the polarization of the particles of matter, to be abandoned, and the difficulties raised by Hare to be avoided. Difficulties of course remained; there was the problem of the "medium" in which lines of force existed,[134] and the hoped-for unification of gravitational, electrical, and magnetic actions[135] was not without its attendant problems.[136]

It must be emphasized that Faraday's concept of matter filling all space continuously by its forces did not involve the identification of matter—or force—with space. He pointed out in 1850 that in arguing

[131] *Ibid.*, par. 3361.
[132] *Ibid.*, par. 3307.
[133] *Ibid.*, par. 3249.
[134] For the necessity of a "magnetic medium", see *Electricity*, iii, par. 3277, 3361. Though Faraday did consider the possibility that the lines of forces were transmitted by an action which was "a function of the aether" (*ibid.*, par. 3075), he was sceptical as to the existence of the aether (*ibid.*, 451).
[135] Faraday endeavoured to explain gravitation by supposing lines of gravitational force spread out through space (*Electricity*, iii, 574). Maxwell echoed this hope in a letter to Faraday of 9 November 1857. This letter is at the Institution of Electrical Engineers, London, and was published in L. Campbell and W. Garnett, *Life of James Clerk Maxwell* (2nd edn., London, 1884), 202-204. For a discussion of this, see my paper cited in (14).
[136] *Electricity*, iii, 572, and "On the Conservation of Force", *Experimental Researches in Chemistry and Physics* (London, 1859), 443-463.

that "the lines of magnetic force can traverse pure space" he did not wish "to confound space with matter" for "Mere space cannot act as matter acts",[137] and he emphasized that "space therefore comports itself independently of matter".[138]

I have tried to show how Faraday's conceptual framework changed after Hare's intervention, and to indicate the possible sources of Faraday's theory of matter in the "Speculation". There can be no doubt of the close association between Faraday's theories of matter and his theories of electricity, and his work can be seen to illustrate Priestley's remark that

"Hitherto, philosophy has been chiefly conversant about the more sensible properties of bodies; electricity, together with chymistry, and the doctrine of light and colours, seems to be giving us an inlet into their internal structure, on which all their sensible properties depend. By pursuing this new light, therefore, the bounds of natural science may possibly be extended, beyond what we can now form an idea of."[139]

---

[137] *Electricity*, iii, par. 2787.
[138] *Ibid.*, par. 2789.
[139] Joseph Priestley, *The History and Present State of Electricity* (3rd edn., 2 vols., London, 1775), i, xiv. Cf. Faraday in the "Speculation": "Light and electricity are two great and searching investigators of the molecular structure of bodies" (*Electricity*, ii, 286).

VII

»Geometry and Nature«: Leibniz and Johann Bernoulli's Theory of Motion

I

This paper is a study of Johann Bernoulli's *Discours sur les loix de la communication du mouvement* (1727)[1], one of the major contributions to the *vis viva* controversy. The historiographical tradition that stresses the significance of the *vis viva* controversy has emphasized arguments about whether "force" was to be measured by the "quantity of motion" (mv) or the *vis viva* (mv^2), regarding the participants in the "controversy" as ranged behind one or the other of these two mechanical concepts.[2] There is, however, a further dimension to the discussions of the conceptual status of these concepts in early eighteenth-century mechanics; for while it is true that arguments about the measure of "force" were important, nevertheless the problem at issue was not confined to disagreements over which of two competing concepts was to be employed for the measure of "force" but was also concerned with the dynamical function and ontological status of the *vis viva* concept. The construal of Bernoulli's *Discours sur le mouvement* in the context of the *vis viva* controversy has had the consequence that the conceptual status of his *vis viva* principle has not been fully delineated.[3]

It has become customary to describe the *Discours sur le mouvement* as displaying the "Leibnizian" character of Bernoulli's dynamics,[4] but this description is ambiguous. Although his intentions—in affirming the elasticity of matter and the conservation of *vis viva* or in attempting to provide a mathematical proof of the distinction between *vis mortua* and *vis viva*[5] and of the measure of *vis viva* by means of a discussion of the

© 1977 Munksgaard International Publishers Ltd., Copenhagen, Denmark.

expansion of elastic springs—may be regarded as being an explication of a theory of motion in consonance with Leibniz's natural philosophy, yet the extent to which Bernoulli's ideas were directly derivative upon Leibniz's dynamics or were essentially original remains unclear. Moreover, the extent and significance of Bernoulli's differences from Leibniz have not been gauged. Bernoulli's dynamical theory of the relation between *vis mortua* and *vis viva* viewed as the counterpart to the relation between infinitesimals and finite quantities was undoubtedly based on Leibnizian arguments, but Bernoulli's view of the ontological status of infinitesimals and of the conceptual status of *vis mortua* and *vis viva* differed significantly from that of Leibniz. There is therefore some ambiguity over the extent and limit of Bernoulli's adoption of Leibnizian principles in his *Discours sur le mouvement*, and the aim of this paper is to provide an analysis of this treatise on motion in the context of Bernoulli's relationship with Leibniz, so as to permit an assessment of Bernoulli's intentions and of the nature and limit of his debt to Leibnizian dynamics.

The conservation of *vis viva* was a fundamental principle in both Leibniz's and Bernoulli's dynamics, but the acceptance and use of the *vis viva* concept by eighteenth-century scientists did not entail a commitment to Leibniz's natural philosophy. As will be shown below, in contrast to Johann Bernoulli, Daniel Bernoulli employed the *vis viva* concept as a mathematical and dynamical quantity without accepting Leibniz's view of its status as a dynamical concept; and Colin MacLaurin, while vehemently rejecting all claims of the generality and special status of the principle of the conservation of *vis viva*, nevertheless considered it to be a principle applicable to certain special problems. The complexity of attitudes to the function and status of the *vis viva* concept in early eighteenth-century dynamics is obscured when views of the principle are considered in terms of the battle lines of the "*vis viva* controversy". This complexity of the interpretations of the principle stems in part from its historical origins. The conservation of the quantity mv^2 was first stated by Huygens: "when two bodies strike each other the sum of the products of the magnitude of each body multiplied by the square of their velocities is always the same before and after impact".[6] For Huygens the quantity mv^2 was merely a number, without ontological significance. This becomes clear in his discussion of the compound pendulum in his *Horologium Oscillatorium* (1673), his demonstration that the distance through which the centre of gravity of a body or system of bodies will fall under the action of gravity is equal to the height to which it can ascend as a result of the velocity acquired in the fall; there is thus an equality between actual descent and potential ascent of the centre of gravity of a system of moving bodies.[7] From Galileo's law of falling bodies the descent of each body is proportional to the square of its velocity, and the conservation of the quantity mv^2 follows from Huygens' "chief principle of mechanics",[8] the equality of descent and ascent of the centre of gravity of a system bodies. The quantity mv^2 became for Leibniz the fundamental entity in his science of dynamics; termed *vis viva* it was, together with *vis mortua* (*mdv*), the phenomenal manifestation of the primitive active force which, unlike extension and motion, was "real"[9] and substantially present in all corporeal entities. Leibniz declared that "the concept of *forces* or *powers* ... for whose explanation I have set up a distinct science of *dynamics*, brings the strongest light to bear upon our understanding of the true concept of substance".[10] For Leibniz, his science of dynamics emphasized the special dynamical status of *vis viva*.

In his *De vera notione virium vivarum* (1735) Johann Bernoulli asserted that *vis viva* was to be considered as a "power of acting" rather than as action itself, for it subsisted even if it was not actually manifested. *Vis viva* was "a real and substantial entity, which subsisted by itself in as much as it is in it to do so [*quantum in se est*]"; *vis viva* was "absolute and without a correlate," existing independently of all other entities, and hence was always conserved.[11] Bernoulli was almost certainly echoing Descartes and Newton in using the phrase *quantum in se est*[12]; just as Newton employed this expression to stress the close conceptual associations between *vis insita* (the force innate in matter) and *vis inertiae* (the force exerted by a body during a change of its state),[13] later stating that *vis inertiae* was an essential property of matter,[14] in using the expression Bernoulli emphasized the conceptual status of *vis viva* as a real, substantial and conserved dynamical entity. It is apparent, as Bernoulli himself pointed out,[15] that his view of the dynamical status of the *vis viva* concept displays Leibnizian rather than Huygenian echoes.

Johann Bernoulli's *De vera notione virium vivarum* was not only intended as a supplement to the *Discours sur le mouvement* but was an attempt to provide conceptual foundations for his use of the *vis viva* concept in a paper (written in 1727) containing theorems illustrating the conservation of *vis viva*.[16] Bernoulli pointed out[17] that his solution of the vibrating string problem was included among these theorems and that he had grounded his analysis, as he had demonstrated in a later paper,[18] on the principle of the conservation of *vis viva*. Bernoulli's use of this principle in his treatment of the vibrating string shows that he considered that the *vis viva* concept could be employed as a mathematical theorem, without regard to the question of its ontological status. For Bernoulli the *vis viva* concept had a dual aspect: in terms of its phenomenal effects and quantitative equivalence, as a mathematical quantity which could be employed in the solution of certain problems; and as a fundamental dynamical concept, its conceptual status being made intelligible by Bernoulli's adoption of the categories of Leibnizian dynamics.

Daniel Bernoulli employed the conservation of *vis viva* as a dynamical theorem in his *Hydrodynamica* (1738), but he rejected Johann Bernoulli's view of its ontological status. Daniel Bernoulli referred to Johann Bernoulli's *Discours sur le mouvement* and to his theorems on the application of the *vis viva* principle, but adopted the *vis viva* principle in the manner formulated by Huygens as "the equality between actual descent and potential ascent," emphasizing that he "preferred to adopt this hypothesis in the words of Huygens rather than of my father [Johann Bernoulli]" because of the controversies raging over the Leibnizian doctrine of the conservation of *vis viva*.[19] The fundamental dynamical principle of Daniel Bernoulli's *Hydrodynamica* is the application to a fluid of Huygens' principle of the equality between actual descent and potential ascent, the distance through which the centre of gravity of the particles of the fluid fall being equal to the height to which it can ascend as a result of the velocity acquired in the fall, from which followed the conservation of mv^2.[20] Daniel Bernoulli thus considered the *vis viva* concept as expressing the mechanical principle of the equality between actual descent and potential ascent rather than the principle of the conservation of *vis viva* as formulated by Leibniz, and maintained this view in a later paper on the *vis viva* principle,[21] refusing to accept the ontological overtones of the *vis viva* concept fundamental to Johann Bernoulli's formulation of the principle of the conservation of *vis viva*.

MacLaurin firmly rejected Johann Bernoulli's view of the *vis viva* principle. MacLaurin directed many arguments against Bernoulli's *Discours sur le mouvement*, and concluded that the principle of the conservation of *vis viva* "is not to be held a general principle or law of action,"[22] but he went on to argue that the conservation of the quantity mv^2 applied to the special case of perfectly elastic bodies, those bodies which after collision "restore themselves with the same force with which they are compressed".[23] Moreover, MacLaurin argued that the principle of the conservation of *vis viva* of Leibniz and Johann Bernoulli was "much the same"[24] as "the principle, which, by Mr *Huygens*, was called the *conservatio vis ascendentis*",[25] the conservation of the quantity mv^2 in the descent and ascent of the centre of gravity of a system of bodies. The principle of the conservation of *vis viva* was thus applicable only to special cases, and though "it may be of use in several enquiries concerning the motion of bodies [it] ... is not [a] general" principle of motion.[26]

This account of the different attitudes to the *vis viva* principle of Daniel Bernoulli and MacLaurin highlights Johann Bernoulli's view of the principle as expressing a fundamental and general dynamical law. Given the importance of the Leibnizian context the analysis of Bernoulli's *Discours sur le mouvement* from the perspective of its apparent Leibnizian framework is fundamental for an understanding of Bernoulli's theory of motion. The comprehension of Bernoulli's objectives thus requires an analysis of his relationship with Leibniz, and the nature and limits of his indebtedness to Leibnizian dynamics may be judged from his reactions to Leibniz's published papers and from the discussions in their correspondence.

II

In his *Theoria motus abstracti* (1671) Leibniz expressed his rejection of Cartesian mechanical philosophy in terms which indicate a fundamental feature of his dynamics. Arguing that mechanical explanations based on the principles of matter and motion lacked the precision of geometry, he looked to a science, *physica*, which would be both "real and exact".[27] The science of *physica* would unite the Cartesian attempt to describe physical reality and the rigour of geometry. In this early work "Leibniz was completely under the spell of indivisibles",[28] the problem of the relation between the continuum and its infinite number of infinitesimal parts, and distinguished between the infinitely small elements of motion, *conatus*, and motion (continuous change) itself, arguing that "*conatus* is to motion as a point to space, or as one to infinity, for it is the beginning and end of motion".[29] The geometry of indivisibles was thus to be applied to the study of motion: the continuum of motion was to be analysed in terms of the "rudiments" of motion, *conatus*.[30] The analysis of the motion of bodies in terms of the relation between infinitesimal and finite quantities was to be fundamental to Leibniz's dynamics. This approach was to be shared by Johann Bernoulli who was familiar with the *Theoria motus abstracti*[31] and its conceptual framework was to be echoed in Bernoulli's *Discours sur le mouvement*.

In his *Brevis demonstratio erroris memorabilis Cartesii* (1686) Leibniz distinguished between the "motive force" of a moving body and its "quantity of motion" (mv), declaring that the "force" of a body could not be estimated from the "quantity of motion" but "is to be estimated from the quantity of the effect it can produce". Moreover, the "motive force" was conserved: "it is reasonable that the sum of motive force should be conserved in nature and not be diminished".[32] In a published reply in 1687 to criticisms by Catelan, Leibniz amplified his remark that force was to be measured by its effect, stating a "metaphysical" axiom which "provides the means of reducing the forces to geometrical calculation". This was the law of causality: "we ought to establish ... [a] law of nature which I hold as being most universal and most inviolable ... that there is always a perfect equivalence between the full cause and the total effect ... each entire effect is equivalent to the cause".[33] The conservation or equivalence of forces was thus grounded on the equality of causes and effects; this justification of the conservation of force by an appeal to the law of causality was to be essential to the argument of Bernoulli's *Discours sur le mouvement*.

Leibniz gave a mature statement of his *"new science of dynamics"*[34] in his *Specimen Dynamicum* which was published in the *Acta Eruditorum* in 1695, and which immediately excited Bernoulli's interest and led to his lengthy correspondence with Leibniz on dynamics. Leibniz began by emphasizing that his dynamics was based on his theory of substance, asserting that "there is something besides extension in corporeal things ... there is something prior to extension, namely a natural force everywhere implanted by the Author of Nature ... [which] must constitute the inmost nature of body, since it is in the character of substance to act". The Cartesian principles of extension and motion could not be the defining characteristics of material substance, for extension was a manifestation of substance, "only the continuation or diffusion of an already presupposed acting and resisting substance", and motion was relational being merely continuous change in space and time, and hence could not be considered as "real", as a defining characteristic of substance: "motion taken in an exact sense never exists", for "there is nothing real in motion itself except that momentaneous state which must consist of a force striving toward change".[35] Leibniz rejected the Cartesian conception of body as essentially extension as being "incomplete", and claimed that "something more than magnitude and impenetrability must be assumed in body, from which an interpretation of forces may arise",[36] and thus argued that force, not extension and motion, was the defining characteristic of substance, and that "whatever there is in corporeal nature besides the object of geometry, or extension, must be reduced to this force".[37]

Leibniz distinguished between active and passive forces, and between primitive and derivative forces. While primitive active force was "in all corporeal things as such ... [and] corresponds to the *soul* or *substantial form*", the derivative active forces, *vis mortua* and *vis viva*, were "exercised in various ways through a limitation of primitive force resulting from the conflict of bodies with each other". Although the primitive force characterized the nature of substance, the primitive force "relates only to general causes which cannot suffice to explain phenomena". In rejecting the "crude concept of corporeal substance" proposed by the Cartesians Leibniz thus emphasized that he was not returning to Aristotelian explanations of phenomena in terms of substantial forms, for though the concept of substantial forms had the "proper function of revealing the sources of things" nevertheless the primitive force cannot explain "the specific and special causes of sensible things" and "cannot provide reasons for the laws of nature which apply to derivative force".[38] Primitive passive force is termed *materia prima*—Leibniz again employing Scholastic terminology, this being the Aristotelian primary matter, the substratum, matter without form—and is manifested phenomenally as the derivative passive forces, the impenetrability of bodies and their resistance to motion. Derivative forces are thus the phenomenal manifestations of primitive forces, and the science of dynamics is concerned with derivative forces alone, the forces by which "bodies actually act and are acted upon by each other".[39] A derivative force such as *vis viva* is thus considered to be a *phenomenon bene fundatum* (well-founded appearance), which is part of the order of nature and subject to the laws of nature but does not possess the status of primitive forces which characterize the nature of substances.[40] While Leibniz stressed the phenomenal status of *vis viva*, its conceptual status and intelligibility as a dynamical principle is grounded on his metaphysical explication of the relations between derivative forces and the nature of substances.

Leibniz's clear restriction of his dynamics to the formulation of the physics of derivative forces is basic to his programme of scientific explanation and is important for an understanding of the relation between Bernoulli's *Discours sur le mouvement* and Leibnizian dynamics. Bernoulli's discussion of the *vis viva* principle and the laws of motion in the *Discours sur le mouvement* was confined to the physics of Leibnizian derivative forces, but Bernoulli evinced considerable interest in Leibniz's theory of substance. In his initial response to the *Specimen Dynamicum* in a letter of June 1695 he raised questions about Leibniz's doctrine of primitive force and substantial forms, and about Leibniz's theory of the relation between primitive force and the phenomenal manifestations of substances.[41] In a later letter, prompted by his discussions with de Volder on the nature of substance, Bernoulli remarked that he did not reject Leibniz's metaphysics and that he would accept Leibniz's metaphysical ideas as readily as his dynamics if Leibniz would express himself more clearly complaining that Leibniz's statements were too laconic, being definitions rather than explanations.[42] Bernoulli went on to express agreement with Leibniz's view that natural bodies arose from the interaction of primitive forces, but argued that terms such as *materia prima* were best avoided in discussions with Cartesians,[43] a view with which Leibniz concurred.[44] Bernoulli's separation of dynamical concepts from their metaphysical foundations may be seen as being in accord with the argument of the *Specimen Dynamicum*.

On turning to a discussion of derivative force—the "force which is connected with motion"[45]—in *Specimen Dynamicum*, Leibniz distinguished between *conatus*, the infinitely small element of motion, an infinite number of which comprise movement itself; *impetus*, the quantity "which the Cartesians usually call the quantity of motion [mv]", the measure of motion at a given instant; and the quantity which he here— contrary to customary Cartesian usage— terms the "quantity of motion" to refer to motion extended through time. The relation between *conatus* and *impetus* is grounded on the relation between infinitesimals and finite quantities; just as motion through time arises from an infinite number of momentaneous motions (*impetus*), *impetus* itself arises from a succession of an infinite number of impressed motions (*conatus*). In a similar way, derivative active force is of two kinds: *vis mortua* (mdv) which arises in the tendency or solicitation of a body to motion, and *vis viva* which arises in "actual motion" such as the collision or fall of bodies, and which "arises from an infinite number of continuous impressions of *vis mortua*"[46] and is measured by the quantity mv^2.[47] The difficult conceptual relations between *impetus, conatus* and *vis viva* need not be examined further here,[48] because the crucial point of the argument, as Bernoulli perceived,[49] was that *vis mortua* and *vis viva* were related by means of concepts drawn from the infinitesimal calculus. *Vis viva* was thus to be considered as arising from an infinite number of infinitesimal impulses of *vis mortua*, and the new science of dynamics was founded on the theory of substance and was in harmony with "geometry": it was both "real and exact".[50]

In *Specimen Dynamicum* Leibniz remarked that in referring to infinitesimal quantities such as *conatus* he did "not mean that these mathematical entities are really found in nature as such, but merely that they are the means of making accurate calculations".[51] Leibniz's view that in employing infinitesimal quantities such as *vis mortua* he was not ascribing existential status to such infinitesimals is in consonance with his general view of the nature of infinitesimals.[52] The problem of the existential status of infinitesimals was discussed by Bernoulli and Leibniz in a series of letters in 1698–9. Leibniz argued that "infinitesimals are imaginary [quantities] yet fitted for determining real entities ... even though they have no existence in the parts of matter";[53] claiming that infinitesimals did "not exist in nature",[54] he advanced the view that because an infinite series contained "infinitely many terms it does not follow that there must also be an infinitesimal term ... [for] we can conceive an infinite series consisting merely of finite terms".[55] Bernoulli rejected Leibniz's view that infinitesimals were imaginary and developed the argument that the existence of an infinite series implied the existence of infinitesimals: "if there are an infinite number of terms in the series ... 1/2, 1/4, 1/8, 1/16 ... [so that] if there are ten terms, then there exists one tenth ... therefore if the number of terms is infinite [then] there exists the infinitesimal".[56]

These mathematical arguments have a close bearing on Bernoulli's dynamics. As Leibniz stressed in a letter to Bernoulli of 1698, his dynamics — grounded on the relation between *vis mortua* and *vis viva* and hence on the relation between infinitesimals and finite quantities — was in harmony with the "law of continuity".[57] Leibniz referred Bernoulli to a paper he had published in 1687 in reply to criticisms by Malebranche, where he had argued that the Cartesian laws of collision supposed that in collision bodies would pass instantaneously from motion to rest or from motion in one direction to motion in another direction, and that this "large leap from one extreme to another"[58] violated the law of continuity, a principle that was fundamental to both "geometry" and nature. In his letter to Bernoulli, Leibniz stressed the implications of the law of continuity, the law that "no change occurs through a leap", for dynamics and the nature of matter. Leibniz asserted that the supposition of hard atoms was incompatible with the law of continuity, which held that "no change occurs instantaneously ... without passing through all intermediate degrees". Hard bodies, being inflexible, would rebound after colliding with an instantaneous transition from one state of motion to another. The law of continuity implied that "motion does not change by a leap", and the elasticity of matter and the theory of *vis viva* as arising from successive infinitesimal impulses of *vis mortua* were in consonance with the law of continuity; hence a body would not change from one state of motion to another without passing through all intermediate degrees of motion.[59] Leibniz thus asserted that the mathematical law of continuity had its counterpart in nature. Bernoulli accepted this argument, affirming in reply that the law of continuity implied that all changes of motion occurred "through all intermediate degrees ... through successive increasing or decreasing quantities".[60] This principle was to be fundamental to the argument of Bernoulli's *Discours sur le mouvement*, and his dynamics—grounded on the relation between *vis mortua* and *vis viva* in terms of *vis viva* arising from infinitesimal impulses of *vis mortua*—was thus derived from the *Specimen Dynamicum* and his correspondence with Leibniz. Bernoulli's acceptance of Leibniz's doctrine of the harmony between mathematics and nature and his view of the existential status of infinitesimals suggests that he differed with Leibniz in considering that infinitesimals such as *vis mortua* possessed real, physical existence.

In the *Specimen Dynamicum* Leibniz justified his claim that his dynamics was a "new science" by distinguishing between *Mechanica* (statics) and *Dynamica*, declaring that the ancients only had knowledge of the former —concerned with the lever, the pulley, and the inclined plane— and hence only had knowledge of *vis mortua*, for in these phenomena only *conatus* was manifested. Moreover, the Cartesians had confused *vis mortua* and *vis viva* in taking *mv* as the measure of force; for example, in the case of falling bodies *vis mortua* (*mdv*) is proportional to *m* and *v*, but the Cartesians had been misled by this special case of the "beginning of motion" when the distance of descent was "infinitely small" and proportional to the *conatus*. But when the body has fallen further *vis viva* is produced, and (from Galileo's law of falling bodies) the distance of descent is proportional to the square of the velocity.[61] Leibniz thus stressed that the new science of dynamics distinguished the operations of *vis viva* from the familiar phenomena of statics known since antiquity in which only *vis mortua* was manifested; and he emphasized that the relation between *vis viva* and *vis mortua*, and hence between *Dynamica* and *Mechanica*, was grounded on the relation between finite and infinitesimal quantities. Bernoulli echoed this distinction in a letter to Euler in 1737, commenting on the title of Euler's *Mechanica* (1736). Bernoulli remarked that the word *Mechanica* had been accepted since antiquity and was associated with *vis mortua*, but that he preferred the term *Dynamica* that Leibniz had employed to refer to the phenomena in which *vis viva* was manifested.[62] This Leibnizian distinction between statics and dynamics was developed further in Bernoulli's *Discours sur le mouvement*.

The problem of collision was of primary importance in seventeenth century mechanics, and Leibniz was concerned to formulate a statement of the laws of impact which would incorporate and establish the principle of the conservation of *vis viva* as a fundamental dynamical theorem. In a letter to Bernoulli in 1696 Leibniz provided a clear statement of his laws of collision, in a form that was to be repeated by Bernoulli in his *Discours sur le mouvement*. Supposing that A and B are the masses of two bodies, their velocities before collision being v and y and their velocities after collision being x and z, respectively, Leibniz stated three laws, the "law of the conservation of absolute forces" (the conservation of *vis viva*): $Avv + Byy = Axx + Bzz$; the "law of the conservation of direction" (the conservation of momentum): $Av + By = Ax + Bz$; and the "law of the conservation of relative velocity" before and after impact: $v - y = x - z$. Leibniz argued that because the relative velocity was the same before and after impact, the bodies were perfectly elastic.[63] The Leibnizian laws of collision thus assert the elasticity of matter, a theory which follows—as Leibniz empasized to Bernoulli in 1698—from the law of continuity, and which provides the physical basis for the fundamental law of the conservation of force. This explication of motion in terms of the law of continuity was to be the distinctive feature of Bernoulli's theory of motion.

III

The conceptual kernel of Bernoulli's *Discours sur le mouvement* was his adherence to the fundamental presupposition of Leibnizian dynamics, the law of continuity, and hence to the principle that the mathematical concept of infinitesimals had its counterpart in nature. Bernoulli noted "the perfect conformity which prevails between the laws of nature and those of geometry; a conformity which is observed so constantly and in all circumstances, that it appears that nature has consulted geometry in establishing the laws of motion".[64] He affirmed the operation of a "general law which nature observes constantly in all operations", which was an "immutable and perpetual order established since the creation of the universe"; this was the Leibnizian "law of continuity ... *natura non operatur per saltum*", in consequence of which all change occurs "by infinitely small degrees ... [for] nothing can pass from one extreme to the other without passing through all the intermediate degrees". Bernoulli illustrated this statement of the law of continuity by referring to the problem of motion, rejecting the idea that "nature can pass from one extreme to the other ... from [a state of] rest to motion [or] from motion to rest, or from motion in one direction to motion in the opposite direction, without passing through all the insensible motions which lead from one to the other". He echoed Leibniz's principle of sufficient reason in arguing that only by explaining the transition from a state of rest to a state of movement in terms of the intermediate sequence of states of motion between the state of rest and the state of motion—and hence in terms of the "necessary connection between the two states"— was it possible to explain the "reason" for the "production of one thing rather than another".[65] The law of continuity thus rendered the order of nature intelligible.

In turning to a discussion of collision, he empasized that the supposition of the "partisans of atoms" that bodies possessed the property of the "absolute" hardness of their "elementary corpuscles" was "absolutely impossible", being in conflict with the law of continuity. If two hard bodies were to collide they would either come to rest instantaneously or rebound in different directions to their original motions; it was "contrary to the law of continuity" to suppose that bodies could either pass "suddenly from motion to rest" or from motion in one direction to another without passing through the states of motion intermediate to them. Thus the "alleged perfectly solid atoms, which some philosophers propose ... are imaginary corpuscles".[66] The Leibnizian cast of these arguments is clear. Leibniz had pointed out to Bernoulli that the law of continuity implied the elasticity of matter, and Bernoulli sought to provide a physical model to make this concept of matter intelligible. Supposing that the particles of bodies were like "balloons filled with compressed air" he suggested that bodies could be considered as consisting of an infinite number of such balloons in a common envelope.[67] Bernoulli argued that hardness was only a relational condition of body, and he introduced the concept of "stiffness" to represent "perfect elasticity"; although there were no natural bodies which were "perfectly hard"[68] the "perfect hardness" of a body was synonymous with its "infinite stiffness".[69] Bernoulli thus defined the concept of a hard body in terms of the elasticity of matter.

Bernoulli's theory of motion was based on the Leibnizian law of continuity and hence on the harmony between the laws of nature and those of geometry; and his explication of motion in terms of *vis mortua* and *vis viva* followed from Leibniz's arguments in the *Specimen Dynamicum*. Bernoulli defined *vis mortua* as the force "which a body not in motion receives when solicited or pressed towards motion";[70] consisting in a "simple endeavour" or tendency to movement, an example of *vis mortua* was the force exerted by gravity: "at each instant, gravity impresses on bodies on which it acts, an infinitesimal velocity", and this "endeavour of gravity" is *vis mortua*.[71] *Vis viva* was quite different, being "neither created nor destroyed instantaneously like *vis mortua*". Unlike *vis mortua*, which was an infinitesimal impulse, "time is needed to produce *vis viva* in a body ... [and] time is also required to destroy this force". Thus "*vis viva* is produced successively in a body" when a pressure acts on the body, so that "motion is acquired by infinitely small degrees and becomes a finite and determinate quantity".[72] Bernoulli thus follows Leibniz in supposing that motion is produced in infinitely small degrees—in accordance with the law of continuity—and hence that *vis viva* is produced as a result of an infinite number of infinitesimal impulses of *vis mortua* and is "inherent in a body when it is in uniform motion".[73]

Bernoulli adduced support for this theory by an appeal to the Leibnizian law of causality, declaring that *vis viva* is "equivalent to that part of the cause that is consumed in producing it ... the whole efficient cause is equivalent to the full effect which it produced". The conservation of *vis viva* is thus consequent on "the equality between the effect and the efficient cause". Moreover, the relationship between *vis mortua* and *vis viva* is analogous to the difference "between a line and a surface, or between a surface and a solid".[74] Bernoulli thus emphasized the harmony between nature and geometry in consonance with his acceptance of the categories of Leibniz's *Theoria motus abstracti* and his assumption of the Leibnizian law of continuity: the concept of infinitesimals thus had its counterpart in nature.

Bernoulli illustrated his theory of the transference of motion by supposing that a "hard" body encountered an elastic spring fixed at one end against an immovable surface, the spring being "repelled" in the same direction and with the same speed as the moving body. Bernoulli explained the conservation of *vis viva* in terms of the equality of "action and reaction" and of motion being transferred in each successive instant and by "infinitely small" degrees from the moving body to the spring, and concluded that "all action develops successively and by elements" and can be considered as consisting of "an infinite number of infinitely small parts".[75] Bernoulli sought justificatory sanction for the theory of the conservation of *vis viva* by an appeal to the equality of action and reaction and the law of continuity, supposing the transference of motion in infinitesimal increments. The *vis viva* principle was viewed as being in consonance with the equality of causes and effects and the equality of action and reaction.[76]

Bernoulli justified his distinction between *vis mortua* and *vis viva* by means of an argument based on the compression and expansion of elastic springs. Supposing that an elastic spring pressed against a movable object (a ball), he argued that the "pressure" or "endeavour" of the spring to expand was the *vis mortua* and that this would be the same whatever the size of the spring. As the spring expanded *vis viva* was produced in the ball set in motion by the expansion of the spring; and because the velocity imparted to the ball would be greater the larger the spring, the *vis viva* will depend on the size of the spring. Hence while the "energy" of the *vis mortua* is proportional to the infinitesimal velocity imparted to the ball as the spring began to expand, the *vis viva* is proportional to the finite or "actual" velocity of the ball.[77] Bernoulli then applied this discussion of the expansion of elastic springs to demonstrate that the measure of *vis viva* was mv^2. Representing the "pressure" or *vis mortua* in the spring by p, this produced an increment of velocity dv in an increment of time dt by the expansion of the spring through a space dx.

Stating "the well-known law of acceleration", $dv = pdt$, he obtained the relation $vdv = pdx$, and this "by integration gives $\frac{1}{2}vv = \int pdx$". If two springs of unequal size acting on two balls of equal mass are compared, then the ratio between the *vires vivae* will depend on the ratio between the squares of the velocities acquired by each ball; and "if the balls are of unequal mass, it is apparent that their *vires vivae* are as the product of the masses by the square of the velocities".[78]

It seems likely that Bernoulli derived the idea of employing elastic springs to illustrate the difference between *vis mortua* and *vis viva* from Leibniz, although his quantitative argument was original. In the *Specimen Dynamicum* Leibniz had observed that the "force" with which a compressed elastic spring began to expand was an example of *vis mortua*,[79] and in a letter to Bernoulli in 1695 he suggested—in the context of a discussion of the cause of gravity—that the action of gravity on a body could be represented by supposing the body to penetrate a medium which was considered as a series of "equal and similar springs placed at equal intervals", so that the force experienced by the body penetrating the medium —the force of gravity—was determined by the compression of the springs.[80] While Bernoulli preferred to regard the mechanism of gravity in terms of "the impulses of an ambient medium"[81] rather than by the compression of elastic springs, his correspondence with Leibniz made him aware of the idea of representing force by the compression of springs. Bernoulli's argument in the *Discours sur le mouvement* can thus be regarded as an elaboration of a Leibnizian model. Leibniz's elastic spring analogy can also be traced to Bernoulli's discussion of inelastic collision in his 1735 paper *De vera notione virium vivarum*. The apparent loss of *vis viva* in inelastic collisions had been discussed by Leibniz and Bernoulli in 1695. Referring to the collision of a soft inelastic body such as clay Leibniz had argued that the "greater part of the force will be absorbed and transferred to the insensible parts of the soft matter, not restored to the whole mass".[82] Force was thus not destroyed but was transferred to the insensible parts of the body. In discussing this problem in 1735 Bernoulli advanced an alternative explanation to account for the apparent loss of *vis viva*, suggesting that the *vis viva* apparently lost in inelastic collision was consumed in deforming the bodies. Drawing on the idea that a "uniformly elastic medium" could be represented by means of elastic springs[83] he suggested that imperfectly elastic bodies were analogous to springs that were prevented from re-expanding, so that "some part of the *vis viva*, which appears to perish, is consumed in the compression of the bodies".[84] Bernoulli's correspondence with Leibniz was thus crucial to the dynamical arguments of the *Discours sur le mouvement*.

Further parallels between Bernoulli's theory of motion and Leibnizian dynamics can be seen in his acceptance of Leibniz's view that the erroneous theories that the "quantity of motion" was the measure of the "force" of a body and that there was "always an equal quantity of motion in the universe" arose from a confusion between *vis mortua* and *vis viva*.[85] Moreover, Bernoulli also implied that this error arose from a confusion between statics and dynamics. Bernoulli pointed out that the condition of equilibrium of simple machines was determined by a principle that he termed the "ordinary principle of statics and mechanics", that "two agents are in equilibrium ... when their absolute forces are in a reciprocal ratio of their virtual velocities [*vitesses virtuelles*]", the "virtual velocity" being the "element of the velocity that each body gains or loses in an infinitely small time".[86] In applying this principle in determining conditions of equilibrium Bernoulli argued that it was necessary to distinguish between infinitesimal (or virtual) velocities and finite (or actual) velocities. Because any finite motion would disturb the "equilibrium of powers", this "fundamental principle of statics" established the condition of equilibrium by considering infinitesimal increments in velocity.[87] The distinction between statics and dynamics was a consequence of the distinction between the infinitesimal velocity with which a body is "pressed" towards motion and the "finite and determinate velocity" which is acquired by "infinitely small degrees".[88] To suppose that the "force" of a body in motion was measured by the "quantity of motion (mv)" was to confuse the "force" of a body in motion, and hence moving with a finite velocity, with *vis mortua* (mdv). The science of statics involved infinitesimal velocities and *vis mortua* and was not to be confused with the science of dynamics which involved finite velocities and *vis viva*. Thus to suppose that the "force" of a body in motion was to be measured by the "quantity of motion" was to confuse infinitesimal and finite velocities and the distinction between statics and dynamics.

Bernoulli stressed the conceptual significance of the *vis viva* principle as a fundamental law of nature in his statement of the Leibnizian laws of collision. He adopted Leibniz's three conservation laws, the "law of conservation of relative velocity before and after impact", the law of the "conservation of the quantity of direction", and the law of "the conservation of *vis viva*",[89] clearly adopting Leibniz's own terminology. Moreover, Bernoulli stated these three laws in the mathematical form employed by Leibniz in his letter to Bernoulli in 1696,[90] and emphasized—following Leibniz's remark that the laws could be derived from each other by algebraic manipulation[91]—that the third and fundamental law of the conservation of *vis viva* could be derived from the other two laws and hence had a "necessary connection with the other two conservation laws".[92] He asserted that this third law of collision stated that the quantity of *vis viva* was "absolutely unalterable by the impact of bodies",[93] and was not a "simple corollary" of the first two laws and without further significance. Bernoulli contrasted his own—and by implication Leibniz's—statement of the law of the conservation of *vis viva* with Huygens' statement of the principle of conservation of the quantity mv^2, remarking that Huygens had regarded the mv^2 conservation principle as a theorem, a mere formula, without realizing its fundamental status as a natural law, asserting that "without recourse to nature and first principles, the most important theorems degenerate into simple speculations".[94] While Bernoulli was aware of the utility of the principle regarded merely as a mathematical theorem, he stressed the dynamical and ontological significance of the law of the conservation of *vis viva*. As Lagrange pointed out, for Huygens "the principle ... was regarded as a simple mechanical theorem", but Bernoulli, who "adopted the distinction established by Leibniz between *vis mortua* ... and *vis viva*", considered the "principle ... [of] the conservation of *vis viva* ... [to be] a general law of nature".[95] As Bernoulli emphasized, if "the quantity of *vis viva*, the single source of the continuation of motion in the universe were not conserved ... all nature would fall into disorder".[96]

It is apparent that Bernoulli was indebted to Leibniz for his theory of motion: many of the distinctive ideas of the *Discours sur le mouvement*, and of the later paper *De vera notione virium vivarum*, were drawn directly from Leibniz's published papers and from his correspondence with Bernoulli. There is thus good reason to regard Bernoulli's *Discours sur le mouvement* as a "Leibnizian" treatise on motion, not only in intention but also in that Bernoulli drew directly on Leibniz's own arguments, frequently elaborating and developing them further. However, there are important differences between Bernoulli's theory of motion and Leibniz's natural philosophy; and the analysis of Bernoulli's *Discours sur le mouvement* from the perspective of the Bernoulli-Leibniz relationship permits not only an appreciation of Bernoulli's direct indebtedness to Leibniz, but also enables the significant differences between their conceptions of motion to be delineated, differences which are important for an understanding of Bernoulli's intentions.

The Leibnizian law of continuity was essential to Bernoulli's assertion of the harmony between geometry and nature; indeed, this principle was the kernel of his theory of motion, providing the conceptual foundation of his theory of *vis viva* as arising from successive infinitely small impulses of *vis mortua*. As his correspondence with Leibniz attests, Bernoulli's view of the ontological status of infinitesimals differed significantly from Leibniz's; for Bernoulli, infinitesimals possessed the same existential status as finite quantities. The discussion of the existential status of infinitesimals in the Bernoulli-Leibniz correspondence bears upon Bernoulli's dynamics, given the relation between his assumption of the law of continuity and his use of infinitesimals and his commitment to the supposition that the mathematical concept of infinitesimals had its counterpart in nature. Hence their discussion of the status of infinitesimals relates directly to Leibniz's claim, in the *Specimen Dynamicum*, that the infinitesimal entities posited in his dynamics did not possess the ontological status of physical, existent entities, but were merely mathematical quantities. Bernoulli's view of the ontological status of infinitesimals and his assumption of the harmony between mathematics and nature thus implies the physical reality of *vis mortua* in his dynamics.[97] This view of *vis mortua* as a real, physical entity is in consonance with Bernoulli's characterization of *vis viva* as a "real and substantial entity",[98] a view that conflicts with Leibniz's theory of *vis viva* as a *phenomenon bene fundatum*, an entity which did not possess the status of substance.

It is apparent that there are important differences between Bernoulli's view of dynamics as a science of physical reality and Leibniz's theory that dynamics was confined to the study of phenomenal entities. Nevertheless, Bernoulli's correspondence with Leibniz quoted above indicates that he was sympathetic to Leibniz's theory that natural bodies arose from the interaction of primitive forces. Whereas Bernoulli may have accepted the Leibnizian principle that while metaphysical arguments concerning the relation between primitive and derivative forces were necessary to render dynamical concepts intelligible, dynamics itself was confined to the study of derivative forces such as *vis viva*, he did not adopt Leibniz's view that derivative forces were merely phenomenal. On the contrary, Bernoulli's dynamical writings elaborate a view of *vis mortua* and *vis viva* as real, physical entities.

It is apparent that despite its "Leibnizian" character, Bernoulli's dynamics cannot be unambiguously described as "Leibnizian". The construal of Bernoulli's theory of motion from the perspective of Leibniz's dynamics and metaphysics serves to illuminate Bernoulli's intentions, and to provide the basis for the reconstruction of possible influences and analogies between the two thinkers, whilst at the same time demonstrating the important differences between them, differences which provide the basis for the delineation of Bernoulli's own objectives. These differences, and the distinctive features of Bernoulli's theory of dynamics, were obscured by the polemics of the "*vis viva* controversy".

IV

Colin MacLaurin highlighted the distinctively Leibnizian kernel of Bernoulli's dynamics in his *Account of Sir Isaac Newton's Philosophical Discoveries*, where he pointed out that the only way to render Leibniz's theory that "the essence of substance ... [is] action or activity"[99] and hence that "force or vigour" is conserved scientifically intelligible, was to suppose that "all the bodies in the world had a perfect elasticity",[100] declaring that Bernoulli had established this Leibnizian view on the basis of an appeal to the "law of continuity".[101] In contesting Bernoulli's theory of nature, MacLaurin stressed that in this application of the law of continuity Bernoulli had attempted "to take benefit from the infinite order of infinitesimals in philosophy, that is claimed by some geometricians".[102] In his *Treatise of Fluxions* MacLaurin had subjected the concept of infinitesimals to a characteristically Newtonian critique. He directed his attention explicitly to the relation between "geometry" and nature in Bernoulli's theory of motion, pointing out that "from geometry the infinites and infinitesimals passed into philosophy ... Nature is confined in her operations to act by infinitely small steps. Bodies of a perfect hardness are rejected, and the old doctrine of atoms treated as imaginary, because in their actions and collisions they might pass at once from motion to rest or from rest to motion, in violation of this law [of continuity]". Hence "the doctrine of infinites is interwoven with our speculations in geometry and nature".[103] Noting that while "Leibniz owns them [infinitesimals] to be no more than fictions", others "place them on a level with finite quantities and endeavour to demonstrate their reality",[104] MacLaurin contended that the concept of infinitesimals itself—whatever view was adopted of the existential status of infinitely small quantities—was confused, and that in using infinitesimals mathematicians have "involved themselves in the mazes of infinity".[105] Echoing Newton's arguments in *De Quadratura Curvarum*, MacLaurin urged the rejection of infinitesimals as not being "founded on accurate principles agreeable to ancient geometry"; by contrast, Newton's concept of fluxions "requires the supposition of no quantities but such as are finite, and easily conceived".[106] Affirming the conceptual superiority of Newton's mathematical methods, MacLaurin declared that Newton "considers the simultaneous increments of the flowing quantities [fluxions] as finite, and then investigates the ratio which is the limit of the various proportions which these increments bear to each other, while he supposes them to decrease together till they vanish".[107] MacLaurin thus claimed that infinitesimals were not to be employed in mathematical arguments, alleging that their use by Bernoulli had led to the development of a false system of natural philosophy: "we ought to guard against abating from ... [the] strictness [of geometry]", for "an absurd philosophy is the natural product of a vitiated geometry".[108] MacLaurin's critique thus delineated the kernel of Bernoulli's theory of motion; as Bernoulli stressed to Euler—with reference to this methods in his *Hydraulica*—the "principle of *continuity*" was for him the fundamental principle,[109] and hence, as he expressed it in the *Discours sur le mouvement*, "it appears that nature has consulted geometry in establishing the laws of motion".[110]

Acknowledgement: I wish to thank the Royal Society for financial support in obtaining source materials during the preparation of this paper.

NOTES

1. Johann Bernoulli, "Discours sur les loix de la communication du mouvement", *Opera Omnia, tam antea sparsim edita, quam hactenus inedita*, 4 vols. (Lausanne and Geneva 1742), Vol. III, pp. 1–107. Bernoulli's treatise was first submitted to the Paris Académie des Sciences for the 1724 contest on hard bodies; disqualified, it was resubmitted (with a supplementary chapter) for the 1726 contest on elastic bodies, and was first published in 1727 in Paris. See also: *Recueil des pièces qui a remporté les prix de l'Académie Royale des Sciences, Tome Premier* (Paris 1732). All references to Bernoulli's papers will be to the collected edition of his works edited by G. Cramer.

2. The Cartesian "quantity of motion" is the product of the magnitude of the body and its speed, not "momentum". As will be seen, both Leibniz and Bernoulli accepted the "conservation of momentum" while rejecting the measure of "force" by "quantity of motion". For statements of the conservation of momentum see: John Wallis, 'A Summary Account of the General Laws of Motion', *Philosophical Transactions of the Royal Society*, 1669, *3*, 864–866; C. Wren, 'Lex Naturae de Collisione Corporum', *ibid.*, 867f; Christiaan Huygens, 'Régles du mouvement dans la rencontre des corps', *ibid.*, 1669, *4*, 925–928; and for Newton's 1665 statement in his *Waste Book*, see: John Herivel, *The Background to Newton's "Principia"* (Oxford 1965), pp. 142f.
3. Useful recent discussions of the *vis viva* controversy include: Thomas L. Hankins, "Eighteenth-century attempts to resolve the *vis viva* controversy" *Isis*, 1965, *56*, 281–297; L. L. Laudan, "The *vis viva* controversy, a post mortem", *ibid.*, 1968, *59*, 131–143; Wilson L. Scott, *The Conflict between Atomism and Conservation Theory, 1644–1860* (New York and London 1970), chapters 1–4; Carolyn Iltis, "D'Alembert and the *vis viva* controversy", *Studies in History and Philosophy of Science*, 1970, *1*, 135–144; Carolyn Iltis, "Leibniz and the *vis viva* controversy", *Isis*, 1971, *62*, 21–35; Carolyn Iltis, "The decline of Cartesianism in mechanics: the Leibnizian-Cartesian debates", *ibid.*, 1973, *64*, 356–373; Carolyn Iltis, "The Leibnizian-Newtonian debates: natural philosophy and social psychology", *Brit. J. Hist. Sci.*, 1973, *6*, 343–377.
4. Wilson L. Scott, *op. cit.*, chapter 2; Carolyn Iltis, "The decline of Cartesianism in mechanics", pp. 363–366. Scott and Iltis discuss Bernoulli's *Discours sur le mouvement*, both focusing on his theory of elastic bodies and Iltis giving an analysis of his elastic springs theory. Both these accounts note the "Leibnizian" cast of Bernoulli's treatise, and the present paper aims to supplement them by a more complete analysis of Bernoulli's intentions in the context of the Leibniz-Bernoulli relationship.
5. In his *Discours sur le mouvement* Bernoulli used the French equivalents of these terms, *force vive* and *force morte*, but for consistency the Latin terms will be employed throughout in this paper.
6. *Œuvres complètes de Christiaan Huygens*, 22 vols. (The Hague 1888–1950), Vol. XVI, p. 73. This statement was made in Huygens' *De motu corporum ex percussione*, first published in B. de Volder and B. Fullenius, eds., *Christiani Huygeni Opuscula Posthuma* (Leiden 1703). Bernoulli was familiar with this work (see *Opera omnia*, Vol. III, p. 58n).
7. *Œuvres complètes de Huygens*, Vol. XVIII, pp. 147, 247, 255. See also Erwin N. Hiebert, *Historical Roots of the Principle of Conservation of Energy* (Madison 1962), pp. 73–77; Richard S. Westfall, *Force in Newton's physics* (New York and London 1971), chapter 4.
8. *Œuvres complètes de Huygens*, Vol. VIII, p. 499.
9. G. W. Leibniz, "Specimen Dynamicum, pro admirandis naturae legibus circa corporum vires et mutuas actiones detegendis et ad suas causas revocandis" [*Acta Eruditorum*, 1695, *14*, 145–157], *Mathematische Schriften*, 7 vols., ed. C. I. Gerhardt (Berlin and Halle: 1849–1863 [reprinted Hildesheim 1960–1961]), Vol. VI, p. 235. Quotations from the "Specimen Dynamicum" are from the translation in G. W. Leibniz, *Philosophical Papers and Letters*, ed. Leroy E. Loemker, second edition (Dordrecht 1969), pp. 435–444.
10. G. W. Leibniz, "De Primae Philosophiae Emendatione, et de Notione Substantiae"

[*Acta Eruditorum*, 1694, *13*, 110–112], *Die philosophischen Schriften von G. W. Leibniz*, 7 vols., ed. C. I. Gerhardt (Berlin: 1875–1890 [reprinted Hildesheim 1960–1961]), Vol. IV, p. 469.
11. Johann Bernoulli, "De vera notione virium vivarum earumque usu in dynamicis" [*Acta Eruditorum*, 1735: 210–230] *Opera omnia*, Vol. III, pp. 239–241. I have quoted D. T. Whiteside's translation of the phrase *quantum in se est*: see *The Mathematical Papers of Isaac Newton*, ed. D. T. Whiteside (Cambridge 1967-continuing), Vol. VI, p. 93.
12. R. Descartes, *Principia Philosophiae*, in *Œuvres de Descartes*, ed. C. Adam and P. Tannery, 13 vols. (Paris 1897–1913), Vol. VIII part 1, p. 66; I. Newton, *Mathematical Principles of Natural Philosophy*, ed. and trans. A. Motte and F. Cajori (Berkeley 1934), p. 2. See I. B. Cohen, "*Quantum in se est*: Newton's concept of inertia in relation to Descartes and Lucretius", *Notes and Records of the Royal Society*, 1964, *19*, 131–155.
13. Newton, *op. cit.*, p. 2.
14. Newton, *op. cit.*, pp. 398f.
15. Bernoulli, "Discours sur le mouvement", *Opera omnia*, Vol. III, p. 58.
16. Johann Bernoulli, "Theoremata selecta, pro conservatione virium vivarum demonstranda et experimentis confirmanda" [*Commentarii academiae petropolitanae* 1727, *2*, 200–207], *Opera omnia*, Vol. III, pp. 124–130.
17. Bernoulli, "De vera notione virium vivarum", *Opera omnia*, Vol. III, pp. 255f.
18. Johann Bernoulli, "Meditationes de chordis vibrantibus" [*Commentarii academiae petropolitanae*, 1728, *3*, 13–28], *Opera omnia*, Vol. III, pp. 198–210. For a discussion of this paper see C. Truesdell, "The rational mechanics of flexible or elastic bodies, 1638–1788", *Leonhardi Euleri Opera Omnia* (Series II), Vol. XI, part 2 (Zurich 1960), pp. 132–136.
19. Daniel Bernoulli, *Hydrodynamica, sive de viribus et motibus fluidorum commentarii* (Strasbourg 1738), p. 12.
20. *Ibid.*
21. Daniel Bernoulli, "Remarques sur le principe de la conservation des forces vives, près un sens général", *Mémoires de l'Académie Royale des Sciences de Berlin*, 1748, *4*, 353–364.
22. Colin MacLaurin, *An Account of Sir Isaac Newton's Philosophical Discoveries* (London 1748), p. 194.
23. *Ibid.*, p. 184.
24. Colin MacLaurin, *A Treatise of Fluxions*, 2 vols. (Edinburgh 1742), Vol. II, p. 438n.
25. MacLaurin, *loc. cit.* (n. 22).
26. MacLaurin, *loc. cit.* (n. 24).
27. G. W. Leibniz, "Theoria motus abstracti" [Mainz 1671], *Mathematische Schriften*, Vol. VI, p. 74.
28. Joseph E. Hofmann, *Leibniz in Paris, 1672–1676: his growth to mathematical maturity* (Cambridge 1974), p. 8.
29. Leibniz, *op. cit.* (n. 27), p. 68. On the origins of Leibniz's concept of *Conatus* see Martial Gueroult, *Leibniz: dynamique et métaphysique* (Paris 1967), pp. 70–75.
30. Leibniz, *op. cit.* (n. 27), p. 68.
31. Bernoulli was familiar with Leibniz's *Theoria motus abstracti*, quoting the phrase "corpus est mens momentanea" (*ibid.*, p. 69) in his letter to Leibniz of 8/18 June 1695,

see Leibniz, *Mathematische Schriften*, Vol. III, p. 188. I am grateful to Dr. H. Bos (Utrecht) for this reference.
32. G. W. Leibniz, "Brevis demonstratio erroris memorabilis Cartesii" [*Acta Eruditorum*: 1686, *5*, 161–163], *Mathematische Schriften*, Vol. VI, pp. 117f.
33. G. W. Leibniz, reply to Catelan [*Nouvelles de la république des lettres*, 1687, *9*, 131–144], *Philos Schriften*, Vol. III, pp. 45f.
34. G. W. Leibniz, "Specimen Dynamicum", *Mathematische Schriften*, Vol. VI, p. 234 (for full reference see above n. 9).
35. *Ibid.*, p. 235.
36. *Ibid.*, p. 241.
37. *Ibid.*, p. 235. *Cf.* Leibniz's letters to de Volder of 24 March/3 April 1699 and 23 June 1699 in Leibniz, *Philos. Schriften*, Vol. II, pp. 169, 184. See also Gueroult, *op. cit.* (n. 29) on Leibniz's metaphysics and theory of force, and Gerd Buchdahl, *Metaphysics and the Philosophy of Science. The Classical Origins: Descartes to Kant* (Oxford 1969), chap. 7.
38. Leibniz, "Specimen Dynamicum", *Mathematische Schriften*, Vol. VI, p. 236.
39. *Ibid.*, p. 237.
40. See Buchdahl, *op. cit.* (n. 37), p. 410.
41. Bernoulli to Leibniz, 8/18 June 1695, *Mathematische Schriften*, Vol. III, p. 188.
42. Bernoulli to Leibniz, 8 November 1698, *ibid.*, p. 545.
43. *Ibid.*, p. 547.
44. Leibniz to Bernoulli, 18 November 1698, *ibid.*, p. 552.
45. Leibniz, "Specimen Dynamicum", *ibid.*, Vol. VI, p. 237.
46. *Ibid.*, p. 238.
47. *Ibid.*, p. 245.
48. See Gueroult, *op· cit.* (n. 29), pp. 34–46.
49. See Bernoulli to Leibniz, 8/18 June 1695 in Leibniz, *Mathematische Schriften*, Vol. III, p. 188f.
50. Leibniz, *loc. cit.* (n. 27).
51. Leibniz, "Specimen Dynamicum", *Mathematische Schriften*, Vol. VI, p. 238.
52. *Cf.* Leibniz to Pierre Varignon, 20 June 1702: "infinitely small quantities could not be considered as other than as ideal entities, or as well-founded fictions", Leibniz, *Mathematische Schriften*, Vol. IV, p. 110; and Leibniz to Varignon, 2 February 1702: "everything takes place, in geometry, and even more in nature, as if they [infinitesimals] were perfect realities", *ibid.*, p. 93. See also Jürgen Mittelstrass, *Neuzeit und Aufklärung: Studien zur Entstehung der neuzeitlichen Wissenschaft und Philosophie* (Berlin and New York 1970), pp. 489–501.
53. Leibniz to Bernoulli, 7 June 1698, *Mathematische Schriften*, Vol. III, p. 499.
54. Leibniz to Bernoulli, 18 November 1698, *ibid.*, p. 551.
55. Leibniz to Bernoulli, 21 February 1699, *ibid.*, p. 575.
56. Bernoulli to Leibniz, 7 January 1699, *ibid.*, p. 563. See also Bernoulli to Leibniz, 6 December 1698, *ibid.*, p. 555.
57. Leibniz to Bernoulli, 20/30 September 1698, *ibid.*, p. 544.
58. G. W. Leibniz, reply to Malebranche [*Nouvelles de la république des lettres*, 1687, *9*, 744–753], *Philos. Schriften*, Vol. III, p. 53.

59. Leibniz to Bernoulli, 20/30 September 1698, *Mathematische Schriften*, Vol. III, p. 544. *Cf.* Leibniz, "Essay de dynamique", *ibid.*, Vol. VI, pp. 228–231.
60. Bernoulli to Leibniz, 8 November 1698, *ibid.*, Vol. III, p. 548.
61. Leibniz, "Specimen Dynamicum", *ibid.*, Vol. VI, p. 239.
62. Bernoulli to Euler, 6 November 1737, in G. Eneström, "Der Briefwechsel zwischen Leonhard Euler und Johann I. Bernoulli", *Bibliotheca Mathematica* (Series III), 1904, *5*, pp. 263f.
63. Leibniz to Bernoulli, 8/18 March 1696, *Mathematische Schriften*, Vol. III, pp. 260f. *Cf.* Leibniz, "Essay de dynamique", *ibid.*, Vol. VI, pp. 226–228 (on which see Gueroult, *op. cit.*, p. 50). It has been suggested by Pierre Costabel, *Leibniz et la dynamique* (Paris 1960), p. 20, that this "Essay de dynamique" was not written before 1698. This suggestion is borne out from a study of the Johann Bernoulli-Leibniz correspondence. Leibniz's statement of the laws of collision in this letter of March 1696 was clearly preliminary to his more articulated formulation in the "Essay de dynamique", which is closer to Leibniz's statement of these laws in a letter to Jacob Bernoulli of April 1703 (Leibniz, *Mathematische Schriften*, Vol. III, p. 69), in that here he refers to the equations as linear, plane and solid, as in the "Essay de dynamique", *ibid.*, Vol. VI, p. 227. *Cf.* also n. 59 above and n. 82 below for other points of comparison between Leibniz's letters to Bernoulli from 1695 to 1698 and this "Essay de dynamique".
64. Johann Bernoulli, "Discours sur le mouvement", *Opera omnia*, Vol. III, p. 58.
65. *Ibid.*, p. 9. *Cf.* Scott, *op. cit.* (n. 3) p. 23.
66. Bernoulli, "Discours sur le mouvement", *Opera omnia*, Vol. III, pp. 9f.
67. *Ibid.*, pp. 12f. See Iltis, "The decline of Cartesianism in mechanics", *op. cit.* (n. 3), pp. 363f., for a full discussion of Bernoulli's physical model. Iltis points out that this model was derived from Descartes' aether theory. Bernoulli's use of Cartesian physical concepts is an important feature of his thought, but cannot be considered here. For a valuable treatment of Bernoulli's Cartesian vortical theory in the 1730's, see E. J. Aiton, *The vortex theory of planetary motions* (New York and London 1972), pp. 214–219, 228–235.
68. Bernoulli, "Discours sur le mouvement", *Opera omnia*, Vol. III, pp. 13f.
69. *Ibid.*, p. 81.
70. *Ibid.*, p. 23.
71. *Ibid.*, p. 35.
72. *Ibid.*, p. 36.
73. *Ibid.*, p. 23.
74. *Ibid.*, pp. 38f.
75. *Ibid.*, 15f.
76. MacLaurin contested Bernoulli's justification of the *vis viva* principle in terms of the equality of action and reaction and the law of causality. MacLaurin argued that *vis viva* was not the cause of effects: for Newton's second law implies that the "impressed force" is "considered as the cause", and "the change of motion produced by it is the effect that measures the cause", *Account of Newton*, p. 137. MacLaurin declared that Bernoulli misunderstood Newton's third law "when he tells us that the preservation of the sum of the absolute motions of bodies, in their collisions, is so immediate a consequence of the equality of *action* and *reaction*", for according to Newton "it is

not the sum of their absolute motions or forces, but this sum estimated in a given direction, that is preserved unaltered in their collisions, in consequence of the third law of motion", *ibid.*, pp. 118f. Hence only "momentum" is conserved, *ibid.*, p. 133.
77. Bernoulli, "Discours sur le mouvement", *Opera omnia*, Vol. III, p. 45.
78. *Ibid.*, p. 47. *Cf.* Iltis, "The decline of Cartesianism in mechanics", *op. cit.* (n. 3), pp. 365f. The mathematical relations $Fdx = mvdv$ and $Fdt = mdv$ (where F is the force, m the mass), were first stated by Pierre Varignon, "Manière générale de déterminer les forces, les vitesses, les espaces et les temps", *Mémoires de Mathématique et de Physique . . . de l'Académie Royale des Sciences*, 1700, pp. 23, 27. Johann Bernoulli first stated these relations in the "Extrait" of his letter of 10 January 1711 "touchant la manière de trouver les forces centrales dans les milieux resistans", *ibid.*, 1711, p. 47 (*Opera omnia*, Vol. I, p. 502).
79. Leibniz, "Specimen Dynamicum", *Mathematische Schriften*, Vol. VI, p. 238.
80. Leibniz to Bernoulli, 24 June 1695, *ibid.*, Vol. III, pp. 193f.
81. Bernoulli to Leibniz, 24 August/3 September 1695, *ibid.*, p. 215.
82. Leibniz to Bernoulli, 28 December 1695, *ibid.*, p. 228. *Cf.* Leibniz, "Essay de dynamique", *ibid.*, Vol. VI, pp. 229–231; and also Leibniz's remarks in his correspondence with Clarke: see *The Leibniz-Clarke Correspondence*, ed. H. G. Alexander (Manchester 1956), pp. 87f.
83. Bernoulli to Leibniz, 17 July, 1695, *Mathematische Schriften*, Vol. III, p. 202.
84. Bernoulli, "De vera notione virium vivarum", *Opera omnia*, Vol. III, pp. 242f.
85. Bernoulli, "Discours sur le mouvement", *ibid.*, p. 38.
86. *Ibid.*, p. 23. *Cf.* Bernoulli's statement of the principle of virtual velocities in his letter to Varignon, quoted in Pierre Varignon, *Nouvelle mécanique ou statique*, 2 vols. (Paris 1724), Vol. II, pp. 174ff. See also Hiebert, *op. cit.* (n. 7), pp. 82–84 and Thomas L. Hankins, *Jean d'Alembert: Science and the Enlightenment* (Oxford 1970), pp. 198–203.
87. Bernoulli, "Discours sur le mouvement", *Opera omnia*, Vol. III, p. 38.
88. *Ibid.*, p. 36.
89. *Ibid.*, p. 56.
90. *Ibid.*, p. 57.
91. Leibniz to Bernoulli, 8/18 March 1696, *Mathematische Schriften*, Vol. III, p. 261.
92. Bernoulli, "Discours sur le mouvement", *Opera omnia*, Vol. III, p. 58.
93. *Ibid.*, p. 56.
94. *Ibid.*, p. 58.
95. J.-L. Lagrange, *Mécanique Analytique*, 2 vols. (Paris 1965), Vol. I, p. 226. Scott, *op. cit.* (n. 3), pp. 38f. gives a different analysis of this point.
96. Bernoulli, *loc. cit.* (n. 92).
97. This argument assumes the constancy of Bernoulli's view from the time of his discussion of these points with Leibniz. Given the continuity between this early correspondence with Leibniz and the *Discours sur le mouvement*, such a constancy of thought seems likely.
98. Bernoulli, *loc. cit.* (n. 11).
99. MacLaurin, *Account of Newton*, p. 82 (see n. 22 for full reference).
100. *Ibid.*, pp. 85f.

101. *Ibid.*, p. 87.
102. *Ibid.*
103. MacLaurin, *Treatise of Fluxions*, Vol. I, p. 39 (see n. 24 for full reference).
104. *Ibid.*, pp. 39f. In a footnote, MacLaurin refers (*ibid.*, p. 45n) to passages in Leibniz's *Théodicée* where Leibniz had stated his view of infinitesimals as "fictions" (see Leibniz, *Philos. Schriften*, Vol. VII, p. 90).
105. MacLaurin, *Treatise of Fluxions*, Vol. I, p. 38. *Cf.* Leibniz to de Volder, 19 January 1706, where Leibniz refers to the problems of infinitesimals and the continuum as the "labyrinth of the continuum", *Philos. Schriften*, Vol. II, p. 282.
106. MacLaurin, *Treatise of Fluxions*, Vol. I, p. 49.
107. *Ibid.*, Vol. II, p. 420. *Cf.* Newton's remarks in his *De Quadratura Curvarum*, in *The Mathematical Works of Isaac Newton*, ed. D. T. Whiteside (New York 1964), Vol. I, pp. 141–143. Whiteside gives an account of the various editions of this work in the early eighteenth-century in his introduction to this volume.
108. MacLaurin, *Treatise of Fluxions*, Vol. I, p. 47.
109. Bernoulli to Euler, 7 March 1739, in G. Eneström, "Der Briefwechsel zwischen Leonhard Euler und Johann I. Bernoulli", *Bibliotheca Mathematica* (Series III) 1905, 6, p. 20.
110. Bernoulli, "Discours sur le mouvement", *Opera omnia*, Vol. III, p. 58.

VIII

DYNAMICS AND INTELLIGIBILITY: BERNOULLI AND MACLAURIN

Abstract. This essay discusses the role of metaphysical argument in the *vis viva* controversy. The debate between Johann Bernoulli and Colin MacLaurin over the *vis viva* concept and Leibnizian dynamics is reviewed. Special emphasis is placed on Bernoulli's appeal to the Leibnizian metaphysical principles of causality and continuity in supporting his theory of motion, and to the special status he accords the principle of the conservation of *vis viva* in dynamics. MacLaurin's critique of Bernoulli is reviewed, with special emphasis on his discussion of the law of continuity, and his defence of Newton's concept of fluxions and his disparagement of the status of infinitesimal quantities in Leibniz's mathematics and Bernoulli's dynamics. The physical and metaphysical arguments he deploys in criticising the principle of the conservation of *vis viva* are discussed, his approach being essentially Newtonian in inspiration.

1. INTRODUCTION

All natural philosophers who wished to proceed mathematically in their work had therefore always (though unknown to themselves) made use of metaphysical principles and were obliged to make use of them, even though they otherwise solemnly protested against any claim of metaphysics on their science.... (Kant, *Metaphysical Foundations of Natural Science* ([13] *4*, 472)).

The discussion of the metaphysical components of scientific theories has been a guiding theme of Gerd Buchdahl's work. In particular, he has discussed the role of regulative maxims such as the law of causality and criteria of analogy and continuity in the articulation of Newton's concept of gravitation, and analysed the attempts to justify the intelligibility of gravity by explications of the meaning of the concepts of matter and force ([4], [5]). Buchdahl has emphasised that these metaphysical arguments were intended to supplement the physical content of the theory of gravity; by emphasising the metaphysical components of scientific theories he has stressed the interaction between the physical and metaphysical components in the articulation of scientific theories. Buchdahl's studies of the debates over the conceptual status of concepts of force and gravity, from Newton to Kant, have amply illuminated his treatment of this philosophical theme, which is deeply Kantian in inspiration.

R. S. Woolhouse (ed.), *Metaphysics and Philosophy of Science in the Seventeenth and Eighteenth Centuries*, 213–225.
© 1988 *by Kluwer Academic Publishers.*
Reprinted by permission of Kluwer Academic Publishers

Following Buchdahl, I have myself argued that reference to metaphysical foundations is constitutive of the conceptual development of classical physics ([7]; [10]); and in particular that debates over the status of the concepts of force and inertia were integral to reception of Newton's physics ([7] 8—80; [8]; [9]). In this essay I will further illustrate this theme by reviewing the debate between Johann Bernoulli and Colin MacLaurin over the *vis viva* concept and the Leibnizian law of continuity (see also [11]).

The correspondence between Leibniz and Samuel Clarke in 1715—16 had given public expression to the disagreement between Newton and Leibniz about the status of the concept of gravitational attraction, and also reawakened Bernoulli's interest in Leibnizian dynamics. The publication of Leibniz's "Specimen dynamicum" (1695) had led to a flourishing correspondence with Bernoulli, who became deeply involved in Leibniz's priority quarrel with Newton over the invention of the calculus, to which the correspondence between Leibniz and Clarke was a tailpiece ([6]). In 1716 Leibniz drew Bernoulli's attention to his debate with Clarke and Newton, whom he considered to be his real adversary lurking behind the scenes. Leibniz criticised Newton's doctrine of the "spontaneous diminution of active forces and final cessation in the world", pointing out to Bernoulli that by the Leibnizian principle of the conservation of *vis viva* ("living force") the "same quantity of forces is always preserved" ([14] *3*, 964). Leibniz thus sees the principle of the conservation of *vis viva* as refuting Newton's claim, in Query 23 of the Latin edition of the *Opticks* (1706), that because motion is constantly being dissipated, for example in the collision of inelastic or partially elastic bodies, it was apparent that "some other principle is necessary for conserving the motion": "the variety of motion which we find in the world is always decreasing, [and hence] there is a necessity of conserving and recruiting it by active principles" ([18] 397—401). While active principles were laws of nature, they were also conceived as the mediating agents by which God conserved motion and gravity in the cosmos. Clarke therefore rejected Leibniz's concept of the conservation of *vis viva* on theological grounds, maintaining that to deny (as did Leibniz) that "every action is the giving of a new force to the thing acted upon" would be to suppose that God is "quite excluded from the government of the natural world". Clarke affirms the Newtonian doctrine that "there must be a continual increase and decrease of the whole quantity of motion in the universe" which had the consequence

DYNAMICS AND INTELLIGIBILITY

that "every thing be not mere absolute mechanism" ([15] 110). In his reply to Leibniz, Bernoulli however expresses agreement with the Leibnizian view of the sufficiency (for purposes of the scientific explanation of phenomena) of mechanical laws, arguing that "no force is destroyed, without giving rise to an equivalent effect"; the "effect is nothing other than the transformed force", and hence "it is necessary that the same quantity of force be preserved" ([14] 3, 966). Leibniz and Bernoulli reject any claim that there are certain natural phenomena — gravity or the collision of inelastic bodies — that "cannot be explained mechanically".[1]

These physical and metaphysical arguments are fully developed in Bernoulli's memoir "Discours sur les loix de la communication du mouvement" (1727), submitted for the 1724 prize of the Paris Académie Royale des Sciences on the laws of the collision of hard bodies. Bernoulli's entry was disqualified on the grounds that he had denied that hardness or inflexibility was a fundamental property of bodies, and the prize was won by the young Scottish mathematician and supporter of Newtonian physics and mathematics, Colin MacLaurin. Bernoulli's memoir was however subsequently published, and collected with other papers submitted to the Académie, and provided a systematic account of the law of the conservation of *vis viva*.[2] MacLaurin consequently took Bernoulli's memoir as a substantive statement of Leibnizian dynamics in his *Treatise of Fluxions* (1742) and his *Account of Sir Isaac Newton's Philosophical Discoveries* (1748), works which established his reputation as the leading British defender and populariser of Newton's physics and mathematics. I will begin with an account of Bernoulli's "Discours sur ... mouvement", and will then turn to an examination of MacLaurin's critique of this work, with an especial emphasis on Bernoulli's appeal to the Leibnizian metaphysical axioms of causality and continuity, and MacLaurin's response.

2. BERNOULLI'S THEORY OF MOTION

Bernoulli presents his memoir "Discours sur les loix de la communication du mouvement" as a systematic elaboration of the Leibnizian science of dynamics, remarking that he was the first natural philosopher for 28 years (since the publication of "Specimen dynamicum" in 1695) to espouse Leibnizian dynamical principles. Based on Leibniz's metaphysical principles of causality and continuity, the elasticity of matter, and the conservation of *vis viva*, Bernoulli's work provides a detailed presentation of Leibnizian dynamics, bringing together in a systematic and coherent fashion themes which Leibniz himself never fully developed. Most fundamentally, Bernoulli adheres to the fundamental presupposition of Leibnizian dynamics, the law of continuity, that "no change occurs through a leap". In correspondence with Bernoulli in 1698 Leibniz had stressed that the law of continuity had profound implications for his dynamics: the mathematical law of continuity had its counterpart in the physical world ([14] *3*, 544).

In his "Discours sur ... mouvement" Bernoulli follows Leibniz in supposing that motion is produced in "infinitely small degrees" in accordance with the law of continuity; therefore *vis viva* is a "finite and determinate quantity" and is produced as a result of an infinite number of infinitesimal impulses of *vis mortua* ("dead force"), and is "inherent in a body when it is in uniform motion" ([2] *3*, 23, 36, 39). The Leibnizian law of continuity implies the harmony between the order of nature and the mathematical relation between infinitesimal and finite quantities. Bernoulli notes the "perfect conformity which prevails between the laws of nature and those of geometry; a conformity which is observed so constantly and in all circumstances, that it appears that nature has consulted geometry in establishing the laws of motion" ([2] *3*, 58). The "law of continuity ... *natura non operatur per saltum*" is an "immutable and perpetual" general law of nature, which explains the generation of motion in terms of the transition of a body from a state of rest to a state of motion by a transition "through all the insensible motions which lead from one to the other". Moreover the law of continuity establishes the "necessary connection" between the states of motion and rest, rendering the order of nature intelligible ([2] *3*, 9—10).

Bernoulli applies this concept of motion to the analysis of the collision of bodies. He follows Leibniz in maintaining that the assumption of the "absolute hardness" of the elementary corpuscles of matter by the partisans of the atomic theory of matter (notably Newton) was "absolutely impossible". It was of course his denial of this assumption, that led to the disqualification of his essay from the 1724 Paris competition. Bernoulli however proceeds to give an account of hardness, as a property of matter, in Leibnizian terms, rejecting the Newtonian view that hardness (along with extension, impenetrability, mobility and inertia) was to be construed as an essential or fundamental property of matter. Bernoulli supposes that matter is inherently elastic,

VIII

DYNAMICS AND INTELLIGIBILITY

and that the hardness of a body is not to be conceived as a fundamental property of matter but as a relational condition. Matter therefore is fundamentally elastic and the hardness of bodies is explained in terms of the relative stiffness and rigidity of inherently elastic matter. He illustrates this concept of the essential elasticity of matter by representing bodies as elastic springs. On collision motion is transferred between bodies *qua* elastic springs by infinitely small degrees. Thus motion is transferred from one body to another "successively and by elements", in consonance with the Leibnizian concept of the transference of motion in accordance with the law of continuity, that "no change occurs through a leap" ([2] *3*, 9—10, 15—16).

Bernoulli develops this model of matter as an elastic spring to give a physical and mathematical representation of the relation between *vis mortua* and *vis viva*. He follows Leibniz in supposing that the force manifested when a compressed elastic spring begins to expand is an example of *vis mortua*, and argues that as a spring expands *vis viva* is generated. While *vis mortua* is proportional to the infinitesimal velocity as the spring begins to expand, the *vis viva* is proportional to a finite or "actual" velocity. Bernoulli develops the argument to demonstrate that the measure of *vis viva* is mv^2. Representing the "pressure" or *vis mortua* in the spring, corresponding to the "endeavour" of the spring to expand, by p, this produces an increment of velocity dv in an increment of time dt by the expansion of the spring through a space dx. From "the well-known law of acceleration" $dv = pdt$ (a result first stated by Varignon and subsequently used by Bernoulli himself), he obtains the relation $vdv = pdx$, and this "by integration gives $\frac{1}{2}vv = \int pdx$". If the action of two springs of unequal size pressing against two balls of equal mass are compared, then the ratio between the *vires vivae* will depend on the ratio between the square of the velocities acquired by each ball; and "if the balls are of unequal mass, it is apparent that their *vires vivae* are as the product of the masses by the square of the velocities" ([2] *3*, 45—7).

Bernoulli gives metaphysical support for his theory of motion by an appeal to the Leibnizian law of causality. The concept of *vis viva* is the true measure of force in nature because *vis viva* is "equivalent to that part of the cause that is consumed in producing it". Because "the whole efficient cause is equivalent to the full effect which is produced", the conservation of *vis viva* follows from "the equality between the effect and the efficient cause" ([2] *3*, 38). The principle of the conservation of *vis viva* is a fundamental natural law expressing the order and harmony of nature: if the quantity of *vis viva*, the "single source of the continuation of motion in the universe", were not conserved then "all nature would fall into disorder". He explicitly contrasts this Leibnizian expression of the self-sufficiency of nature, as grounded on the preservation and conservation of *vis viva* in mechanical processes, with the Newtonian doctrine of the diminution of activity in the collisions of bodies ([2] *3*, 58). Bernoulli's theory of motion is justified by the appeal to the metaphysical principles of causality and continuity, and to the harmony between mathematics and nature as expressed by the generation of *vis viva* from *vis mortua*.

Bernoulli made it plain that his theory of motion and concept of *vis viva* was essentially Leibnizian in inspiration. He contrasts his own statement of the law of the conservation of *vis viva* with Huygens' formulation of the conservation of the quantity mv^2 in collisions. For Huygens the quantity mv^2 was merely a number, without any fundamental dynamical significance. In his *Horologium Oscillatorium* (1673) Huygens demonstrates that the distance through which the centre of gravity of a body or system of bodies will fall under the action of gravity is equal to the height to which it can ascend as a result of the velocity acquired in the fall; there is an equality between actual descent and potential ascent of the centre of gravity of a system of moving bodies. From Galileo's law of falling bodies the descent of each body is proportional to the square of its velocity; the quantity mv^2 is conserved in the descent and ascent of the centre of gravity of a system of bodies ([12] *18*, 147, 247, 255). Bernoulli remarks that Huygens had regarded his theorem of the conservation of mv^2 as a mathematical proposition, a mere formula, without realizing its fundamental status as a general dynamical natural law. Indicating his own espousal of Leibnizian dynamics, he declares that "without recourse to nature and first principles, the most important theorems degenerate into simple speculations" ([2] *3*, 58).

While Bernoulli presents his "Discours sur ... mouvement" as a treatise on the motions and collisions of bodies which was essentially Leibnizian in inspiration, there are important differences between his argument and Leibniz's own presentation in "Specimen dynamicum". Bernoulli's discussion is confined to the physics of Leibnizian derivative forces. The Leibnizian theory of substance is basic to Leibniz's own science of dynamics; derivative forces are phenomenal analogues of the primitive forces which define the nature of substances, while being conceived as part of the order of nature and expressing the mechanical laws of nature. This plays no part in Bernoulli's exposition of the theory of motion. Bernoulli's differences with Leibniz over the status of infinitesimals are also important. Writing to Bernoulli in 1698 Leibniz had declared that "infinitesimals are imaginary [quantities]" and did "not exist in nature"; the representation of *vis viva* as generated from infinitesimal impulses of *vis mortua* is a mathematical model ([14] *3*, 499, 551). In "Specimen dynamicum" he declares that the infinitesimals posited in his dynamics are "mathematical entities" which were not "really found in nature as such" but were "the means of making accurate calculations" ([14] *6*, 238). In his correspondence with Leibniz Bernoulli had diverged from Leibniz's view that infinitesimals are imaginary, declaring that "the infinitesimal exists" ([14] *3*, 563). In a later essay "De vera notione virium vivarum" (1735) he declares that he conceives *vis viva* as a "real and substantial entity", as a fundamental "absolute" quantity, an existent quantity which is inherent in substances ([2] *3*, 239—41). This concept of *vis viva* contrasts with Leibniz's view of *vis viva* as a derivative force which is a phenomenal analogue of the primitive forces which define substances. In Bernoulli's dynamics it is implied that both *vis mortua* and *vis viva* have the status of real, existent quantities though their dynamical status differs: while *vis mortua* is transient *vis viva* is conserved and undiminished.

Despite these differences with Leibniz, Bernoulli's work can be seen as Leibnizian in its physics and in its appeal to metaphysical axioms of continuity and causality. Bernoulli certainly intended that this should be so, but of course he was too powerful a personality and too creative a mathematician to be merely the follower of another's metaphysical system, a system moreover which he apparently found impenetrably obscure ([14] *3*, 545, 547, 556).

3. MACLAURIN'S "NEWTONIAN" CRITIQUE

In his *Treatise of Fluxions* (1742) MacLaurin develops a presentation of Newton's concept of fluxions by appealing to the method of first and last ratios of nascent and vanishing quantities approaching their limits. The book was written as a response to George Berkeley's *The Analyst* (1734), and MacLaurin took the opportunity to subject the concept of infinitesimals to a characteristically Newtonian critique. MacLaurin's

An Account of Sir Isaac Newton's Philosophical Discoveries (1748) was apparently begun after Newton's death in 1727, but only published posthumously, and is a wide-ranging discussion of Newtonian natural philosophy, and includes a critique of Leibnizian dynamics. Bernoulli's theory of motion is discussed in both *Fluxions* and *Newton*, where Bernoulli is taken as Leibniz's main protagonist, "the most learned and skilful advocate for the new [Leibnizian] doctrine" ([17] 118), whose elements are described in the following terms in *Fluxions*:

> From geometry the infinites and infinitesimals passed into philosophy, carrying with them the obscurity and perplexity that cannot fail to accompany them. An actual division, as well as a divisibility of matter *in infinitum*, is admitted by some. Fluids are imagined consisting of infinitely small particles, which are composed themselves of others infinitely less; and this subdivision is supposed to be continued without end. Vortices are supposed, for solving the phaenomena of nature, of indefinite or infinite degrees, in imitation of the infinitesimals in geometry; that, when any higher order is found insufficient for this purpose, or attended with an insuperable difficulty, a lower order may preserve so favourite a scheme. Nature is confined in her operations to act by infinitely small steps. Bodies of a perfect hardness are rejected, and the old doctrine of atoms treated as imaginary, because in their actions and collisions they might pass at once from motion to rest, or from rest to motion, in violation of this law. Thus the doctrine of infinites is interwoven with our speculations in geometry and nature. Suppositions, that were proposed at first diffidently, as of use for discovering new theorems in this science with the greater facility, and were suffered only on that account, have been indulged, till it has become crowded with objects of an abstruse nature, which tend to perplex it and the other sciences that have a dependence upon it ([16] *1*, 39).

This powerful passage covers the main elements of Leibniz's physics, planetary theory and mathematics. Here I will omit all discussion of Leibniz's "Tentamen de motuum coelestium causis" (1689), where he applied the general principles of his differential calculus to the problem of planetary motion, where a rotating vortex provides a mechanism for the necessary forces ([1] 125—51). MacLaurin grasps the close link between Leibnizian dynamics and the Leibnizian metaphysical axiom of continuity, and in *Newton* he discusses this point with explicit reference to Bernoulli's "Discours sur . . . mouvement":

> We have another instance of the art by which they support their schemes, in the pretended demonstration they give against the possibility of atoms, or of any perfectly hard and inflexible bodies. According to what they call the law of *continuity*, all changes in nature are produced by insensible and infinitely small degrees; so that no body can, in any case, pass from motion to rest, or from rest to motion, without passing

through all possible intermediate degrees of motion; from which they conclude that atoms, or any perfectly hard bodies, are impossible; because if two of them should meet with equal motions, in contrary directions, they would necessarily stop at once, in violation of the law of *continuity* ([17] 87—8).

In response MacLaurin seeks to turn the notion of "continuity" against Leibniz and Bernoulli. He observes that his opponents suppose a distinction between two kinds of "forces": "when the velocity is finite, how small soever it may be, the force is measured by the square of the velocity; but when the velocity is infinitely little (as it is, according to the favourers of the new opinion) in consequence of the first impulse of the power that generates the motion, the force is simply as the velocity [thus: as dv]; and we cannot but observe, that this sudden change of the law does not appear to be consistent with the favourite principle of *continuity*, so zealously maintained by the same philosophers" ([17] 132). The supposition of two kinds of "forces", which Bernoulli himself had conceived to be "heterogeneous" ([2] *3*, 37) is therefore in contradiction to the concept of continuity; there must be a continuity and hence identity between the "forces" at the commencement of motion and when motion is established. Similar critiques of Leibniz and Bernoulli were made by Euler in his paper "De la force de percussion et de sa véritable mésure" (1745), and by Kant in his *Gedanken von der wahren Schätzung der lebendigen Kräfte* (1747) ([7] 63—4).

In section 1 of the *Principia*'s first book Newton justifies his infinitesimal arguments by the method of prime and ultimate ratios of nascent and vanishing finite quantities approaching their limits. He claims that he does not suppose indivisible magnitudes but finite limit ratios: "by the last ratio of vanishing quantities you must understand not the ratio of quantities before they vanish, not that afterwards, but that with which they vanish". He claims that the determination of this limit is a "geometrical problem" ([19] *1*, 87—8). These claims shape MacLaurin's defense of Newton and critique of the Leibnizian calculus. He notes that the proponents of the Leibnizian calculus differed among themselves about the status of infinitesimals. While Leibniz supposed infinitesimals to be "no more than fictions", others (such as Johann Bernoulli) "place them on a level with finite quantities and endeavour to demonstrate their reality". He maintains that these views are confused: mathematicians have "involved themselves in the mazes of infinity". While he concedes that "the computations in [Newton's] method are the same as in the [Leibnizian] method of infinitesimals", he urges that Newton's method is to be preferred as being "founded on accurate principles agreeable to ancient geometry". Newton's method "requires the supposition of no quantities but such as are finite and easily conceived" ([16] *1*, 38—49). He explains that "Newton considers the simultaneous increments of the flowing quantities as finite, and then investigates the ratio which is the limit of the various proportions which those increments bear to each other, while he supposes them to decrease together till they vanish" ([16] *2*, 420). While MacLaurin blurs the similarities between Newtonian and Leibnizian infinitesimal methods, his concern was with the justification of these methods, appealing to the canons of classical geometry ([3]).

MacLaurin contests the Leibnizian theory of matter as adopted by Bernoulli, which formed the basis of Bernoulli's representation of collision in terms of the action of elastic springs. He argues that "there never has been discovered as yet any one body whose elasticity is perfect; and when any two bodies meet with equal motions, they rebound with less motions, and there is always force lost by their collision". It is MacLaurin's case that Bernoulli's arguments apply to the special case of "perfectly elastic bodies only . . . not one of which has hitherto been found in nature" ([17] 86). On turning to an examination of the problem of the collision of bodies, MacLaurin argues that "Mr *Bernoulli* has resolved only a very limited case of this problem in his *Essay* on motion, *Paris* 1726; for he supposes the bodies to be perfectly elastic" ([17] 192). Moreover, Bernoulli's treatment of collision in terms of the action of elastic springs is erroneous: "it is the last spring only, which is in contact with the body, that acts upon it, the rest serving only for sustaining it in its action; so that any change produced in the body, by whatever name it be called, ought to be determined from the action of this last spring only, and in just reasoning ought to be computed from it alone" ([17] 134—5).

MacLaurin therefore concludes that the Leibnizian principle of the conservation of *vis viva*, which Bernoulli had sought to explicate, "is not general". The principle is of use in the case of the collision of perfectly elastic bodies: "They who hold this principle to be general confine this theory too much to one sort of bodies, which for any thing appears from nature have no prerogative above others". MacLaurin does however allow that the principle of the conservation of *vis viva* is applicable to special cases in the theory of mechanics. He observes that "the principle which Mr. Huygens calls the *conservatio vis ascendentis*

VIII

DYNAMICS AND INTELLIGIBILITY

[the conservation of the quantity mv^2 in the descent and ascent of the centre of gravity of a system of bodies] ... and which seems to be much the same with what is called the *conservatio vis viva* of late, obtains indeed in many cases besides those he has considered, and may be of use in several inquiries concerning the motions of bodies that have no elasticity, as well as those that are perfectly elastic, but is not general" ([16] 2, 438n.). Equating the Leibnizian *vis viva* principle with Huygens' concept, MacLaurin sought to deny Bernoulli's special claim of the dynamical and ontological significance of the principle. MacLaurin thus rejects Bernoulli's metaphysical justification (by the law of continuity) of Leibnizian dynamics, the theory of matter by which Bernoulli supports his representation of collision, and Bernoulli's claim that the principle of the conservation of *vis viva* is a fundamental law of nature, not merely a special theorem as Huygens had supposed.

MacLaurin's claim in *Newton* that the principle of the conservation of *vis viva* "is not to be held a general principle or law of motion" ([17] 194) provides the basis for his general defence and presentation of the truth of the Newtonian system of natural philosophy. In rejecting the Leibnizian principle, espoused by Bernoulli, that "the quantity of force is for ever the same in the universe", MacLaurin affirms the Newtonian view, stated by Clarke in his correspondence with Leibniz, that "it may be better that the Author of the world should act immediately in it, cherishing and governing his work, and sometimes changing or renewing it". Leibnizian dynamics, which rests on the principle of the conservation of *vis viva* which establishes the self-sufficiency of nature, denies Newton's "opinion that the fabrick of the universe, and course of nature, could not continue for ever in its present state, but would require, in process of time, to be re-established or renewed by the same hand that formed it". Thus "the capital doctrine of this philosophy that represents the universe as a perfect machine, such as may continue for ever by mechanical laws in its present state, is, that the same quantity of force and vigour remains always in it, and passes from one portion of matter to another, without undergoing any change in the whole" ([17] 84—6). MacLaurin's critique of Bernoulli thus forms part of a more general attack on Leibnizian dynamics and theology, an element in his thoroughgoing defence of Newtonian principles. This entailed a denial of the possibility of the sufficiency of mechanical laws in explaining the structure of the universe, and rejection of the appeal by Leibniz (in his correspondence with Clarke) and

Bernoulli (in his "Discours sur ... mouvement") to the principle of the conservation of *vis viva* as establishing the self-sufficiency and intelligibility of nature. To Bernoulli's claim that if "the quantity of *vis viva*, the single source of the continuation of motion in the universe were not conserved ... all nature would fall into disorder" ([2] *3*, 58), MacLaurin countered with the Newtonian argument that "tho' the course of nature was to be regular, it was not necessary that it should be governed by those principles only which arise from the various motions and modifications of unactive matter, by mechanical laws" ([17] 84).

MacLaurin's *Newton* concludes with discussion of the concept of gravity, where these physico-theological arguments are further deployed. Following Newton and Clarke he claims that gravity "seems to surpass mere mechanism" ([17] 387). Buchdahl has discussed the complex of arguments arising from this claim, and writes that for Newton

> the argument operates however at two different levels, a physical ... and a metaphysical level. It is physical when Newton argues that the growing irregularities in astronomical motions, as well as the continual "loss of motion" [in inelastic collisions], require a power that will "reform" the parts of the universe at suitable moments in time. ... On the other hand, the "metaphysical" argument is quite different. ... He contends that the existence of gravitational phenomena becomes rational (and thus real) only on the supposition that they are an expression of divine providence, often described as an "active principle" ... ([5] 179—80).

As in the case of the intelligibility of dynamics, this metaphysical argument was intended to supplement and justify the concept of gravity, a dimension to scientific theorizing highlighted in Buchdahl's studies of Newtonian themes.

NOTES

[1] Leibniz, 'Specimen dynamicum' (1695) ([14] 6, 242).
[2] Bernoulli, Jean, 'Discours sur les loix de la communication du mouvement', in *Recueil des pieces qui a remporté les prix de l'Académie des Sciences, Tome premier* (Paris, 1732); reprinted in [2] *3*, 7—107.

REFERENCES

1. Aiton, E. J., *The Vortex Theory of Planetary Motions* (London: Macdonald, 1972).
2. Bernoulli, Jean, *Opera omnia*, 4 vols (Lausanne and Geneva, 1742).
3. Bos, H. J. M., 'Differentials, higher-order differentials and the derivative in the Leibnizian calculus', *Archive for History of Exact Sciences 14* (1974), 1—90.

4. Buchdahl, Gerd, 'Gravity and intelligibility: Newton to Kant', in *The Methodological Heritage of Newton*, eds. R. E. Butts and J. W. Davis (Oxford: Blackwell, 1970), 74—102.
5. Buchdahl, Gerd, 'Explanation and gravity', in *Changing Perspectives in the History of Science*, eds. M. Teich and R. M. Young (London: Heinemann, 1973), 167—203.
6. Hall, A. R., *Philosophers at War. The Quarrel between Newton and Leibniz* (Cambridge: Cambridge Univ. Press, 1980).
7. Harman, P. M., *Metaphysics and Natural Philosophy. The Problem of Substance in Classical Physics* (Brighton: Harvester Press, 1982).
8. Harman, P. M., 'Force and inertia: Euler and Kant's *Metaphysical Foundations of Natural Science*', in *Nature Mathematized*, ed. W. R. Shea (Dordrecht: Reidel, 1983), 229—49.
9. Harman, P. M., 'Concepts of inertia: Newton to Kant', in *Religion, Science and Worldview. Essays in Honour of Richard S. Westfall*, eds. M. J. Osler and P. L. Farber (Cambridge and New York: Cambridge Univ. Press, 1985), 119—33.
10. Heimann [Harman], P. M., 'Helmholtz and Kant: The metaphysical foundations of Über die Erhaltung der Kraft', *Studies in History and Philosophy of Science 5* (1974), 205—38.
11. Heimann [Harman], P. M., '"Geometry and nature": Leibniz and Johann Bernoulli's theory of motion', *Centaurus 21* (1977), 1—26.
12. Huygens, Christiaan, *Oeuvres complètes*, 22 vols (The Hague: Nijhoff, 1888—1950).
13. Kant, Immanuel, *Kants gesammelte Schriften*, 29 vols in 32. Ed. Königliche Preussische Akademie der Wissenschaften (Berlin: Reimer and de Gruyter, 1902—83).
14. Leibniz, G. W., *Mathematische Schriften*, 7 vols, ed. C. I. Gerhardt (Berlin and Halle, 1849—60).
15. Leibniz, G. W., *The Leibniz-Clarke Correspondence*, ed. H. G. Alexander (Manchester: Manchester Univ. Press, 1956).
16. MacLaurin, Colin, *A Treatise of Fluxions*, 2 vols (Edinburgh, 1742).
17. MacLaurin, Colin, *An Account of Sir Isaac Newton's Philosophical Discoveries* (Edinburgh, 1748).
18. Newton, Isaac, *Opticks* (4th ed., London, 1730; repr. London: Dover, 1952).
19. Newton, Isaac, *Isaac Newton's Philosophiae Naturalis Principia Mathematica: The Third Edition (1726) with Variant Readings*, 2 vols, eds. A. Koyré and I. B. Cohen (Cambridge: Cambridge Univ. Press, 1972).

IX

Concepts of inertia: Newton to Kant

In his *Force in Newton's Physics,* Richard S. Westfall described Newton's concept of inertia as paradoxical, for there are striking ambiguities in Newton's designation of the concept of inertia as the "force of inertia *[vis inertiae]."* In the *Principia,* the force of motion of a body is defined as the cause of a change of motion, whereas inertia is held to preserve a body in a state of rest or uniform rectilinear motion. For Newton to link his concepts of force and inertia in denoting the "force of inertia" would therefore seem to be anomalous.

Despite this terminological ambiguity, Newton does not confuse his concepts of impressed force and inertia in his usage in the *Principia;* but the "paradox of Newton's *vis inertiae*"[1] may be seen as the tip of the iceberg of problems concerning matter and force, which Newton carefully excluded from consideration in his treatise on the mathematical principles of motion, but which are nevertheless central issues in his natural philosophy. The problem of force and its relation to inertia remained at the heart of the debates on the foundations of physics in the eighteenth century, and in this essay I shall seek to illuminate the problematic status of *vis inertiae* as perceived by Leibniz, Euler, and Kant, and to review their attempts at conceptual clarification. Although subsequent discourse about the role of forces in natural philosophy was fundamentally shaped by Newton's physics, Newton's treatment of

---

[1] Richard S. Westfall, *Force in Newton's Physics: The Science of Dynamics in the Seventeenth Century* (London and New York, 1971), p. 450.

the concepts of force and inertia was subjected to searching criticism by his successors.

The problems these natural philosophers were seeking to resolve had their origin in the debates surrounding the mechanical philosophy of the late seventeenth century. These issues concerning the conceptual foundations of physics were not put to rest by Newton's *Principia,* despite the importance of the transformation in the conceptual structure of physics brought about by the establishment of the Newtonian laws of motion and concept of universal gravitation. Debates over the status of the concepts of force and inertia not only continued to flourish but were integral to the development of natural philosophy in the eighteenth century. My intention here is not to discuss this theme systematically but to illustrate some of its salient features by focusing upon the problem of Newton's concept of *vis inertiae.*

It should be appreciated that Leibniz, Euler, and Kant approached these matters with different intentions, though it is not possible here to properly characterize their diverse objectives and worldviews. Leibniz aimed to refute the conceptual framework of the *Principia* and to create his own distinctive science of "dynamics"; Euler sought to elaborate an essentially Newtonian mechanics by clarifying the ambiguities of the Newtonian concept of *vis inertiae;* whereas Kant sought to justify the intelligibility of Newtonian physical laws by reconstructing the metaphysical foundations of Newtonian science.[2]

FORCE AND INERTIA IN NEWTON'S PHYSICS

Newton based his first law of motion in the *Principia* on a relationship between *force,* as an external action generating change of motion, and *inertia,* conceived as a fundamental property of matter by which bodies resist changes in their state of rest or uniform rectilinear motion. Whereas the separation of his mathematical theory of the motion of bodies from a physical interpretation is fundamental to the strategy of Newton's argument, the laws of motion provide a physical basis for the mathematical theory of motion. On one level of explanation, Newton considered "forces

---

[2] For a broader discussion of these themes, see P. M. Harman, *Metaphysics and Natural Philosophy: The Problem of Substance in Classical Physics* (Brighton, Sussex, and Totowa, N. J., 1982).

Concepts of inertia: Newton to Kant

not physically but merely mathematically" and maintained that the concept of force, as defined by its usage in the mathematical formalism of the *Principia*, does not imply any "physical cause or reason" for the motions of bodies.[3] But at the same time he emphasized that the treatment of the motion of bodies in the *Principia* is to be given a physical interpretation by means of the laws of motion. The laws of motion thus provide the physical rationale of the mechanics of the *Principia*, and are based on concepts of force and inertia.

Newton's interpretation of force and inertia as physical concepts had its origin in his reading of Descartes's theory of the motion and collision of bodies. In particular, Newton reformulated Descartes's first two laws of motion to establish the basis of the first law of motion of the *Principia*. In expounding his own laws of motion, Descartes explained the tendency of a body to persevere in a state of rest or a state of motion in terms of the "force" of a body to remain at rest, and its "force" to remain in a state of motion; force is therefore conceived as the cause that maintains the existence of a body in any particular state, whether of rest or motion.[4]

In developing his own theory of mechanics, Newton adapted and significantly transformed the Cartesian concept of force. Newton's arguments show significant development from his early writings on the theory of mechanics in the 1660s (which show a pronounced Cartesian influence) to the mature formulation in the *Principia*.[5] The key feature of this transformation is the introduction of two concepts, *impressed force* and *inertia*, to explain the motion of bodies. Newton adopted the term *inertia* from Descartes who had employed the word to denote the sluggishness of bodies. Newton, however, used *inertia* to denote the internal power by which a body tends to persevere in a state of rest or uniform rectilinear motion.[6] In the *Principia*, Newton employed the concept

---

[3] *Isaac Newton's Philosophiae Naturalis Principia Mathematica: The Third Edition (1726) with Variant Readings*, ed. A. Koyré and I. Bernard Cohen, 2 vols. (Cambridge, Mass., 1972), I, 46.
[4] A. Gabbey, "Force and Inertia in the Seventeenth Century: Descartes and Newton," in *Descartes: Philosophy, Mathematics and Physics*, ed. S. Gaukroger (Brighton, Sussex, and Totowa, N. J., 1980), pp. 230–320.
[5] J. W. Herivel, *The Background to Newton's 'Principia'* (Oxford, 1965); Westfall, *Force in Newton's Physics*, pp. 424–67.
[6] I. Bernard Cohen, *The Newtonian Revolution* (Cambridge, Engl., 1980), pp. 189, 333–4.

of *impressed force* to denote causes generating change of motion or rest, the "action exerted on a body to change its state either of resting still or moving uniformly straight on." The disjunction between the concepts of impressed force and inertia expresses a distinction between an external cause generating changes in the motion of a body, which consists in "action alone, and does not endure in the body after the action is over," and the internal, inherent power of inertia, by which bodies resist changes in their state of rest or uniform rectilinear motion.[7]

Newton's designation of the concept of inertia as the "force of inertia" is ambiguous but reflects his early (Cartesian) conception of force as the principle maintaining a body in a state of rest or motion. To denote the power of matter by which a body persists in its state of rest or uniform rectilinear motion, Newton had used the term *vis insita* (innate force), which in seventeenth-century usage meant natural power or inherent force, ultimately introducing *vis inertiae* and declaring that "the innate force may be called, by a very significant name, the force of inertia."[8] Newton's ambiguous terminology in designating inertia as a *force* reflects contemporary usage, but in his later writings especially, he seeks to differentiate sharply between the status of the concepts of inertia and impressed force.

The concept of inertia is fundamental to the meaning of Newton's first law of motion, providing an explanation of the natural tendency of a body to persevere in the same state of rest or uniform rectilinear motion. He supported his view of the physical significance of the concept of inertia by claiming that inertia is proportional to the mass of a body: Inertia defines the materiality of bodies. In the third rule of philosophizing, appended to the second edition of *Principia* (1713), Newton listed inertia together with extension, hardness, impenetrability, and mobility as the "universal" qualities of matter, the essential properties an entity would have to possess as a necessary and sufficient condition of its materiality.[9] Inertia is thus a defining property of material substances; and in contrast to inertia, impressed force is held to be "not essential to body" and to be external to the material substance of bodies.[10]

[7] Newton, *Principia*, I, 40–1.
[8] Newton, *Principia*, I, 40. See Cohen, *Newtonian Revolution*, pp. 190–1, 334.
[9] Newton, *Principia*, II, 552.
[10] Newton, *Principia*, I, 41 (an unpublished annotation to the text of the second edition).

Despite his general disparagement of metaphysical arguments, he supported his statement of the physical significance of inertia by appeal to philosophical principles. In support of this claim that inertia is essential to matter, Newton declared that the universal qualities of bodies, including inertia, are known through experience to be essential properties of matter. He justified their universality, their ascription to the imperceptible indivisible particles of bodies, by appeal to the "analogy of nature," and declared that the ascription of these qualities to all bodies in nature is the "foundation of all philosophy."[11] The universal qualities are conceived as being those that could not change without affecting the materiality of bodies. Unlike nonessential qualities like heat and cold, these qualities do not manifest continuous and successive gradations of intensity: Were inertia to change, then a body would necessarily change its essential nature. The ascription of essential qualities to the fundamental particles of matter is justified by an appeal to the uniformity and homogeneity of nature.[12] The primordial atoms thus differ from observable particles only in size, not in their possession of essential properties such as inertia.

The definition of inertia as an essential property of matter contrasts with Newton's definition of force as external to matter. Newton's denial in his letter to Richard Bentley in 1693 that the force of gravity is "innate inherent and essential" to matter[13] emphasized that gravity was in a different category from inertia, reflecting Newton's distinction between force as external to the material substance of bodies and as acting to bring about change of motion, and inertia as a "universal" or "essential" property of matter. Hence unlike inertia, gravity is not an inherent or essential property of matter.

In the *Opticks*, Newton contrasted inertia as a "passive principle by which bodies persist in their motion or rest" with "active principles, such as are the cause of gravity." Matter in itself does not have the capacity to sustain motion; the motion and activity of bodies in nature is therefore seen in terms of forces and the causal agency of "active principles." Newton referred to active principles

---

[11] Newton, *Principia*, II, 552–4.
[12] J. E. McGuire, "Atoms and the 'Analogy of Nature': Newton's Third Rule of Philosophising," *Studies in History and Philosophy of Science*, 1 (1970), 3–57; E. McMullin, *Newton on Matter and Activity* (Notre Dame and London, 1978), pp. 13–21.
[13] Newton to Bentley, 25 February 1692/3, in *The Correspondence of Isaac Newton*, ed. H. W. Turnbull, J. F. Scott, A. R. Hall, and L. Tilling, 7 vols. (Cambridge, Engl., 1959–77), *3*, 254.

both as being the "cause of gravity" and as being "general laws of nature . . . such as is that of gravity," and it would seem that active principles functioned both as laws of nature (though not "passive" laws of matter) and as the mediating agents by which God conserved motion and gravity in the cosmos.[14] The operations of active principles in nature were not reducible to the passive principles of matter such as inertia.[15]

The introduction of a conceptual disjunction between active and passive principles is clearly intended as a clarification of the status of gravity: Gravity, not being an essential property of matter, could not be explained in terms of passive principles of matter. But the introduction of active principles to explain gravity raised further difficulties. Leibniz ridiculed the appeal to a theory of gravity "performed without any mechanism" or "by a law of God" as tantamount to supposing gravity" an unreasonable occult quality."[16] Newton was accused of reviving the discredited notion of occult qualities, a view of nature vehemently contested by the mechanical philosophers of the seventeenth century.

Newton's introduction of his famous aether theory in the 1717 *Opticks* was probably governed by his attempt to refute Leibniz's charges, developed at length in Leibniz's correspondence with Samuel Clarke in 1715–16. Rejecting the reducibility of gravity to a contact–action model based on the impact of particles, which would have given gravity the status of a "passive" principle, Newton endowed the aether with active properties, which enabled it to function as a cause of gravity. The aether is composed of material particles and would ostensibly appear to fall under the category of passive principles. But Newton sought to distinguish between the passivity and inertia of ordinary matter and the active properties of ether.[17] The use of aether as an "active" principle thus threatened the active–passive dualism of Newton's natural philosophy, just as the ambiguous term "force of inertia" blurred the conceptual distinction between inertia as a passive property of matter and force as an external action generating change.

[14] Isaac Newton, *Opticks: or a Treatise of the Reflexions, Refractions, Inflexions and Colours of Light*, 4th ed. (1730; reprint ed., London, 1952), pp. 397–401.
[15] J. E. McGuire, "Force, Active Principles, and Newton's Invisible Realm," *Ambix*, 15 (1968), 154–208.
[16] Quoted in A. Koyré, *Newtonian Studies* (London, 1965), p. 141.
[17] P. M. Heimann [Harman], "Ether and Imponderables," in *Conceptions of Ether: Studies in the History of Ether Theories 1740–1900*, ed. G. N. Cantor and M. J. S. Hodge (Cambridge, Engl., 1981), pp. 61–83.

LEIBNIZ AND THE CONCEPT OF FORCE

In his *Specimen Dynamicum* (1695), Leibniz sought to resolve the difficulties (as he perceived them) arising from Newton's dualist ontology by elaborating a theory of motion that was not based on a dualism of forces acting to bring about change and matter passively resisting change. By contrast, Leibniz proposed to explain motion in terms of a monism of force. Forces act to bring about change of motion; the resistance to motion, *inertia,* was explained in terms of forces resisting change of motion. Leibnizian dynamics revoked the disjunction between the concepts of force and inertia in Newton's physics. Leibniz rejected Newton's supposition that inertia is an essential property of matter: As a resisting power of matter, inertia does not define the nature of substances but is conceptualized as a "force." By supposing a monism of force, Leibniz aimed to resolve the ambiguities of the Newtonian disjunction between impressed force and inertia (conceived as a defining property of matter).

Leibnizian dynamics rested upon a theory of substance which differed radically from that held by Newton. Leibniz did not envisage a dualism between matter and force: In his view, substances are characterized by fundamental forces, and the forces of empirical physics are conceived as phenomenal analogues of these fundamental forces. The relationship between substances and empirical forces was thus conceived in quite different terms from the ontological dualism proposed by Newton.[18]

Leibnizian dynamics was thus grounded on a distinctive theory of substance, and Leibniz emphasized the importance of explaining the relations between ontological foundations and the laws of empirical physics. Unlike Newton, Leibniz maintained that the formulation of an intelligible natural philosophy requires explicit appeal to metaphysical principles. Leibnizian dynamics, concerned with empirical forces, was thus shown to be intelligible by a metaphysical explication of the relation between substances and empirical forces.

Leibniz criticized the Cartesian theory of substance, the thesis that matter is defined by spatial extension. In Leibniz's view, spatial extension is merely a manifestation of substance, not its defin-

---

[18] For general discussion, see Gerd Buchdahl, *Metaphysics and the Philosophy of Science. The Classical Origins: Descartes to Kant* (Oxford, 1969), pp. 388–469; Westfall, *Force in Newton's Physics,* pp. 283–322.

ing property. The inherent activity of substances, caused by forces, is the most fundamental characteristic of bodies, and force therefore defines the nature of substances. Leibniz termed the fundamental forces that characterize substances "primitive forces," but he denied that these fundamental forces could be invoked to explain the laws of empirical physics. Primitive forces explain the ultimate "sources of things" but not the "reasons for the laws of nature." The laws of empirical physics are explained in terms of "derivative" forces, the forces "by which bodies act on one another or are acted upon by each other." Derivative or empirical forces, which alone provide the basis for physical theorizing, were conceived as phenomenal analogues of the primitive forces that define the nature of substances.[19]

In characterizing the laws of nature, Leibniz distinguished between "active" and "passive" derivative forces, these terms having a distinctive meaning in his dynamics. The derivative active forces, which generate and sustain motion, were termed "living" and "dead" forces. The explanation of their relationship, based on an appeal to the metaphysical principle of the law of continuity, that "all change occurs gradually," forms the core of the Leibnizian theory of dynamics, based on the relationship between infinitesimal and finite quantities.[20] Living force, which measures the force of motion of a body, arises from an infinite number of infinitesimal impulses of dead force – the force that arises in the tendency of a body to achieve its state of motion. The conservation of living force in the mechanical interaction of bodies was for Leibniz a fundamental law expressing the inherent activity of nature and the order and self-sufficiency of natural processes.[21]

The derivative passive forces were the impenetrability of bodies and their resistance to motion, constituting the effort of bodies to remain in their state of rest or motion. For Leibniz, the resistance of bodies to motion (inertia) was not, as with Newton, explained by appeal to the essential nature of matter. Resistance to motion, or "natural inertia," was explicated in terms of the manifestation

---

[19] G. W. Leibniz, *Specimen dynamicum* [1695], in *Leibnizens Mathematische Schriften*, ed. C. I. Gerhardt, 7 vols. (Berlin and Halle, 1849–63; reprinted Hildesheim, 1960–1), 6, 233–8.
[20] Leibniz, *Mathematische Schriften*, 6, 241.
[21] P. M. Heimann [Harman], " 'Geometry and nature': Leibniz and Johann Bernoulli's Theory of Motion," *Centaurus*, 21 (1977), 1–26.

of "forces."[22] Impenetrability and "inertia" were not conceived as essential or defining properties of matter, but were explicated as derivative passive forces, conceived as the phenomenal manifestation of primitive forces that define substances. The Newtonian dualism between force and matter was therefore avoided. For Leibniz, *inertia* represented a power of matter: Whereas active force generates motion, passive force resists motion. Bodies therefore resist motion by the derivative passive forces of impenetrability and inertia. In Leibnizian dynamics, the motion of bodies is explained by the interplay between active and passive derivative forces, whereas in Newton's physics, the theory of motion is based on the dualism of force and matter (defined by fundamental properties of inertia and impenetrability).

Living and dead forces, i.e., impenetrability and resistance to motion, were thus explicated as falling under different categories of *force*. Whereas living and dead forces (*active* forces) generate motion, inertia (*passive* force) resists motion. The Newtonian dualism of force and inertia conflates to a monism of force, an interaction of active and passive derivative forces. The relation between active and passive derivative forces was not envisaged as analogous to the Newtonian disjunction between impressed force and inertia; hence Leibniz sought to avoid the problems of the Newtonian *vis inertiae*. The notion of inertia as a resisting power is made intelligible in terms of the Leibnizian category of derivative force; and primitive forces, not inertia, define the essential nature of substances.

EULER'S CRITIQUE OF "FORCE OF INERTIA"

In an essay "Recherche sur l'origine des forces" (1750), Leonhard Euler's concern lay in analyzing the foundational questions arising from Newton's concept of force. Euler contested the Leibnizian science of dynamics, which explicated empirical forces as phenomenal manifestation of fundamental forces; and he also rejected the view of D'Alembert, who sought to eliminate forces from the science of mechanics on the ground that the concept of force was obscure and metaphysical. In Euler's view, the concept of force was neither redundant nor "primitive" (in the Leibnizian sense);

---

[22] Quoted in Westfall, *Force in Newton's Physics*, p. 318.

adopting a Newtonian theory of force, he nevertheless recognized that "force" required conceptual explication.[23]

Euler perceived that there is an ambiguity in Newton's notion of "force of inertia." He argued that for Newton, force is the cause of a change of motion of a body, whereas inertia is defined in terms of the perseverance of a body in its state of rest or uniform rectilinear motion. Euler emphasized that strictly speaking, the concepts of *force* and *inertia* were therefore "directly contrary to one another." He concluded that to define *inertia* in terms of a *force* is therefore self-contradictory.

Euler nevertheless agreed with Newton's claim that inertia and impenetrability are defining properties of matter. Euler alluded to Newton's argument in the third rule of philosophizing of the *Principia,* that the essential properties of matter, such as impenetrability and inertia, are not subject to alteration of degrees of intensity, for he claimed that "impenetrability does not admit of degrees." Euler thus maintained that impenetrability is an absolute quality of bodies: "If a body is not completely impenetrable, it is penetrable." Because of the "absolute impossibility" of bodies to admit penetration by other bodies, impenetrability is an essential property of matter.[24] For Euler, the property of impenetrability is fundamental, providing a basis for his explication of force as arising from the impenetrability of bodies, manifested when bodies collide.

These arguments were developed further in Euler's *Lettres à une princesse d'Allemagne* (1768–72), in which he asserted that impenetrability is a "necessary property of all bodies" and defined body as an "impenetrable extension." Inertia, too, was conceived as a defining property of matter: "It would be impossible for a body to exist without inertia." Defining inertia as "a repugnance to everything that tends to change the state of bodies," he contrasted inertia with force, the "external cause," which signifies "everything that is capable of changing the state of bodies." Whereas inertia, like impenetrability, is essential to matter, force is not *"inherent* in matter." Thus the term "force of inertia" is an abuse of language, because inertia is "the opposite of a force." By rejecting

---

[23] S. Gaukroger, "The Metaphysics of Impenetrability: Euler's Conception of Force," *British Journal for the History of Science,* 15 (1982), 132–56.

[24] L. Euler, "Recherches sur l'origine des forces" [1750], in *Leonhardi Euleri opera omnia,* 2nd ser., vol. 5, ed. J. O. Fleckenstein (Lausanne, 1957), 112–15.

Newton's ambiguous term *vis inertiae*, Euler sought to clarify the Newtonian concept of inertia.

Euler sought to explain the origin of forces in terms of the fundamental concept of impenetrability. He took collision, contact-action, as the basic mode of change in nature. He suggested that bodies act on one another "no more than is necessary to prevent penetration." Hence collision is the source of "all the changes which occur in the world," and he concluded that the impenetrability of bodies is "the great spring by which nature works all her effects." He argued that forces, which arise from the impenetrability of bodies, are manifested only in resisting penetration. Forces are therefore dispositional, for although the impenetrability of matter gives rise to force, matter is not "endowed with a determinate force" but is "rather in a condition to manifest force" necessary in order to prevent penetration.[25] Thus the "origin of forces is based on the impenetrability of bodies." Euler therefore sought to clarify Newton's arguments, rejecting the term *vis inertiae* as self-contradictory, and affirming the (Newtonian) disjunction between the concepts of force and inertia.

KANT AND THE CONCEPT OF INERTIA

In his *Metaphysische Anfangsgründe der Naturwissenschaft* (1786), Kant aimed to provide an analysis of the presuppositions about matter and force that underlie Newton's statement of the laws of motion and the concept of universal gravitation. Kant therefore sought to appraise the relationship between Newtonian physical laws and the false metaphysical assumptions that he believed were fundamental to Newton's statement of his physics in the *Principia*. Kant declared that all natural philosophers who sought to create a mathematical physics had in fact "made use of metaphysical principles and were obliged to make use of them, even though they otherwise [like Newton] solemnly protested against any claim of metaphysics on their science."[26]

---

[25] L. Euler, *Lettres à une princesse d'Allemagne sur divers sujets de physique et de philosophie*, 3 vols. (St. Petersbourg, 1768–72), in *Leonhardi Euleri opera omnia*, 3rd ser., vol. 2, ed. A. Speiser (Zürich, 1960), 150–71.

[26] Immanuel Kant, *Metaphysische Anfangsgründe der Naturwissenschaft* [1786], in *Kants gesammelte Schriften. Herausgegeben von der Königlich Preussischen Akademie der Wissenschaften*, 24 vols. (Berlin, 1902–38), 4, 472.

Kant contested Newton's atomistic ontology and the doctrine that impenetrability and inertia are defining properties of matter. By reappraising metaphysical foundations, by defining matter in terms of inherent forces of attraction and repulsion, Kant sought to establish the fundamental status of the concept of force (which he believed was confused in Newton's account) and thus to demonstrate the intelligibility of Newton's concept of the attractive force of gravity. Rejecting Newton's philosophical argument that inertia is an essential property of matter, Kant nevertheless sought to clarify the status of the Newtonian concept of inertia as a physical principle. Indeed, Kant claimed that only by rejecting Newton's metaphysical arguments could the status of inertia as a physical principle be adequately justified.

The argument of Kant's book is elaborate and at times discursive; its unifying theme is the application of the a priori categories of the *Critique of Pure Reason,* which he regarded as being constitutive of all experience, to the concept of matter. Although Kant claimed that there are links between physical theory and the a priori principles of cognition, he did not claim that the validity of Newtonian physics – the law of gravitation and the laws of motion – can be derived from a priori premises. Kant's aim was rather to establish the intelligibility of Newtonian physical concepts by demonstrating links between the categories and Newtonian physical laws.[27] In Kant's view, this enterprise involved a total reappraisal of Newton's dualistic ontology of matter and force: Only then would gravity and inertia be shown to be intelligible as physical concepts. Kant's reappraisal of Newton's dualistic ontology of force and matter was based on a metaphysical argument, which proceeded by the application of the categories of cognition to the concept of matter. The metaphysical argument was intended to establish the possibility of physical concepts and laws, not their actuality, yielding principles of constraint on possible physical hypotheses.

Kant's critique of Newton's theory of matter was developed in the second chapter of his book, on "Dynamics." He rejected the doctrine of essential qualities proposed by Newton and Euler, that impenetrability and inertia were the defining properties of all material substances. Kant maintained that forces define the essence of matter: "Matter fills space, not by its mere existence, but by a

---

[27] Buchdahl, *Metaphysics and the Philosophy of Science,* p. 678.

special moving force." Matter fills space by repulsive or extensive forces, which form the "basis of its impenetrability." The property of impenetrability is derivative not fundamental and "rests on a physical basis," the repulsive force. Kant went on to assert that "the possibility of matter requires a force of attraction as the second essential fundamental force of matter," a force that limits the extensive effect of the repulsive force.[28]

The dynamic account of matter was formulated with reference to the categories of reality, negation, and limitation, which correspond analogically to the account of matter in terms of fundamental forces of attraction and repulsion, which counteract or limit each other and determine the "degree of the filling of space" by matter. Kant rejected the concept of "absolute impenetrability": the repulsive force has "a degree which can be overcome," and the filling of space by matter is dependent on the "degree of compression" or "relative impenetrability" of matter. The dynamic theory of matter supposes that extension and impenetrability are derivative properties of matter, and that these qualities can change by degrees of intensity; impenetrability is derivative, being grounded on the "fundamental forces" which define the essence of matter.[29]

Kant claimed that in Newton's "mathematico-mechanical" philosophy, "forces were philosophized away," being superadded to matter, which was defined by the "empty concept" of "absolute impenetrability." By contrast, the Kantian "metaphysico-dynamical" theory made forces fundamental, avoiding the problems raised by Newton's dualistic matter–force ontology.[30] Moreover, the Kantian scheme provided an explanation of the intelligibility of the concept of gravity. By its attractive force, matter acts through empty space on other matter: The attractive force is extended through the universe. Thus in establishing that the "possibility of matter requires a force of attraction," Kant claimed that he (unlike Newton) had thereby justified the notion of action at a distance, the concept of gravitational attraction.[31] Kant's argument thus avoided the need to appeal to a physicotheological argument to justify the concept of gravity (as in Newton's reference to "active principles") or to an aether model (as in Newton's anomalous aether concept).

Kant's discussion of Newton's first law of motion in his chapter

---

[28] Kant, *Schriften*, 4, 497, 502, 508.   [29] Kant, *Schriften*, 4, 501, 502, 525.
[30] Kant, *Schriften*, 4, 524–5.   [31] Kant, *Schriften*, 4, 516–17.

IX

on "Mechanics" sought to clarify the meaning of Newton's concept of inertia. Having established that matter is defined by fundamental forces of attraction and repulsion, and that impenetrability is a relative and derivative concept, Kant aimed to show that inertia should be construed as a law of mechanics, not as a defining property of matter. As before, the argument in the chapter on "Mechanics" is based on the application of the categorical principles to the concept of matter. The principle of causality states that "every change has a cause"; applied to the concept of matter, it yields a metaphysical "law of mechanics" that "every change of matter has an external cause." This metaphysical law of mechanics establishes the possibility of Newton's first law of motion (though not its physical actuality), as Kant indicated by placing brackets around his added statement of Newton's first law of motion. Kant did not seek to prove Newton's first law of motion but to establish that "all change of matter is based on an external cause" and that matter "undergoes no changes except by motion."[32]

Kant described this law of mechanics as the "law of inertia," which denotes the passivity of matter, its inability to "determine itself to motion or rest." Kant therefore denied that matter possesses an "internal principle," an inherent power or "special force of matter under the name of the force of inertia." The supposition that matter possesses an "internal principle" or force would contradict the law of inertia, which proves that matter does not possess an inherent power. Kant was thus in agreement with Euler in rejecting the "designation force of inertia" as contradictory.

Kant's reappraisal of the metaphysical foundations of Newton's physics thus aimed to clarify Newton's *vis inertiae*: Inertia is not an inherent or essential property of matter nor is inertia a "special and entirely peculiar force [of resistance]." The law of inertia merely signifies that all changes of matter require an external cause.[33] Kant's rejection of the notion that matter possesses an inherent principle or force of resistance (which he believed to be implied by the term "force of inertia") also signals his rejection of the conceptual framework of Leibnizian dynamics. Although he disagreed with Euler about the relative status of the concepts of inertia, impenetrability, and force he echoed Euler's critique of the term "force of

---

[32] Kant, *Schriften*, 4, 543. See Buchdahl, *Metaphysics and the Philosophy of Science*, pp. 676–8.
[33] Kant, *Schriften*, 4, 543–4, 549–51.

inertia."³⁴ Kant's intention was to reconstruct the relationship between Newton's physical laws and the assumptions about matter and force which underlie the physics of *Principia*. The clarification of Newton's concept of inertia was central to this endeavor and required the Kantian critique of Newton's "mathematico-mechanical" philosophy of nature. Kant's analysis and reappraisal of the metaphysical foundations of Newtonian physics thus resolved the paradox of Newton's *vis inertiae*.

---

[34] P. M. Harman, "Force and Inertia: Euler and Kant's *Metaphysical Foundations of Natural Science*," in *Nature Mathematized*, ed. W. R. Shea (Dordrecht and Boston, 1983), pp. 229–49.

X

FORCE AND INERTIA: EULER AND KANT'S
METAPHYSICAL FOUNDATIONS OF NATURAL SCIENCE

The conceptual problems of natural philosophy remained a subject of enduring interest for Kant. Despite shifts in outlook, engendered by a deeper understanding of natural philosophy and the transformation in philosophical perspective which led to the development of the critical philosophy, the conceptual status of 'force' and the relationship between 'force' and 'matter' remained at the core of Kant's treatment of the problems of natural philosophy. These issues pervade the chapters on 'Dynamics' and 'Mechanics' in the *Metaphysical foundations of natural science* (1786), Kant's mature and most systematic discussion of natural philosophy, where he elaborated the ways in which the transcendental categories of the *Critique of pure reason* (1781) were to be applied to the concept of matter. It has become a commonplace to describe Kant's intentions as an attempt to demonstrate the validity of Newtonian physics, but as Buchdahl has emphasised Kant's 'metaphysics of nature' purports to demonstrate links between physical theory and the transcendental principles rather than to claim that the actual inductive validity of Newtonian physics can be derived from *a priori* premises.[1] Moreover, in the *Metaphysical foundations* Kant's examination of the metaphysical foundations of Newtonian physical concepts led him to a reappraisal of the conceptual status of 'force', 'matter' and inertia' in physical theory. The argument of the *Metaphysical foundations* thus has a complex relationship to the conceptual structure of Newtonian natural philosophy.

In this paper I propose to follow a single strand in the complex of problems associated with the status of 'Newtonian physics' in Kant's philosophy, tracing his changing attitude to the relationships between the concepts of 'force', 'matter' and 'inertia' from his early writings on natural philosophy to the mature formulation in the *Metaphysical foundations*. To do so necessarily imposes limitations, both historical and philosophical, but may serve to highlight some important features of Kant's treatment of natural philosophy. In focusing on the conceptual status of 'force' and 'inertia' in Kant's natural philosophy, I shall emphasise the impact of Johann Bernoulli's theory of 'living force' and of Euler's treatment of the conceptual status of 'force' and 'inertia' on Kant's discussions of physical theory.[2] While Kant's discussions of natural philosophy display a marked divergence from the theories of nature formulated by Bernoulli and Euler, he drew important insights from their work which influenced his construal of the problems of natural philosophy. In the *Metaphysical foundations* Kant follows Euler in stressing the disjunction between the concepts of 'force' and 'inertia', but rejects Euler's view that 'inertia' was a defining property of 'matter', maintaining that 'forces' were the defining characteristics of material substances. Nevertheless, the arguments of Bernoulli and Euler helped to shape Kant's treatment of natural philosophy. For Euler, and for the Kant of the *Metaphysical foundations*, the problems posed by Newton's concepts of 'force' and 'inertia' were of crucial importance, and in particular Kant seeks to provide an analysis of the conceptual framework of natural philosophy, the assumptions about 'matter' and 'force' which underlie Newton's statement of the laws of motion and the concept of universal gravitation. Kant's examination of the metaphysical foundations of 'Newtonian' physical concepts led him to a reappraisal of the conceptual status of 'force' and 'inertia' in physical theory, and to reject the 'Newtonian' concept of 'inertia' as a defining property of 'matter' in favour of the ontological priority of 'force' over the concept of 'matter'. In the *Metaphysical foundations* this re-location of the conceptual relations between 'force', 'inertia' and 'impenetrability' was developed under the formal guidance of the categorial principles, and fostered by Euler's critique of Newtonian natural philosophy. Kant's account of the 'metaphysics of nature' yields a framework of principles which differs from the philosophical assumptions of Newton's theory of nature, providing a reappraisal of the conceptual structure of 'Newtonian' natural philosophy.

Before turning to an account of relevant aspects of Kant's early writings on natural philosophy and an examination of Euler's critique of Newton's discussion of the concept of 'force of inertia [*vis inertiae*]' and its impact on Kant's argument in the *Metaphysical foundations*, some preliminary remarks on Kant's notion of 'metaphysical' foundations' are necessary. Kant's treatment of the 'metaphysics of nature' sought to remedy a crucial deficiency in his early writings on natural philosophy, viz. the gap between a mathematical theory of nature and physical reality. In the 'Preface' to the *Metaphysical foundations* he makes a distinction between the general part of the metaphysics of nature (in the *Critique*), concerned with the general 'laws which make possible the concept of a nature in general', and a 'special metaphysics of nature' (the subject-matter of the *Metaphysical foundations*), in which the transcendental concepts and principles are applied to the empirical concept of matter. Kant maintains that the demonstration of the possibility of 'determinate natural things', as distinct from the demonstration of the possibility of the concept of a nature in general, requires the metaphysical 'construction of concepts', to show that mathematics can be applied to 'determinate natural things'. Kant emphasises that mathematical physics 'presupposes metaphysics of nature' because 'principles of the construction of concepts that belong to the possibility of matter in general must precede' and 'make possible the application of mathematics' to the concept of matter.[3] However Kant denies that 'forces' are entities that can be constructed, and while his 'special metaphysics of nature' sought to bridge the gap between physical reality and the mathematical representation of nature, Kant does not claim to establish that matter can be represented by 'mathematical construction', but only purports to show 'the possibility of a mathematical doctrine of nature'.[4]

I

In his *Thoughts on the true estimation of living forces* (1747) Kant was concerned to analyse the arguments about whether 'force' was to be measured by the 'quantity of motion' or by the 'living force [*vis viva*]', a controversy that had occupied leading natural philosophers in the 1720s and was still the subject of debate, Daniel Bernoulli, Euler, Boscovich and d'Alembert all making contributions to the argument in the 1740s. Kant believed that the 'Cartesian' measure of 'force' ('quantity of motion') could be established by mathematical argument, while the 'Leibnizian' measure of 'force' ('living force'), not being subject to the principle of the conservation of force (in Kant's view) was 'found to be false in mathematics'.[5] Nevertheless he maintained that the 'Leibnizian' measure of 'force' provided a true description of physical reality: 'I will maintain that living forces are really to be found in nature' he declared.[6] Kant emphasised the disjunction between mathematics and physical reality, arguing that 'the mathematical concepts of the properties of bodies and their forces are quite distinct from the concepts found in nature'.[7] There was therefore a gap between mathematics and nature, and Kant set himself the task of resolving this problem, maintaining that while 'living forces' would remain concealed from mathematical argument they would be revealed by a 'metaphysical investigation'.[8] By a 'metaphysical' investigation here Kant did not mean the demonstration of a 'metaphysics of nature' in the sense of the *Metaphysical foundations*. While Kant's concern in the *Metaphysical foundations* was to establish that mathematics could be applied to physical entities, in *Living forces* he stresses the disjunction between the 'mathematical' status of 'force' and its ontological status as a 'physical' entity existing in nature. By a 'metaphysical' investigation in the *Living forces* essay Kant means an analysis of the conceptual status of 'force' as a physical entity.

Kant was conversant with the extensive literature on 'living forces' published during the controversies of the 1720s, and his distinctive view of the conceptual status of 'living forces' cannot be understood without reference to these works, notably the authoritative essays by Johann Bernoulli to which Kant refers on several occasions, and which had been reprinted in the collected edition of Bernoulli's works published in 1742.[9] Kant's theory of 'living force' displays striking contrasts to the arguments of Leibniz and Bernoulli. In Leibniz's dynamics the conceptual status of 'living force' and its intelligibility as a dynamical principle was grounded on his theory of substance. He argued that 'living force' was a phenomenal manifestation of the 'primitive active force' which, as he put it in *Specimen dynamicum* (1695), unlike extension and motion was 'real' and substantially present in all corporeal entities. 'Derivative' forces such as 'living force' were the phenomenal manifestations of 'primitive' forces, and the science of dynamics was concerned with 'derivative' forces alone, the forces by which 'bodies actually act and are acted upon by each other'. A 'derivative' force such as 'living force' was thus considered to be a 'well-founded appearance' which was part of the order of nature and subject to the laws of nature but which did not possess the status of 'primitive' forces which characterised the nature of substances.[10]

Leibniz's mathematical argument was based on a distinction between 'living force' and 'dead force [*vis mortua*]', both being conceived as 'derivative' forces. Leibniz maintained that 'dead force' (mdv) arose in the tendency of a body to motion, whereas 'living force' (mv^2) arose in 'actual motion' such as the collision or fall of bodies, and 'arises from an infinite number of continuous impressions of dead force'. 'Living force' was thus to be considered as arising from an infinite number of infinitesimal impulses of 'dead force'. Leibniz emphasised that in referring to infinitesimal quantities such as 'dead force' he did 'not mean that these mathematical entities are really to be found in nature as such, but merely that they are the means of making accurate calculations'.[11]

These remarks in the *Specimen dynamicum* remained among Leibniz's few public statements of his concept of 'living force' and the existential status of infinitesimal entities; and his view of infinitesimals as 'well-founded fictions', as he expressed it in a letter to Varignon,[12] and of the relationship between 'dead force' and 'living force' as a purely mathematical model was not echoed by Johann Bernoulli in his writings on 'living forces'. Substantial portions of Bernoulli's mathematical and philosophical correspondence with Leibniz were published in 1745,[13] and in correspondence with Bernoulli Leibniz had maintained that the theory of 'living force' as arising from successive infinitesimal impulses of 'dead force' was in consonance with the 'law of continuity', which implied that 'motion does not change by a leap' and hence that a body would not change from one state of motion to another without passing through all the intermediate degrees of motion.[14] In formulating his theory of living forces Bernoulli drew directly on Leibniz's arguments, though he rejected Leibniz's view of 'living force' as a 'well-founded phenomenon'.

The conceptual kernel of Bernoulli's treatise on the *Laws of the communication of motion* (1727) was his adherence to the fundamental presupposition of Leibnizian dynamics, the law of continuity, and hence to the principle that the mathematical concept of infinitesimals had its counterpart in nature. The law of continuity established the harmony between nature and mathematics, the 'perfect conformity which prevails between the laws of nature and those of geometry'.[15] Bernoulli thus follows Leibniz in supposing that motion is produced in infinitely small degrees in accordance with the law of continuity, and hence that 'living force' is produced as a result of an infinite number of infinitesimal impulses of 'dead force' and was 'inherent in a body when it is in uniform motion'.[16] Bernoulli's concept of 'living force' was explained mathematically, and his theory of motion contrasts with Kant's disjunction (in *Living forces*) between the mathematical and physical representations of 'force'. Bernoulli did not however repeat Leibniz's claim that the infinitesimal entities posited in Leibniz's dynamics were merely mathematical quantities, and did not possess the ontological status of physical entities. In correspondence with Leibniz, Bernoulli had affirmed the view that infinitesimal quantities were physically existent entities, and given his assumption of the harmony between mathematics and nature, it is likely that he intended to imply the physical reality of 'dead force'.[17] In an essay *On the true concept of living forces* (1735) Bernoulli amplified his account of the theory of living forces, characterising 'living force' as a 'real and substantial entity',[18] a view that conflicts with Leibniz's statement of the ontological status of 'living force' as a 'well-founded phenomenon', an entity which did not possess the status of substance. Bernoulli's dynamical writings elaborate an interpretation of 'living force' and 'dead force' as real physical entities.

In his essay on *Living forces* Kant quoted with approval Bernoulli's formulation of 'living force' as a 'real and substantial entity' persisting in natural bodies. While Bernoulli had 'expressed his meaning as a mere geometer' his argument was nevertheless 'completely intelligible': 'this formulation expresses my view to no small advantage'. However Kant believed that Bernoulli was mistaken in seeking to establish the physical status of 'living force' by appeal to the Leibnizian law of continuity, the mathematical relation between infinitesimals and finite quantities.[19] Kant criticised the Leibnizian distinction between the 'beginnings of motion' and 'actual motion', arguing that 'whatever is valid when a body has been in motion for some time ... must also apply at the commencement of motion'. Assuming that both the 'forces' possessed by the body in these two states of motion were real physical entities (as Bernoulli had done), Kant turned the 'law of continuity' against Leibniz and Bernoulli, asserting that 'if a body possesses living force when it has been in motion for some time (for however small a time increment), then it must also have that force when it begins to move'.[20] For Kant there was a continuity and hence identity between the 'forces' in these two states of motion; he rejected the conceptual basis of the Leibnizian distinction between 'dead force' and 'living force'. He concluded that the Leibnizian measure of 'force' was disproved by mathematical argument, and that the geometrical arguments of the Leibnizians — Bernoulli, Bilfinger and Hermann — which purported to demonstrate the law of the conservation of 'living force' were invalid.[21]

There are parallels between Kant's critique of Leibnizian theory and arguments advanced by Euler in a paper on *The force of impact and its true measure* (1745), a notable contribution to the debate on the conceptual status of 'force'. Euler notes that according to Leibniz impact occurred in an instant giving rise to 'dead force'; 'living force' then arose from an infinite number of impressions of 'dead force'. The two 'forces' were therefore 'heterogeneous', a term which had been used by Bernoulli.[22] Euler questions the 'heterogeneity' of 'living' and 'dead force' by turning the 'law of continuity' against the Leibnizian argument. According to this 'supremely constant law of nature, in virtue of which nothing occurs suddenly', impact would require a time interval; and so he argues that both 'living' and 'dead force' must arise in the same way, in a time interval, and hence have the same quantitative measure. Euler concludes that 'the fundamental principle, on which rests the measure of living force, is not only unsteady, but falls entirely in ruin; for it is demonstrated that the effect of impact of two or more bodies is not produced in an instant, but that it requires a certain interval of time'. Euler concludes that Newton's first law of motion, the law of inertia, defined the measure of 'force': 'there is no other force but inertia, by which [a body] conserves its state, and this force is always the same, whether a body remains at rest or whether it moves'.[23]

In a very similar fashion Kant concluded that 'mathematics does not permit a body to be endowed with a force ... that is not the external cause of its motion ... this is the fundamental law of mechanics ... for which there is no other measure [of force] than the Cartesian'. Newton's first law of motion thus established the 'Cartesian' measure of 'force' by mathematical argument. However, he went on to claim that a 'natural body' possessed a 'quite different property', the capacity of 'increasing in itself' the 'force' which was the external cause of its motion, so as to attain 'a degree of force that does not arise from the external cause of motion'. This property of physical bodies, Kant maintained, could not be reconciled with the mathematical theory of 'force': 'the mathematical concepts of the properties of bodies and their forces are quite distinct from the concepts found in nature'.[24]

Kant therefore stresses the disjunction between the mathematical status of 'force' and its ontological status as an entity occurring in nature. He explicitly concurs with Bernoulli's characterisation of 'living force' as a 'real and substantial entity' and, by implication, rejects Leibniz's distinction between 'primitive' (substantial) and 'derivative' (physical) 'forces'; and he contests the 'Leibnizian' justification of the 'living force' concept by the appeal to the mathematical relation between infinitesimals and finite quantities. In stressing the disjunction between mathematics and physical reality, Kant faced the question: 'how is it that a law which is found to be false in mathematics can occur in nature?'[25] Thus, the central issue of the essay on *Living forces* became the relationship between mathematics and physical reality. Kant's answer to this question took the form of a 'metaphysical investigation', viz. a conceptual analysis of 'living force' that would demonstrate the intelligibility of the concept as denoting something physical. He declared that 'we must connect the metaphysical laws with the rules of mathematics in order to determine the true measure of force in nature'.[26] To do so he provides an 'estimation of living forces' which, though not purporting to yield a mathematical explanation in the sense of the Leibnizian theory of 'living force' as arising from an infinite number of infinitesimal impulses of 'dead force', nevertheless attempted to provide a mathematical illustration of 'living force' as a physical entity existing in nature.

Kant's 'estimation' of 'living force' is based on his introduction of a concept which he terms 'intension', the 'basis of activity' of physical bodies, representing their 'perpetual endeavour to action', the property of physical bodies which, Kant had maintained, could not be explained by the mathematical theory of 'force'. 'Force' was measured by the product of 'intension' and velocity. At the commencement of motion the striving towards motion ('intension') is indeterminate, so the 'force' is proportional to the velocity (corresponding to the Leibnizian 'dead force'). Once motion is established, the 'intension' is finite, so the 'living force' is proportional to the product of 'intension' and velocity. If velocity and 'intension' are each represented by a line, then the 'force' at the commencement of motion would be represented by a line, but the 'living force' would be represented by a square, corresponding to the square of the velocity and the representation of 'living force' as mv^2.[27] The comparison between 'dead force' and 'living force' as between a 'line and a surface' had been drawn by both Bernoulli and Euler.[28] The difference between the 'force' at the commencement of motion and when motion was established was thus due to the way in which the 'intension' of bodies was manifested, not (as in Leibnizian dynamics) as a result of a disjunction between the two states of motion, a heterogeneity which Kant believed was contrary to the law of continuity.

In Kant's 'estimation' of 'living force' the concept of 'living force' is explained as a physical property of bodies. He juxtaposes the mathematical and physical explanations of 'force', one yielding a 'Cartesian' and the other a 'Leibnizian' measure of 'force'. Kant did not succeed in resolving the controversy over the meaning of 'force', only in highlighting the tension in his own theory of nature, the disjunction between the mathematical definition of 'force' and its ontological status as a physical entity.

Kant's essay on *Physical monadology* (1756) provided an important elaboration and development of his view of the ontological status of 'force'. He now asserted that bodies were constituted of 'monads' or 'simple substances' which possessed inherent 'forces'. Kant's view of the physical reality of the 'force' possessed by the 'monads' constituting physical bodies resembles Wolff's theory of monads as indivisible points rather than Leibniz's theory of monads as 'metaphysical points' characterising the nature of 'substance'.[29] Kant's theory of monads as possessing inherent 'forces' which defined their physical reality is in consonance with his acceptance of Bernoulli's view of 'living force' as a 'real and substantial entity' in his *Living forces* essay; but the introduction of the concept of 'monads' as an explication of the physical status of 'living force' probably reflects his response to the controversy over the Wolffian 'monad' theory in the late 1740,[30] an emphasis that was foreshadowed in his essays on fire and cosmology of 1755, where he enunciated a theory of an 'inherent striving' of nature.[31]

In *Physical monadology* Kant argues that the monads constituting physical bodies possess an inherent 'force of inertia'; and that while the 'inertia' of

X

FORCE AND INERTIA

bodies was due to an inherent 'force', the contact action of bodies was explained in terms of the 'forces of impenetrability'. Kant now introduces the 'Newtonian' notion of attractive and repulsive forces, which he interprets as being inherent in matter and which determined the properties of bodies; the conjunction and degree of these 'forces' determined the limit of the extension of bodies.[32] The use of attractive and repulsive 'forces' here is of fundamental importance in Kant's natural philosophy. In the *Metaphysical foundations* he attempts to clarify the relationship between the concepts of 'force' and 'inertia' under the formal guidance of the categorial principles. While he remained committed to one of the central assumptions of the *Physical monadology*, that of the primacy of 'force' over the concepts of solidity and impenetrability, in the *Metaphysical foundations* he denies that 'inertia' was due to an inherent 'force', in favour of a concept of 'inertia' as denoting the passivity of matter, an argument that was foreshadowed in his *New conceptual study of motion and rest* (1758) where he denied that 'inertia' was 'an inner force of nature'.[33] Now this reappraisal of the conceptual status of 'inertia' reflects Kant's indebtedness to Euler's critique of the Wolffian monadology and of the conceptual status of 'force', 'impenetrability' and 'inertia' in Newton's natural philosophy. Although Kant did not accept Euler's view that 'inertia' was a defining characteristic of matter, his restructuring of the relation between the concepts of 'force' and 'inertia' suggests the influence of Euler's critique of the expression 'force of inertia'. Before turning to an examination of Euler's arguments, I will first briefly review Newton's discussion of 'inertia', to provide a perspective for the analysis of Euler's examination of the intelligibility of Newton's concept of 'inertia'.

II

The main sources of Newton's concept of 'inertia' for eighteenth-century natural philosophers were Definitions III and IV of *Principia* (1687) and the third Rule of Philosophising that Newton appended to the second edition of *Principia* (1713). In Definition III Newton states that 'force innate [*vis insita*] in matter is the power of resisting whereby each individual body, inasmuch as it is in it to do so, perseveres in its state of resting or of moving uniformly straight on', adding that because the 'innate force' did not differ from the 'inertia' of the mass of the body other than in the manner of our conceiving it, the 'innate force' could be called the 'force of inertia [*vis inertiae*]'. In Definition IV Newton added that a body persevered in each state of motion by its 'force of inertia' alone.³⁴ In Rule III he listed 'inertia' together with extension, hardness, impenetrability and mobility as the 'universal' qualities of matter, the essential properties an entity would have to possess as a necessary and sufficient condition of its materiality.³⁵ As commentators have noted, Newton's use of the term *force* of 'inertia' and his association of 'inertia' and the 'innate force' of matter bristles with difficulties. Newton referred to 'inertia' both as a passive property of matter and as an inherent active 'force' of matter, an innate power of resisting, actualised when bodies interacted with one another.³⁶ If Newton considered matter to be totally passive, then the use of the expression 'force of inertia' was ambiguous; yet Newton stressed that a body perserved in each state of motion by its 'force of inertia'. The first law of motion of *Principia*, that 'every body perserves in its state of resting or moving uniformly straight on, except inasmuch it is compelled by impressed forces to change that state',³⁷ was thus grounded, it seemed, on a concept of 'inertia' that lacked adequate explication.

Whatever Newton's intentions, this is how the issue was construed by Euler, subjecting Newton's concepts of 'force' and 'inertia' to a sharp critique in an essay *On the origin of forces* (1750). Euler emphasises that strictly speaking the concepts of 'force' and 'inertia' were 'directly contrary to one another'; while 'force' was the cause of a change of motion, 'inertia' preserved a body in a state of motion or rest. Hence the expression 'force of inertia' was self-contradictory. Euler however follows Newton in emphasising the importance of impenetrability as a defining property of matter, arguing that impenetrability was as essential a property of bodies as extension and inertia. In his third Rule of Philosophising Newton had distinguished the 'universal' qualities of matter such as impenetrability and inertia from other properties of matter (including gravity) by arguing that the 'universal' qualities of matter were not subject to alteration of degrees of intensity, and Euler again follows Newton in arguing that 'impenetrability does not admit of degrees'. Euler was firmly committed to Newton's concept of matter and to Newton's philosophical criterion by which the doctrine of the 'universal' qualities of matter was established. He concluded that 'if a body is not completely impenetrable, it is penetrable'; impenetrability was an absolute quality of bodies, consisting in 'an absolute impossibility to admit penetration', and hence it was 'impossible for two bodies, or only two of their smallest particles, to exist at the same time in the same place'.³⁸ Euler claims that there is a close conceptual association between 'force' and 'impenetrability', that 'force' is 'inseparable from' impenetrability. Forces were necessary to maintain the impenetrability of bodies and 'derive their origin from the impenetrability of bodies'.³⁹ In the *Metaphysical foundations* Kant inverts Euler's assumption that the concept of 'force' was grounded on impenetrability, rejecting Euler's assumptions about the nature of matter, and arguing that 'forces', not extension and solidity, were the defining properties of material substance.

Euler developed his views on 'force' and 'inertia' at greater length in his *Letters to a German Princess* (1768–72), again emphasising that impenetrability was 'a necessary property of all bodies', and defining 'body' as an 'impenetrable extension'. Euler therefore agrees with Newton rather than Descartes in maintaining that while extension was a necessary characteristic of bodies, 'extension and mobility alone do not constitute the nature of bodies' for 'something may be extended without being a body'. Another property was required, that of 'impenetrability', without which 'extension cannot be body'. The concept of 'impenetrability' was fundamental to Euler's theory of motion. He argues that the motion of bodies was changed in collisions 'no more than is necessary to prevent penetration'; because collision was the source of 'all the changes which occur in the world' impenetrability was therefore 'the great spring by which nature works all her effects'.[40]

When Euler turns to a discussion of 'inertia' and its relation to 'force' he states that 'inertia' is 'as necessary to bodies as extension and impenetrability'. 'Inertia' was a defining characteristic of material bodies: 'it would be impossible for a body to exist without inertia'. He defines 'inertia' as 'a repugnance to everything that tends to change the state of bodies', to be contrasted with 'force' which was the 'external cause' which signifies 'everything that is capable of changing the state of bodies'. Unlike 'inertia' which was 'essential' to matter, 'force' was not *inherent* in matter'. Euler thus rejects the Wolffian monad theory which had held that bodies make a continual effort to change their state by means of an inherent force. That doctrine clearly contradicted his account of 'inertia'. Moreover, the term 'force of inertia' was an abuse of language; as already noted, 'inertia' was 'the opposite of a force'.[41]

Euler then attempts to explain the origin of 'force', for despite the fact that 'force' was not inherent in matter it was apparent that 'forces' were associated with material entities. He finds the explanation in the property of 'impenetrability'; the impenetrability of bodies 'always exerts the force necessary to change their state . . . [so as] to prevent penetration'. Hence the 'impenetrability of bodies' was the source of the 'true origin of the forces which continually change the state of bodies in the world'. Collision, contact action, was the basic mode of change in nature. The 'force' arising from 'impenetrability' was only manifested in resisting penetration: 'it is only to prevent penetration, that impenetrability becomes active', that is, 'provides a force sufficient for the required effect'. While 'impenetrability' was an essential property of body, the 'force' to which it gave rise was dispositional: 'though impenetrability provides these forces' it was not 'endowed with a determinate force; it is rather in a condition to manifest force' necessary in order to prevent penetration. The 'impenetrability' of bodies, a quality necessary to their materiality, would therefore manifest the 'forces' sufficient to prevent the mutual penetration of bodies. The concept of 'force' was thus explicated in terms of the more fundamental property of 'impenetrability': the 'origin of forces is based on the impenetrability of bodies'.[42]

In the *Metaphysical foundations* Kant follows Euler in rejecting the theory that bodies make a continual effort to change their state by means of an inherent 'force', accepting Euler's strictures against the term 'force of inertia' as a linguistic and conceptual confusion.[43] In his essay on *Living forces* he expounded his disjunction between mathematical and physical theories of nature by contrasting the concepts of 'inertia' and 'living force', the former concept expressing a mathematical law while the latter was conceived as an inherent active 'force', a physical entity persisting in natural bodies. Euler had criticised the doctrine that bodies possessed 'internal forces' as contradicting the concept of 'inertia', and in seeking to establish the intelligibility of a unified natural philosophy, bridging the gap between the mathematical and the physical representations of nature proposed in *Living forces*, in the *Metaphysical foundations* Kant rejects the concept of 'living force' in favour of 'inertia'. In the *Metaphysical foundations* he seeks, under the guidance of the categories, to clarify the distinction between the concepts of 'force' and 'inertia', rejecting the theory of 'force' propounded in *Living forces*, that bodies possessed inherent 'activity', a 'perpetual endeavour to action'.[44]

Kant does not however accept the Newton-Euler doctrine that 'inertia' and 'impenetrability' were 'essential' properties of matter. In the *Metaphysical foundations* he conceives 'inertia' as a law of mechanics which implied the passivity of matter, not as an 'essential' or defining property of material substance. As in his essay on *Physical monadology* he conceives the concept of 'force' as ontologically prior to 'impenetrability', and emphasises that 'forces' were the defining properties of matter. While Kant did not accept Euler's views uncritically, Euler's writings on the conceptual foundations of mechanics were clearly instrumental in deepening his understanding of the problems of natural philosophy, bringing about a re-structuring of the relations between the concepts of 'force', 'inertia' and 'impenetrability' in the *Metaphysical foundations*.

FORCE AND INERTIA

III

In the *Metaphysical foundations* Kant elaborates a 'special metaphysics of nature' which considered 'matter' as 'it must be represented in accordance with the universal laws of thought'. The four chapters of the book, 'Phoronomy', 'Dynamics', 'Mechanics' and 'Phenomenology' correspond to the categories of quantity, quality, relation and modality, which subsume 'all determinations of the universal concept of matter in general'.[45] While an early commentator maintained that the terms 'Phoronomy', 'Dynamics' and 'Mechanics' had little significance, merely deriving from Hermann's *Phoronomia* (1716), d'Alembert's *Dynamique* (1743) and Euler's *Mechanica* (1736),[46] this assertion is clearly mistaken. The term *phoronomia* had been used by Leibniz to denote motion as considered merely geometrically, precisely the sense of Kant's 'Phoronomy'.[47] The term *dynamica* has clear Leibnizian echoes, denoting Leibniz's theory of 'forces'; and in the chapter on 'Dynamics' Kant is concerned with the concept of 'force'. The term *mechanica*, however, probably does relate to Euler's treatise, though the connection is a substantive one, for in 'Mechanics' Kant is concerned to discuss the laws of motion, corresponding to Euler's attempt to construct an axiomatic science of mechanics based on the concepts of mass and force.

The discussion of the concepts of 'force', 'impenetrability' and 'inertia' which Kant gives in the chapters on 'Dynamics' and 'Mechanics' in the *Metaphysical foundations*, indicates in a very interesting fashion some of the distinctive features of Kant's 'special metaphysics of nature', in the context of his reconstruction of the relationships between these physical concepts, and his attempt to avoid the disjunction between mathematical and physical representation that had dominated his essay on *Living forces*. The chapter on 'Dynamics' begins with the fundamental 'dynamical explication' of, as Kant emphasises, the 'empirical concept' of 'matter' as 'the movable insofar as it fills a space'. This 'dynamical' treatment of matter has been preceded, and presupposes, its 'phoronomic' explication as 'the movable in space' now supplemented by having 'the capacity of resisting a motion within a certain space'.[48] As I have already observed, Kant rejects the 'Newtonian' doctrine (also espoused by Euler) of 'essential' qualities, that 'solidity' and 'impenetrability' were defining characteristics of material substances. He maintains that 'forces' define the essence of matter, that 'force' is 'inherent in matter'.[49]

The 'dynamical' account of 'matter' supposes that 'matter fills a space, not by its mere existence, but by a special moving force'. Matter fills space by 'repulsive' or 'extensive' forces which resist the penetration of other forces and which thus form the 'ground of its impenetrability'. The property of 'impenetrability' thus 'rests on a physical basis', for the 'extensive force makes matter itself, as something extended filling its space, first of all possible'.[50] Moreover Kant claims that 'the possibility of matter requires a force of attraction, as the second essential fundamental force of matter', a force limiting the dispersive effect of the repulsive force. Kant argues that the 'possibility of matter' requires the assumption of 'an original force of matter acting in the opposite direction to the repulsive [force]', an 'attractive force' which 'belongs to all matter as a fundamental force appertaining to its essence'. Without the attractice force matter would 'disperse itself to infinity'; and without repulsive force 'all parts of matter would approach one another without hindrance and diminish the space that matter occupies'. Hence both attractive force and repulsive force belong to the 'essence of matter', and 'one cannot be separated from the other in the concept of matter'.[51]

This 'dynamical' explication of matter is carried out with an eye to the categories of 'quality' ('reality, negation and limitation').[52] These categories are clearly meant to correspond analogically to the account of 'matter' in terms of attractive and repulsive 'forces', and the limiting or balance between these 'forces' which determined the 'degree of the filling of space' by matter. There is thus the suggestion of a correspondence between these categories and explication of matter in terms of attractive and repulsive 'forces': 'attractive force as a penetrative force ... in combination with its counteracting one, namely, repulsive force [and] the limitation of this latter'. This 'dynamical' account thus demonstrates the 'possibility of a space filled in a determinate degree' by matter.[53]

Kant rejects the concept of 'absolute impenetrability' (as expounded by Euler), the doctrine that 'matter, insofar as it is matter, resists all penetration unconditionally and with absolute necessity'. In place of this Newtonian 'mathematico-mechanical' concept of matter Kant proposes his 'metaphysico-dynamical' mode of explanation, which supposes that 'impenetrability rests on a physical basis', being grounded on the 'extensive' or repulsive force. He argues that this force 'has a degree which can be overcome, and hence matter's space of extension can be diminished' by a 'compressive force' counteracting the repulsive force. Hence the filling of space by matter must be dependent upon the 'degree of compression' or 'relative impenetrability' of matter. Thus the 'extension' and 'impenetrability' of matter could change by degrees of intensity, both being accounted for in terms of the concept of 'force'. In contrast with Newton's doctrine, according to which 'impenetrability' could not change by degrees, and impenetrability, like extension and solidity, was an absolute quality defining the materiality of matter, Kant maintains that impenetrability and extension are derivative, being dependent on the fundamental 'forces' which define the concept of 'matter'. As I have already pointed out, Kant thus inverts Euler's treatment of the relationship between 'force' and 'impenetrability'.[54]

In emphasising that 'the possibility of matter requires a force of attraction' Kant arrives at a conclusion of fundamental importance, the justification of the possibility of the action of matter at a distance, a concept which (as Kant remarks) had given such offence to Newton's contemporaries and even to Newton himself. Kant sought to justify the notion of 'action at a distance' as being 'possible without the mediation of matter lying in between', thus demonstrating the intelligibility of Newton's theory of gravitational attractive force. The justification of the possibility of the concept of gravity is given in terms of the 'metaphysico-dynamical' concept of matter, which supposes that 'matter occupies a space without filling it' by means of an attractive force, by which 'matter acts through empty space upon other distant matters'.[55]

It should be noted in particular that Kant's 'metaphysico-dynamical' approach is not in any way intended to yield any specific empirical laws of 'forces' by which nature is regulated, nor is it claimed that the physical actuality of the 'forces' follows deductively from the general categorial scheme. The metaphysical argument establishes only the possibility of matter in general as composed of fundamental 'forces' of attraction and repulsion, not that one can 'presume to assume either of them as actual'. Kant emphasises that 'one must guard against going beyond what makes the universal concept of matter in general possible and against wanting to explain a priori the particular or even specific determination and variety of matter'. He declares that 'no law whatever of attractive or of repulsive force may be risked on a priori conjectures; but everything, even universal attraction as the cause of gravity, must, together with the laws of such attraction, be concluded from data of experience'.[56]

Kant rejects the view of 'Lambert and others', presumably including Euler, who considered 'solidity' to be a defining property of matter, an ultimate concept which entailed the resistance of matter to penetration. He argues that the proponents of this 'mathematico-mechanical' theory suggested that 'solidity' was a concept which could not be 'further constructed' because it was 'an initial datum of the construction of the concept of matter', and that they implied that 'solidity' was 'incapable of any mathematical construction in order thereby to prevent a return to the first principles of natural science'.[57] Kant maintains that his 'metaphysico-dynamical' explication of 'matter' has exposed the confused nature of this argument, by demonstrating that 'solidity' and 'impenetrability' were not ultimate concepts but were derivative, being dependent on the 'fundamental forces'. While he admits that the 'mathematico-mechanical mode of explication' had the advantage of explaining a 'great specific multiplicity of matters', he regards the conceptual foundations of this schema as being unsatisfactory. Kant maintains that 'force' is the 'initial datum' of construction, and he argues that the 'metaphysico-dynamical' mode of representation contrasted favourably with the 'mathematico-mechanical' theory, for the latter was a 'merely mathematical physics' based on the 'empty concept' of 'absolute impenetrability', a conception of nature in which 'forces were philosophised away'. In the 'mathematico-mechanical' theory 'forces' were arbitrarily superadded to matter whereas the 'metaphysico-dynamical' mode of representation was based on the 'proper forces of matter' which were conceived as being essential to matter.[58]

Nevertheless Kant was careful not to claim too much for his 'metaphysico-dynamical' argument. He denies that his 'dynamical' explication established the 'possibility of fundamental forces' because 'all means are wanting for the construction of this concept [of force]'. Kant argues that 'forces' cannot be constructed because they are 'fundamental' and 'cannot be further derived from any source', and also because they are empirical and are known from the 'data of experience' and cannot be exhibited *a priori*.[59] 'Forces' can therefore only be 'assumed', and Kant does not claim to have established a mathematical physics based on the supposition of 'fundamental forces'. In seeking to establish the intelligibility of a unified natural philosophy based on the 'fundamental concept' of 'force', bridging the gap between physical reality and the mathematical representation of nature proposed in the essay on *Living forces*, Kant denies that 'forces' could be constructed, and thus emphasises that the metaphysical argument only establishes the 'possibility of a mathematical doctrine of nature'.[60]

In the next chapter of the *Metaphysical foundations*, on 'Mechanics', Kant gives an account of the relationship between the concepts of 'force' and 'inertia', demonstrating the application of the categories of 'relation' ('subsistence', 'causality' and 'community') to the concept of 'matter'.[61] The principle of 'causality', as enunciated in the 'second analogy' of the *Critique*, states (as Kant puts it in the *Metaphysical foundations*) that 'every change has a cause'. Applied to the concept of 'matter' it yields Kant's 'second law of mechanics: every change of matter has an external cause'. Kant places brackets round his appended statement of Newton's first law of motion to which this metaphysical 'law of mechanics' analogically corresponds, implying that the metaphysical argument merely suggests the possibility of Newton's first law of motion, not its physical actuality. Nor does his 'proof' of the 'second law of mechanics' purport to validate Newton's first law of motion, but to establish that all changes of matter are 'based on an external cause' and that matter 'undergoes no changes except by motion', postulating a link between the category of 'causality' and Newton's first law of motion. Newton's first law of motion is therefore construed as the empirical embodiment of the principle of 'causality'.[62] The metaphysical argument thus only establishes the 'possibility of a mathematical doctrine of nature'.

Kant describes his 'second law of mechanics' as the 'law of inertia', because the 'inertia of matter is and signifies nothing but its lifelessness', its inability to 'determine itself to motion or rest as change of its state'. He refers to the capacity of a substance to change its state by an 'internal principle' as 'hylozoism', the capacity of living things to determine to act by means of thought, and he argues that only living things could manifest a 'positive effort' to change or maintain their state. He concludes that the doctrine that matter possesses an 'internal principle' of 'inertia', the concept of a 'special force of matter under the name of the force of inertia', would entail 'hylozoism' and would therefore contradict the 'law of inertia'. Kant's rejection of the supposition of an 'internal principle of a substance to change its state' was fundamental to his proof of the 'law of inertia': because 'matter has no absolutely internal determinations' hence 'all change of matter is based upon an external cause'.[63]

Kant therefore is an agreement with Euler in rejecting the construal of 'inertia' as a 'special force of matter'. He maintains that the 'designation force of inertia' was self-contradictory: 'a special and entirely peculiar force merely to resist, but without being able to move a body, would under the name force of inertia be a word without meaning'. The expression 'force of inertia', employed in his essay on *Physical monadology*, was therefore abandoned. To suppose that matter possesses an 'internal principle' of 'inertia', which he considers to be implied by the term 'force of inertia', would contradict the 'law of inertia' which entails the denial that matter possesses an inherent power enabling it to change its state. Kant's interpretation of the connotations of the term 'force of inertia' in the *Metaphysical foundations* does however give a misleading impression of his use of the concept of 'force of inertia' in his essay on *Physical monadology*, where 'hylozoism' (as defined in the *Metaphysical foundations*) was not implied.[64]

Kant's argument illustrates his reconstruction of the concepts of his earlier period, following his re-interpretation of the relationship between 'force' and 'inertia' under the guidance of the categorial principles. In the *Metaphysical foundations* his 'metaphysico-dynamical' explication of 'force' as the ontological basis of 'matter' replaces his 'physical monadology' in which bodies were supposed to be constituted of 'monads' endowed with inherent 'forces'. The notion of inherent activity came to be associated strictly with living things; and the concept of an 'internal principle' or 'force of inertia' was abandoned together with the concept of 'living force' as an inherent active 'force' persisting in physical bodies. The 'law of inertia' thus entailed the denial of the principle that the cause of any change of matter could be 'internal'.[65]

Nevertheless this did not imply an acceptance of the Newton-Euler doctrine that 'inertia' was a defining property of 'matter'. Kant regards the concept of 'inertia' as a 'law of mechanics' which implied the passivity of matter, not as a defining property of matter. He retains his commitment to the ontological priority of 'force' over the concept of 'matter', though in the *Metaphysical foundations* he expounds this theory in terms of his 'metaphysico-dynamical' explication of 'fundamental forces'. Kant's shift from the assertion of his 'physical monadology' to his formulation of his 'metaphysico-dynamical' theory of matter thus demonstrates his reconstruction of the relationship between the concepts of 'force' and 'inertia' under the guidance of the categorial principles; whilst his reinterpretation of these concepts manifests his changed approach to natural philosophy under the influence of Euler.

ACKNOWLEDGEMENTS

I wish to express my gratitude to Gerd Buchdahl for several helpful discussions during the preparation of this paper, for his detailed comments on the draft, and for suggesting some valuable improvements.

I also wish to thank the Royal Society for financial support in obtaining source materials during the preparation of this paper, and the British Academy for an overseas conference grant enabling me to attend the Third International Conference on the History and Philosophy of Science in Montreal in August 1980, where this paper was presented.

FORCE AND INERTIA   247

NOTES

[1] G. Buchdahl, *Metaphysics and the philosophy of science: the classical origins. Descartes to Kant*, Blackwell, Oxford, 1969, p. 678.
[2] H. E. Timerding: 'Kant und Euler', *Kant-Studien* **23** (1919), 18–64.
[3] I. Kant, *Metaphysische Anfangsgründe der Naturwissenschaft* [1786], in *Kant's gesammelte Schriften herausgegeben von der Königlichen Preussischen Akademie der Wissenschaften*, Vol. 4, Reimer, Berlin, 1911, pp. 469–72. I have used the recent translation by J. Ellington of Kant's *Metaphysical foundations of natural science*, Bobbs-Merrill, Indianapolis and New York, 1970. Quotations from the *Metaphysische Anfangsgründe* in this paper are taken, with occasional modifications, from this translation; and all page references are to the *Akademie* edition, page numbers in that edition being given as marginal numbers in Ellington's translation.
[4] Kant, *Schriften*, Vol. 4, pp. 473, 476. See G. Buchdahl: 'The conception of lawlikeness in Kant's philosophy of science', *Synthese* **23** (1971), 24–46.
[5] I. Kant, *Gedanken von den wahren Schätzung der lebendigen Kräfte* [1747], in *Kant's gesammelte Schriften*, Vol. 1, Berlin, 1902, p. 139. For especially relevant background on the *vis viva* controversy, see: T. L. Hankins: 'Eighteenth-century attempts to resolve the *vis viva* controversy', *Isis* **56** (1965), 281–97; R. Calinger: 'The Newtonian – Wolffian confrontation in the St. Petersburg Academy of Sciences (1725–1746), *Journal of World History* **11** (1968), 417–35; and C. Iltis: 'Madame du Châtelet's metaphysics and mechanics', *Studies in History and Philosophy of Science* **8** (1977), 29–48.
[6] Kant, *Schriften*, Vol. 1, p. 59.
[7] *Ibid.*, p. 107.
[8] *Ibid.*, p. 60.
[9] *Ibid.*, pp. 57, 91, 150. Bernoulli's writings on 'living force' were collected in the third volume of his *Opera Omnia*, 4 vols., Bousquet, Lausanne/Geneva, 1742.
[10] G. W. Leibniz: 'Specimen Dynamicum', *Acta Eruditorum* **14** (1695), 145–57; in Leibniz, *Mathematische Schriften*, 7 vols. C. I. Gerhardt (ed.), reprinted: Olms, Hildesheim, 1960–61, Vol. 6, pp. 235–7; trans. by L. E. Loemker in Leibniz, *Philosophical papers and letters*, D. Reidel Publ. Co., Dordrecht, Holland, 1969, pp. 435–444.
[11] Leibniz, *Mathematische Schriften*, Vol. 6, p. 238.
[12] Leibniz to Varignon, 20 June 1702, *Mathematische Schriften*, Vol. 4, p. 110. Cf. J. Mittelstrass, *Neuzeit und Aufklärung: Studien zur Enstehung der neuzeitlichen Wissenschaft und Philosophie*, de Gruyter, Berlin, New York, 1970, pp. 489–501.
[13] *Got. Gul. Leibnitij et Johan Bernoullij commercium philosophicum et mathematicum*, 2 vols., Lausanne/Geneva, 1745. A more complete collection of the Leibniz-Bernoulli correspondence is in Leibniz, *Mathematische Schriften*, Vol. 3, parts 1 and 2.
[14] Leibniz to Bernoulli, 20/30 September, 1698, *Mathematische Schriften*, Vol. 3, p. 544.
[15] J. Bernoulli: 'Discours sur les loix de la communication du mouvement' [1727], *Opera omnia*, Vol. 3, p. 58.
[16] Bernoulli, *Opera omnia*, Vol. 3, p. 23.
[17] Bernoulli to Leibniz, 6 December, 1698 and 7 January, 1699, in Leibniz, *Mathematische Schriften*, Vol. 3, pp. 555 and 563. On Bernoulli's relation to Leibniz see

P. M. Heimann: '"Geometry and nature': Leibniz and Johann Bernoulli's theory of motion', *Centaurus* **21** (1977), 1–26.

[18] J. Bernoulli: 'De vera notione virium vivarum earumque usu in dynamicis' [*Acta Eruditorum* (1735), 210–30], *Opera omnia*, Vol. 3, pp. 239–41. *Cf.* Heimann, *op. cit.*, for a full account of Bernoulli's theory of 'living force'.

[19] Kant, *Schriften*, Vol. 1, pp. 150–1. *Cf.* E. Adickes, *Kant als Naturforscher*, 2 vols., Berlin, 1924–25, Vol. 1, p. 98. While Adickes correctly contrasts Kant's and Bernoulli's theories ot 'living force', he fails to note Kant's reference to Bernoulli, which has a significant bearing on the relationship between them. The account of Kant's 'living forces' paper by Buchdahl, *op. cit.*, (note 1), pp. 553–6 provides a valuable analysis, but ignores Kant's relation to Bernoulli, and hence gives a slightly misleading account of the status of Kant's 'living force' concept.

[20] Kant, *Schriften*, Vol. 1, pp. 34, 139.

[21] J. Hermann: 'De mensura virium corporum' and G. Bilfinger: 'De viribus corporum moto insitis', *Commentarii Academiae Scientiarum Imperialis Petropolitanae* **1** (1728), 1–42 and 43–121. See Kant, *Schriften*, Vol. 1, pp. 43–5, 79–84.

[22] Bernoulli: 'Discours sur le mouvement', *Opera omnia*, Vol. 3, p. 37.

[23] L. Euler: 'De la force de percussion et de sa véritable measure', *Mémoires de l'Académie Royale des Sciences de Berlin* **1** (1745, [published 1746]), 21–53 (on pp. 29–31).

[24] Kant, *Schriften*, Vol. 1, pp. 107, 140.

[25] *Ibid.*, p. 139.

[26] *Ibid.*, p. 107. *Cf.* Buchdahl, *op. cit.* (note 1), pp. 553f.

[27] Kant, *Schriften*, Vol. 1, pp. 26, 141–8.

[28] Bernoulli: 'Discours sur le mouvement', *Opera omnia*, Vol. 3, p. 37; Euler: 'Force de percussion', *op. cit.* (note 23), p. 29. *Cf.* Leibniz to de Volder (undated, late 1698), in *Die Philosophischen Schriften von G. W. Leibniz*, 7 vols., C. I. Gerhardt (ed.), reprinted: Olms, Hildesheim, 1960–61, Vol. 2, p. 154, comparing 'living force' to 'dead force' as a 'line' to its 'elements'. Leibniz had compared 'living force' to 'dead force' as a 'surface to a line' in a manuscript, *Mathematische Schriften*, Vol. 6, p. 121.

[29] J. Ecole: 'Cosmologie wolffienne et dynamique leibnizienne', *Les études philosophiques* **19** (1964), 3–10.

[30] I. Polonoff, *Force, cosmos, monads and other themes in Kant's early thought*, Bouvier Verlag Herbert Grundmann, Bonn, 1973, pp. 77–89; R. Calinger: "The Newtonian – Wolffian controversy (1741–1759)', *Journal of the History of Ideas* **30** (1969), 319–30, and also *idem*: 'Kant and Newtonian science: the pre-critical period', *Isis* **70** (1979), 349–62. Euler had taken a strongly anti-Wolffian stance in these controversies, in his *Gedanken von die Elementen der Cörper*, Berlin, 1746, so in the mid-1750s Kant's position was anti-Eulerian, a view he was ultimately to invert.

[31] Kant, *Schriften*, Vol. 1, p. 226. On these issues see S. Schaffer: 'The phoenix of nature: fire and evolutionary cosmology in Wright and Kant', *Journal for the History of Astronomy* **9** (1978), 180–200.

[32] I. Kant: 'Monadologia Physica', *Schriften*, Vol. I, pp. 473–87.

[33] I. Kant: 'Neuer Lehrbegriff der Bewegung und Ruhe' [1758], *Schriften*, Vol. 2, p. 20.

[34] D. T. Whiteside, ed., *The mathematical papers of Isaac Newton*, Vol. 6, Cambridge University Press, Cambridge, 1974, p. 93.

FORCE AND INERTIA

[35] I. Newton, *Mathematical principles of natural philosophy*, ed. and trans. A. Motte and F. Cajori, University of California Press, Berkeley, 1934, p. 399. *Cf.* J. E. McGuire: 'The origin of Newton's doctrine of essential qualities', *Centaurus* **12** (1968), 233–60.

[36] *Cf.* A. Gabbey: 'Force and inertia in seventeenth century dynamics', *Studies in History and Philosophy of Science* **2** (1971), 1–67; R. S. Westfall, *Force in Newton's physics: the science of dynamics in the seventeenth century* Macdonald, London, 1971, pp. 448–56; E. McMullin, *Newton on matter and activity*, University of Notre Dame Press, Notre Dame/London, 1978, pp. 33–43.

[37] Whiteside, *op. cit.* (note 34), p. 97.

[38] L. Euler: 'Recherches sur l'origine des forces', *Mémoires de l'Académie des Sciences de Berlin* **6** (1750 [published 1752]), 419–47; in *Leonhardi Euleri opera omnia*, series II, Vol. 5, J. O. Fleckenstein (ed.), Orell Füssli, Lausanne, 1957, pp. 112–5.

[39] *Ibid.*, pp. 116, 131.

[40] L. Euler, *Lettres à une princesse d'Allemagne sur divers sujets de physique et de philosophie*, 3 vols., St. Petersburg, 1768–72; in *Leonhardi Euleri opera omnia*, Series III, Vol. II ed. A. Speiser, Orell Füssli, Zürich, 1960, pp. 150–3.

[41] *Ibid.*, pp. 161–6.

[42] *Ibid.*, pp. 167–71.

[43] *Cf.* Timerding; *op. cit.* (note 2), p. 50.

[44] Euler, *op. cit.* (note 40), p. 172; Kant, *Schriften*, Vol. 1, pp. 26, 141.

[45] Kant, *Schriften*, Vol. 4, pp. 473, 476, 477.

[46] *Gehler's physikalishes Wörterbuch neu bearbeitet*, 10 vols., Leipzig, 1825–44, Vol. 2, p. 715.

[47] G. W. Leibniz, *Theoria motus abstracti*, Mainz, 1671; in Leibniz, *Mathematische Schriften*, Vol. 6, p. 71. *Cf.* R. Palter: 'Kant's formulation of the laws of motion', *Synthese* **24** (1972), p. 111.

[48] Kant, *Schriften*, Vol. 4, pp. 472, 480, 496.

[49] *Ibid.*, p. 502.

[50] *Ibid.*, pp. 497, 502, 508.

[51] *Ibid.*, pp. 508, 509, 511.

[52] *Ibid.*, p. 523.

[53] *Ibid.*, pp. 518, 519.

[54] *Ibid.*, pp. 501, 502, 525.

[55] *Ibid.*, pp. 508, 511, 512, 516.

[56] *Ibid.*, pp. 524, 534, *Cf.* Buchdahl, *op. cit.* (note 4).

[57] Kant, *Schriften*, Vol. 4, pp. 497, 498.

[58] *Ibid.*, pp. 498, 524, 525.

[59] *Ibid.*, pp. 513, 525, 534.

[60] *Ibid.*, pp. 473, 524.

[61] *Ibid.*, p. 551.

[62] *Ibid.*, p. 543. *Cf.* Buchdahl, *op. cit.* (note 1), pp. 676–8.

[63] Kant, *Schriften*, Vol. 4, pp. 543, 544, 549.

[64] *Ibid.*, pp. 549, 550, 551.

[65] *Cf.* Buchdahl, *op. cit.* (note 1), p. 556.

XI

Mayer's Concept of "Force": The "Axis" of a New Science of Physics

Mayer's conception of nature has received inadequate attention from historians. His works tend to be regarded as speculative, confused, and obscure, yet containing strong elements of positive science which justifies his inclusion among the "pioneers" of energy conservation.[1] The analysis of Mayer's ideas from the perspective of the "simultaneous discovery" of energy conservation presupposes that though the intentions of the different pioneers may have been different, their ideas can be understood in terms of concepts common to them all.[2] Mayer's first published paper, "On the Forces of Inorganic Nature" in 1842,[3] which is traditionally regarded as his first publication on the conservation of energy, opened with the statement that "the purpose of the following pages is to seek the answer to the question: what are we to understand by 'forces' and how are these interrelated?"[4] Mayer's claim, as he informed his friend the physician Wilhelm Griesinger later that year, was to have represented "the connection of many phenomena much more clearly than has been seen hitherto," and to have given "a clear and good idea of what a force

*Department of History, Furness College, University of Lancaster, Bailrigg, Lancaster, LA1 4YG, England.

[1] D. S. L. Cardwell, *From Watt to Clausius* (London, 1971), pp. 229 ff.

[2] This is the approach adopted by Thomas S. Kuhn in his important study, "Energy Conservation as an Example of Simultaneous Discovery," in *Critical Problems in the History of Science,* ed. M. Clagett (Madison, 1959), pp. 321–356. The crucial feature of Kuhn's analysis is his claim to have pointed to factors that are *specific* to the period 1830 to 1850 and hence to have explained simultaneous discovery. Kuhn's approach is discussed, with reference to his stress on the interconversion of forces as one such specific factor, in P. M. Heimann, "Conversion of Forces and the Conservation of Energy," *Centaurus, 18* (1974), 147–161.

[3] J. R. Mayer, "Bemerkungen über die Kräfte der unbelebten Natur," *Ann. d. Chem. u. Pharm., 42* (1842), 233–240. I have used the reprint of this and other papers of Mayer's in J. J. Weyrauch, ed., *Die Mechanik der Wärme in gesammelte Schriften von Robert Mayer* (Stuttgart, 1893). Mayer's correspondence and unpublished papers are collected in Weyrauch, *Kleinere Schriften und Briefe von Robert Mayer* (Stuttgart, 1893). These two volumes are cited below as Weyrauch, *1* and Weyrauch, *2,* respectively. All translations from these volumes are my own.

[4] Weyrauch, *1,* 23.

is."[5] The kernel of Mayer's thought is his concept of force and his theory of the relations between forces, and its understanding is essential to our comprehension of Mayer's fundamental intentions. It is this kernel that is obscured or distorted by the search for correspondences and connections between Mayer's ideas and those of other "pioneers" of energy conservation.

The distortion of Mayer's intentions goes back to nineteenth century controversies over the scientific merits and priority of Mayer's papers and his claim to be judged as an originator of the law of the conservation of energy. Central to this claim was the discussion of the value and validity of Mayer's calculation in 1842 of the mechanical equivalent of heat. Mayer based his claim to scientific originality on this calculation, and indeed it would distort Mayer's view that "numbers are the sought-for foundation of an exact natural science"[6] to fail to note the significance of his calculation. Mayer drew attention to his statement of the "law of the equivalence of heat and motion" and his derivation of "its numerical expression, the mechanical equivalent of heat,"[7] by noting that "the celebrated English physicist Joule was led to the thesis that the phenomena of heat and motion rest essentially on the same principle, or, as he expresses it in a similar way to myself, that heat and motion can be transformed into one another."[8] John Tyndall, in defending Mayer's claim to be a pioneer of energy conservation, respected Mayer's theory of nature and drew attention to the analogy between Mayer's doctrine of the indestructibility and transformability of forces and Joule's notion of the indestructibility and convertibility of natural powers.[9] The priority controversy led to a blurring of the conceptual basis of Mayer's calculation, for Mayer rejected what was central to Joule's work, the mechanical theory of heat; analogies between Mayer's and Joule's papers have limited validity. By contrast, Joule's champion P. G. Tait poured relentless scorn on Mayer's theory of nature. He called it "entirely subversive of common sense and logic in an experimental science," being "without experimental bases."[10] Mayer's intentions

---

[5] Weyrauch, 2, 181.
[6] J. R. Mayer, "Bemerkungen über das mechanische Aequivalent der Wärme" [1851], in Weyrauch, 1, 237.
[7] Weyrauch, 1, 272.
[8] Ibid.
[9] John Tyndall, "Remarks on the Dynamical Theory of Heat," Philosophical Magazine, 25 (1863), 380.

were obscured by polemics whose purpose was as limited as their conceptual finesse and historical acumen. Moreover, those who have attempted to view Mayer as one of the pioneers of energy conservation have judged his importance almost solely on the basis of that work that seemed relevant to energy conservation.

The present paper attempts to escape from this historiography by focusing on the primary intentions of Mayer's natural philosophy. The genesis of Mayer's ideas lay in physiology, which is essential to recognize if we wish to understand how the fundamental feature of his thought came to be a clarification of the concept of "force." The apparent obscurity of Mayer's conception of nature has led to considerable confusion over Mayer's philosophical indebtedness. Although claims that Mayer was a Kantian owing to his appeal to the law of causality,[11] or an adherent of Schelling's philosophy,[12] or that he "generalized" Leibniz' concept of force[13] may be fanciful, the confusion surrounding his natural philosophy is conducive to claims of this kind. The present paper, which aims at a clarification of Mayer's concept of force, will conclude with a brief discussion of the validity of such claims.

Mayer's account of his observation, which he made while performing a venesection in Java in 1840, that venous blood in the tropics was unusually bright red—so bright that he thought he had struck an artery—is a familiar story. Arguing that this observation implied that a person living in the tropics needed less oxygen than one living in a cooler climate for the maintenance of body heat, he speculated on the transformation of food material into body heat and on the relation between this transformation and the performance of bodily exertion.[14] From this speculation he derived his concept of the equivalence of heat and mechanical motion and his theory of the transformability and indestructibility of forces. Although Mayer in

---

[10] P. G. Tait, "On the History of Thermodynamics," *ibid.*, 28 (1864), 292.

[11] Charles C. Gillispie, *The Edge of Objectivity* (Princeton, 1960), pp. 375, 385.

[12] Erwin Hiebert, in his comments on Kuhn's paper on energy conservation, in Clagett, *op. cit.* (note 2), p. 394.

[13] Alwin Mittasch, *Julius Robert Mayers Kausalbegriff* (Berlin, 1940), pp. 40 ff.

[14] J. R. Mayer, "Die organische Bewegung in ihren Zusammenhange mit dem Stoffwechsel" [1845], in Weyrauch, *1*, 105 ff.

his first two papers—the second of which was published in Justus Liebig's *Annalen der Chemie und Pharmacie* in 1842—did not mention this physiological observation and its implications, he alluded to his derivation of the concept of the transformation of forces from physiological investigations in a letter to his friend the physicist Carl Baur on 24 July 1841.[15] The first clear reference to this derivation is in a letter to Griesinger on 14 June 1844, in which Mayer emphasized that his theory was not concocted at the writing table but arose from observations of the "changed physical condition" in the tropics, and to his reflections on "the conditions of the blood [which] directed my thoughts primarily to the production of animal heat by the respiratory process."[16] Mayer gave a full account of the biological origins of his theories in his 1845 paper, "Organic Motion in Its Relation to Metabolism." His reason for not having done so earlier was in part because his 1842 paper was a short note intended as a priority claim[17] and because, as he told Griesinger, "if one wants to achieve clarity on physiological questions, a knowledge of physical matters is essential if one does not choose to consider the question metaphysically, to which I have an infinite distaste."[18] Mayer thus believed that it was essential to provide a general physical rather than physiological framework for his concept of the indestructibility and transformability of forces.

Mayer's interpretation of the brighter color of venous blood in the tropics in terms of animal heat reflected contemporary thinking. Indeed, his account of his observation in 1845 shows that he drew upon Liebig's *Animal Chemistry* (1842) for much of his discussion of animal heat, which suggests that his interpretation of his observation made in 1840 may well owe something to retrospective reconstruction. Liebig asserted that "the mutual action between the elements of the food and the oxygen conveyed by the circulation of the blood to every part of the body is the source of animal heat."[19] The experimental basis of his argument that respiration was the only source of animal heat was not original but was founded on Lavoisier's

[15] Weyrauch, *2*, 110.
[16] *Ibid.*, pp. 212 f.
[17] Weyrauch, *1*, 246 f.
[18] Weyrauch, *2*, 213.
[19] Justus Liebig, *Animal Chemistry or Organic Chemistry in its Application to Physiology and Pathology*, trans. W. Gregory (1842; Johnson reprint: New York and London, 1964), p. 17.

conclusion that respiration was a chemical process comparable to the combustion of carbon.[20] Later experimental work had left the combustion theory of animal heat in an ambiguous state; C. Despretz and P. L. Dulong implied on experimental grounds that the chemical theory of animal heat was inadequate.[21] Liebig's attempts to meet such criticisms were unsatisfactory, though two of his arguments—that anomalies occurred as a result of the physical situation of the experimental animals[22] and that inaccurate data were used for the heats of combustion[23]—were employed by Mayer in an attempt to support Liebig.[24]

Mayer's use of Liebig's arguments here shows that when he wrote his account of physiological problems in 1845 he made use of Liebig's extended discussion of animal heat. But there are more significant affinities between their writings. Liebig had supported his firm statement of the respiratory theory of animal heat by a series of examples, each purporting to illustrate the relation between the quantity of food consumed, the supply of oxygen, and the amount of heat given off by the animal. He claimed that "our clothing is merely an equivalent for a certain amount of food," so that "the more warmly we are clothed the less urgent becomes the appetite for food, because the loss of heat by cooling, and consequently the amount of heat to be supplied by the food, is diminished." Thus, he argued that if men living in temperate zones were to go naked they would need to consume enormous quantities of food, and that the loss of appetite experienced by Europeans resident in the tropics was owing to their diminished need for food.[25] Liebig's assumption was that an animal needed a smaller amount of oxygen in warmer climates, for there was a relation between the amount of oxygen supplied to the animal and the difference between the temperature of the environment and that of the animal. The smaller the temperature

[20] For an account of work on animal heat at this time, see F. L. Holmes' Introduction to the Johnson reprint of *Animal Chemistry.*

[21] C. Despretz, "Recherches expérimentales sur les causes de la chaleur animale," *Ann. chim. phys.,* 26 (1824), 337-364; P. L. Dulong, "Mémoire sur la chaleur animale," *ibid.,* 1 (1841), 440-455.

[22] Liebig, *op. cit.* (note 19), p. 36. For comments, see Holmes' Introduction, p. xxxiii.

[23] J. Liebig, "Ueber die thierische Wärme," *Ann. d. Chem. u. Pharm.,* 53 (1845), 63-77.

[24] See Mayer's comments in his 1845 paper, Weyrauch, *1,* 81ff.

[25] Liebig, *op. cit.* (note 19), pp. 21 ff.

difference, the less oxygen the animal needed, and hence a smaller quantity of nutrients would be oxygenated.[26] Mayer used the same argument in his account of his 1840 observation of the bright red color of venous blood in the tropics. He explained the red color by relating the difference between the temperature of the environment and that of the animal to the amount of oxygen supplied to the animal. He saw the color difference between arterial and venous blood as "an expression of the magnitude of the oxygen consumption," so that the unusually red color of venous blood in the tropics implied that a smaller amount of oxygen was supplied to the body.[27] Because of the smaller temperature difference between the animal and the environment in the tropics, a smaller quantity of nutrients was oxygenated and a smaller quantity of oxygen was supplied to the blood: "nature had the task of decreasing the chemical process [the oxygenation of food] to a corresponding degree."[28] Mayer's interpretation of his observation used terms that show his adherence to Liebig's theory of animal heat. Although there seems no good reason to doubt Mayer in claiming that his 1840 observation was the starting-point of his speculations, it is clear that the 1845 account of this observation was explicitly couched in Liebig's terms.

As in the case of Mayer's theory, Liebig's theory of animal heat was part of a general theory of the transformation and indestructibility of natural agents. Although there would thus seem to be obvious affinities between the two theories, the affinities are superficial. Liebig's theory of animal heat was part of a general chemistry of physiological processes, in which the chemical "force" supplied from respiration was the source of animal heat, which in turn was responsible for the work done by bodily exertion. Moreover, Liebig argued that a special vital force was essential to the explanation of bodily phenomena such as growth, motion, and resistance to disease.[29] The vital force was one of several "forces" that were equivalent in the sense that one force could generate another. The existence of the vital force was known from its distinct effects: "it is a peculiar force, because it exhibits manifestations which are found in no other

[26] *Ibid.*, p. 19.
[27] Weyrauch, *1*, 106.
[28] *Ibid.*, p. 107.
[29] See T. O. Lipman, "The Response to Liebig's Vitalism," *Bull. Hist. Med., 40* (1966), 511-524, and *idem*, "Vitalism and Reductionism in Liebig's Physiological Thought,"*Isis, 58* (1967), 167-185.

known force."[30] Just as the phenomena of gravity were ascribed to a gravitational force, vital phenomena were to be ascribed to a vital force. The laws of vitality and gravitation were to be studied by investigating the effects of these forces, and scientific analysis could not extend to the study of the nature of life any more than it could to that of the nature of gravity.[31] Moreover, "no force, no power can come of nothing,"[32] so that forces could be transformed into one another but could not be annihilated.[33]

Mayer vehemently rejected the concept of a vital force; he considered that the appeal to a vital force was an appeal to a miracle and a return to mysticism,[34] and he included Liebig among those he attacked for their vital force explanations.[35] Having accepted Liebig's chemical theory of animal heat, Mayer argued that physiological processes could be completely explained in chemical terms.[36] He argued that Liebig's application of the law of the transformation, equivalence, and indestructibility of forces to the vital force did not render the concept of vital force intelligible. He regarded the use of vital force to explain the special characteristics of organisms as gratuitous and without foundation. In his 1845 paper Mayer stated that only the following "forces" could be held to exist: "fall force" (the force which caused the fall of bodies), motion, heat, magnetism, electricity, and chemical force.[37] The operations of nature were determined by the transformation of these forces into one another, and Mayer specifically excluded the vital force from the operations of nature. He also believed that Liebig's notion of forces as causes was confused. Mayer argued that since Newton had considered gravity as a *causa mathematica* and that since the "fall force" was the *causa physica*, Liebig's notion of the gravitational force as the physical cause of the fall of bodies contradicted Newton.[38] Mayer's theory

---

[30] Liebig, *op. cit.* (note 19), p. 221.
[31] *Ibid.*, p. 7.
[32] *Ibid.*, p. 28.
[33] *Ibid.*, p. 196.
[34] See his comments in his 1845 paper, Weyrauch, *1*, 81, 84.
[35] *Ibid.*, pp. 132-138, in passages which Mayer omitted from the 1867 reprint of his papers (*Die Mechanik der Wärme*) so as not to detract from the significance of Liebig's achievement by old polemics: see a letter of Mayer's to H. Schaaffhausen, 20 August 1867, Weyrauch, *2*, 412.
[36] Weyrauch, *1*, 88 ff.
[37] *Ibid.*, p. 71.
[38] *Ibid.*, p. 59.

of the indestructibility of forces was grounded on the equality of causes and effects, and his critique of Liebig's view of the causal principle was uncompromising and highlights the difference between their conceptions of nature. Mayer wryly noted to Griesinger in a letter in December 1842 that Liebig had written to him that the nature of force and of cause and effect was a confused question, as if Liebig "knew himself to be long ago elevated above the general confusion"; Mayer was satisfied that Liebig was not so elevated.[39] Despite superficial similarities, Mayer's conception of nature was essentially different from Liebig's; the basis of this difference in worldview lay in Mayer's concept of force, an analysis of which provides the key to an understanding of Mayer's thought.

Mayer's first paper on the nature of force, "On the Quantitative and Qualitative Determinations of Forces,"[40] which he wrote in 1841, provides an insight into his primary intentions. His declaration that "all bodies are subject to changes . . . [which] cannot happen without a cause . . . [which] we call force," that "we can derive all phenomena from a basic force [*Urkraft*]," and that "forces, like matter are quantitatively invariable" is the key to his natural philosophy. His intention was to create a new science of physics concerned with "the nature of the existence of forces." He compared physics with chemistry, which was concerned with the existence of matter. The basic principle of both chemistry and physics was that "the quantity of [their] entities [was] invariable and only the quality of these entities [was] variable."[41] Although the forces of nature might change their form, they could not change their magnitude. Mayer's meaning is clarified by letters he wrote to Baur in this period, in which he emphasized that forces are determined by principles analogous to the basic principles of chemistry. Just as "the chemist has to deal with a given quantity of matter, the physicist [deals] with a given quantity of force," so that both chemistry and physics "must be based on the same principles."[42] The basic principle of chemistry was the "indestructibility of substance" during chemical changes: "when H and O are destroyed (become qualitatively zero) and HO

[39] Weyrauch, *2*, 190.
[40] J. R. Mayer, "Ueber die quantitative und qualitative Bestimmung der Kräfte," Weyrauch, *2*, 100-107.
[41] *Ibid.*, pp. 100 ff.
[42] Weyrauch, *2*, 121.

[water] ensues ... the chemist is not permitted to accept that H and O really become zero." Forces must be discussed in the same way; they are "as indestructible as a substance, for in combining with one another they are destroyed in their old form (to become qualitatively zero),"[43] though they remain quantitatively indestructible. Mayer's distinction between quantitative and qualitative differences was clarified by a chemical analogy: "Chemistry teaches us to recognize the qualitative changes that matter undergoes," for "in chemical processes only the *form* and not the *magnitude* of the given matter is changed."[44] In an analogous way the forces—the subject matter of physics—could change their qualitative form, but not their quantitative magnitude.

Mayer attempted to demonstrate his argument that forces were quantitatively invariable by examining the inelastic collision of two bodies. Although his argument suffers because he defined the "force" or "motion" of the bodies quantitatively as mass multiplied by velocity and because he asserted that there was a loss of "force" in collision, his basic conceptual point remains clear enough: from the "presupposition of the invariability of the quantity of force,"[45] the "neutralized" force apparently "lost" in collision was not really lost; it was heat. There was no quantitative loss, but only a qualitative transformation of force. Mayer concluded that "motion, heat and ... electricity are phenomena which can be explained by a single force ... and can be transformed into one another in accordance with definite laws. Motion is transformed into heat by being neutralized by an opposite motion."[46]

Despite the weakness of Mayer's attempt at a quantitative argument, his 1841 paper contains a major insight: mechanical losses could be quantitatively equated with the evolution of heat. Moreover, from the first Mayer realized that he was creating a new science that would develop the implications of the interconnection of heat and mechanical processes. His intention was further clarified in his second paper, "On the Forces of Inorganic Nature," which he published in 1842. From this paper it is clear that the analogy he had

[43] *Ibid.*, pp. 110 ff.

[44] See his 1845 paper, Weyrauch, *1*, 48. Mayer's stress on the chemical analogy is noted by George Rosen, "The Conservation of Energy and the Study of Metabolism," in *The Historical Development of Physiological Thought*, ed. C. M. Brooks and P. F. Cranefield (New York, 1959), pp. 243-263.

[45] Weyrauch, *2*, 103.

[46] *Ibid.*, p. 105.

drawn between chemistry and physics—the former as the science of matter, the latter as the science of force—was not merely a heuristic metaphor, but expressed a fundamental feature of his conception of nature: nature constituted a duality of matter and force. Mayer remarked that whereas matter was readily characterized by properties such as weight and volume, the nature of force remained "unknown, impenetrable, hypothetical." From the outset he declared it his intention to explicate the framework of a science of forces. His paper was "an investigation to make the concept of force as exact as that of matter," so as to create a science of physics that would be as exact as that of chemistry.[47] Hence, as he told Baur, "my first endeavor now is to secure for the science of forces the axis around which the science of matter rotates."[48]

It is significant that one of the crucial steps in the argument—one which was contained in two passages which Mayer omitted from the 1867 reprint of the 1842 paper—involved an appeal to chemical principles. "Chemistry," he noted, "whose problem is to elaborate the existing causal relations between material entities, teaches us that a material cause has a material effect."[49] In a letter to Griesinger later in 1842, he indicated that the principle of the relation between material causes and material effects in chemistry expressed the indestructibility of substances in chemical processes that was known from chemical experiments. "The law which unconditionally governs all ponderable entities (matter)," he stated, "is that no given material entity is ever reduced to nothing and none arises out of nothing; material substances change into one another and assume different manifestations."[50] Because of the analogy between the laws of matter and those applicable to the operations of force, the proof of the law of the indestructibility of forces could be seen to depend on the relation between causes and effects. The indestructibility of forces was grounded in the equivalence of causes and effects: "forces are causes," he declared in his 1842 paper, so "with them we may make full use of the principle: *causa aequat effectum* . . . this first property of all causes we call their indestructibility."[51]

This statement of the indestructibility of force in terms of the

[47] Weyrauch, *1*, 23.
[48] Weyrauch, *2*, 121.
[49] Weyrauch, *1*, 31.
[50] Weyrauch, *2*, 176.
[51] Weyruach, *1*, 23.

equality of causes and effects expresses the kernel of Mayer's concept of force. The relationship between his concept of causality and the quasi-substantial concept of force may be illustrated by reference to Leibniz' statement of the causal principle, for Mayer's view of the law of causality resembles Leibniz' doctrine that "there is always a perfect equivalence between the full cause and the whole effect ... each entire effect is equivalent to the cause."[52] In discussing Leibniz' statement of the equality of causes and effects, Emile Meyerson pointed out that the equality was "none other than the principle of identity applied to objects in time."[53] Mayer's statement of the indestructibility of forces in terms of the law of causality exemplifies Meyerson's thesis that the quantitative equality of causes and effects implies their ontological status as substantial entities. Mayer asserted that "to force as a cause corresponds force as an effect,"[54] and that hence "a force is no less indestructible than a substance";[55] he concluded that force possessed the property of "substantiality."[56] His claim that the indestructibility of force was grounded on the equality of causes and effects was thus fundamental to his view of the ontological status of force. Given the parallels between Mayer's causal principle and Leibniz', it may be noted that Leibniz' close association of the notion of cause and the principle of sufficient reason is perhaps echoed in Mayer's appeal to the "general laws of human thought ... the principle of logical reason [*Satz vom logischen Grunde*]."[57] Mayer's appeal was in support of his claim that the indestructibility of forces was dependent on the relation between causes and effects; in 1845 he grounded the indestructibility of forces in "the laws of thought" and in "experience," by which he meant the principle of causality and the law of the indestructibility of matter, respectively.[58]

Mayer's statement of the analogy between the laws applicable to matter and those applicable to force and his statement of the "substantiality" of force did not entail the material status of force. The

---

[52] Leibniz' reply to Catelan (1687), quoted in Pierre Costabel, *Leibniz et la Dynamique* (Paris, 1960), p. 33.
[53] Emile Meyerson, *Identity and Reality* (London, 1930), p. 43.
[54] Weyrauch, *1*, 31.
[55] Weyrauch, *2*, 115.
[56] Weyrauch, *1*, 73. See also Meyerson, *op. cit.* (note 53), chapter 5.
[57] Weyrauch, *2*, 177.
[58] Weyrauch, *1*, 59. See also Gerd Buchdahl, *Metaphysics and the Philosophy of Science* (Oxford, 1969), pp. 40 ff.

central feature of his 1842 paper was his attempt to explicate a concept of force as a substantial, yet nonmaterial, entity. Whereas matter possessed the properties of weight and impenetrability, force did not, and Mayer concluded that forces were nonmaterial, or "imponderable," entities. Employing his distinction between quantitative and qualitative changes in nature, Mayer defined "causes" as "(quantitatively) *indestructible* and (qualitatively) *transformable entities.*" This definition covered both material and "imponderable" entities, and Mayer asserted that no transitions could occur between the two classes of entities. Matter was ontologically distinct from forces, which were *"indestructible, transformable, imponderable* entities."[59] The concept of force was characterized by the *"union* of indestructibility and transformability."[60] The transformation of forces implied that "in innumerable cases we see motion cease without having caused another motion"; nevertheless, "a force once in motion cannot be annihilated, but can only change into another form."[61] The transformability of forces was thus associated with their indestructibility. Moreover, forces which were transformed one into the other were "two different manifestations of one and the same entity";[62] it was this commitment to the notion of the different forces of nature as phenomenal manifestations of a single force, an *Urkraft* as he had termed it in 1841, that led Mayer to argue that to view one force as the cause of another did not entail that any one phenomenal force could be reduced to any other.

The nonreducibility of phenomenal forces to one another bore on Mayer's conception of the transformation of mechanical motion into heat. He emphasized in 1842 that though "we prefer the assumption that heat is caused by motion to the assumption of a cause without an effect and an effect without a cause," we should not infer from this causal relation any similarity between heat and motion other than that they both belonged to the category of force: "for it to become heat," he stated, "motion must cease to be motion."[63] From this statement it is clear that Mayer did not affirm the mechanical theory of heat, and he did not presuppose it in his calculation of the mechanical equivalent of heat. His denial that heat consisted of mo-

---

[59] Weyrauch, *1*, 24.
[60] *Ibid.*, p. 25.
[61] *Ibid.*, p. 26.
[62] *Ibid.*, p. 24.
[63] *Ibid.*, p. 28.

tion followed directly from his understanding of the nature of force. Motion and heat had the same ontological status, each a different manifestation of a single *Urkraft*. The causal relation between forces only implied their indestructibility and transformability, not the reducibility of one to the other.

Mayer elaborated on this point in a letter to Griesinger in November 1842, in which he affirmed that "what heat, what electricity etc. are in their essence I do not know, as little as I know of the inner essence of a material substance." As a result of his investigations he felt that "I know this, that I see the connection of many phenomena much more clearly than has been seen hitherto, and that I can give a clear and good idea of what a force is."[64] Mayer was arguing that the intelligibility of his concept of force was grounded in his account of the connection between phenomena and hence of the connection between forces, but his claim that he made no attempt to specify the "essence" of force is ambiguous. Mayer did not speculate on the nature of the *Urkraft* or on the nature of matter, as is indicated by his disavowal of knowledge of the "inner essence" of matter, and his claim that he did not know the "essence" of the different forces reflects his concern to give an account of the connection between forces rather than to discuss the nature of, say, heat. However, he was concerned to specify the ontological status of force: in the mature statement of his theory in 1845, he stated that force possessed the property of "substantiality," adding that "there is no immaterial matter"[65] and emphasizing that the substantiality of forces did not grant them the status of material entities. There is clear disharmony between his claim that he refused to speculate on or had knowledge of the essence of force and was only concerned to define the relations between forces and his statement that force was a nonmaterial, yet substantial, entity. There is disharmony between his discussion of the substantive and of the relational aspects of force.[66]

Mayer stressed not only the ontological status of force, but also the quantitative expression of force. In 1842 he argued that force was to be measured by the Leibnizian *vis viva*, noting, as had Leibniz,

[64] Weyrauch, *2*, 180 ff.
[65] Weyrauch, *1*, 73.
[66] In stressing Mayer's emphasis on the relational aspects of force, Ernst Cassirer failed to do justice to the complexity of Mayer's ideas. See Cassirer's interesting discussion of this point in *The Philosophy of Symbolic Forms* (New Haven, 1957), *3*, 461 ff.

that "the law of the conservation of *vis viva* is based on the general law of the indestructibility of causes."[67] The law of the conservation of *vis viva*, which applied to mechanical motions, was a special case of Mayer's law of the indestructibility of forces. In 1842 he associated *vis viva* with the measure of "fall force," the force which caused the fall of bodies, and in 1845 he extended that measure to the force of "motion."[68] These two forces, as he pointed out in 1841, were associated with changes in the spatial relations of material entities,[69] and hence the Leibnizian *vis viva* had obvious application to them. From the first, Mayer had distinguished these "mechanical forces," as he later termed them,[70] from the forces associated with electrical, thermal, and chemical phenomena.[71] Given Mayer's emphatic statement of the view that one kind of force could not be regarded as constituting the essence of another and that the causal relation between forces only implied their transformability, the way in which the Leibnizian *vis viva* was related to forces such as heat remained obscure. Nevertheless, in calculating the mechanical equivalent of heat he made no attempt to specify the way the nature of heat was related to its quantitative expression.[72] It was in this sense that Mayer's theory of the indestructibility of force required no statement of the "essence" of force.

Despite his claim to have clarified the concept of force by an explication of the phenomenal manifestations of and connections between forces, Mayer's papers and correspondence show his continued concern to define the nature of force. In a letter to Baur of July 1842 he argued that "from the actual state of experience we are able to consider only five forces in inorganic nature as being objective: these are fall force, motion, heat, electricity and chemical difference of matter. These five forces stand in such connection that one can transform into another."[73] He amplified this view in a letter to Griesinger the following December, in which he explained that the

[67] Weyrauch, *1*, 25. Kuhn is mistaken in supposing that Mayer employs $1/2mv^2$ as the measure of force (*op. cit.* [note 2], p. 349).
[68] Weyrauch, *1*, 62.
[69] Weyrauch, *2*, 101.
[70] Weyrauch, *1*, 71.
[71] Weyrauch, *2*, 101.
[72] For interesting comments on the failure of eighteenth century scientists to perceive this relation, see Erwin Hiebert, *Historical Roots of the Principle of Conservation of Energy* (Madison, 1962), pp. 2, 92-94, 103.
[73] Weyrauch, *2*, 134 ff.

transformability of these five forces into one another was a consequence of the fact that they were "one and the same entity in different manifestations."[74] He published his five fold division of forces in 1845, noting again that they were "in truth only a single force."[75] He explained to Griesinger that forces could be defined simply in terms of their capacity to produce effects: forces were "causes which produce motion."[76] He elaborated on this point in his 1845 paper, declaring that "an entity which through its expenditure brings motion we call force."[77] These statements illustrate the ambiguity and dual nature of Mayer's discussion of force: forces were defined as possessing "substantiality" and as manifestations of the *Urkraft*, yet they were also defined in terms of their phenomenal effects and quantitative equivalence. The basis of Mayer's claim to have clarified the concept of force can thus be seen in his demonstration of the transformability of forces from the indestructibility of causes and in his explication of the phenomenal manifestations of force.

The obscurity surrounding Mayer's conception of nature has led to some confusion as to what he meant by saying that forces were causes and why he emphasized the role of forces in maintaining the operations of nature. In this connection, there has been some speculation as to Mayer's probable philosophical sources. The preceding analysis permits an assessment of the conceptual similarities between Mayer's natural philosophy and philosophical traditions and of the possible influence of such traditions on his theory of nature.

The preceding analysis shows that the principle that causes are equivalent to their effects was fundamental to Mayer's natural philosophy. His theory "in no way rests on an unusual and arbitrary definition of the causality condition," he assured Griesinger in 1844.[78] Kant's importance in the German cultural sphere at this time and the central place of the causal principle in Kant's philosophy might seem to suggest Mayer's adherence to Kant's philosophy. But the analysis of Mayer's concept of causality above shows that although Mayer may have been indebted in some sense to Kant for his causal principle, his view of causality was different from Kant's. For

[74] *Ibid.*, p. 201.
[75] Weyrauch, *1*, 48.
[76] Weyrauch, *2*, 201.
[77] Weyrauch, *1*, 47.
[78] Weyrauch, *2*, 226.

Kant the principle of causality established the law-likeness of nature: nature is dependent upon the causal principle "as the original ground of its necessary conformity to law."[79] There is no suggestion in Mayer's writings that causality is to be considered as a condition of the law-likeness of nature; rather, Mayer regarded the causal principle as asserting the indestructibility of causes and the equivalence of causes and effects.[80]

The conceptual analogies between Mayer's view of the causal principle and Leibniz' doctrine of the equality of causes and effects, Mayer's adoption of the Leibnizian concept of *vis viva*, and the possible programmatic analogy between Mayer's attempt to create a new science of physics and Leibniz' attempt to create a "new *science of dynamics*"[81] hardly justify our viewing Mayer as a Leibnizian. Leibniz emphasized that force was something different from size, figure, and motion, and that it corresponded to something real in bodies.[82] Leibniz' science of dynamics was the culmination of his critique of the Cartesian conception of body as essentially extension: "the concept of *forces* or *powers*," he wrote, "for whose explanation I have set up a distinct science of *dynamics*" was to bring "the strongest light to bear upon our understanding of the concept of *substance*."[83] Hence, for Leibniz a true science of bodies would be concerned with the nature of force. His science of dynamics was a consequence of his theory of substance, in which his metaphysics differs so demonstrably from that of Mayer's natural philosophy. For Leibniz the nature of material substance was to be understood in terms of the concept of force, not in terms of impenetrability and extension, which he considered to be an "incomplete" and "analyzable and relative concept"; whereas extension was an "attribute resulting from many substances existing continuously at the same

---

[79] I. Kant, *Critique of Pure Reason*, trans. N. Kemp Smith (London, 1929), p. 173.

[80] See Gerd Buchdahl, "The Conception of Lawlikeness in Kant's Philosophy of Science," *Synthese, 23* (1971), 24–46.

The Kantian approach is fundamental to Helmholtz' philosophy of nature: for a full analysis, see P. M. Heimann, "Helmholtz and Kant: the Metaphysical Foundations of Über die Erhaltung der Kraft," *Studies in History and Philosophy of Science, 5* (1974), 205–238. For a discussion of these two different senses of the principle of causality, see Meyerson, *op. cit.* (note 53), chapter 1.

[81] Gottfried Wilhelm Leibniz, *Philosophical Papers and Letters*, ed. L. E. Loemker (Dordrecht, 1969), p. 435.

[82] *Ibid.*, p. 315.   [83] *Ibid.*, p. 433.

time,"[84] force was "absolutely real."[85] The primitive active force was substantially present in all corporeal entities and was manifested phenomenally as the derivative active force—the "force by which bodies actually act and are acted upon by each other"—which appeared either as "dead force" or as "living force [*vis viva*]."[86] The conservation of *vis viva* expressed on the phenomenal level the unfolding activity of the monads which constituted the essence of material substances. Leibniz' concept of force as a defining characteristic of material substance stands in sharp contrast to Mayer's matter-force duality. For Mayer, force possessed the property of "substantiality," but was ontologically distinct from matter.

Mayer's emphasis on the role of forces has led to the suggestion that *Naturphilosophie* influenced his thought. As this philosophical movement is often held to have had an influence on science,[87] some discussion of its possible relation to Mayer's work is in order. The fundamental aim of Schelling's philosophy was to discover certain a priori principles that were inaccessible to empirical cognition. His physics was concerned with the inner essence of nature in contrast to empirical physics which was concerned with phenomenal principles. For Schelling, empirical physics was the science of the "surface" of nature, whereas the aim of *Naturphilosophie* was to comprehend a level of reality that by definition was known only a priori.[88] Schelling's conception of physics stands in sharp contrast to that of Mayer, who sought to render the concept of force as empirically meaningful as the concept of matter. Schelling conceived of nature as the product of two opposing tendencies, productive activity and the limitation of that activity; physical objects were the result of the interaction of these tendencies.[89] The tendencies were manifested on the empirical, phenomenal level as two primitive forces, known as

[84]*Ibid.*, pp. 516, 520.   [85]*Ibid.*, p. 445.

[86]*Ibid.*, pp. 436 ff. For an analysis of the relations between Leibniz' dynamics and metaphysics, see Martial Gueroult, *Leibniz, Dynamique et Métaphysique* (Paris, 1967); Costabel, *op. cit.* (note 52); Carolyn Iltis, "Leibniz and the *Vis Viva* Controversy," *Isis, 62* (1971), 21-35.

[87]For a useful general discussion, see Barry Gower, "Speculation in Physics: The History and Practice of *Naturphilosophie*," *Stud. Hist. Phil. Sci., 3* (1973), 301-356.

[88]F. W. J. Schelling, "Einleitung zu dem Entwurf eines Systems der Naturphilosophie," in Schelling, *Sämmtliche Werke*, ed. K. F. A. Schelling (Stuttgart, 1857), *3*, 275.

[89]*Ibid.*, p. 288.

Grundkräfte, so that the principles that characterize the inner essence of reality, though only known a priori, had empirical counterparts. Schelling's theory of the polarity of forces as an expression of the tension between productivity and its limitation has no parallel in Mayer's writings. The general thrust of the writings of *Naturphilosophen* such as Ritter was to account for phenomenal changes by an appeal to inner essences, and their notions of the unity of nature and the polarity of forces bear only a remote analogy to Mayer's concept of the transformation of forces.

Mayer felt that his work had forced "the twaddle of the *Naturphilosophen* to stand in wretched nakedness in the pillory,"[90] if for no other reason than because of the quantitative content of his work. "A single number," he exclaimed, "has more real and lasting value than a costly library of hypotheses."[91] Statements of this kind do not disprove the possibility that Mayer was influenced by the *Naturphilosophen*. It seems that he was familiar with their speculations, and it is possible that the influence of *Naturphilosophie* was so pervasive in this period that it was implicit in all scientific activity concerned with the unity and conversion of "forces"; indeed, Mayer's reference to an *Urkraft* and to the unity of forces suggests an indebtedness to the ideas of the *Naturphilosophen*. But while such an influence is possible, it must be emphasized that in other respects Mayer's conception of nature was fundamentally at variance with the ideas of the *Naturphilosophen*. His matter-force duality and stress on the concept of force as an empirical quantity suggest that there would be little reason to attribute to *Naturphilosophie* any substantive role in shaping Mayer's natural philosophy. His intentions were fundamentally opposed to those of the *Naturphilosophen,* and claims for the influence of their ideas on Mayer's work must therefore be regarded with some suspicion.

Mayer provided one clue in connection with his indebtedness to philosophical traditions. He hinted that he had been influenced by the notion of attractive and repulsive forces as postulated by the "Kantian school of natural philosophy."[92] Mayer's intentions, however, show little correspondence with Kant's central concern in the *Metaphysische Anfangsgründe der Naturwissenschaft* (1786), which was to discuss the ways in which the a priori, transcendental cate-

---

[90] Weyrauch, 2, 181.
[91] *Ibid.,* p. 226.
[92] *Ibid.,* p. 378.

gories of the *Critique* were to be applied to the empirical concept of matter. Kant's metaphysics of nature was to be in "unison with the mathematical doctrine of motion"[93] and to show that the explication of the concept of matter demonstrates the possibility of Newtonian science. Mayer's reference to the Kantian "school" is difficult to interpret. It is unlikely that he had in mind J. F. Fries, whose *Mathematische Naturphilosophie* (1822) was an attempt to develop the Kantian approach in opposition to the *Naturphilosophie* of Schelling. Fries' exposition of Kant's metaphysics and stress on a firm link between mathematics and metaphysics has no counterpart in Mayer's natural philosophy.[94] It would seem likely that Mayer's reference to the Kantian theory of forces reflected no more than an awareness—possibly at second-hand—of Kant's explication of matter in terms of attractive and repulsive forces in the chapter on "Dynamics" in the *Metaphysische Anfangsgründe*. Kant had argued there that the dynamical concept of matter was to be explicated in terms of an attractive force limiting the repulsive force, so that the quantity of matter present in a given space was determined by the limiting or balance of the repulsive force by the attractive force. Mayer's reference to the Kantian emphasis on attractive and repulsive forces— even though he only made this remark in an "Autobiographical Note" written as late as 1863[95]—suggests that he was indebted to the Kantian notion of the limiting or balance of forces for his concept of the interconversion and equivalence of forces, but there is no substantive affinity between the Kantian discussion of attractive and repulsive forces and Mayer's conception of nature.

In attempting to clarify the confusion over Mayer's indebtedness to philosophical traditions, this analysis has underlined the conceptual individuality of Mayer's natural philosophy. Nevertheless, the possibility of the influence of the Kantian notion of the balance of forces or of the unity of forces of *Naturphilosophie* cannot be discounted, however limited this influence and tenuous the filiation of ideas and despite the major differences between these philosophical traditions and Mayer's work. It would be a mistake to conclude that Mayer's intellectual development can be understood out of all con-

---

[93] I. Kant, *Metaphysical Foundations of Natural Science*, trans. J. W. Ellington (Indianapolis and New York, 1970), p. 17.

[94] For a discussion of Fries, see Heimann, *op. cit.* (note 80), pp. 230 f.

[95] For comments on the dating of this note, see Weyrauch, 2, 376.

text; for textual analysis, though necessary, is not a sufficient condition for historical understanding.

ACKNOWLEDGMENTS

I wish to thank Gerd Buchdahl, Karl Figlio, and Russell McCormmach for comments on a draft of this paper.

XII

HELMHOLTZ AND KANT: THE METAPHYSICAL FOUNDATIONS OF ÜBER DIE ERHALTUNG DER KRAFT

I believe ... that perfection may in time be obtained by a cleverer hand when, stimulated by this sketch [the *Metaphysische Anfangsgründe der Naturwissenschaft*], mathematical investigators of nature may find it not unimportant to treat the metaphysical portion—which cannot be got rid of anyway—as a special fundamental part of general physics, and to bring it into unison with the mathemathical doctrine of motion.[1]

THIS study is an analysis of a work by tradition regarded as one of the first enunciations of the principle of the conservation of energy, Hermann Helmholtz's *Über die Erhaltung der Kraft* of 1847.[2] The tendency to stress the correspondences and connections between Helmholtz's ideas and those of other 'pioneers' of energy conservation such as J. P. Joule and J. R. Mayer, has inevitably led to some distortion of the central features of Helmholtz's paper. Helmholtz's intentions have been obscured by the attempt to stress aspects of his work which have parallels in the thought of men such as Joule and Mayer, the tendency to assess his work in terms of criteria held to be appropriate for a pioneer of energy con-

I wish to express my thanks to Gerd Buchdahl for a number of helpful discussions during the preparation of this paper and for suggesting some valuable improvements, and to Russell McCormmach for comments on a draft of the paper.

[1] Immanuel Kant, *Metaphysische Anfangsgründe der Naturwissenschaft* [1786], *Kant's gesammelte Schriften herausgegeben von der Königlichen Preussischen Akademie der Wissenschaften*, IV (Berlin: G. Reimer, 1911), 478. I have used the recent translation by James Ellington (Kant, *Metaphysical Foundations of Natural Science*, translated with Introduction and Essay by James Ellington (Indianapolis and New York: Bobbs-Merrill, 1970)). Quotations from the *Metaphysische Anfangsgründe* in this paper are taken, with occasional modifications, from this translation; and all page references are to the *Akademie* edition, page numbers in that edition being given as marginal numbers in Ellington's translation.

[2] Hermann Helmholtz, *Über die Erhaltung der Kraft, eine physikalische Abhandlung* (Berlin: G. Reimer, 1847), in *Wissenschaftliche Abhandlungen von Hermann von Helmholtz*, 3 vols., I (Leipzig: Barth, 1882–95), 12–68, page numbers of the original publication being given as marginal numbers in this edition. Helmholtz's *Wissenschaftliche Abhandlungen* will be denoted as *WA*. I have consulted Tyndall's translation, 'On the Conservation of Force', *Scientific Memoirs, Natural Philosophy*, J. Tyndall and W. Francis (eds.) (London: Taylor and Francis, 1853), 114–62, and a translation in R. Kahl, *Selected Writings of Hermann von Helmholtz* (Middletown, Connecticut; Wesleyan University Press, 1971), 3–55, though I frequently differ from both these translations.

Reprinted with permission from *Studies in History and Philosophy of Science* 5. © 1974, Pergamon Press PLC, Oxford.

servation.³   William Thomson, writing in 1852, considered Helmholtz's monograph as being a 'treatise on the principle of mechanical effect';⁴ *Über die Erhaltung der Kraft* was commonly regarded as providing a mathematical formulation of the principle of energy conservation. Helmholtz himself was quick to note the significance of his contribution to the emergent law of the conservation of energy. Writing in 1856 he pointed out⁵ that his terms *lebendige Kraft* and *Spannkraft* were synonymous with the terms 'actual [kinetic] energy' and 'potential energy' introduced in 1853 by W. J. M. Rankine,⁶ and in a lecture (written in English) on the 'Law of the Conservation of Force' in 1861⁷ he noted with approval Rankine's introduction of the expression 'conservation of energy'. He suggested that this should be the preferred usage rather than his own expression 'conservation of force [*Erhaltung der Kraft*]' because the law in question 'does not mean that the intensity of the natural forces is constant; but it relates more to the whole amount of power which can be gained by any natural process, and by which a certain amount of work can be done'. The law of the conservation of energy stated that 'the power of the whole system in which these operations take place is neither exhausted nor increased in quantity, but only changed in form'.⁸ In nevertheless here retaining the use of the expression the

³ This distortion of intentions follows from the attempt to explain the emergence of the principle of energy conservation as 'an example of simultaneous discovery', as Kuhn expresses it. See Thomas S. Kuhn, 'Energy Conservation as an example of Simultaneous Discovery', *Critical Problems in the History of Science*, M. Clagett (ed.) (Madison: Wisconsin University Press, 1959), 321–56. Kuhn's paper remains the most successful interpretation of the emergence of energy conservation as a group phenomenon: it is supposed that though the intentions of different pioneers may have been different, yet their ideas can be understood in terms of concepts common to the group. This sociological approach needs to be supplemented by analytic studies which examine the intentions of the individuals: for a discussion of Mayer, see P. M. Heimann, 'Mayer's Concept of Force', *Historical Studies in the Physical Sciences*, 6, in press. Moreover, I believe that there are significant difficulties in maintaining Kuhn's formulation, in which he delineates factors which he regards as *specific* to the period 1830–50 and which explain the simultaneous discovery of energy conservation: for a discussion of the concept of the interconversion of forces, which is one of Kuhn's specific factors, see P. M. Heimann, 'Conversion of forces and the conservation of energy', *Centaurus*, 18, (1974), 147-161.
⁴ William Thomson, 'On the Dynamical Theory of Heat', *Mathematical and Physical Papers*, I (Cambridge: Cambridge University Press, 1882), 182–3n. This footnote was added to the 1852 reprint of the paper (*Philosophical Magazine*, 4 [1852], 8-12, 105-17, 168-76); the paper was first published in the *Transactions of the Royal Society of Edinburgh*, 20 (1851), 261–88.
⁵ H. Helmholtz, 'Theorie der Wärme', *Fortschritte der Physik im Jahre 1853*, ix. *Jahrgang* (Berlin: G. Reimer, 1856), 407.
⁶ W. J. M. Rankine, 'On the General Law of the Transformation of Energy', *Philosophical Magazine*, 5 (1853), 106.
⁷ Helmholtz, 'On the Application of the Law of the Conservation of Force to Organic Nature', *WA*, III, 565–80.
⁸ *Ibid.*, 565f. For the expression 'conservation of energy' see Rankine, *op. cit.*, note 6.

'law of the conservation of force' Helmholtz indicated that this was an appropriate expression to denote the indestructibility of 'natural forces': although the expression 'conservation of force', or 'constancy of force [*Constanz der Kraft*]'[9] as he originally termed it, denoted the principle of the indestructibility and transformability of natural agents, referring to the 'conservation of energy' gave a more precise description of the quantities which were conserved. Helmholtz thus indicated that the principle of *Erhaltung der Kraft* denoted both the 'indestructibility of natural forces' (thus resembling the principles enunciated in the writings of Justus Liebig, Joule and Mayer) and the 'conservation of energy' (as formulated by Rankine).

However, to fasten on these aspects of *Über die Erhaltung der Kraft* omits the most individual and indeed almost the cardinal feature of the paper: Helmholtz's attempt to demonstrate that the principle of the conservation of energy could be expressed in terms of an explanatory framework which posited an ontology of matter and of the forces associated with material entities. Moreover, he argued that these forces were Newtonian central forces so that 'the problem of physical science is to reduce natural phenomena to unalterable forces of attraction and repulsion, whose intensity depends on the distance'. In using the term '*Kraft* [force]' here, he thus introduced an additional use of this term to mean 'force' in the sense of Newtonian attraction and repulsive forces; these forces were not held to be subject to the conservation principle denoted by the principle of *Erhaltung der Kraft*.[10] Helmholtz's formulation of the

---

[9] See Helmholtz's letters to du Bois-Reymond of 21 December 1846, 12 February 1847 and 21 July 1847 (this last, two days before the paper was read to the Berlin Physikalische Gesellschaft) in all of which the paper is referred to as being concerned with the *Constanz der Kraft*. Helmholtz's letters to du Bois-Reymond are at the Staatsbibliothek Preussischer Kulturbesitz, Berlin.

[10] Helmholtz, *WA*, I, 16. The common interpretation of Helmholtz's paper, which owes its origin to the attempt to assimilate Helmholtz to the other 'pioneers' of energy conservation, that the concept of *Kraft* really meant 'energy' (for example: D. S. L. Cardwell, *From Watt to Clausius* [London: Heinemann, 1971], 235), is clearly vitiated by Helmholtz's usage. The interpretation maintained by Y. Elkana, 'Helmholtz's' "Kraft": An Illustration of Concepts in Flux', *Historical Studies in the Physical Sciences*, 2 (1970), 263–98, that both 'force and energy were not at all clearly defined separate entities, but rather different guises of a vaguely defined "Kraft" that Helmholtz thought of as being conserved', *op. cit.*, 266, is also incorrect. The problem in interpreting the concept of *Kraft* arises from Helmholtz's use of the term in several different ways. For example, Helmholtz's *lebendige Kraft* corresponds to the concept of 'kinetic energy', the meaning of the term as an 'energy' term being clear from its contextual scientific function. But the term *Kraft* could also mean both 'Newtonian force' and 'natural agent'—again, the meaning being clear from the context. The expression *Erhaltung der Kraft* could mean both the 'conservation of energy' and the 'indestructibility of natural agents', but there was no confusion with the sense of *Kraft* to mean 'Newtonian force'. Elkana assumes that Helmholtz used the term *Kraft* to denote a single concept, and hence did not distinguish force and energy terms.

principle of *Erhaltung der Kraft* was inextricably linked to his assumption that natural phenomena were reducible to central forces. In the first part of this paper I shall suggest that *Über die Erhaltung der Kraft* emerged from Helmholtz's concern with the problem of animal heat which persuaded him of the necessity of formulating a principle of the 'constancy of force' which would entail the denial of perpetual motion. In the second part of the paper I shall show that in representing the impossibility of perpetual motion mathematically he formulated the principle of the conservation of energy in a way such that his principle of *Erhaltung der Kraft* was dependent on the central force principle as a necessary condition of its validity. The assumption that natural phenomena were reducible to central forces of attraction and repulsion was thus basic to his formulation of the principle of *Erhaltung der Kraft*.

Now, in the Introduction to *Über die Erhaltung der Kraft* Helmholtz declared that the implementation of the central force principle was of significance for the 'central and ultimate aims of physical science',[11] since the subsumption of natural phenomena under central force explanations was for him 'the condition of the complete comprehensibility of natural phenomena' and was therefore 'the necessary conceptual form for understanding nature'.[12] The philosophical argument of the Introduction, whose analysis is the major concern of this study, attests to his belief that the claim concerning the central force principle being the presupposition of the complete intelligibility of nature, could not be established by reference to empirical evidence but required independent justification. It thus became his concern to provide an account of the intelligibility of the central force principle by demonstrating that the conformity of nature to Newtonian laws was the only possible explanatory system. In the furtherance of this end he makes a major appeal to Kant's metaphysics of nature. Though the argument involves some distortion of Kant's architectonic, its Kantian basis is unmistakable.[13]

It thus becomes clear that the primacy of the central force concept

[11] Helmholtz, *WA*, I, 12.
[12] *Ibid.*, 16f.
[13] That there are Kantian strains in Helmholtz's reference to the law of causality in the Introduction is commonly accepted: see R. S. Turner, 'Helmholtz', *Dictionary of Scientific Biography*, VI, C. C. Gillispie (ed.) (New York: Scribner's, 1972), 234, and J. W. Ellington, 'Kant', *ibid.*, VII (1973), 234. I shall be in part concerned with this aspect of the Kantian affinities of the paper, for which I will attempt to provide a systematic analysis, but my analysis is mainly concerned with Helmholtz's attempt to justify his central force principle. Following Helmholtz's own remark (*WA*, I, 68) the Kantian affinities of his matter-force ontology have on occasion been noted, but Helmholtz's argument requires full analysis for its content and implications to be understood.

Helmholtz and Kant

was reinforced by being grounded on the argument of the Introduction, which is meant to provide a metaphysical foundation for the concept of central forces so as thereby to demonstrate its intelligibility as a scientific concept.[14] According to his biographer Helmholtz studied Kant in the early 1840s,[15] and he himself later indicated that the argument of the Introduction had been strongly influenced by Kant's philosophy,[16] so there is good reason to view the Introduction in relation to Kantian philosophy. I will contend that whilst *Über die Erhaltung der Kraft* originally emerged from Helmholtz's concern with physiological problems, the explication of the principle of *Erhaltung der Kraft* led Helmholtz to the enunciation of a world view more comprehensive than that of *Erhaltung der Kraft* itself: the universal validity of the mechanical view of nature. In *Über die Erhaltung der Kraft* the intelligibility and necessity of the ontology of the mechanical view of nature was supposed to be given justificatory sanction by an appeal to more general philosophical principles.

I

The origins of *Über die Erhaltung der Kraft* in part lie in Helmholtz's background in medicine and interest in physiology, and in his specific concern with the problem of animal heat in the mid-1840s. The genesis of his ideas arose from his sustained interest in Liebig's *Thier-Chemie, oder die Chemie in ihrer Anwendung auf Physiologie und Pathologie* (1842), in 'Liebig's attempt to derive physiological phenomena from known physical and chemical laws',[17] as Helmholtz put it in a paper published in 1845. Helmholtz emphasized that Liebig's theory that respiration was the only source of animal heat was part of a general statement of the chemical principles underlying physiological processes, in which the chemical 'force' supplied from respiration was the source of animal heat which in turn was responsible for bodily exertion. Despite the ambiguities of the experimental evidence[18] Helmholtz concluded in favour of the

---

[14] In his paper cited in note 10, Elkana claims to establish his interpretation by an analysis of Helmholtz's use of *Kraft* in the Introduction to *Über die Erhaltung der Kraft*, comparing this usage with the use of *Kraft* later in the paper. However, in the Introduction Helmholtz was referring to Newtonian attractive and repulsive forces in the sense of Kant's *Metaphysische Anfangsgründe*, not to the concept of *Kraft* as denoted by the principle of *Erhaltung der Kraft*. Although he recognizes that there are Kantian strains in Helmholtz's paper, Elkana does not appreciate their significance and implications.

[15] Leo Koenigsberger, *Hermann von Helmholtz*, F. A. Welby (trans.) (Oxford: Clarendon Press, 1906), 18.

[16] Helmholtz, *WA*, I, 68.

[17] Helmholtz, 'Über den Stoffverbrauch bei der Muskelaction', *WA*, II 735.

[18] The experimental basis of Liebig's argument was founded on work by Lavoisier in which

XII

chemical theory of animal heat, for he felt that this was the only possible theory, but stated that the intelligibility of Liebig's argument was dependent on the validity of the principle of the constancy of force. The doctrine that 'heat as a principle ... can be derived from other forces and not out of nothing' supposed the validity of the 'principle of the constancy of the force equivalents by the excitation of one force by another'. Helmholtz pointed out that this theory was 'hitherto neither completely decided or acknowledged nor empirically supported',[19] and concluded that it was necessary to provide a justification for Liebig's principle that 'no force, no power can come of nothing',[20] so that forces could be transformed into one another but could not be annihilated. Liebig had argued that a vital force, essential for the explanation of bodily phenomena such as growth and the resistance to disease, was part of this web of forces,[21] and Helmholtz noted that the question 'whether organic life is the effect of a self-perpetuating, unique force, or the result of forces operating also in inorganic nature but modified by the particular manner of their continual operation'[22] had been raised by Liebig's attempt to derive physiological phenomena from physical and chemical laws. Helmholtz did not reject Liebig's use of vital forces, and appears to have interpreted Liebig's approach to physiology as being that in which organic life was held to be the result of forces which were in some sense modifications of those operative in the inorganic world. The crucial problem for Helmholtz was the subsumption of the forces which regulated the physiology of organisms under the framework of the laws determining inorganic forces. In Helmholtz's view, this would be the case if the operations of all forces were subject to the law of the constancy of force. His approach to physiology was clearly affirmed in his 1861 lecture, where

it was concluded that respiration was a chemical process comparable to the combustion of carbon. Later experimental work (C. Despretz, 'Recherches expérimentales sur les causes de la chaleur animale', *Annales de chimie et physique*, 26 (1824), 337–64; P.-L. Dulong, 'Mémoire sur la chaleur animale', *ibid.*, 1 (1841), 440–55) implied that the chemical theory of heat was inadequate. Liebig's attempts to meet such criticisms were unsatisfactory: in a paper in 1845 he argued that anomalies to the combustion theory arose from the fact that Dulong and Despretz had employed inaccurate data (J. Liebig, 'Über die thierische Wärme', *Annalen der Chemie und Pharmacie*, 53 (1845), 63–97). For further discussion see F. L. Holmes' Introduction to the reprint of *Animal Chemistry* (New York: Johnson reprint, 1964).

[19] Helmholtz, 'Bericht über die Theorie der physiologischen Wärmeerscheinungen für 1845', [*Fortschritte der Physik im Jahre 1845*, (Berlin: Reimer, 1847), 346–55.]; *WA*, I, 6.

[20] J. Liebig, *Animal Chemistry*, *op. cit.* note 18, 29.

[21] Liebig argued that the existence of the vital force was known from its effects: 'it is a peculiar force, because it exhibits manifestations which are formed in no other known force', *ibid.*, 221. For a discussion of Liebig's use of vital forces see T. O. Lipman, 'Vitalism and Reductionism in Liebig's Physiological Thought', *Isis*, 58 (1967), 167–85.

[22] Helmholtz, *op. cit.* note 17, 735.

Helmholtz and Kant

he tacitly agreed with Liebig in stating that 'there may be other agents acting in the living body than those agents which act in the inorganic world', but that these forces 'must be of the same character as inorganic forces, in this at least, that their effects must be ruled by necessity, and must be always the same, when acting in the same conditions',[23] because for Liebig vital forces did have the same character as other forces since the vital force could not arise from nothing and would generate an equivalent amount of another force. For this reason Helmholtz could claim, in 1845, that Liebig's theory depended on the as-yet-unproven assumption of the constancy of forces. However, Helmholtz did object to a vital force principle in the sense in which a vital force could be regarded as 'self-perpetuating' and hence would not be subject to the principle of the constancy of force. In his 1861 lecture he asserted that the supposition of such a vital force was contrary to the principle of the 'conservation of force' because this implied that 'the physical forces in the living body . . . could be suspended or again set free, at any moment by the influence of the vital principle'.[24] In the sense that a vital force implied perpetual motion its operation was not determined by he 'principle of the constancy of force equivalents', as he put it in 1845, and it could not be considered within the ontology consequent on the conservation principle.

The denial of perpetual motion was clearly associated, in Helmholtz's view, with the commitment to the principle of the constancy of force. In his 1845 review of work on animal heat he indicated that Liebig's doctrine that forces could only be 'derived from other forces and not out of nothing' supposed the as-yet-unproven principle of the constancy of force, and he formulated his intention in *Über die Erhaltung der Kraft* as being that of applying the principle that 'it is impossible by any combination of natural bodies to produce force continually from nothing'[25] to all parts of physics. The problem which led Helmholtz from his physiological studies to the composition of *Über die Erhaltung der Kraft* was thus the problem of perpetual motion. His intention was to demonstrate that forces could not be derived out of nothing by a rigorous formulation of 'the principle of the constancy of force equivalents'.

The physiological context of *Über die Erhaltung der Kraft* provides the basis for the clarification of Helmholtz's conceptual framework and

[23] Helmholtz, *WA*, III, 579.
[24] *Ibid.*
[25] Helmholtz, *WA*, I, 17.

terminology. Writing in 1845, that is, prior to the formulation of the paper, Helmholtz used Liebig's terminology quite unselfconsciously. Natural phenomena were associated with natural agents termed forces; one force could generate another such force, and the total system of these forces was regarded as being subject to the principle of the constancy of force. It was this sense of 'force' that was meant by the 'law of the conservation of force' in the 1861 lecture, this new expression replacing the earlier expression 'constancy of force' and both being used to denote the indestructibility and transformability of natural agents. Helmholtz emphasized his use of the term 'force' to mean 'natural agent' and of the expressions 'law of the constancy of force' and 'law of the conservation of force' to mean the indestructibility and transformability of natural agents in his 1861 lecture, stating that 'we may express the meaning of the law of conservation of force by saying that every force of nature when it effects any alteration, loses and exhausts its faculty to effect the same alteration a second time'. Nevertheless, he continued,

while, by every alteration in nature, that force which has been the cause of this alteration is exhausted, there is always another force which gains as much power of producing new alterations in nature as the first has lost . . . the power of the whole system in which these alterations take place is neither exhausted nor increased in quantity, but only changed in form.[26]

Though the phraseology of this exposition of his views in 1861 may possibly reflect his awareness of J. R. Mayer's papers, in which the doctrine of the indestructibility and transformability of force was expounded at length and its application to physiology given some prominence,[27] these passages are consonant with Helmholtz's 1845 position. When Helmholtz discussed in his 1861 lecture the physiological problems which first led him to write *Über die Erhaltung der Kraft*, it was perfectly natural for him to use expressions such as 'the physical forces in the living body' which meant 'the agents acting in the living body'.[28] His relation to Liebig thus clarifies the meaning of the 'law of the conservation of force [*Erhaltung der Kraft*]' here.

Helmholtz concluded *Über die Erhaltung der Kraft* with some remarks on physiological problems. His purpose in writing the paper was to

---

[26] Helmholtz, *WA*, III, 566.
[27] Helmholtz reviewed Mayer's *Bemerkungen über das mechanische Aequivalent der Würme* (Heilbronn, 1851), Mayer's lengthy summary of his work of the early 1840s, in his 'Theorie der Wärme', *Fortschritte der Physik in Jahren 1850 und 1851, vi. und vii. Jahrgang* (Berlin: Reimer, 1855), 566f.
[28] Helmholtz, *WA*, III, 579.

demonstrate the principle of *Erhaltung der Kraft* by a mathematical investigation of the physical quantities which were conserved. In so doing the concept of *Erhaltung der Kraft* acquired a sense additional to that in which it denoted the indestructibility and transformability of natural agents: that of the conservation of energy. When Helmholtz turned to a discussion of the respiratory theory of animal heat, an analysis of the relation between combustion of nutrients, animal heat and bodily exertion, it is hardly surprising to find that he employed the concepts he used in the paper to denote the physical quantities conserved as a consequence of the 'constancy' of these 'forces'. He thus refers to *chemische Spannkräfte* being consumed and *mechanische Kräfte* being generated (that is, chemical potential energy and work).[29] These new terms denote the quantities which are conserved. Nevertheless, it still remained meaningful to refer to 'forces [*Kräfte*]' in the sense of natural agents and to *Erhaltung der Kraft* in the sense of the conservation of natural agents. But the emergence of the new sense of *Erhaltung der Kraft* to mean the 'conservation of energy' arose directly from the problem as Helmholtz conceived it in 1845: to subsume all 'forces' under the law of the constancy of force—which entailed the denial of perpetual motion.

II

It is apparent that the ambiguity of Helmholtz's terminology arose in part from the physiological origins of his work and his consequent tendency to assimilate certain aspects of Liebig's conceptual framework and terminology. Helmholtz employed the term *Kraft* in the sense of 'natural force' in the first sentence of the first part of *Über die Erhaltung der Kraft*, stating that 'we will set out with the assumption that it is impossible, by any combination of natural bodies, to produce force [*bewegende Kraft*] continually from nothing'.[30] The use of *Kraft* here, to mean natural force, would have seemed quite reasonable to Helmholtz because of the way his formulation of the problem arose from his view that the principle of the constancy of force was consequent on the denial of perpetual motion. Moreover, his use of the term *bewegende Kraft* was to be expected, for he went on to state that Carnot and Clapeyron had employed this principle—that *bewegende Kraft* could not be produced from nothing—citing the German translation of Clapeyron's version of Carnot's memoir,

[29] Helmholtz, *WA*, I, 66.
[30] *Ibid.*, 17.

in which the term *bewegende Kraft* was used as a translation of the French *puissance motrice*.[31]

In addition to this sense of *Kraft*, to mean natural power, and of *Erhaltung der Kraft* to mean the indestructibility of natural powers, Helmholtz employs terms such as *lebendige Kraft* and *Spannkraft*, their usage demonstrating that they are 'energy' terms and that it is the conservation of these quantities which is denoted in one sense of the expression *Erhaltung der Kraft*. However, Helmholtz also employs the term *Kraft* in the sense of 'force' in Newtonian mechanics, and one of the central features of his paper is his claim to demonstrate that the principle of the conservation of *vis viva* [*lebendige Kraft*] was only valid when the acting forces [*Kräfte*] were central forces between point centres, that is they acted in the direction of the lines which unite the point centres and their intensity was dependent only upon the distance between these point centres.

Helmholtz began his paper by stating that his derivation of the *Erhaltung der Kraft* principle could be approached from two starting-points, either from the principle that it was impossible to obtain an unlimited amount of 'work force [*Arbeitskraft*]' by any combination of natural bodies, or from the hypothesis that all actions in nature were reducible to 'forces of attraction and repulsion [*anziehende und abstossende Kräfte*]', the intensity of the forces depending only on the distances between the points between which they acted.[32] Declaring that it was his intention to demonstrate the identity of these two principles, he represented the first of these principles in terms of the conservation of *vis viva*, so that if any number of material points are set in motion solely by the forces which they exert on one another, or are directed against fixed centres, then the total sum of the *vires vivae* would be the same at all times when the points occupied the same relative positions. Discussing the case in which the *vis viva* is applied to raise a system of masses to a given height, he noted that here the 'mechanical work [*mechanische Arbeit*]' would be equal when the points occupied the same relative positions. However, he argued that this principle was 'not applicable to all possible kinds of forces' for it could be derived from the principle of virtual velocities which 'could only be established with respect to material points endowed with attractive or repulsive forces'.[33] He thus attempted to link his

---

[31] B. P. E. Clapeyron, 'Über die bewegende Kraft der Wärme', *Annalen der Physik und Chemie*, **59** (1843), 446–51, 566–86; a translation of Clapeyron's 'Mémoire sur la puissance motrice de la chaleur', *J. Ec. polytech.*, **14**, cahier 23 (1834), 153–90.

[32] Helmholtz, *WA*, I, 12.   [33] *Ibid.*, 17ff.

XII

Helmholtz and Kant

principle with Jean Bernoulli's principle that, for a system of forces in equilibrium which are given a small movement, each of the forces will either advance or recede, and a quantity Bernoulli called *Energie* (denoted by the product of the forces and the displacements), will be conserved; the system of forces will adjust itself so that the algebraic sum of the products of the forces and their displacements will be zero.[34] Helmholtz went on to argue that when the principle of the conservation of *vis viva* is applied the forces are central forces between material points, showing that the direction and magnitude of the forces acting between a mass point m and a system of forces A are only functions of the position of m with respect to A, and that in the case of two mass points acting upon one another the direction and magnitude of the force is solely a function of the distance between them. He thus concluded that if the principle of the conservation of *vis viva* [*lebendige Kraft*] applied, then all forces [*Kräfte*] were central forces.[35] It is clear that there is no confusion between 'force' and 'energy' terms in this argument.[36]

Helmholtz then went on to provide a more general formulation of his argument, showing that the difference between the *vires vivae* possessed by a mass point m at two different distances r and R from a second mass point was equal to a quantity $\int_r^R \phi \, dr$, where ϕ is the intensity of the force. Helmholtz denoted this quantity by the term 'sum of the tensional forces [*Summe der Spannkräfte*]',[37] and argued that for the motion of a point under a system of central forces the increase of *vis viva* was equal to the sum of the tensional forces which correspond to the alteration of its distance, concluding that 'the sum of the tensional forces and *vires vivae* is always constant' and calling this the 'principle of the conservation of force [*Erhaltung der Kraft*]'.[38] This was a generalization of the principle of the conservation of *vis viva*, and the term '*Spannkraft*' corresponds to the 'energy' term of potential energy. The principle of *Erhaltung der Kraft* thus expressed the conservation of *lebendige Kraft* and of *Spannkraft*. He argued that if the forces between two mass points were brought to a condition of equilibrium by the action of external forces on these points, the equilibrium would not be destroyed if a rigid connection were to be substituted for the forces which the points exerted on one another. Arguing

---

[34] See Pierre Varignon, *Nouvelle mécanique ou statique*, II (Paris, 1725), 174ff.
[35] Helmholtz, *WA*, I, 19ff.
[36] There is no implication that the principle of *Erhaltung der Kraft* signified the conservation of *Kraft* as used in the sense of 'Newtonian force'. See also note 10 above.
[37] Helmholtz, *WA*, I, 22. I have employed the term 'tensional force' with Kahl, *op. cit.* note 2, in preference to Tyndall's 'tension', for Helmholtz's *Spannkraft*.
[38] Helmholtz, *WA*, I, 25.

that the forces applied to two points of a rigid straight line could only be in equilibrium if they were themselves in that line, he concluded that these forces must act in the direction of the line which connected them, and hence that they were forces of attraction or repulsion. This enabled him to state his general principle of *Erhaltung der Kraft* in its relation to the central force principle:

> whenever natural bodies act upon each other by forces of attraction or repulsion [*anziehende oder abstossende Kräfte*], which are independent of time and velocity, the sum of their *vires vivae* and tensional forces [*lebendigen und Spannkräfte*] must be constant; the maximum quantity of work [*Arbeitsgrösse*] which can be obtained from them is therefore fixed, finite.

Moreover, he stated that if these conditions did not obtain then the principle of *Erhaltung der Kraft* would not be valid: 'the combinations of such bodies are possible in which force [*Kraft*, in the sense of *lebendige Kraft* or *Spannkraft*] may be lost or gained *ad infinitum*'.[39] It is clear that despite his ambiguous use of the term *Kraft* here, and indeed, in having earlier referred to *Spannkraft* as a *Kraft*,[40] the context shows that the use of the term *Kraft* has the reverberations of his statement that it was impossible to produce 'force [*bewegende Kraft*]' from nothing: the term *Kraft* here meant natural 'force' or 'agent'. His adoption of the term *Spannkraft*, which was a term in use in the theory of elasticity to mean 'elastic force',[41] emphasized the relationship between this concept and that of *lebendige Kraft*, just as his use of the expression *Erhaltung der Kraft* echoed the older principle of *Erhaltung der lebendigen Kraft*. In neither case was it implied that Newtonian 'force' was being conserved: the context made it clear that 'energy' was being conserved.

The fundamental point to Helmholtz's discussion was that he regarded the central force principle as a necessary condition for the validity of *Erhaltung der Kraft*, asserting that if the forces were not central forces, then *Erhaltung der Kraft* would not hold. Moreover, in the Introduction he declared that the reduction of phenomena to central forces was a condition of the intelligibility of nature. Given the fundamental importance of the central force principle in Helmholtz's demonstration of *Erhaltung der Kraft*, the analysis of the argument of the Introduction is crucial to an understanding of his intentions.

[39] Helmholtz, *WA*, I, 27.
[40] *Ibid.*, 22.
[41] See article 'Elasticität', *Gehler's Physikalisches Wörterbuch, neu bearbeitet von Brandes, Gmelin, Horner, Muncke, Pfaff*, III (Leipzig, 1827), 167.

III

In the Introduction Helmholtz stated that though his paper was developed in the form of a physical assumption independently of philosophical foundations, nevertheless the two propositions which were the starting point of his analysis—that of the impossibility of obtaining an unlimited amount of work force [*Arbeitskraft*] from any combination of bodies, and that of the reduction of phenomena to central forces—had a strong bearing on the ultimate aims of physical science, and he argued that their philosophical implications were significant. Indeed, Helmholtz's motive for asserting the importance of philosophical foundations was that his condition that the explanation of natural phenomena in terms of the physical principles of motion—by the central force hypothesis—was at the same time the condition of the 'complete comprehensibility [*vollständige Begreiflichkeit*]'[42] of nature and would thus yield knowledge of 'the ultimate and invariable causes of natural phenomena'.[43] The physical principles could thus not be separated from their philosophical foundations: nature was completely intelligible only on condition of the postulation of central forces.

In the course of his argument Helmholtz distinguishes between the discovery of general rules [*allgemeine Regeln*] such as Boyle's law which were no more than generic concepts [*Gattungsbegriffe*] by which phenomena could be collected and which could be discovered by means of experiment, and the elaboration of a theoretical science which aims to ascertain the unknown causes of natural phenomena by comprehending them under the law of causality [*begreifen nach dem Gesetze der Causalität*], and thus to discover the ultimate causes of phenomena acting 'according to invariable laws'. Since the principle of causality was thus a presupposition [*Voraussetzung*] of the intelligibility of nature, it followed that the discovery of ultimate and invariable causes presupposed the law of causality.[44] Thus far Helmholtz's argument purports to demonstrate that the possibility of scientific explanation requires nature to be considered as structured in accordance with causal laws; but from this he now moves to the quite separate and more specialized claim that nature is in fact regulated by Newtonian laws involving central forces. In other words, he wants to demonstrate that the discovery of the invariable causes by which nature

---
[42] Helmholtz, *WA*, I, 16.
[43] *Ibid.*, 12.
[44] *Ibid.*, 13.

XII

can be rendered intelligible requires the reduction of the phenomena to central forces of attraction and repulsion; hence this becomes the condition of the 'complete comprehensibility' of nature. Now, his attempt to prove this latter claim can be shown to involve four separate contentions.

1. The existence of matter corresponds to our awareness of a passive, unchanging reality which is characterized by the category of quantity (mass). Matter in itself, viewed as such a passive entity, can only be subject to one change, *viz.* motion.

2. The application of the concept of matter furthermore requires consideration of the qualitative differences apparent in natural phenomena. These differences cannot be explained in terms of the motion of a merely passive entity; the explanation of the qualitative differences of matter requires us to take note of the capacity which matter possesses for the production of effects and this can only be ascribed to the action of forces. Helmholtz contends that in considering matter as an entity capable of producing effects the concepts of materiality and force are inseparable: a force cannot be regarded as having an existence separate from matter. For although existent entities as such may be called 'matter', the concept of matter cannot but be considered as a description of the capacity of natural entities to produce effects: 'we perceive matter only through its forces, not in and of itself'.

3. Natural phenomena must thus be referred back to unalterable, ultimate causes which are to be sought in entities possessing 'unchangeable forces (ineradicable qualities)', as found in chemical elements. The universe is therefore to be considered as consisting of chemical elements possessing unchangeable qualities. Since the only possible changes in such a system are spatial changes the forces involved are moving forces [*Bewegungskräfte*] whose action is determined by their spatial relations. Natural phenomena are thus to be reduced to the motions of matter endowed with inalterable moving forces.

4. When bodies are considered with respect to our experience of them it is apparent that motion is a change of spatial relations and can thus only take place among extended bodies; hence it follows that motion can only be experienced as a change in the spatial relations of at least two bodies relative to one another. Moreover, force, which is the cause of such changes, can only be conceived in terms of the relations between at least two bodies and is thus to be defined as the tendency [*Bestreben*] of two bodies to change their relative positions. It follows that since the

XII

Helmholtz and Kant

spatial relations of two points have reference solely to their distance apart, the force which two mass points exert on one another must be such as to cause an alteration in the distance between them; the force is thus a force of attraction or repulsion whose intensity is dependent solely upon the distance between the two mass points.[45]

Helmholtz therefore concluded that the problem of the physical sciences was the reduction of natural phenomena to unchangeable forces of attraction and repulsion, contending that this would provide the condition for the complete intelligibility of nature. Moreover, it was the 'necessary conceptual form for understanding nature'[46] and indeed was in conformity with the 'principle of sufficient reason';[47] for only one direction is specified between two points—that of the line between them—so the forces they exert on one another must be directed along this line.[48] Hence this formulation was 'the only possible one which the phenomena would allow'.[49]

On editing *Über die Erhaltung der Kraft* for publication in his *Wissenschaftliche Abhandlungen* in 1881, Helmholtz appended a note which has direct bearing on the argument of the Introduction.[50] Helmholtz there points out that the philosophical discussion in the Introduction had been considerably influenced by Kant. However, this claim needs careful evaluation if we are to understand it correctly, for he significantly adds that the argument had been 'more strongly influenced by Kant's epistemological insights than I would now consider still as correct'. What this can mean may be gleaned from what Helmholtz now offers as a replacement of the original argument, and which is intended to provide a new justification for his appeal to the causal principle in support of the central force principle. Helmholtz now states that 'only later' had he come to grasp that there exists a much closer connection, of a purely conceptual kind, between the nature of law, force and matter than he had originally assumed to be implied by his 'Kantian' position concerning causality in the Introduction. On the one hand, he now holds that the principle of causality is simply equivalent to the lawlikeness [*Gesetzlichkeit*] of all natural phenomena. But 'law', understood in the sense of 'objective power', *is* just what we call force. On the other hand, the term 'cause'

---

[45] *Ibid.*, 14f.
[46] *Ibid.*, 17.
[47] *Ibid.*, 15.
[48] *Ibid.*, 15f. Clausius was later to criticize this argument: see below.
[49] Helmholtz, *WA*, I, 17.
[50] *Ibid.*, 68.

[*Ursache*] etymologically also denotes the permanent beneath the change of appearances, *viz.* matter [*Stoff*], whose law of action is—as just stated—nothing other than force. Hence, whilst (as he notes) Helmholtz had argued already in the 1847 Introduction for the impossibility of conceiving 'force' and 'matter' in isolation from one another, on his later view this is simply due to the close conceptual connection that both notions bear to that of law. For the concept of law, in the sense of *law* of action, demands that such *action* be necessarily grounded in the action of *matter*, and he thus concludes that force taken in abstraction from matter would be tantamount to an hypostatization of law, lacking the required conditions for exercising causal efficacy.

This move, from the universal lawlikeness of nature to its expression in terms of the material action of forces, was evidently thought to provide a stronger justificational foundation for the central forces principle. But it makes it difficult to interpret Helmholtz's assertion that his 1847 argument of the Introduction had been influenced by Kant, with the implication that the new argument is now to replace it. For not only does the new argument display distinct affinities with some of Kant's remarks in the Second Analogy,[51] concerning the relations between causality, force and matter, but one may wonder what Helmholtz during both the earlier and the later periods imagined Kant's arguments actually to have been. Here, one can only surmise, and reconstruct from the tenor of the 1881 note. Presumably, at the start, Helmholtz believed (together with many of his Kantian contemporaries) that Kant had given a definitive transcendental proof of the principle of causality; whether or not at that period he was directly influenced by the Kant of the *Metaphysische Anfangsgründe*—to which I shall turn presently—he would have understood Kant to have made a fairly sharp distinction between his treatment of causality and the construction of the foundations of New-

---

[51] It is curious that Helmholtz's 1881 remarks—which he clearly intended to be a replacement for the Kantian Introduction of 1847—have parallels with some of Kant's remarks in the Second Analogy in the *Critique of Pure Reason*, N. Kemp-Smith (trans.) (London: MacMillan, 1929). Kant argues that phenomenal changes were manifested as actions: 'action signifies the relation of the subject of causality to its effect' (A205/B250), and the succession of appearances is manifested as forces, for 'causality leads to the concept of action, [and] this in turn to the concept of force' (A204/B249). Kant thereupon claims that this presupposes the permanence of substance, stating that 'wherever there is action—and therefore activity and force—there is substance, and it is in substance alone that the seat of this fruitful source of appearance must be sought'. The manifestation of forces, that is, the phenomenal appearances of changes, supposes an 'ultimate subject' which is 'the substratum of everything that changes', and this is 'the *permanent*, that is, substance', for actions themselves cannot be found in a subject which itself changes (A205/B250).

tonian dynamics, as is indeed the case. Nevertheless, I will contend, Helmholtz's words in 1881 notwithstanding, that the approach during *both* periods is broadly Kantian in outline; a fact which is sufficient justification for the attempt at a reconstruction of possible influences and analogies between the two thinkers, whether the influence was direct, or indirect only, mediated by the philosophical climate of Helmholtz's time.

Helmholtz's admission that his use of the principle of causality was indebted to Kant does not establish by itself any substantive influence and might imply no more than a ceremonial gesture, invoking the support of Kantian philosophy for Helmholtz's general argument in 1847 on the lawlikeness of nature, especially since he seems to imply that the 1881 argument from the law of causality to the dynamic interpretation of matter is original. However, the analysis of Helmholtz's claim that his reference to the law of causality in the Introduction had at that time received its supposed sanction from Kant's philosophy is aided by consideration of one of Helmholtz's mature philosophical statements, which gives a more extended discussion of the law of causality in which the Kantian influence is explicitly acknowledged. In the third volume of his *Handbuch der Physiologischen Optik* (1867) Helmholtz claims, using characteristically Kantian phraseology, that the law of causality is a 'law of our thinking' which is 'prior to all experience'.[52] Thus the possibility of our comprehending nature presupposes that the law of causality is 'a characteristic function of the intellect' as a result of which it 'can conceive of the world only as being in causal connexion'.[53] Now this is evidently an explication of a view of the law of causality which accords with Kant's concept of causality as a transcendental condition, which I will term 'transcendental lawlikeness'.[54] In the *Critique of Pure Reason* Kant claims that the principle of causality is valid for all objects of experience, being 'itself the ground of the possibility of such experience'.[55]

[52] H. Helmholtz, *Handbuch der Physiologischen Optik* (Leipzig: Voss, 1867), 453. See also H. Helmholtz, 'Über das Sehen des Menschen' [1855], *Vorträge und Reden*, I (Braunschweig: Vieweg, 1884), 85–117.   [53] H. Helmholtz, *op. cit.* note 52, 455.
[54] For a discussion of 'transcendental lawlikeness' see Gerd Buchdahl, 'The Conception of Lawlikeness in Kant's Philosophy of Science', *Synthese*, 23 (1971), 24–46, and in: *Kant's Theory of Knowledge*, L. W. Beck (ed.) (Dordrecht: Reidel, 1974), 128–50. Buchdahl there uses the terms 'transcendental' and 'empirical' lawlikeness to distinguish causality as a transcendental condition from causality as a condition justifying actual causal inferences. (He now suggests the term 'theoretical' in preference to 'empirical' [personal communication].) See also Strawson, *op. cit.* note 62. This terminology accords well with Helmholtz's conception of 'theoretical science' a being concerned with the establishment of invariables causes in the attempt to make nature intelligible (*WA*, I, 13).
[55] Kant, *op. cit.* note 51, B247.

XII

The category of causality, as a transcendental principle, then becomes one of the necessary grounds for the possibility of 'nature' as such, and indeed of all experience in general. Thus Kant argues that 'the order and regularity in the appearances, which we entitle *nature*, we ourselves introduce ... [the] unity of nature has to be a necessary one ... [so that the] subjective grounds of [this] unity [must be] contained *a priori* in the original cognitive powers of our mind'.[56] Moreover, the principle of causality not only makes experience possible but experience itself in some sense comes to possess a lawlike character. Kant thus asserts that the principle of causality (together with the other categories) establish the transcendental lawlikeness of nature: 'nature ... is dependent upon these categories as the original grounds of its necessary conformity to law'.[57]

This conception of transcendental lawlikeness may be distinguished from the view according to which nature is held to be lawlike in the sense of being subject to empirical laws. This is the sense in which Helmholtz claimed that nature could be rendered completely intelligible only in terms of invariable causal laws, and may be termed 'theoretical lawlikeness'.[58] Helmholtz alludes to this in his treatment of causality in the *Handbuch* in arguing that 'we have to proceed on the assumption that phenomena are comprehensible ... that natural phenomena are to be subsumed under a definite causal connexion', because if 'we cannot trace natural phenomena to a law, and therefore cannot make the law objectively effective as being the cause of the phenomena, the very possibility of comprehending such phenomena ceases'.[59] This notion of 'theoretical lawlikeness' thus makes the claim that the possibility of the construction of a framework of theoretical science presupposes that nature be considered as being causally and systematically structured. It is this sense of 'theoretical lawlikeness' which Kant suggests in arguing that empirical laws are considered to be lawlike and hence necessary in the sense that their necessity relates to their scientific systematization: it is a consequence of the regulative function of the reflective judgment (or 'reason' in its 'hypothetical employment', as he calls this in the *Critique*), which ascribes to nature a causal order which is the grounds of its theoretical lawlikeness.[60] Theoretical lawlikeness is thus a presupposition of

---

[56] Kant, *op. cit.* A125.
[57] *Ibid.*, B165.
[58] See Buchdahl, *op. cit.* note 54.
[59] Helmholtz, *op. cit.* note 52, 455. For reference to Kant see *ibid.*, 456.
[60] Buchdahl, *op. cit.* note 54. See Kant, *op. cit.* note 51, A647, for the reference to the regulative function of 'reason'.

Helmholtz and Kant

the comprehensibility of empirical laws *qua* laws: 'without this presupposition we should have no order of nature in accordance with empirical laws'.[61]

Now, it seems most unlikely that Helmholtz ever distinguished clearly between causality as a transcendental condition and causality as a condition of the possibility of empirical laws as members of systematic theories: like most commentators, it is more than likely that he conflated these two senses.[62] What is clear is that both senses of lawlikeness (transcendental and theoretical) appear in his treatment of the causal principle in the *Handbuch*, and that his indication of Kant's influence there does have textual support. Moreover, the notion of 'theoretical lawlikeness' does correspond to Helmholtz's 1847 claim that the law of causality was a necessary condition for the intelligibility of nature. There would thus seem to be reasonable grounds for accepting Helmholtz's statement that his discussion of causality in 1847 was influenced by Kant. Moreover, the ease with which Helmholtz could slide from 'transcendental' to 'theoretical' lawlikeness in the *Handbuch* does suggest that the argument in the Introduction embodied a similar but implicit conflation. It is apparent that whatever Helmholtz's confusion as to the intricacies of Kant's views on the principle of causality, there is some textual support for the view that Helmholtz's 1881 comment reflects more than the admission of a vague awareness of Kant's position on causality when he wrote the Introduction, although clearly not embodying the 'dynamic' version of this position as it appears in some of Kant's discussions in the Second Analogy and more, in the *Metaphysische Anfangsgründe*.

Helmholtz's argument in the Introduction is in two parts: the first is the claim that the intelligibility of nature requires that nature be considered as regulated by causal laws, and the second is the claim that nature is in fact regulated by central force laws. It is this second part of the argument which is the most significant for Helmholtz, for it is this argument, as shown above, which provides the justification for his enunciation of the *Erhaltung der Kraft* principle in terms of central force laws. I will suggest that Helmholtz's argument displays remarkable parallels to the argument of Kant's *Metaphysische Anfangsgründe*. Though

---
[61] I. Kant, *The Critique of Judgement*, J. C. Meredith (trans.), (Oxford: Clarendon Press, 1928), 25.
[62] The view that Kant conflates causality as a transcendental condition with causality as a condition justifying actual causal inferences is maintained by P. F. Strawson, *The Bounds of Sense* (London: Methuen, 1966), 137; *cf.* Gerd Buchdahl, *Metaphysics and the Philosophy of Science. The Classical Sources: Descartes to Kant* (Oxford: Blackwell, 1969), 660–5.

there is no documentary evidence to confirm that Helmholtz was even familiar with Kant's *Metaphysische Anfangsgründe*, it is curious that the exposition of Helmholtz's demonstration of the intelligibility of the central force principle given above is suggestive of Kant's fourfold metaphysical explication of the concept of matter in the *Metaphysische Anfangsgründe*, so that given the form in which I cast Helmholtz's argument there would seem to be structural analogies between this account of Helmholtz's argument and the *Metaphysische Anfangsgründe*. Indeed, Helmholtz's intention in the Introduction—to demonstrate that the intelligibility of nature requires the reduction of phenomena to Newtonian laws of central forces—has affinities to Kant's intention in the *Metaphysische Anfangsgründe*, to demonstrate the possibility of Newtonian science. Though I will admit that Helmholtz did not adhere rigidly to the Kantian framework, the parallels between the Introduction and the Kantian approach suggest that it would be instructive to construe Helmholtz's argument from the perspective of the Kantian framework, in order to appreciate the nature of Helmholtz's own objectives in the Introduction. Moreover, this would have the added advantage of presenting us with an example of the provision of metaphysical foundations. I therefore suggest that an understanding of Helmholtz's attempt to provide justificatory sanction for the central force principle in the Introduction requires analysis of its relation to the argument of the *Metaphysische Anfangsgründe*.

A full understanding of the parallels between Helmholtz's attempt to establish his claim that nature is regulated by central force laws and the argument of the *Metaphysische Anfangsgründe* thus demands some discussion of Kant's intentions in that work.[63] Kant's central concern in this work is to discuss the ways in which the categorial framework of the *Critique* is to be applied to the empirical concept of matter rather than to the concept of nature in general. The *Metaphysische Anfangsgründe* is thus concerned with the elaboration of what Kant terms a 'special metaphysics of nature'.[64] Kant suggests that the elaboration of such a metaphysics of nature would require 'a complete analysis of the concept of matter' which would involve the application of the *a priori* transcendental principles of the operations of thought to the empirical concept

---

[63] I have found the following works helpful in reading Kant's *Metaphysische Anfangsgründe*: Jules Vuillemin, *Physique et métaphysique Kantiennes* (Paris: Presses Universitaires de France, 1955); Lothar Schäfer, *Kants Metaphysik der Natur* (Berlin: de Gruyter, 1966); Hansgeorg Hoppe, *Kants Theorie der Physik* (Frankfurt: Klostermann, 1969); J. W. Ellington, 'The Unity of Kant's Thought in His Philosophy of Corporeal Nature' in his translation of the *Metaphysische Anfangsgründe*, *op. cit.* note 1; and Gerd Buchdahl, *op. cit.* note 54.

[64] Kant, *Metaphysische Anfangsgründe*, *op. cit.* note 1, 470.

Helmholtz and Kant

of matter, so that metaphysics is no longer a mere 'invention' but is taken from 'the essential nature of the thinking faculty itself'.[65] Kant wants to demonstrate that the metaphysics of nature is 'in unison with the mathematical doctrine of motion'.[66] Thus the creation of a mathematical physics cannot be separated from the elaboration of metaphysical principles, and in the *Metaphysische Anfangsgründe* Kant is concerned to show that the explication of the concept of matter by this special metaphysics of corporeal nature demonstrates the possibility of Newtonian science. This involves the application of mathematical construction to the concept of matter and hence the establishment of a system based on concepts whose possibility has thereby been established. Obviously, in a quite analogous way, Helmholtz was concerned to establish the claim that the invariable laws which render nature intelligible were Newtonian laws: to this end he attempted to explicate an ontology of matter and central forces of attraction and repulsion.

The argument of the *Metaphysische Anfangsgründe* has a fourfold structure, corresponding to the categories of quantity, quality, relation and modality,[67] which in turn are clearly meant to correspond to the principles of pure understanding—axioms of intuition, anticipations of perception, analogies of experience and postulates of empirical thought —functioning as rules for the employment of the categories.[68] Arguing that 'in metaphysics the object is considered merely as it must be represented in accordance with the universal laws of thought',[69] Kant claims that 'under the four classes of quantity, quality, relation, and finally modality, all determinations of the universal concept of matter in general and, therefore, everything that can be thought *a priori* respecting it, [and] that can be presented in mathematical construction' can be subsumed.[70] The metaphysical explication of the concept of matter is carried out in accordance with the fourfold classification of the categories, and hence the *Metaphysische Anfangsgründe* has four chapters.

The first may be called *Phoronomy*, and in it motion is considered as pure quantum, according to its composition, without any quality of the matter. The second may be termed *Dynamics*, and in it motion is regarded as belonging to the quality of the matter under the name of an origina' moving force. The third emerges under the name of *Mechanics*, and in it matter with this dynamical

---
[65] *Ibid.*, 472.
[66] *Ibid.*, 478.
[67] Kant, *Critique, op. cit.* note 51, B95, B106.
[68] *Ibid.*, B200.
[69] Kant, *op. cit.* note 1, 473.
[70] Kant, *ibid.*, 475f.

XII

quality is considered as by its own motion to be in relation. The fourth is called *Phenomenology*, and in it matter's motion or rest is determined merely with reference to the mode of representation, or modality.[71]

This fourfold metaphysical explication of the concept of matter has, it appears to me, considerable suggestive analogies to my exposition of Helmholtz's demonstration of the intelligibility of the central force principle as a four-part explication of his matter-force ontology. A full understanding of the extent and significance of this analogy may therefore derive some considerable benefit from a further analysis of Kant's argument.[72]

1. In *Phoronomy* Kant considers matter as being 'the movable in space',[73] its only changes being those arising from its motion. Phoronomy is concerned with matter as the movable in space. Its object is to construct velocity as an extensive magnitude, which falls under the category of quantity and its corresponding principle of the axioms of intuition, that 'all intuitions are extensive magnitudes',[74] and then to derive various rules for the composition of velocities.

2. In *Dynamics* matter is considered as 'the movable insofar as it fills space'.[75] The analysis of the concept of matter in this section presupposes the concept of matter as being movable, but this is now supplemented by the property of resisting motion into a certain space. Kant argues that 'matter fills a space not by its mere existence, but by a special moving force'.[76] Matter is held to fill space by its repulsive forces, and the dispersion of matter is counteracted by an attractive force. The dynamical concept of matter is explicated in terms of the attractive force limiting the repulsive force, so that the repulsive force can vary in degree with regard to the same attractive force. This is the metaphysical analogue of the anticipations of perception, which establish that the objects of experience have intensive magnitude. The dynamical principle of repulsion is opposed by attraction and hence the perceptible degree of a filling of space is determined by the limiting or balance of the first force by the second, these principles corresponding to the category of quality (its subdivisions being reality, negation and limitation).[77] The

---

[71] *Ibid.*, 477.
[72] For a detailed analysis of the fourfold structure of the *Metaphysische Anfangsgründe* see also Schäfer, *op. cit.* note 63, and Ellington, *op. cit.* note 63.
[73] Kant, *op. cit.* note 1, 480.
[74] Kant, *op. cit.* note 51, B202.
[75] Kant, *op. cit.* note 1, 496.
[76] *Ibid.*, 497.
[77] Kant, *op. cit.* note 51, B106.

XII

Helmholtz and Kant

principles of dynamics thus establish that the qualitative differences of matter are to be explained by means of its forces.

3. In *Mechanics* matter is considered as 'the movable insofar as it is something having a moving force', so that the mechanical explication of matter is concerned with matter in motion. Kant states that while 'the merely dynamical concept could also regard matter as at rest' here the 'force of a material entity set in motion is regarded as present in order to impart this motion to another material entity'.[78] The concern in Mechanics is to analyse the relations of material objects with one another by means of their motions. The mechanical explication presupposes the dynamical, for 'the communication of motion takes place only by means of such moving forces as also inhere in a material entity at rest',[79] and the transfer of motion is explained simply in terms of the motion of the moving forces, in terms of spatial changes, so that matter is said to act by means of its moving forces of attraction or repulsion. Kant's laws of mechanics, 'the laws of the subsistence, the inertia and the reaction of matter'[80] are concerned with the relations between material entities and correspond to the categories of relation.

4. In *Phenomenology* matter is regarded as 'the movable insofar as it can as such be the object of experience',[81] and Kant is here concerned with the relation of matter to our experience of it. He states that matter can only be experienced in terms of its motion, that motion cannot take place without the influence of moving forces, and that the communication of motion depends on the 'relation of the moved in space to every other thing thereby movable'.[82] Hence our experience of the motion of matter is determined with regard to Phoronomy (motion), Dynamics (moving forces) and Mechanics (the relation of the moving forces).[83]

It would be misleading to suggest a strict correspondence between the argument of Helmholtz's Introduction and Kant's metaphysical explication of the concept of matter. Nevertheless, comparison of the fourfold argument of the *Metaphysische Anfangsgründe* with my account of Helmholtz's demonstration of the intelligibility of the central force principle as a four-part exposition of his matter and central forces ontology, suggests some affinities between Kant's argument and Helmholtz's

---

[78] Kant, *op. cit.* note 1, 536.
[79] *Ibid.*, 551.
[80] *Ibid.*, 551.
[81] *Ibid.*, 554.
[82] *Ibid.*, 558.
[83] *Ibid.*, 556, 558.

Introduction. (i) Kant's concern with matter as an extensive magnitude corresponding to the category of quantity, so that matter is viewed solely in terms of its movability, has analogies with Helmholtz's view of matter in terms of its motion. (ii) Like Kant, Helmholtz supplements the concept of matter as being movable with an analysis in terms of quality, expressing its qualitative differences in terms of its forces and stressing the inseparability of matter and force. (iii) Both Helmholtz and Kant view the interactions of matter in terms of its moving forces. (iv) Helmholtz concludes his discussion by arguing that we experience bodies through their motions, their forces, and through the relations between their moving forces, his argument having some analogy to Kant's discussion in Phenomenology.

There exist therefore clear structural analogies between the argument of the *Metaphysische Anfangsgründe* and Helmholtz's attempt to provide justificatory sanction for the intelligibility of his central force principle. Though Helmholtz did not construct his argument with explicit reference to the Kantian architectonic, the textual affinities which I have noted strongly suggest that he had this architectonic in mind. Helmholtz's intention in the Introduction, to demonstrate that the reduction of phenomena to Newtonian laws of central forces would render nature intelligible, would give a motive for drawing upon Kant's demonstration of the possibility of Newtonian science.

Nevertheless, quite apart from dissimilarities in detail, there are some important differences in intention which need to be noted. Indeed, in the absence of historical evidence for any direct influence on the part of the *Metaphysische Anfangsgründe* on Helmholtz, these differences provide an important reason for this tentative reconstruction of a possible influence; for these differences provide the basis for the delineation of Helmholtz's own objectives. Kant's purpose was to use the fourfold classificatory analysis to demonstrate the *possibility* of Newtonian science, and the argument should not be taken as implying that the actual inductive validity of Newtonian physics was meant to follow from the transcendental principles:[84] 'one must guard against going beyond what makes the universal concept of matter in general possible and against wanting to explain *a priori* the particular or even specific determination and variety of matter'.[85] So the metaphysical argument provides the guide to the metaphysical construction of matter[86] and is meant to establish only

[84] See Buchdahl, *op. cit.* note 54.
[85] Kant, *op. cit.* note 1, 524.
[86] *Ibid.*, 517.

the possibility of Newtonian science, not its inductive validity; the metaphysical foundations are meant to yield principles of constraint on possible physical hypotheses. By contrast, Helmholtz clearly believed that his own account of the metaphysics of corporeal nature would demonstrate the actual conformity of nature to Newtonian laws. For him, Newtonian laws of central forces were 'the necessary conceptual form for understanding nature . . . the only possible one which the phenomena would allow',[87] and his appeal to Kantian metaphysics was an attempt at justification of these claims. But the position here implied, I contend, had for Helmholtz the strength of a quasi-deductive demonstration, a consequence of the insufficient recognition of the Kantian distinction between actuality and possibility. His fundamental assumption was that the reduction of phenomena to central forces was the condition of the complete intelligibility of nature, and Helmholtz's appeal to Kantian argument was an acknowledgement that this claim could not be established empirically but demanded independent justification. Nevertheless, the global nature of Helmholtz's epistemological claims for the reduction of phenomena to central forces, by relating his physical arguments more closely to a metaphysical treatment, was meant to justify these claims and in consequence the physical actuality of the central force laws themselves.

In the absence of unambiguous documentary evidence, this interpretation must remain tentative; yet it does provide some insight into the manner in which Helmholtz interpreted the significance of his attempt to justify his central force principle. Helmholtz's application of Kant's metaphysics of nature was less systematic, whilst at the same time being less tentative and exploratory than Kant's own exposition. Helmholtz grounded his argument on the Kantian scheme but his reference to the Kantian architectonic is not formulated systematically. What is important is to see that he believed that his claim of the complete intelligibility of nature in virtue of the reducibility of phenomena to central forces could be supported by an appeal to metaphysical foundations.

Helmholtz's belief that his metaphysics of nature demonstrated the conformity of nature to Newtonian laws, though apparently going further than Kant's view that metaphysics is rigidly limited to a demonstration of the possibility of Newtonian science, is actually far more consonant with interpretations of Kant's philosophy of science current in the period, suggesting a further reason for holding that something

---

[87] Helmholtz, *WA*, I, 17.

like Kant's doctrine of the metaphysical foundations of science had reached him at least indirectly via certain contemporary sources. A comparison with the writings of J. F. Fries, whose works were explicitly concerned with the metaphysical foundations of science developed along Kantian lines, may serve to illustrate this.[88] Fries' philosophy was an attempt to develop the Kantian approach as an alternative to the *Naturphilosophie* of Schelling and Hegel, his most significant work, composed directly in the shadow of the *Metaphysische Anfangsgründe*, being the *Mathematische Naturphilosophie* (1822). Though his elaboration of Kant's ideas over-systematized the Kantian framework, his claim to demonstrate the union of mathematics and metaphysics was in line with Kant's own intentions. Claiming that the 'general basic laws of all explanations for corporeal phenomena' demonstrated the 'necessary general laws of motion and of moving forces' and 'the kind of possible motions and moving forces',[89] he developed a systematic form—far more rigid than Kant's own—of the Kantian fourfold metaphysical explication of matter, emphasizing that the justificatory force of this analysis lay in its dependence on the categorial table of the *Critique*[90] and that it corresponded to Newton's mathematical formulation. For example, in the chapter on Mechanics he declares that 'Newton's laws of motion are of metaphysical origin' and asserts that this followed from the three analogies of experience, so that 'changes of state must be determined by causes based on necessary laws'.[91] Fries followed Kant in claiming a connection between the metaphysical laws of mechanics and Newton's laws; his third proposition corresponds to Proposition 3 of Kant's chapter on Mechanics in stating that every change of matter had an external cause (Kant calls this the 'second law of mechanics'[92]), and Fries followed Kant in labelling this the 'law of inertia'.[93] However, Fries' approach represents a hardening of Kant's rather more tentative drawing of the lines of connection between the 'metaphysical' demonstration and the Newtonian laws, claiming that the actual Newtonian laws follow directly from the categories, so that Newton's laws could be regarded as comprising

[88] For a discussion of a different aspect of Fries's thought, and of its influence on Mathias Schleiden, see Gerd Buchdahl, 'Leading Principles and Induction: the Methodology of Mathias Schleiden', *Foundations of Scientific Method: the Nineteenth Century*, R. N. Giere and R. S. Westfall (eds.) (Bloomington: Indiana University Press, 1973), 23–52.
[89] Jakob Friedrich Fries, *Die mathematische Naturphilosophie nach philosophischer Methode bearbeitet* (Heidelberg: Mohr und Winter, 1822), 400.
[90] *Ibid.*, 410f.
[91] *Ibid.*, 500.
[92] Kant, *op. cit.* note 1, 543.
[93] Fries, *op. cit.* note 89, 502.

the 'necessary metaphysical-mathematical presupposition of all science'.[94] By contrast, though for Kant the Newtonian laws display affinities to his metaphysical laws of mechanics, the metaphysical analysis merely demonstrates 'the principles of the possibility of a mathematical doctrine of nature',[95] so that metaphysical construction did not have the force of inductive demonstration. The thrust of Fries' stress on a firm link between mathematics and metaphysics was emphasized by his lengthy treatment of mathematical problems, the chapter on Mechanics including an account of the principles of momentum, least action and virtual velocities.

If Helmholtz had read Fries, his well-known aversion to *Naturphilosophie* would have been reinforced by Fries' diatribes against the 'dreams' of *Naturphilosophie*,[96] and Fries' view that scientific explanation was to be obtained 'through the application of pure mathematical representations grounded on philosophical concepts'[97] was certainly shared by Helmholtz. Though Fries' analysis involves a hardening of Kant's position, as mentioned, his belief that metaphysical analysis would prove the conformity of nature to Newtonian laws does again have clear parallels to Helmholtz's use of metaphysical argument. Emphasis on the metaphysical foundations of science is to be found in writings other than those of philosophers at this time. The article on *Materie* in the sixth volume of *Gehler's Physikalisches Wörterbuch* (1836) includes an account of Kant's philosophy of science, where an account is given of Kant's representation of the concept of matter in terms of four classes—magnitude, quality, relation and modality—and after an explanation of the fourfold framework of the *Metaphysische Anfangsgründe* there follows an account of the four divisions of matter corresponding to the fourfold division of the metaphysics of corporeal nature.[98] The author singles out the final paragraph[99] of the *Metaphysische Anfangsgründe*—it is called a 'memorable expression'[100]—in which Kant had declared that because reason could never conceive anything except insofar as the latter is determined under given conditions ... nothing remains for it ... but to turn back from objects to itself in order to investigate and determine the ultimate boundary of the capacity given it.

This account of Kant, though brief, is generally favourable, contrasting

[94] *Ibid.*, 539.
[95] Kant, *op. cit.* note 1, 473.
[96] Fries, *op. cit.* note 89, 506.
[97] *Ibid.*, 509.
[98] G. W. Muncke 'Materie', *Gehler's Physikalisches Wörterbuch*, VI (Leipzig, 1836), 1410f.
[99] Kant, *op. cit.* note 1, 564f.
[100] *Op. cit.* note 98, 1412.

again with the obligatory diatribes against the *Naturphilosophen*, and Kant's claim for the importance of the metaphysical foundations of science for science itself was treated sympathetically.

It is thus apparent that Helmholtz's stress on the metaphysical foundations of mechanics was by no means idiosyncratic, and his appeal to Kantian principles, however transformed, to provide justificatory sanction for his claim that the representation of phenomena by Newtonian laws was both necessary and complete, was in line with some contemporary views on science and its philosophy. The Introduction to the paper thus provided the grounds for the incorporation of the principle of *Erhaltung der Kraft* within the framework of Helmholtz's programme of scientific explanation, the reduction of phenomena to Newtonian laws of central forces.

IV

Helmholtz was never in any doubt as to the scope and significance of his principle of *Erhaltung der Kraft*. He wrote the report of his paper in the *Fortschritte der Physik* himself, stating that his principle demonstrated that 'the sum of the tensional forces and *vires vivae* present is constant', adding that 'the quantity of force [*Kraft*] in the world is as indestructible as that of matter',[101] a statement which is not to be found in *Über die Erhaltung der Kraft* itself. This latter remark suggests that Helmholtz had become aware of J. R. Mayer's work when he wrote the report in the *Fortschritte der Physik*, for Mayer made the principle that the indestructibility of force was analogous to the indestructibility of matter fundamental to his demonstration of the transformation of forces.[102] However, Helmholtz's view of the significance of his work was not universally admitted. The story of Gustav Magnus' disinclination to recommend the paper to Poggendorff and its consequent rejection by the *Annalen der Physik* is well known,[103] and Helmholtz undoubtedly hoped to establish his work as a major contribution to physics by his report in the *Fortschritte der Physik*. In this too he was thwarted, finding to his dismay that his lengthy discussion of *Über die Erhaltung der Kraft* had been included in his article on animal heat, despite his express instructions to the contrary. 'I have received the first part of the physics annual report' he informed du Bois-Reymond,

---

[101] H. Helmholtz, 'Physiologische Wärmeerscheinungen betreffende Arbeiten aus dem Jahre 1847', *Fortschriffe der Physik in Jahre 1847* (Berlin: Reimer, 1850), 236.
[102] See P. M. Heimann, 'Mayer's Concept of Force', *op. cit.* note 3.
[103] Koenigsberger, *op. cit.* note 15, 38.

and was not a little surprised to see my *Erhaltung der Kraft* placed by Karsten [the editor] along with physiological heat phenomena, although I had forwarded it worked up separately. You would have received a letter of thanks for your work these days even if your letter had not arrived. It is one more proud pursuit on the part of the resolute Magnus.[104]

According to a letter of Helmholtz's at the time, one of the reasons given for the rejection of the paper was that it was felt that the argument did not differ substantively from papers by Clapeyron and Holtzmann (on the production of heat by mechanical work).[105] Though Helmholtz himself stated in 1881 that he had not at the time considered the paper to be an original research but to be an attempt at critical analysis,[106] his statements during the period itself indicate that though he was indeed concerned with critical analysis—as in his emphasis on the metaphysical foundations of the central force principle—he also believed that he had something original and indeed revolutionary to say to physicists. 'The principal contents of the present memoir are intended principally for physicists', he declared in the opening sentence of the paper,[107] and his anger was aroused when he believed that Magnus, after evincing little enthusiasm for the paper in the first place, should try to restrict its import to physiology. The paper may have had its origin in Helmholtz's concern with animal heat, but as it stood it was intended as a contribution to physical science. As an ironic twist, Helmholtz obtained an implicit admission of this point, for in the years following he contributed review articles to the *Fortschritte der Physik* on the work of such men as Joule, Mayer and Rankine, in which he spelt out the relation of their papers to *Über die Erhaltung der Kraft*—in the section on the 'theory of heat'.[108] Helmholtz was further vindicated by the gratifying recognition by luminaries such as William Thomson for his contribution to the emergent law of the conservation of energy.

However, for Helmholtz himself, the recognition of his principle of *Erhaltung der Kraft* represented the acceptance of only one aspect of his

[104] Helmholtz to du Bois-Reymond (15 January 1850): 'Die physikalischen Jahresberichte 1^n Abth. habe ich empfangen und mich nicht wenig gewundert, meine Erhaltung der Kraft von Karsten zu den physiologischen Wärmeercheinungen gestellt zu sehen, obgleich ich sie abgetrennt bearbeitet eingeliefert hatte. Für Dein Werk hättest Du in diesen Tagen ein Dankschreiben bekommen, auch wenn Dein Brief nicht eingetreffen wäre. Es ist eine noch stolze Fortsetzung von dem kühnen Magnus'. See note 9 for the location of this letter. The *Fortschritte* for 1847 was not published until 1850 (see note 101).

[105] Helmholtz to du Bois-Reymond (6 August 1847). See Clapeyron, *op. cit.* note 31, and Helmholtz's discussion in *Über die Erhaltung der Kraft*, *WA*, I, 37ff.

[106] Helmholtz, *WA*, I, 74.

[107] *Ibid.*, 12.

[108] For example, see Helmholtz, *op. cit.* note 5 and *op. cit.* note 27.

paper. His attempt to reduce phenomena to central forces was basic to his intentions, and it was precisely this aspect of *Über die Erhaltung der Kraft* which was made the subject of attack in the years following the publication of the paper. The initial criticisms were confined to probings into the validity of Helmholtz's claim to have established the central force principle in relation to the law of the conservation of energy, but in due course the issues widened beyond the consideration of the validity of specific arguments in *Über die Erhaltung der Kraft*. Helmholtz's espousal of and continued commitment to the central force principle was to be challenged by later developments in physics, but Helmholtz not only stood his ground in rejecting any attempt to modify what were for him fundamental mechanical principles, but responded with a renewed assertion of the mechanical view of nature.

The first assault on this aspect of *Über die Erhaltung der Kraft* was made by Rudolf Clausius in 1853. Clausius struck at the very foundations of Helmholtz's theory, the principle that the reduction of phenomena to central forces was the only possible explanation of nature. In criticizing Helmholtz's claim to demonstrate that the principle of the conservation of *vis viva* was only valid when the acting forces were central forces,[109] Clausius correctly located the source of Helmholtz's assumption that the central force principle was a necessary condition for the validity of the conservation of *vis viva* in his more general claim, in the Introduction to the paper, that since the spatial relations of points were determined by their distance apart, then the force which two mass points exert on one another could only effect an alteration in the distance between the points, that is, it could only be a force of attraction or repulsion, its magnitude dependent on the separation of the mass points.[110] Clausius claimed that even though the central force principle was possible physically, it was not mathematically necessary as a condition of the validity of the principle of conservation of *vis viva*, for it was not inconceivable that forces could act from a point in several directions, and hence the magnitude of the forces acting need not be a function of the distance between the mass points.[111] In his reply Helmholtz suggested[112] that Clausius' criticisms were not substantive, because his own proof had only

---

[109] Rudolf Clausius, 'Ueber einige Stellen der Schrift von Helmholtz "Über die Erhaltung der Kraft"', *Annalen der Physik und Chemie*, **89** (1853), 574.

[110] *Ibid.*, 575.

[111] Clausius, *op. cit.* note 109, 577.

[112] H. Helmholtz, 'Erwiderung auf die Bemerkungen von Hrn. Clausius', *Annalen der Physik und Chemie*, **91** (1854), 241–60; *WA*, I, 76–93.

been concerned with the consideration of the principle of *vis viva* in terms of the relative positions of the moving masses, and he justified this by arguing that physics was only concerned with the inter-relations of existent physical entities and not in the relation to imaginary coordinate systems.[113] Clausius' response to this was simply to note that he had been concerned with Helmholtz's claims of the necessity of the central force principle,[114] clearly referring to Helmholtz's view of the central force principle as the condition of the complete intelligibility of nature. Helmholtz's only reply was in a report on the controversy in the *Fortschritte der Physik*, where he emphasized that 'points' and 'corporeal elements' should be clearly distinguished,[115] and he argued that his argument was concerned only with the latter, that is, with physical actuality, and argued that physical entities had no other relation than that of their positions relative to one another. It is evident that Clausius had successfully probed a sensitive link in Helmholtz's argument, the claim for the universal applicability and necessity of the central force principle.

The second controversy also arose from Helmholtz's statement of the dependence of the principle of *Erhaltung der Kraft* on the central force principle. Helmholtz had argued that if 'bodies possess forces which depend upon time and velocity, or which act in directions other than the lines which unite the two acting mass points ... then combinations of such bodies would be possible in which force [*i.e. lebendige Kraft* or *Spannkraft*] may be either lost or gained *ad infinitum*'.[116] In considering electromagnetic problems later in the paper Helmholtz had referred to Wilhelm Weber's theory in which an attempt was made to explain the phenomena by referring to 'the attractive and repulsive forces of the electric fluids themselves, the intensity of the forces depending on the velocity of approach or recession and upon the increase of velocity'. Helmholtz thus concluded that 'up to the present time no hypothesis has been established by which these phenomena could be reduced to constant central forces',[117] and the implication was clear: that Weber's force law violated the principle of *Erhaltung der Kraft*. The almost inevitable controversy—Weber's response and a protracted exchange of criticisms and replies—did not flare up until 1869,[118] a delay which was sufficient

[113] Helmholtz, *WA*, I, 82.
[114] R. Clausius. 'Über einige Stellen der Schrift von Helmholtz "über die Erhaltung der Kraft," zweite Notiz,' *Annalen der Physik und Chemie*, 91 (1854), 604.
[115] H. Helmholtz, 'Theorie der Wärme', *Fortschritte der Physik im Jahre 1854* (Berlin; Reimer, 1857), 369.   [116] Helmholtz, *WA*, I, 27.
[117] *Ibid.*, 61.
[118] Wilhelm Weber, 'Über einen einfachen Ausspruch des allgemeinen Grundgesetzes der

for Maxwell to adopt Helmholtz's critique of Weber's force law as an argument against any attempt to formulate an action at a distance theory of electromagnetism.[119] The significant feature of the controversy was Helmholtz's continued refusal to countenance any modification of the central force principle. In a paper of 1878 Weber had replied to points raised by Helmholtz by suggesting that the principle of the conservation of energy required modification in its application to electrodynamics,[120] and in the 1860s and 1870s a number of German theorists had suggested interpretations of electrodynamic phenomena which involved significant departures from the world view of Helmholtz's *Über die Erhaltung der Kraft*. Clausius had argued that Newton's law of the equality of action and reaction need not hold for electrodynamic forces,[121] while Bernhard Riemann and Carl Neumann had suggested that electric action was propagated with a finite velocity.[122] Helmholtz responded to these suggestions in the notes he appended to the 1881 reprint of *Über die Erhaltung der Kraft*. He pointed out that his statement that the principle of *Erhaltung der Kraft* would be violated if the acting forces were dependent on time or velocity was only correct if the 'law of the equality of action or reaction is generally valid',[123] noting that if this law was allowed to lapse then Clausius had shown that forces which were velocity-dependent would not produce an infinite amount of mechanical work. However, he went on to reaffirm that any such abrogation of the central force principle, as in current electrical theory (pre-

elektrischen Wirkung', *Annalen der Physik und Chemie*, **136** (1869), 485–9; *Wilhelm Webers Werke*, 6 vols., IV (Berlin: Springer, 1892–4), 243–6.

[119] James Clerk Maxwell, 'On Faraday's Lines of Force' [1856], *The Scientific Papers of James Clerk Maxwell*, 2 vols., I, W. D. Niven (ed.), (Cambridge: Cambridge University Press, 1890), 208; *idem*, 'On Physical Lines of Force' [1861], *op. cit.*, I, 488; *idem*, 'A Dynamical Theory of the Electromagnetic Field' [1864], *op. cit.*, I, 527. Maxwell realized that Helmholtz's 1847 argument was inadequate in 1871: see a letter to P. G. Tait of 7 November 1871, informing Tait that 'Weber has reason...' (Cambridge University Library, Add. MSS 7655). In his *Treatise on Electricity and Magnetism*, 2 vols (Oxford: Clarendon Press, 1873), §§ 853–4, Maxwell accepted Helmholtz's new criticism of Weber, as developed in H. Helmholtz, 'Über die Bewegungsgleichungen der Electricität für ruhende leitende Körper', (1870), *WA*, I 543–628, and *idem*, 'Über die Theorie der Elektrodynamik' (1872), *ibid.*, 636–46. For an analysis of Maxwell's changing theories of reality, see P. M. Heimann, 'Maxwell and the Modes of Consistent Representation', *Archive for History of Exact Sciences*, **6** (1970), 171–213.

[120] W. Weber, 'Elektrodynamische Maasbestimmungen insbesondere über die Energie der Wechselwirkung', *Werke*, IV, 361–419.

[121] R. Clausius, 'Ueber die Ableitung eines neuen elektrodynamischen Grundgesetzes', *Journal für reine und angewandte Mathematik*, **82** (1876), 85–130.

[122] B. Riemann, 'Ein Beitrag zur Elektrodynamik', *Annalen der Physik und Chemie*, **131** (1867) 237–42; C. Neumann, 'Die Principien der Elektrodynamik' [1868], *Mathematische Annalen*, **17** (1880), 400–34.

[123] Helmholtz, *WA*, I, 71.

sumably the theories of Weber, Clausius and Riemann), in which 'the investigations... have been in contradiction... to the established mechanical principles of the equality of action and reaction and of the constancy of energy', would be an abandonment of any prospect of 'the complete solution of scientific problems'.[124] Thus, though he admitted Clausius' theory as being possible mathematically, its acceptance seemed to him to threaten a violation of the principles which were a necessary condition of the intelligibility of nature, and he concluded that such theories should only be adopted 'if all other theoretical possibilities have been exhausted'.[125]

It is evident that Helmholtz would not envisage any deviation from the fundamental principles that he had first expounded in 1847, and it is apparent that his refusal to countenance any relaxation of the applicability of these principles was a consequence of his commitment to the intelligibility of the mechanical view of nature, a world view which, as I have shown, Helmholtz believed to have received a metaphysical grounding and thus possessed a special status. It was surely these philosophical commitments which determined his attempts in the 1880s to develop mechanical foundations for thermodynamics, his intention being to extend the range of the principle of mechanical explanation.[126] A similar concern is evident in his attempt to establish a general formulation of the principle of least action in this period.[127] Arguing that this principle had been expounded only in a manner which presupposed the physical assumptions of Newton's laws of motion and the validity of the law of conservation of energy, he pointed out that this seemed to be a limitation to the range of validity of the least action principle. His own intention was to establish the principle in a general way and to demonstrate its application to a wide variety of electrodynamic and thermodynamic phenomena, and hence to affirm the universality of the mechanical view of nature. He declared that

we may draw the conclusion that the range of validity of the principle of least action has extended far beyond the boundaries of the mechanics of ponderable bodies... it seems that the general validity of the principle of least action is

[124] *Ibid.*, 69f.
[125] *Ibid.*, 70.
[126] H. Helmholtz, 'Principien der Statik monozyklischer Systeme', *Journal für reine und angewandte Mathematik*, **97** (1884), 110–40, 317–36; *WA*, III, 142–62, 179–202. See Martin J. Klein, 'Mechanical Explanation at the End of the Nineteenth Century', *Centaurus*, **17** (1972), 64ff.
[127] H. Helmholtz, 'Ueber die physikalische Bedeutung des Princips der kleinsten Wirkung', *Journal für Mathematik*, **100** (1886), 137–66; *WA*, III, 203–48.

secure... as a heuristic principle and as a guide for the endeavour to formulate the laws of new classes of phenomena.[128]

When Helmholtz's pupil Heinrich Hertz wrote that 'all physicists agree that the problem of physics consists in tracing the phenomena of nature back to the simple laws of mechanics',[129] his statement could possibly have been meant to have some prescriptive force, but this programme undoubtedly characterized Helmholtz's natural philosophy. In *Über die Erhaltung der Kraft* he attempted to establish the mechanical conception of nature by an appeal to the metaphysical foundations of science, treating 'the metaphysical portion... as a special fundamental part of general physics... to bring it into unison with the mathematical doctrine of motion'.[130]

---

[128] Helmholtz, *WA*, III, 209f.
[129] Heinrich Hertz, *The Principles of Mechanics Presented in a New Form*, D. E. Jones and J. T. Whalley (trans.). (London: MacMillan, 1899), Preface.
[130] Kant, *op. cit.* note 1, 478.

INDEX

Alembert, Jean Lerond d': IX 127; X 231, 241
Aristotle: VII 7

Baur, Carl: XI 280, 286
Baxter, Andrew: I 268; VI 253
Bentley, Richard: IX 123
Berkeley, George: I 251–2, 261–3; II 13–14, 22; VIII 219
Bernoulli, Daniel: III 61; VII 2, 4–5; X 231
Bernoulli, Jacob: VII 24
Bernoulli, Johann:
— continuity (principle of): VII 10, 12–14, 18; VIII 214–18, 220–1; X 233–4
— dynamics: VII 1–5, 8–10, 12–20; VIII 215–19, 220–4; X 232–6; XII 215
— infinitesimals: VII 9–10, 12–14, 16; VIII 216–19, 220–2; X 234, 236
— on Leibniz: VII 2–3, 8–11, 12–19; VIII 215–19; X 233–4
— *vis viva* (conservation of): VII 1–5, 6, 12–20; VIII 215–19, 222–3; IX 229–30; X 232–6
Berzelius, J.J.: VI 236
Bilfinger, G.B.: X 234
Black, Joseph: III 75–6, 77
Boerhaave, Hermann: II 10–13, 14–17, 22; III 62, 68–70, 73–4, 83; IV 277; V 150
Boscovich, R.J.: I 277–8; VI 235–7, 244–53; X 231
Boyle, Robert: I 247–8; II 9, 11; III 68; IV 271–2
Buchdahl, Gerd: VIII 213–14, 224; X 229

Carnot, S.: XII 213
Catelan, Abbé F.: VII 6
Cavendish, Henry: III 63, 76
Clapeyron, B.P.E.: XII 213–14, 233
Clarke, Samuel: III 67; IV 273–4, 276, 277, 283; VIII 214, 223–4; IX 124
Clausius, Rudolf: XII 234–7
Colden, Cadwallader: I 303; II 16–17; III 72; IV 277
Coleridge, S.T.: IV 281
Cooper, P.: VI 249

Croll, James: VI 247
Cudworth, Ralph: II 7
Cullen, William: III 74–5

Davy, Humphry: II 23–4; III 78–80; V 148, 152–3
deism: I 292–3; IV 271; IV 282–3
Desaguliers, J.T.: VI 247
Descartes, René: I 235; II 11; III 61–2, 64; IV 272, 275; VII 3, 5–10; IX 121–2, 125; X 231, 235
Despretz, C.: XI 281; XII 210
De Volder, Burchard: VII 8
Du Bois Reymond, Emil: XII 232–3
Dulong, P.L.: XI 281; XII 210

Edwards, Jonathan: I 251–4
energy:
— concepts of: V 148–9; XII 206–7, 213–15
— conservation of: III 80; V 147–59; XI 277–9; XII 205–8, 211–16, 232–3
— *see vis viva*
ether: I 240–5, 289–91, 297–302; II 3–10, 14–17, 19–23; III 61–73, 75; IV 275–8; V 150; IX 124
Euler, Leonhard: III 61; VII 11; VIII 221; IX 119–20, 127–9, 130; X 231, 234, 238–40
Exley, Thomas: I 303–4; VI 247–52

Faraday, Michael:
— on Boscovich: VI 238, 244–6
— conversion of forces: II 24; III 80; V 147–9, 153–5
— field concept: I 237, 305–6; VI 237–43, 254–7
— lines of force: I 305; VI 237, 239–40, 254–6
— matter: I 305–6; VI 237–9, 243–53
field (concept of): I 237, 305–6; VI 237–43, 254–7
Franklin, Benjamin: II 14; III 70–1; IV 277
Freind, John: I 239
Fries, Jacob Friedrich: XI 295; XII 230–1

Galileo, G.: VII 3, 11; VIII 218
Gehler, J.S.T.: XII 216, 231–2
Greene, Robert: I 251, 254–61; III 67; IV 276–7; VI 247
Gregory, James: I 295
Griesinger, Wilhelm: XI 277, 280, 284, 289, 290, 291
Grove, William Robert: II 24; V 147–9, 153, 155–6

Hales, Stephen: III 68–71, 74
Hare, Robert: VI 236, 242–6, 257
Harrington, Robert: I 300; II 23; VI 249
Hartley, David: I 267, 269, 277–80
Hauksbee, Francis: I 243; II 7
Hegel, G.W.F.: XII 230
Helmholtz, Hermann von:
— animal heat: XII 209–12
— causality (law of): XII 217–23
— central forces: XII 207–8, 214–16, 217–19, 223–4, 229, 232, 234–7
— energy (concepts of): XII 206–7, 213–15
— energy (conservation of): XII 205–8, 211–16, 232–3
— mechanical foundations: XII 208–9, 214, 216, 217–19, 223–4, 229, 232–8
— philosophical foundations: XII 208–9, 217–32
— vital force: XII 210–12
Helmont, J.B. van: II 10, 13
Hermann, Jacob: X 234, 241
Herschel, Sir William: I 278, 301
Hertz, Heinrich: XII 238
Higgins, Bryan: I 299; II 22–3; III 76; VI 249, 251
Hobbes, Thomas: I 235, 250
Holtzmann, Karl: XII 233
Hume, David: I 234, 261, 263–5; IV 273, 277–9
Hutchinson, John: II 15
Hutton, Charles: III 78; VI 252–3
Hutton, James: I 234, 236, 281–95, 297–8; II 17–22; III 72, 76–8, 79–80; IV 281–3; V 150–2; VI 247, 249
Huygens, Christiaan: VII 2–3, 5, 17, 21; VIII 218, 222–3

infinitesimals: VII 9–10, 12–14, 16, 18–20, 26; VIII 215–24; X 233–6
Ingenhousz, Jan: II 21

Jones, William: II 15–16, 22
Joule, James Prescott: III 80; V 147–9, 153, 156–7, 158; XI 278; XII 205, 207, 233

Kant, Immanuel:
— causality: IX 132; X 244–5; XI 279, 291–2; XII 219–23
— forces: VI 247; IX 130–1; X 241–6; XI 294–5; XII 226–7
— inertia: IX 130, 131–3; X 240, 244–6
— matter: VI 247; IX 130–1; X 241–4; XII 226–7
— metaphysical foundations: VIII 213, 221; IX 129–33; X 229–32, 235–7, 240–6; XI 294–5; XII 208–9, 223–32
— on Newton: IX 129–33; X 240–1, 242–6
— space: I 255–6
Keill, John: I 239, 242; III 67
Kelvin, Lord: see Thomson, Sir William
Kirwan, R.: III 76
Knight, Gowin: I 296–9, 301; II 14–15; III 71–2; VI 249
Kuhn, Thomas S.: V 147, 157–8, 161

Lagrange, Jean Louis: VII 17
Lambert, Johann Heinrich: III 83; X 243
Lavoisier, Antoine: XI 280–1
Leibniz, Gottfried Wilhelm:
— causality: VII 6, 13–14; VIII 217–18; XI 287
— on Descartes: IV 276; VII 5–11
— divine agency: IV 276, 277, 280–2; VIII 214–15
— dynamics: VII 1–19; VIII 215–19, 220–4; IX 125–7; X 231–4; XI 292–3
— force (primitive): VII 3, 7–8, 18; VIII 219; IX 125–7; X 232–3; XI 279, 292–3
— infinitesimals: VII 9–10, 18, 26; VIII 216–17, 219–22; IX 126; X 233–5
— on Newton: III 65–6, 67; IV 276, 277; VIII 214; IX 124–7
— *vis viva* (conservation of): VII 6–11, 13, 14–19; VIII 214, 216–19, 222–3; IX 126; X 231–5; XI 289–90, 293
Leslie, John: I 295
Leslie, P.D.: I 299–300; II 23; III 75–6
Liebig, Justus von: XI 280–4; XII 207–12
Locke, John: I 235, 248–51, 261–2, 264–7, 269, 294; VI 247

McGuire, J.E.: I 233–306; II 5
MacLaurin, Colin: III 72–3; IV 275; VII 2, 4–5, 19–20, 24–5; VIII 215, 219–24
Macquer, P.J.: III 77, 83
Magnus, Gustav: XII 232–3
Malebranche, N.: I 263; IV 278; VII 9
Martin, Benjamin: III 68

INDEX

Maxwell, James Clerk: I 306; III 81; V 148–9; VI 241, 245, 256; XII 236
Mayer, Julius Robert:
— animal heat: XI 280–4
— causality: XI 286–95
— chemistry: XI 284–6
— energy: V 156, 158; XI 277–9; XII 205, 207, 233
— force: XI 277–96; XII 212, 232
— vital force: XII 283–4
Melloni, M.: V 153
Meyerson, Emile: XI 287
Michell, John: I 277–9; VI 247, 249, 251
More, Henry: II 7
Mossotti, O.F.: VI 247–9

Naturphilosophie: XI 293–5
Newton, Sir Isaac: I 233–7; II 1–3; IV 271–2; VI 247, 251; VII 21
— active principles: I 239–45; II 5–10; III 65–7, 73–7; IV 273–9; V 150; VIII 214; IX 123–4
— ether: I 240–5, 301; II 3–10, 16, 19; III 61–73, 75; IV 275–8; V 150; IX 124
— gravity: I 241–5; II 6–7; III 65–6; IV 273, 275; VIII 213–14, 224; IX 123–4; X 243
— inertia: VII 3; VIII 214; IX 119–25, 127–9, 130, 132–3
— infinitesimals: VII 19; VIII 221–2
— Queries to *Opticks*: I 237–46; II 2–5; III 61, 64–6; VI 247; VIII 214
Nicholson, William: I 275–6; VI 253

Oersted, H.C.: V 153
Oldenburg, Henry: II 8–9, 11; III 64, 66, 68, 73

Paracelsus: II 10
Pemberton, Henry: III 67
Playfair, John: I 294–5; II 21; III 63, 78
Poggendorff, J.C.: XII 232
Priestley, Joseph: I 234, 236–7, 240, 268–80, 302; III 76; IV 279–81, 283; VI 236, 247–53, 257

Rankine, W.J. Macquorn: V 148–9; XII 206, 233
Reid, Thomas: I 234, 251, 265–8; IV 278–9
Riemann, Bernhard: XII 236–7
Ritter, J.W.: XI 294
Robinson, Bryan: I 242; II 4, 14; III 68
Robison, John: I 295; III 63; VI 236, 247
Roget, P.M.: V 154
Rowning, John: I 302; II 17; IV 277; VI 247
Rumford, Count: III 78–9, 83

Schelling, F.W.J.: XI 279, 293–4; XII 230
Schofield, Robert E.: I 235; III 63
Seebeck, T.J.: V 153
Shaw, Peter: II 11–13; III 69, 73–4
Smith, Robert: VI 247
Spinoza, B.: IV 281
Stahl, George Ernst: III 62, 68, 73–4, 83
Stewart, Dugald: I 293–5

Tait, Peter Guthrie: V 155; XI 278
Thomson, Sir William (Lord Kelvin): V 148, 156–7; XII 206, 233
Toland, John: IV 276
Tyndall, John: XI 278

Varignon, Pierre: VII 23, 25
vis viva (conservation of): VII 1–5, 9–11, 13–20; VIII 214–15, 217–19, 221–4; IX 126; X 232–6; XI 289–90; XII 214–16

Walker, Adam: I 300–1; II 23; III 78; V 151–3; VI 249, 251
Wallis, John: VII 21
Watson, William: II 14
Weber, Wilhelm: VI 255; XII 235–7
Westfall, Richard S.: IX 119
Whewell, William: V 154; VI 245, 248
Williams, L. Pearce: VI 235–7
Wilson, Benjamin: II 14; III 70
Wolff, Christian: X 236, 239
Wren, Sir Christopher: VII 21

Young, Robert: I 260, 274–5
Young, Thomas: I 278–9; III 79; VI 247, 251, 252–3

OHIO UNIVERSITY LIBRARY

Please return this book as soon as you have finished with it. In order to avoid a fine it must be returned by the latest date stamped below. All books are subject to recall after two weeks or immediately if needed for reserve.

JAN 19 1995